# DIARY OF A WORLD WAR I
# CAVALRY OFFICER

# The Diary of a World War I Cavalry Officer

## Brigadier General Sir Archibald Home
KCVO, CB, CMG, DSO, CderLH

Editor: Diana Briscoe

Costello, 1985

Published 1985

D.J. Costello (Publishers) Ltd,
43 The High Street, Tunbridge Wells, Kent TN1 1XL.


**British Library Cataloguing in Publication Data**

Home, *Sir,* Archibald
    Diary of a World War I Cavalry Officer.
    1. World War, 1914-1918—Campaigns
    2. World war, 1914-1918—Personal narratives, British
    I. Title
    II. Briscoe, Diana
    940.4'81'41          D546

ISBN 0-7104-3004-3

Maps drawn by Mr James Morrison.

Typeset by Composing Operations Ltd
88a London Road, Southborough, Kent TN4 0PP
Printed and bound in Great Britain by
Biddles Ltd, Guildford and King's Lynn

# Contents

# List of Maps

# FOREWORD

by The Marquess of Anglesey D.Litt, FSA, FRHistS, FRSL

The dozen years which led up to the First World War were in many ways the most extraordinary in the history of the British army. In that short period it emerged with astonishing speed from the hard sheath of its amateur chrysalis to become a fully-fledged professional imago. This metamorphosis was especially pronounced in the Cavalry. It is true that the diehards who believed in the continuing paramouncy of shock tactics and the knee-to-knee charge were still partly in the ascendancy. Yet even French and Haig found themselves as Armageddon approached demanding more professionalism and, particularly, greater proficiency in musketry. By the time hostilities began, it was a fact, as General Rimington, one of the finest of Cavalrymen, wrote in 1912, that 'our British regular Cavalry are at least ten if not fifteen years ahead of any continental Cavalry in rifle shooting, fire discipline and the knowledge of when and how to resort to fire tactics'.

Its performance, especially in the pre-trench warfare days of 1914, proved this to be so. The writer of these diaries gives as truly vivid an account of those anxious first weeks as I've ever read. The Cavalry's part in the operations and especially in the Mons retreat is most brilliantly highlighted. It is still little appreciated how much more reactionary and old fashioned were the Cavalries of Germany and France and, equally, how quickly and efficiently the British came to accept the immobility of trench warfare. These diaries fully illustrate both points.

Another sphere in which the pre-war army advanced professionally well beyond expectations was that of staff training. This was certainly inferior to that of Germany and France, whose higher formations in peace time were always 'in being' and fully staffed. Yet it is remarkable how the Camberley Staff College grew from a pathetic school of theory into an institution which by 1914 had come to rival those great schools on the Continent. Under Rawlinson, Henry Wilson and 'Wully' Robertson as Commandants it became a realistic forcing house for young staff officers of the highest calibre.

Archibald Home, whose fascinating diaries are here published for the first time, was a shining example of this species. He had been a General Staff Officer at Camberley before the war and was thus peculiarly fitted for the increasingly prominent staff appointments to which he was appointed throughout the struggle on the Western Front. It is most instructive to see him gaining that sure-footedness which made him seem indispensable to the various chiefs whom he served. Not the least entertaining and revealing parts of his diaries are those which give incidental character sketches of his generals and colleagues. He emerges as immensely likeable, a soldier of deep feelings and exceptional competence.

There can be no question that this book is a vastly important addition to the literature of the First World War. It illustrates with exceptional clarity and understanding what it was really like to be at the controlling end during the whole of that most awful conflict.

Anglesea,
Penrhyn,
May 1985

8

## ACKNOWLEDGEMENTS

The Editor and Publishers gratefully acknowledge the help and advice of:
Lt Colonel Peter Upton and Lt Colonel Robert Merton at the Royal Hussars Museum,
Winchester; and of Mr Roderick Suddaby, the Department of Documents and the
Department of Photographs at the Imperial War Museum, London.

All photographs in the second section are reproduced Courtesy of the Imperial War
Museum, as are the photographs of the 5th Lancers, the 16th Lancers and 2nd Cav.Div.
transports behind Hollebeke Château in the first section. All other photographs are Courtesy
of the Royal Hussars (PWO) Museum in Winchester.

*The front jacket illustration was supplied by:*
*Military Archive & Research Services, Braceborough, Lincs.*

# BIOGRAPHICAL NOTE

Archibald Fraser Home (pronounced Hume) – commonly known as 'Sally' Home – was born in Kursauli in India (now Pakistan) on 14 September 1874, the elder son of Colonel Frederick Jervis Home CSI, CIE, Royal Engineers and Constance McEwan. He came from an old army family with long associations with India. His great-grandfather was Robert Home the painter, and his grandfather Major-General Richard Home. A great-uncle was Duncan Home who won the Victoria Cross during the assault on the Kashmir Gate in Delhi during the Indian Mutiny.

While still a child, his father was detached to the civil side of engineering and he accompanied his family to Italy, France and Germany. As a result of this early education, he spoke good French and German; while in Germany he attended the Realgymnasium in Kassel, where his father was working on the construction of a dam. He came back to England to school at Aldenham about the age of 12 and from there went to Sandhurst where he was a contemporary of Winston Churchill. In 1895 he was commissioned 2/Lieutenant in the 11th Hussars and joined his regiment in India. During the Boer War, the Regiment was stationed in Cairo returning to this country in 1901. In 1900 he married Violet Mary Bertha D'Arcy, second daughter of W.K. D'Arcy of Mount Morgan Gold and later British Petroleum Co. fame. After passing through the Staff College, he held a number of staff posts both in this country and Ireland until in 1913 he went to the Staff College as an instructor with the rank of Brigade Major.

On the declaration of war in August 1914, he went to France as GSO(2) to the Cavalry Division under General (later Field Marshal Lord) Allenby; then as GSO(1) to De Lisle with the 1st Cavalry Division; then as Brigadier-General of the Cavalry Corps until its disbandment in March 1916. He was posted as GSO(1) to Stuart-Wortley (46th Division), before being posted to the new 9th Corps under Hamilton-Gordon. In September 1916, he was seconded to the (then temporarily reconstituted) Cavalry Corps and served under Kavanagh to the end of the war as his Brigadier-General. During 1914-18 he was mentioned in dispatches seven times, was awarded the DSO in 1915, received the Légion d'Honneur and in 1918 was made a CMG; the following year he was made a CB (1919).

He retired from active service in 1919, as Brigadier-General, and was then associated with the late Field Marshal Lord Haig and other senior officers in founding the (now Royal) British Legion, and the British Empire (now Commonwealth) Service League, which co-ordinated the various ex-servicemen's organisations that were set up at the same time as the Legion throughout the Commonwealth. It may not now be realised that, until then, no such organisations existed to help the discharged serviceman. With so many men being involved in the war – many of whom were grievously disabled – it was decided to do something to help them. He became the first Treasurer and Secretary of the British Empire Service League, and remained in that post until 1947. His work took him to Canada twice (the first time with Haig in 1925), and to New Zealand and Australia in 1934, which included the opening and consecration of the Melbourne War Memorial. He took part in many pilgrimages to the battlefields in France and Flanders, the last time being for the consecration of the Vimy Ridge Memorial to the Canadian forces in 1936.

On his retirement in 1919 he was appointed to the Honourable Corps of Gentlemen-at-Arms (who act as the Sovereign's bodyguard on ceremonial occasions). In 1926 he was made Clerk of the Cheque and Adjutant. In 1933 he was made a KCVO for the work he had done on behalf of ex-servicemen, and in 1938 he became the Lieutenant of the Corps. In 1923 he bought the estate of Cavenham Park in Suffolk, largely for the shooting, as following a riding accident in 1920 he was forbidden to ride a horse again. He was an excellent shot and much in demand, spending the months from August to January in Suffolk, attending to his farming and other interests, coming only to London for official duties and committee meetings. He was a JP and latterly Chairman of the Mildenhall Branch. He was High Sheriff of Suffolk in 1929 and in 1930 was made a Deputy Lieutenant. He was President of his local British Legion Branch.

As the outbreak of the 1939-45 War he was too old for active service to his great regret, but became County Director of the Suffolk Branch, British Red Cross until his retirement for health reasons in 1945. He was also a private in the local Home Guard Unit. In 1939 he succeeded General T.T. Pitman as Colonel of the 11th Hussars, and followed the interests and progress of the Regiment throughout the war and the many campaigns in which they took part. In the Regiment he was always known as 'Sally' – a reference to a celebrated gorilla in the London Zoo. His wife died in 1944 and he became unwell in that year, suffering a severe stroke which incapacitated him completely and caused him to give up his work. He died in 1953.

At Sandhurst, he was a contemporary of Winston Churchill. When the latter became Prime Minister in 1940, AFH remarked 'Now he has achieved all his ambitions!' When asked about this, he said that they had spent an afternoon together on the lake at Sandhurst, during which Churchill had told him all that he hoped to achieve in the future. It is typical of the man and his integrity that he never mentioned this in public until it was achieved, though references do occur in the diaries; but these were a private and personal journal. Sadly, there are omissions in this narrative, on matters which would now be of very great interest, but, because these constituted information which would have been highly sensitive, no reference is made to orders, dispositions or to anything which might have helped the enemy, had the diary got into the wrong hands.

On a personal note: my Father was an extremely handsome man with a courteous approach to all he met, in whatever walk of life. His marriage was a supremely happy one, but he never recovered from my Mother's death in 1944. I think he was genuinely loved by all. One of his greatest virtues – and possibly fault, in a worldly sense – was his loyalty to those he served and worked with, and his unwillingness to push himself forward. Thus the honours which came to him were freely given and never sought. His diaries came to light when Cavenham Park was sold in 1946. When I asked him why he had never written anything about his experiences, he replied that he had originally thought of doing so but 'too many people had written a lot of "bilge" on the subject' and he did not want to add to this. The Home family motto 'True to the End' perhaps summarises his life and attitudes in a way he would not have recognised himself, and which would have greatly embarrassed him if anyone had pointed it out to him. However to my mind, it makes a fitting epitaph.

Teresa Briscoe
Stoke Poges, Bucks
May 1985

# Editorial Note

Faced with extreme inconsistency of spelling, I have elected to correct all place names to their modern French or Belgian equivalents with the few exceptions of such towns as Ypres, Rheims, Dunkirk, etc where the given name is more familiar. Because the Diaries had to be cut, word order has been rearranged in some places, but all editorial interpolations are given in [square] brackets. All dates and abbreviations have been standardised, and obvious spelling errors have been corrected without comment.

The originals of the nine journals are lodged at the Imperial War Museum in London along with a complete (uncorrected) transcript and various associated items of interest. They are mostly written in pencil or ink on the recto side of the page in regulation Army report books, which have squared paper, perforated at the back margin. In cutting them, I have tried to remove items of little interest such as lists of friends seen, repetitions of news from other fronts and/or battles, and repeated speculations as to German tactics as in March 1917.

As far as can be ascertained, AFH never re-read or corrected his Diaries. They were deposited in England when he went home on leave and were probably not even read by his wife; the keeping of such journals was strictly forbidden. TMVB reported that, when she first opened Volume II (?), it had an unmistakable smell of the trenches which she recognised from her nursing experience in World War II. She characterised it as 'a mixture of unwashed bodies, dirty khaki uniforms, and mud' and it vanished within a few days of the volume being exposed to fresh air (the originals were in store between 1945 and 1975).

All footnotes are related to a specific day-entry. Many of them endeavour to expand on AFH's often cryptic references to events elsewhere; they may prove unnecessary for experts on this period, but I hope will be useful for those less aware of events in Russia, the Balkans and Palestine.

Dedicated to those who did not return and to those who gave their mental or physical health in this conflict.

All royalties from this book are being donated to the Royal Hussars Benevolent Fund.

# 1. From Mons to the Marne

**Wednesday 12 August 1914** WAR! August 2nd and a Bank Holiday and mobilisation ordered – but we had expected it and the many histories which will be written will show the why and the wherefore. Myself I must own that I am lucky – A weary year as a teacher at the Staff College has brought its reward and I now find myself a GSO 2nd Grade with the Cavalry Division. The days of mobilization are always wearying, the parting from wife and children must affect the nerves so I must pass from those sad times. On August 11th, I left Southampton on the *Comrie Castle* for Le Havre, or rather I embarked for we did not leave 'till 2.30 am on the 12th: Ludlow the RQMG, Ravenhill (Cashier) and myself as the advanced party of the Cavalry Division. The voyage was uneventful and we arrived at Le Havre at 3.30 pm. On the way across we met only a couple of torpedo boats, the first one passed within 50 yards of us, the second lay more out to sea – a small sign, but a very comforting one when one thinks of submarines and other such horrors. We met very little shipping, a significant sign as the purser told me that on ordinary occasions the Channel is stiff with ships.

We made a triumphant entry into Le Havre itself. People lined the shores and cheered – the soldiers ran up a flag consisting of the Union Jack and Tricoleur combined – the men on the ship sang the Marseillaise, where they had learned it heaven only knows – sirens blew, in fact a greater welcome no soldiers could ever have had. We made fast opposite the wharves of the German Hamburg-America Line, now quite deserted and the disembarkation began. First person I saw was Keddie of the 42nd – he looked very tired, told me he had been up for the whole night. There was certainly a shortage of petrol, for we were told that our car (a beautiful 6 cylinder Siddeley limousine) could not be sent on. We sent the horses to the supply depot for the night and arranged ourselves to sleep in the shed – the horses suffered a good deal on the ship on account of the heat. Passed a bad night, am not used to the smells of a goods' shed yet.

**Thursday 13 August 1914** Lucky day – We left Le Havre at 12 noon, destination unknown, in a train. They gave us an excellent first class carriage – it was very hot. First halting place Rouen – here we stayed an hour. Tommy* was given water, brandy and water and coffee and rum – had to stop men filling water bottles with a mixture of all three. French Officers much amused at this – they said it could not hurt a fly – they don't know Tommy. Had a tremendous reception from the French all the way – bouquets of flowers, flags, cheering and soon stopped at Amiens for one hour.

**Friday 14 August 1914** Reached Busigny at 4.00 am and there learnt our destination to be Maubeuge practically on the Belgian Frontier. Arrived at Maubeuge at 9.00 am and here met by French Officers attached to the Cavalry Division – very kind and did everything for our comfort. Had *dejeuner* at 12.00 and got into cars to go round billeting area. It was a

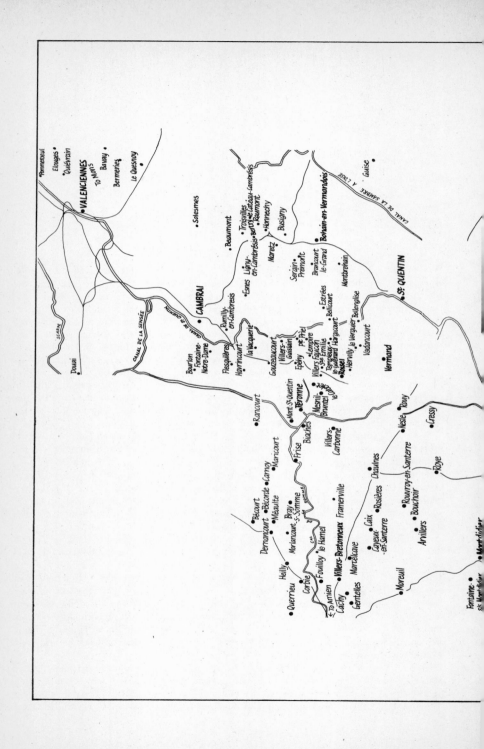

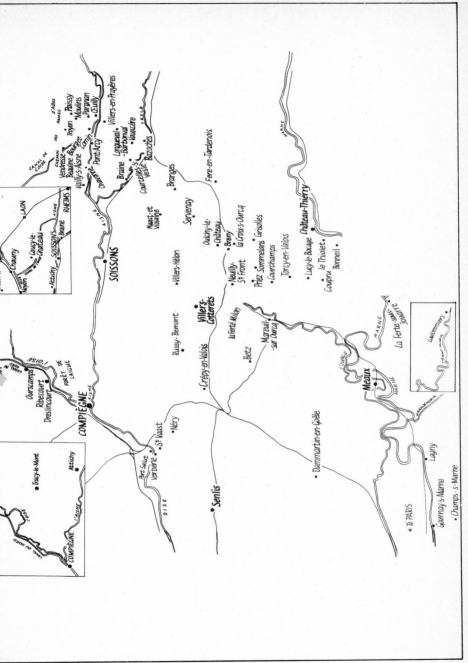

The Retreat from Mons area.

16

triumphant progress, at Solre-le-Château we must have been surrounded by 1,000 people. There are no men in France now, the population is women and children. Every road, bridge and railway is guarded by the old men day and night, they shoot on sight unless one stops motor at once. The harvest lies on the ground, the men are at the war. We motored round area of billets and got back at 7.30 pm. The French Officers are marvels at billeting and did the work very throughly and quickly.

**Saturday 15 August 1914** Spent morning studying maps and talking over operations with French Officers attached to HQ. Got a lot of information out of them. At 2.00 pm motored to Busigny and saw Dawkins and Jebb (GHQ) and many others, 2nd Div.* arriving. French train service wonderful – left at 9.00 pm by **ordinary** train, only two hours late – got to bed 12.20 am. Have got no letters – cannot write as censorship very strict.

**Sunday 16 August 1914** Issued GS instructions for moves to billets. At 4.00 pm did reconnaissance in motor of ground north and east of Jument. Proceeded to Busigny by 8.00 pm train – shall have bad time of it for next two days. It is really Ludlow's job but I know he cannot leave this place. Air Squadron arrives today. Went in motor car into Belgium on reconnaissance – country very much wired and very like England in many places. Belgians most friendly except in one place where we were stopped for one hour by a crusty old man armed with a rusty gun. The reason is that German Officers are supposed to have made a reconnaissance dressed as English and French Officers. Arrived at Busigny at 11.00 pm and slept in the goods shed on sacks of salt – was very tired.

**Monday 17 August 1914** Did not wake 'till 7 am – French porters seemed to be waiting for something. As soon as I got up off the sacks they whisked them on to a cart – very nice of them to wait until I was awake. Spent a bad day – nothing to do but to wait for trains. Was given a billet over a little *auberge* in Busigny.

**Tuesday 18 August 1914** Another day with trains – saw many old friends as Regiments of Cavalry coming through all day – otherwise a very monotonous proceeding. Moving to sudden orders, left by 11.23 train for Maubeuge. Arrived at 2.00 am and woke up Ludlow, very grumpy but everything all right.

**Wednesday 19 August 1914** No news – went to Conference at GHQ at Le Cateau-Cambresis at 12 noon – saw many old friends. Had lunch and returned here at 4.00 pm. Tried to teach my servant the French for a toothbrush, most comic, but he went out and bought one. Got two letters from my own* – not allowed to write as censorship most strict – Sent postcard home. I think there will be some trouble with French Officers – we do not know how to treat them at all – hope it will blow over. It is, to my mind, of the utmost importance to keep friends with them – I dislike R.† – but he is no worse than many of our own people – the British Officer is very insular.

**Thursday 20 August 1914** Moved the HQ to Aibes. Move forward tomorrow – northwards I believe.

**Friday 21 August 1914** Cavalry Division marched at 5.00 am and crossed the border into Belgium. Chetwode [5th Ca.Bde] being moved to Binche at about 8.00 am – we began to get our first news of the Germans. Of course all alarmist reports from the inhabitants, but no doubt fairly true. We moved forward to the line Binche-Mons. I was sent into Fontaine L'Sogne to see General Sordet, he was very polite and punctilious. Their horses were very tired, they had been having a good doing. Came back southwards.

**Saturday 22 August 1914** Up at 3.00 am and did no more 'till 12 noon. At 9.00 am we got news of a squadron of 4th Dragoon Guards (Bridges) having got rich and captured some Germans – everyone very bucked up. German prisoners looked very young. Our first touch of war – our orders were to move west but at 11.00 we got news of Goffy* being engaged with enemy. This was the first fight – Scots Greys† were engaged towards Pommeroeul, I went to stop 4th Bde, found Staff gone and wandered out to find them. Went towards Binche and met Bulkeley Johnson of Greys, said he had had a nice scrap – all very happy and not a bit afraid of Germans. Rode back towards Goffy and met Allenby and Staff – all well. Enemy did not push and we retired west on Quiévrain – 15 miles over paved roads, the worst march I have ever done, on a tired horse and in the dusk. Arrived 11.30 pm – a long day.

**Sunday 23 August 1914** Had promised myself a long lie: result that I was woken at 3 am. Left at 4.30 with General Allenby for Conference at 2nd Army HQ. At 6.00 pm Germans attacked line of Canal* and our troubles began – 5th Div.† heavily attacked. Moved out during night, had half hour's sleep.

**Monday 24 August 1914** Moved out of Elouges at 4.00 am and German attack started at about 4.30, not pushed very hard against us – so moved west thinking 5th Div. retiring; this not the case and had to come back to our first real fight – was greatly surprised because was not nearly as frightened as I thought. Fought for about three hours and helped 5th Div. to get away. 9th Lancers and 4th Dragoon Guards* charged and lost heavily, but not so heavily as one would have thought – Goffy went in too and stopped German attack – 4th Hussars leading. Saw Mockett who had horse shot under him and also Parker (5th Lancers) shot in the leg, he was quite cheerful. It was a beautiful Cavalry action, the men fought splendidly. Our Artillery was excellent, I watched a section working against the Infantry and every shell burst low over them; they stood it for five minutes and then bolted. We retired as soon as our mission was accomplished and hoped to get back to billets to reorganise after the fight. It is difficult to describe the feelings of the ordinary mortal when first under fire.

At 5.00 pm we got to a place called Germimes – there we were told to occupy a position, it had been partly entrenched. Cavalry to occupy a position, if attacked we lose all our mobility, the official reason being that the Infantry was too tired. I got back to my billet at midnight – half hour's sleep in 48 hours. The questions which must be asked are as follows: Why did we advance north only to retire? Were we were short of guns? Perhaps it is part of a general plan, I hope so! It is poor comfort to the rank and file who know little except that they are **retiring**.

**Tuesday 25 August 1914** Up at 3.30 [am]. Had a great hunt to find Allenby and found him at last at about 10.00 am about six miles south-east of Valenciennes. Here met sporting Colonel of French Territorials who had fought the Germans 'till he had run out of ammunition. We told him we would cover him. Moved south and came on Germans, they quickly got our range and commenced shelling us. Shells dropped all round but did not do any damage – met 1st Inf.Bde* and moved south, the rear guards were closely followed up this evening; we came again under heavy shell fire. No orders reached us as regards billets and at 7.00 pm we decided on Beaumont. I went forward on a tired horse, but there was considerable confusion. The Cavalry Division got separated owing to the rear guard being driven south-east, Beaumont being south-west. No food tonight for men or horses. Slept for two hours on a mattress in a small pub, but was woken up every half hour.

**Wednesday 26 August 1914** Moved to Ligny and tried concentrate Cavalry Division, enemy attacked all along line there impossible to do so, remained about Ligny all day. Enemy shell fire very heavy – Hoped that French would co-operate from Cambrai; the Cavalry did so and saved us a lot of trouble in the evening. 4th Div.* hotly engaged and many casualties – it is no fun watching a battle, but without **guns** this sort of fighting is impossible – we only had two and the 4th Bde. At 5.00 pm covered the retirement of 4th Div. and got into billets at Lempire[?] at midnight very tired. Infantry very footsore and weary.

**Thursday 27 August 1914** Moved at 4.00 am to a position of readiness south of Lempire – slept from 7.00 to 8.30 nothing doing. Haldane's [10th] Bde* came through, we got them some food. Moved about 10.00 am on St Emilie and got in touch with Germans – had a small rearguard action and went with Crichton's squadron of Blues†. We now dodge the shell fire – first comes an aeroplane and has a look at us, goes away and about 15 minutes after shells start dropping – now as soon as aeroplane goes away we move and the shells drop in the wrong place. German guns very good, their fuses not so good. Moved into billets at Mesnil-Bruntel south-east of Peronne and got there at 6.00. At 7.00 received orders to move another nine miles south to Rouy-Le-Grand. This was a most trying march, moved at 8.30 and troops never got in at all, men slept in saddles – they had been going for three days – little or no food, little or no sleep. Our one idea is a day's rest to reorganise.

**Friday 28 August 1914** Stopped to rest but at 4.00 am moved south, reached Cressy.

**Saturday 29 August 1914** Enemy advanced in force and 4th and 2nd Bdes retired fighting on Noyon. Cavalry Division HQ moved to Dives.

**Sunday 30 August 1914** Moved to Compiegne – the saddest things of the war are the poor inhabitants, they are terrified of the Germans. You see old men, old and young women and children fleeing along the roads, it is terrible, who wants war? This retirement is a terrible strain, the only thing that keeps one up is the knowledge that Russia is advancing and that Germany must, must beat France before she can turn and cope with Russia. I know this but the men don't – they are wonderful really.

**Monday 31 August 1914** We are to cover more of 2nd Army – we have got De Lisle, Bingham and Briggs* now. The day was a very ordinary one only fight of outposts – very hot. Our billeting orders changed three times – got very little sleep. Allenby is wonderful, he has had an awful week of it and yet he has been kindness itself, it is greatly due to him that the morale of troops has not suffered more.

**Tuesday 1 September 1914** A fighting day – 6.00 am we got message that Briggs [1st Cav.Bde]* heavily attacked at Nery. Moved up at once with 4th Bde and I Battery came under fire as soon as approached village, was very anxious as Regiment† in this Brigade. Story as follows – German 4th Cav.Div. moved up in fog to within 600 yards of village and caught Bays‡ and L Battery outside it, horses stampeded and L Battery most gallantly got into action, they were practically wiped out by shell fire – our advance and that of 10th Inf.Bde caused enemy to quit and we got eight of their guns – took 40 or 50 prisoners. We gave as good as we got that is one thing and got their guns§.

**Thursday 3 September 1914** Retired to Gournay-sur-Marne and went into billets in lovely chateau – we are at last having a day's rest*. Parts of the weeks passed seem to be a nightmare and for two days I firmly believed we should end our existence fighting to get the footsore and tired Infantry back, or else in a German fortress. We started on the line Binche-Valenciennes, we are now back on the Marne. It is only troops such as ours which could have stood the strain, I do not believe Continental conscripts would have had much fight in them after our experiences. It may be a good thing for the Army to experience troubles first and then the good things afterwards but it may also ruin an army. It is a great pity, our men do not fear the German Cavalry in the slightest and in every action, however small, have done well. They have been very steady under shell fire of the most awful kind – I only hope that we shall lead them forward soon. On the other hand we have lost at least 25 per cent of our efficiency during this retrograde movement. Of General Allenby no praise can be too high, we call him 'the Bull' and through all this time he has been absolutely stolid and to the outer world has shown a calm face whatever his thoughts may have been. The French are difficult to understand; there are thousands of them all over the country, yet there is no concerted action on their part whatever.

**Friday 4 September 1914** Good news today – a forward movement at last we hope but it may be dashed at any minute. I only hope that the Germans won't get into here and spoil the place, they are no respecters of persons or places.

**Saturday 5 September 1914** Marched at 4.00 am south, I think that men are rather dispirited, they want to go forward. Reached Brie-Comte Robert about 9.00 am and had the usual tussle about transports and roads. Rumours of French successes, of Joffre playing his trump card – that H.W.* wants to go back behind the Seine and soon – real truth is we must refit. Reached our farm at 11.00 am and there met all the big boys of GHQ; they say we are going forward and we have to move east. Arranged to move at 4.00 pm and arrived in billets at 9.00 pm, bad billets and little or no sleep. Orders arrive and we move **north** tomorrow, everyone quite pleased and jolly.

**Sunday 6 September 1914** Moved north in morning covering right and front of the 1st Army Corps and in touch with French Cavalry Corps on our right. De Lisle [2nd Cav.Bde] leading and he got into touch easily with German Cavalry, near Pècy came under shell fire. HQ had four Officers wounded in about two minutes – the usual story all in a bunch watching the shelling and a shell burst in the middle of them. Long wait for 1st Army Corps to come and fighting in a desultory way all day – French Cavalry talk a lot but do not come on, their horses are terrified, they never get off them at all, it is a wonder they last a week.

Had first personal brush with Uhlans: J.T.† and I motored forward to see the night billets and Jacco of the Signals followed. We were motoring towards Jouy-le Cha when suddenly I saw three Lancers coming down the road about 300 yards away. I swore they were Uhlans but J.T. said 9th Lancers, anyway I got hold of the rifle in the car and we began to turn it at the crossroads. Jacco then came, he had no doubt about the Uhlans and he and I jumped out of the cars and loosed off at them, they made off down the road, **we did not hit one!!!** Then 10 men of the Signal troop came up and we saw about 50 of them on our flank and blazed away at them and got three. They were not enterprising, otherwise they would have bagged the lot of us. It was rotten bad shooting on our part.

**Monday 7 September 1914** Uhlans reported all round us – made a mess of march table and was very sick about it. Hutch* is a bit of a grouser. Met enemy nearly at once at least 2nd Cav.Bde† did, turned out to be Guard Cavalry, they charged but did little good against the rifle and the mounted attack. A good example of the lack of the combination of the two. Had a very long day, we were in touch with the enemy all day. Slow work waiting for the 1st Corps to come up on our left. The country is beautiful and full of orchards, everywhere signs of the German bivouacs – beginning to see signs of retirement, dead horses, accoutrements lying about and so on. Went into billets at La Hante, just a farm, most insanitary and so had dinner in the orchard and slept under a tree.

**Tuesday 8 September 1914** Expected a hard day and got it all right. Started 4.00 am and prepared to cross the Grand Morin at La Ferté-Gaucher. Here we found the bridge broken by the French in the retirement, but mended by the Germans who made a very good job of it. Rather surprised to find no resistance, so we continued north via Pinebard to the Petit Morin river. A German aeroplane here flew over us and we all shot at it, but needless to say without any result at all. Here we heard that the crossing over the Petit Morin were held and found the 2nd Div. (1st Corps) fighting for a crossing at La Tretoire. I was sent over to see Monro and saw Percival*, discussed the situation and checked that the best way we could help was to push across at Sablonnières. Got in touch with the French on our right.

The crossing at Sablonnières proved rather a tough nut and was not carried easily, many Officers and men being wounded. The bridge lies in a valley and it is practically impossible to get any Artillery fire on it. The German troops fought well and I spoke to several prisoners – they told me their orders were to defend the crossing until told to retire. Of course no one told them to retire and so they stayed until killed or captured – their discipline must be very good. We got across after a fight† and pursued for a couple of miles and then were fired on by our own guns, not a pleasant experience – this must happen in modern war. Rained in the evening and a great muddle as to billets – we went into a farm, the Germans had been there the night before and had made hay, pulled every drawer out and thrown all things on the floor, emptied the cellar and so on, makes one very angry at the waste of good stuff. Off early next morning so to bed but not much rest – fleas!!! It is curious how the Germans publish false information to their men; they tell them all sorts of stories and the men believe these implicitly.

**Wednesday 9 September 1914** Spent a horrible night and in the morning moved forward to cross the River Marne, expected opposition here but to our surprise found none. We crossed at Chezy-sur-Marne and found the bridges intact, but everywhere signs of the retiring Germans. After crossing we moved on to a place called Le Thiolet. Here our motors were sniped at from the wood and three of them were hit, we picked up about 30 prisoners from the woods, they looked tired. 3rd Inf.Bde (Landon) came up in the evening and we had a scramble for billets. French not much help today – my opinion of them does not improve. They are never in line – if they had been we should have made a huge bag of Germans, but neither our Infantry or the

French came on. We spent the night at Bonneil – French just as bad as Germans in the way they treat the inhabitants. No casualties reported today for a wonder, every day we fight and generally lose an Officer or two.

**Thursday 10 September 1914** Moved early with objective north-east. Heard firing from the west and south [?] and I got into a motor to see 1st Div. (Lomax). Roads blocked with troops, met Fraser coming back from Lomax and so returned with him. Lomax hotly engaged with Germans at Priez. On return found Cavalry Division moving towards Sommelans and La Croix-sur-Ourcq to protect right of 1st Div. and get round enemy's left. Briggs [1st Cav. Div.» led and on reaching a point south-west of La Croix brought his guns into action. He was at once answered by a concealed German battery and later had a shell pumped into a Squadron of my Regiment (11th). This German battery was well handled and took on two of ours and two French batteries without being knocked out – we could not locate it. Saw a convoy of enemy moving on Breny, Bingham took it on with his guns and the French pursued it with Infantry in motor buses. Many rumours, result not known, evidently up against strong rearguard of Germans. French crossed at Breny, we stayed on south bank of stream, we wanted to go forward but our orders were imperative. Went into billets at Grisolles, everything cleared out.

Two distressing things happened today, both cases of being shelled by our own troops. In one case a Regiment got within 50 yards of a German battery and had practically captured it when it was shelled out by our own people and had some casualties, the second case no one was hurt luckily. Germans still retiring, French Cavalry playing Marceline*. In the middle of the night orders arrived giving direction of march north-east instead of north – there is bound to be confusion.

**Friday 11 September 1914** There was – first we found the HQ of a French Cavalry Corps in Oulchy-le-Château and also a French Cavalry Division. This delayed us for two or three hours. We saw some of the Algerian Cavalry for the first time mounted on tiny Barb ponies, but all quite cheerful. The Officers told me that they feel the cold very much, what our Indian troops will do when they arrive heaven only knows. Poured in torrents all afternoon but we got shelter in a shed. Germans reported from all inhabitants as tired and rather dispirited, but they do not leave many traces behind. Advanced as far as Branges, then went into billets at Servenay. This is not a good day – the feeling is that we are not getting on enough on the heels of the Germans, but perhaps that was the wet and cold.

**Saturday 12 September 1914** Moved forward with intention of crossing La Vesle River at Courcelles and Bazoches – bridge at Courcelles broken but others standing. Bazoches occupied by French Cavalry – so 1st Bde sent across at Braine, village occupied but taken and a good bag of 50 prisoners taken. 5th Bde* came up and saw Haking, quite cheerful. In evening went into billets at Vauxcére – pouring with rain very wet, little or no food, no transport, not a good evening.

**Sunday 13 September 1914** We moved north with the intention of crossing the river Aisne either at Bourg-et-Comin or Pont-Arcy and get the high ground beyond. First thing walked two miles across heavy plough to get my horse and found General* riding it. De Lisle moved forward and occupied Troyon. Looking at this ground from the south side I saw masses of German Cavalry moving all along the skyline on the main Rheims-Soissons road, we watched them for about two or three hours – estimated it a strong Division. We all wished we could be at them but they were too far away. We thought the position a strong one and knowing that the Germans were fighting the French at Soissons, that they would probably hold it as a rearguard and flank guard. We were not far wrong. Infantry took several prisoners and we went into billets at Villeres-en-Prayères for the night.

**Tuesday 15 September 1914** The battle begins – very foggy in the early morning the Infantry moves on Troyon and takes some prisoners and 12 guns. Cavalry moves to the right flank to the Tour de Paissy. We do not do much, just meditate and from time to time are shelled by enemy. Very thankful when the French come up on our right. The Germans have some big guns with a high explosive [shell], we call them the 'Coal Box'* because a lot of black smoke follows the explosion, they make a lot of noise but do not do very much harm unless they happen to hit – the German Gunnery is very good. It is funny how a battle rages round a point, in this case it is a factory chimney on top of a hill. Both sides will not let the other remain there and so the fight goes backwards and forwards. Attack reconnoitre attack – we have not much to do with it.

What a day for a birthday! I told Allenby that it was mine, all he said in his blunt way was that he would not wish me many happy returns of it. Back to the same billets – this is the second time only that we have slept under the same roof. We have seen a lot of the Zouaves and Turcos†, but the cold weather does not seem to agree with them and I don't wonder, they have been sleeping in the open for some nights and their trousers seem to be made of paper. They are very stoical, badly wounded men walk back from the firing line and do not seem to mind. The Infantry I hear have had very hard fighting and many casualties and I suppose many friends have gone. The Black Watch‡ took 12 guns but could not keep them.

**Wednesday 16 September 1914** Returned to our position at 5.00 am, we are getting tired of our shed and wondering when it will become a shell trap. Great noise of firing on our left and the 1st Corps hotly engaged. We have today only the 4th Bde* (Bingham) in, but we have the 32nd Bde (RFA)† which in such a case as this will be of the utmost use. The 1st and 2nd Bdes are with D.Haig and the 1st Corps – we are fighting without any reserves today except a couple of weak Cavalry Brigades. It is curious to see how the French hold such a position – they are as thick as flies on it whilst on the other hand we are as thin as possibly can be. Got lots of letters and parcels and am very pleased with things tonight.

We are still fighting the battle, the 1st and 2nd Corps are still engaged very hotly and the Sugar Factory‡ is once more the scene of the attack. It is strange the emptiness of the modern battle field – you see a few batteries, puffs of smoke dotted here and there, some ambulances, a group or two of men, a burning farm or two and at times a great deal of noise. Very difficult to distinguish friend from foe, at times impossible. It has rained most of the day. Here the roads are as if the bottom had fallen out of them – a foot of liquid mud in places – horses and men all alike perfectly filthy. The roads are full of horses, carts of all sorts, motors and mud everywhere. During the afternoon a very strong attack on the Sugar Factory – we turned all our guns on it to help. It was rather an anxious time and we were very glad when the attack was repulsed. The French on our right have been properly gingered up; Curly Birch is the head gingerer and chucker-out, if they talk of retiring they are at once reported and sent home, we have already got rid of several. Fighting has gone on all day and the Germans kept their guns going last night.

**Thursday 17 September 1914** The battle is still going on, in our little corner the morning broke foggy and with a promise of rain. The promise soon matured for the rain began to come down early and 'till 6.00 pm it simply poured with a biting south-west wind – we were thankful of our shed and kept as warm as we could in the straw. The French had pushed a detachment into Ailles (a village about 1½ miles in front) and that was the trouble – of course pushing out a salient like that was to invite an attack. It came at once and back came the French, men and Batteries, luckily we had the French General* with us so we did not let him think of a retirement but he wanted to, at least this was our impression. Anyhow we sent the 3rd Hussars up who trotted quickly through the retiring Zouaves. As soon as the Zouaves saw this, they turned like a man and went back to the firing line, this was rather curious – it is the old question of morale.

**Friday 18 September 1914** At 7.00 am the Coal Box started – the shells came nearer and nearer – they hit the tower on our right and the farm and went all round our shed, at last it became too warm to be pleasant so we went behind the hay rick, but no good at 8.45 we had to quit. It was quite heavy shell fire from Howitzers, luckily the ground was soft. The General had a narrow escape, a shell going into the earth two yards to his side but did not explode – two men killed and five wounded by one shell which exploded five yards away. There is

22

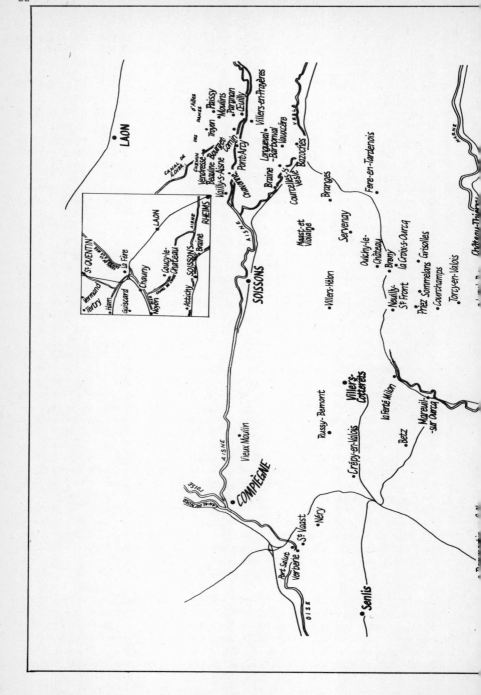

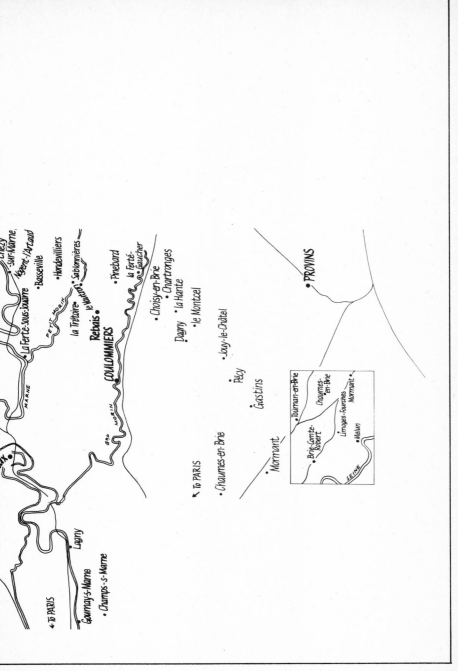

The Battle of the Aisne area.

nothing but shell fire at present, but it is difficult to sit still under it for a long time – the Queens* have been under it for about 12 hours today. After a short time men seem to get used to it and pay no attention to it at all.

**Saturday 19 September 1914** Still at our haystack, the battle still going on. We are now feeding the French on our right they are in the trenches and cannot cook at all. Curly Birch is splendid, he is our Liaison Officer and practically commands the French 10th Corps. I think without him they would have gone back long ago. The old Gentleman* commanding the 38th Div. on our right is a bit of a pessimist, he is a fine old man though but his Staff are like a lot of mutes† at a funeral. Very wet and cold today, but the wet state of the ground is in our favour as it minimizes the effect of the big shells of the German guns.

**Sunday 20 September 1914** A very wet cold day and still at our haystack, the General has a bad cold and has lost his voice but insists on coming out. Hope he will be better later. A day of strong attacks by the Germans. They commenced at 5.00 am and went on all day – the Zouaves gave way a short distance very early in the day and this affected the whole of our right. There was no great cause for anxiety as we had for once some reserves, but it was a very anxious time as we did not know how far the French would hold out. At night we held our trenches again but the French were slightly retired – all was well however by evening although D.H.* very worried by L.† who has nerves. Heavy firing from all sides 'till long after dark. Germans seemed to have attacked all along the line today, their losses must be great. Ravenhill brings us out hot lunch daily this is I think our salvation.

Rode forward to locate the left of the French and our right. Saw the ground over which the Zouaves tried to retake top of ridge – they had many casualties, the slope was dotted with them – they were all from shell fire – it was very accurate. Even as I walked forward several shells bursting quite close – they must have been observing from a captive balloon which we saw, the shells bursting south-east and then enfilading the attack which was moving north-north-east. These black troops although excellent fighters do not like shell fire, I don't wonder. How will it affect our Indian troops?

**Thursday 24 September 1914** The battle of the big guns continues and German attacks which are always beaten back. Tuesday [22nd] they found our haystack and we had to retire, yesterday they found it out with a vengeance and we were under a lot of shell fire, several shells hitting the stack itself, so once more we had to move. It was a very clear day yesterday I think that they could see us from the Sucrerie on top of the hill and thought we were one artillery observation party – anyhow we had to quit. The German spy system is excellent. The French found a man in a farm with an underground telephone, he had been given 30,000 francs and his horses, he was of course shot. A second case our troops saw the hands of a clock on a tower moving and found a man signalling with them. This man I hope was also shot but have not yet heard.

Yesterday the French were to attack all along the line, heavy gun fire everywhere, but I do not think that they did very much – at all events on our immediate right they got back the position which they lost a couple of days ago. We know very little here, the rumour is that Italy has declared war against Austria, that Germany has pushed back Russia. It is difficult to understand but what we do want, looking from the war from a general point of view, is a victory by Russia. Night before last all the Knuts* came to see us, Sir John French, P.A. of Connaught† and they saw Black Maria‡ performing so I suppose they will get the clasp§ for the battle. The weather is now lovely – there is talk about an advance – we **cannot** and **must not** do so until the 2nd and 3rd Corps come up into line with us, the 1st Corps is pushed out as a dangerous salient already – GHQ must see this. I think we shall be here for days – there appears to be no weakening of Germans in front of us, we are the centre and others must pivot on us. Hear French 6th Army doing good work on the West‖.

Sir John French and all the corps commanders are loud in their praises at the way in which the Cavalry have gone into the trenches and done the work of Infantry without a murmur. They have done splendidly, out in the trenches by day and night heartening up Infantry and

Artillery, leading Zouaves forward when they were retiring, I do not think praise is too high for them – unselfishness has been their keyword the whole time. The French General commanding the monkey men (Turcos) is always fussing, we keep him quiet and hearten him up with all good things (R and W)¶. The day finished with the usual performances of Coal Box, but no damage was done to our people – the French batteries suffered. The German aeroplanes are very bold and are always over us, but I hope our planes are going to take them on.

**Friday 25 September 1914** Good news for the Cav.Div. they only want one Regiment up today and I am having a Europe morning*. Shea came over from GHQ and brought us good news as regards our left, hope it proves true. Dalmeny drives him, it is funny how everyone is out here. Great shelling of German aeroplanes this morning but as far as we could see no hits – there is one thing about it however, it frightens them away and they cannot observe in perfect peace. General came back to lunch and we went to see Lomax 1st Div. and I saw Jebb who is now AQMG†. He was full of buck‡ and very glad to get out of GHQ.

We went on to the hill but nothing much doing. Black Maria at work again making a lot of noise and smoke but doing little or no harm – it has on the whole been a quiet day, it may be the calm before the storm – if the French left succeeds we may do some good. Saw 60th [Regiment] moving along road; they look well but it is curious how all Infantry walk with a sort of slouch after a lot of hardship. We are trying hard to get some aeroplanes for the Division at present; they won't give us any so we are trying to steal some from French volunteers. The Remounts§ are again giving trouble. This department seems to collect fat-headed idiots (this is the General's expression) – Too much department with a big 'D' and too little war with a small 'w'. MacAlpine-Leny going down to ginger them up. We have just received the **Kaiser's effusion** – it is quite good reading‖.

**Saturday 26 September 1914** Went on duty up to the hill at 6.00 am and there was a heavy fight going on towards the French 18th Corps on our right and the 2nd Div. on our left. The French 36th Bde had to give ground in the morning whilst our 2nd Div. beat back all attacks with great loss to the enemy. Black Maria was very busy on our hill, she again shelled the HQ out of our cave of vantage and we had at last to retreat to a cave in Pargnan. In front of the 2nd Bde* they came on and were shot down in masses, even the hardened men who have been fighting all the time said it was dreadful – but that is the Prussian system they always say 'We have plenty more. It has been a heavy day's fighting all round, but the Germans have made no impression on our lines or on those of the French. We are very strongly dug in now and quite happy. It was beautifully fine today. The German aeroplanes were very busy, they are gallant fellows. Most of our people are resting and they will be all the better for it.

**Sunday 27 September 1914** Everything much quieter today the German gun fire has certainly decreased in intensity, but it is probably only a lull and we shall have an attack probably tonight. Saw Hutch who was quite chirpy. German prisoner brought in during the morning and found hiding in a haystack, he looked bad, had been there for eight days in fear of his life as he had been told that we shoot all our prisoners. He was awfully scared poor chap. Liaison Officer (Shea) arrived from HQ, news on left not quite so good as Germans produced another Division or Corps, but this must be expected. Nothing doing in our own front today at all. Lewenden drove me over to see Goffy and several others at the 2nd Cav.Div. HQ. Goffy was better but very bored at the inaction – told him all about our work in the trenches and drew him lurid pictures of Black Maria. He told me lots of things which rather opened our eyes, it is funny what a lot of gossip one hears. Got back about 5.00 pm. Lefroy came over from 1st Div.* with an alarmist message – Germans establishing themselves at the Oeuilly-Paissy crossroads – want us to turn them out. The General very funny about it, Cavalry charging a trench or crawling up with rifle in the hand and sword between the teeth like the pirate pictures one sees – this is Infantry work and not Cavalry. Besides I do not think there is any reason to fuss, there are enough guns on Paissy for us to blow any German to pieces who puts his nose over the ridge.

**Tuesday 29 September** 1914 Another quiet day, today our last Regiment in the Moulins Valley has been withdrawn. There is not much activity today among the Germans except with their guns and these are not being used at our trenches but at the valley behind, it seems to be a great waste of ammunition but some day we may know the reason for it. Our food is becoming monotonous and there are lots of partridge and hares about so we are all trying to get scatter guns to go after them, shall borrow a gun and have a dart myself soon. Tried to shoot rabbits with a revolver; it was a very dangerous game, but not for the rabbits. Got a mail in and letters from my own. What a fool Fred Drake* is to talk as he has done – the Regiment are furious with him. Why cannot people keep their tongues quiet? War is not a thing to buck about, one has only to see an attack to keep one quiet for a long time.

Had good news from French left, they are making good progress, but am beginning to take French news with a grain of salt, French are very mercurial. Was passing some Zouaves this morning when one of them called out to me in English. He is a Scot born in France of the name of Menzies. He said the Zouaves loved the English Tommy and Tommy was very good to them and shared food with them – by the bye Tommy has been very well fed this campaign, I think that is the main reason he has fought so well. Black Maria got into the 9th Lancers in their billets at Longueval-Barbonval today, it was a terrible thing 40 casualties, 19 killed and 23 wounded. It is a great misfortune as the 9th have had very bad luck and a great many casualties already.

**Wednesday 30 September** 1914 The last day of September – it seems years since this war started. Had a real holiday today and went into Rheims. We went over in a motor, Baggally, Tomkinson, dear old McCarthy and myself. McCarthy in great form cracking his whip and very Irish. The first thing we saw on approaching were the refugees in hundreds, they leave the town during the day time and go back for the night. All old men, women and children – it was a sad sight – most of the shops were shut, people who were in the street wore a frightened look, the only happy ones seemed to be the boys between six and 12 years of age. We first did some shopping. I bought some underclothing for Barrow, he said he wanted it thick and it was thick, I could not have worn it, but he seemed to think it all right. McCarthy also did some shopping in broad Irish, to pay he simply pulled out a handful of coins and said 'Here take out the amount.'

We then went on to see the Cathedral – it is not as bad as the papers make out – the outside has been considerably damaged and all the beautiful stained glass broken, but the western entrance has hardly been touched. The southern side seems to have suffered most. No one can say that it was not done deliberately, I think it was, as all the houses around except one have been hit and practically demolished. We then went and had a very good lunch at the Hotel; quite a welcome change after our fare here. McCarthy very delighted as he found Guinness' Stout and had the biggest bottle he could get. Returned through the town – more shopping. McCarthy bought wine for his Mess – told the young lady in the shop that as long as she kept her head cool and stomach warm she would be all right – luckily she did not understand English. Drove back and stopped to see Regiment, then home again, had a shock as we saw ammunition columns getting over hill. Thought Black Maria had been at work – but found our home standing. Black Maria sent three shells into Canal behind here, wonder if she will find us tomorrow, but we are well hidden.

**Thursday 1 October** 1914 A frost last night and a lovely morning. Guns still firing but on the whole a quieter morning – wish we could get a move on. Played football in the evening with 32nd Bde (RFA). McCarthy in great form – sorry to say he was leaving us; we shall miss him a good deal. Football great fun and the exercise splendid – only field had been used for grazing cattle and one had to fall rather carefully.

**Friday 2 October** 1914 Great fun over despatches. They must have been called for from GHQ as he [General Allenby] never volunteers them. Brigades sent in long lists so he did great execution with a blue pencil. He goes on the principle that it is up to everyone to do good work without a reward – quite right too – that is the standard to set, but unfortunately it is not the standard throughout the army!! We have had orders to move out of here tomorrow morning. The Battle of the Aisne still continues, I can hear the guns firing now, but not so strongly as before. Does it mean we are going to fight on a new line? I hope so, our eyes must be turned to the northern flank – the line is too long for a success in the centre.

**Saturday 3 October 1914** Marched HQ to the L'Abbataille Château at Braine. Do not like it nearly as much as Villers-en-Prayères. To begin with it is practically in a town and troops have been here for the last three weeks, it must be unhealthy. I wish people in England could see the state of a town after war has passed over it, I think it would open their eyes a bit – the news on the whole is good but Colonel Shea (Liaison Officer) has left us and no new one has been appointed.

**Sunday 4 October 1914** Another week gone, we have at last got orders for a move and we are all very thankful for it. I think that these valleys have got very unhealthy. They have been full of troops for three weeks now and even with the greatest care they become very foul, especially as the Germans were there before us. We move west tonight under cover of darkness – a wise precaution. Left Braine at 8.30 pm with a full moon, it was like marching in daylight no difficulty in finding the road at all. Got to our château at Villers-Hélon at about midnight.

**Monday 5 October 1914** Woke at 8.00 am and found the place a typical French Château, very picturesque. It has the usual moat which is full of huge carp – General de Chauvenet, the old gentleman, is very fond of these and when he whistles they come to be fed. During the German retirement this Château was occupied by the Duke of Mecklenburg, they evidently treated the place well. It is rather funny to think of an old French General who fought in 1870 having a German Duke billeted on him. We hear continual rumours of good French work to the north but nothing official has come in as yet. We move on again tonight and shall reach well known ground – we fought over it during the retreat [from Mons].

**Tuesday 6 October 1914** The Division moved west but I stayed behind with the General and went on by motor at 9.30 am to Russy-Bemont. Took the opportunity of going over the Néry battlefield, it was very sad. We found poor George Ansell's and Cawley's graves. From the position of the German guns it was a marvel anyone escaped. Got a shrapnel bullet as a momento. Went on through Verberie to Port Salut, the proper bridge had been blown down and the French made a temporary bridge by using large barges as pontoons, this worked very well.

It is a curious feeling moving up a road, down which only about five weeks ago we moved thinking sometimes that we were very near a German fortress, to notice the men's faces, to look back and remember how they looked during the retreat, not so much in the Cavalry as the Infantry – the difference in the carriage of a man's body – the way he drags his legs in a retreat and his general forlorn appearance; in the advance the jaunty step and general alertness. Curly Birch arrived with news tonight, he has no opinion of the Frenchman – nor of HQ – he says Castelnau is uneasy about the situation at Roye.

**Wednesday 7 October 1914** First a cypher message during the night that we were to help the French about Roye if absolutely necessary; next a Liaison Officer at 7.00 am asking us to help and lastly Shea from GHQ confirming all this. GHQ must have thought the situation bad as Sir John said that 'should the situation arise every man should be used' – but we must if possible continue our march northwards. We got into a position of readiness about Montdidier just east of the place at about 2.00 pm. All seemed fairly quiet, although guns could be heard to the east. Had a splendid message from Jack* – he said that the French were being heavily attacked and he was reinforcing them with **his troop**!!! 24 men in a line 200 miles long and held probably by 2,000,000 men. Will the whole thing fizzle out? The French held their ground and we went into billets at a château at Fontaine s/s Montdidier.

**Thursday 8 October 1914** I motored on into Amiens to arrange for the passage of the troops through the town. Went to HQ there and had a talk with a voluble old French Officer. Rode through Amiens with 1st Bde and went into billets at Argoeuves. A beautiful day; got a new coat by post and **found V's\* note** in pocket.

28

**Friday 9 October 1914** Marched on to Rèbreuve-sur-Canche; another peace march and a very fine day. Motored on to Frévent, it was full of refugees from Arras. A good deal of fighting going on there. Told about formation of a [Cavalry] Corps – hope shall go on with A.*, but will probably have to remain with the Division. Am glad A. has got the Corps, throughly deserves it.

# 2. The First Battle of Ypres

**Saturday 10 October 1914** Went on to Chelers – A. went off to see French. At 1.00 pm, urgent message from Mandling that we should push on to Bethune so got into a car and went to see if Infantry were going there. Met Gleichen who told me, owing to French not supplying enough motor buses, Infantry would not reach Bethune. Then went on to Briggs and decided to sent patrol forward to see situation. Great fuss going on as our army is concentrating on line north-west of Bethune. Hope all will go well as it is a great chance of regaining incentive. Heard definitely am going to be 1st Grade [GSO in 1st] Cav. Div. Am very lucky and De Lisle going to command.

**Sunday 11 October 1914** Allenby in command of both Divisions – moved up to line of Canal d'Aire, 2nd Corps* moving on Bethune and east of that place. German Cavalry reported north of that place. Allenby told me he had personally recommended me for 1st Grade. Did not know what to say – so thanked him – awfully kind of him. Went into billets at St Venant, the 1st and 2nd Bde in touch with enemy's cavalry on line Vieux Berquin-Hazebrouck. Enemy reported in force north of this line – we always begin a big battle on a Sunday.

**Monday 12 October 1914** Orders for formation of Corps have come out – glorious muddle to begin with. Division ordered to make good line of high ground about Berthen. Both Brigades stopped on line Merris-Vieux Berquin – constant bickering all day – especially round Vieux Berquin. French Cavalry Corps on our right attacked Neuf Berquin but did not do any good, they do not know how to use the rifle. In fact they gave way and exposed Briggs [1st Cav.Bde]'s right. Shall be glad when we are clear of French and with our own Infantry – we can trust them to carry on. Talked over many things with De Lisle and got a lot settled.

**Tuesday 13 October 1914** A day's hard fighting, poor Jack Ainsworth killed near Merris. I am very sorry, he was one of the best subalterns in the Army. Went and saw Briggs at Vieux Berquin – he was being relieved by the Infantry and gave him orders to concentrate behind Strazeele. Then went on to that place and walked over ridge – we must have got into some Germans there – they left only one man dead but must have had many hit. They belonged to 5th Dragoons (King George's Regiment).

We decided to move on Meteren. 2nd Bde ordered to attack that place, 1st Bde on its left on Thieushouck. At 12 noon got orders that 4th Div. to attack Bailleul and to the south, and 6th Div.* Thieushouck – we to co-operate on the left of 6th Div. Attack to commence at 1.00 pm. Meteren ridge strongly occupied by enemy with machine guns – Briggs ordered to attack Thieushouck – Mullins in reserve. Enemy offered a strong resistance and still held ground in evening. Heavy rain and mist and so could not use many guns, poisonous afternoon. A good day's fighting and the situation seems promising as a whole – we are nearly in Belgium again the frontier is only five miles away. Shall have a late night – the worst of a Corps is that orders take so long coming.

**Wednesday 14 October 1914** Back in Belgium again, we left it on 24 August. A day of bickering with the German Cavalry. 2nd Div. started in front but we were soon in line. Captured a few Germans – Infantry got the position about Meteren last night, they got off lightly owing to the fog. If it had not been for that we should have blown them out of their trenches with our guns. Moved on later at about 1.00 pm to Dranouter (oh these Belgian names!) some opposition from German Cavalry – not very much. Caught a young jaeger*, quite an intelligent looking fellow. Moved into billets at Dranouter in a convent school – the Priest most anxious we should take care of the place so issued the strictest orders. I know V. would like this† – shall leave a present for the nuns tomorrow before leaving.

**Friday 16 October 1914** Had orders to attack crossings over Lys River between Armentieres and Pont-Rouge. 2nd Bde ordered forward to do it. There was a dense fog all the morning and in the afternoon one could not see a mile. The result was very slow movement – we got down to the river and found all the crossings defended or the bridges blown up. The Infantry Division were moving up on our right. The 6th Div. got across at Sailly-sur-la-Lys and were up on the right bank. I don't think the Germans mean to hold the line of the river I expect they will be gone tomorrow. The Belgians round here are a poor race, they compare very badly with the French and our own men. In France you see no men, this country is full of them. The Germans will have a bad time retiring through this country as they are not loved by the Belgians who will, I fancy, give a short shrift to any Germans they catch here. We are hunting 15 Uhlans who cannot get back over the river – I think they are hidden in a big wood near here. Hope we move north tomorrow.

**Saturday 17 October 1914** Back again to the river. This sounds like another battle of the Aisne. It is very hard work on the Cavalry man, he goes into the fight with no reserves and occupies a front which four times the number of Infantry would require. He is quite cheerful about it, he only grumbles when he has to come out of it. Moved down to Ploegsteert and established HQ in the house of the priest. Poor young Lumley was killed this morning – as far as I can make out he got up to look through his glasses and the Germans only 300 yards away. He was shot through the lung and died of a haemorrhage. In the evening just as we had arranged billets the 4th Div. came forward and of course turned us out, they advanced two miles that day and we were doing their work on the River the whole day long. Everyone in very bad temper – orders bad, had to go in to Corps HQ at 10.00 pm to see them. Lewenden drove me – at every village a sentry pointed a bayonet at one's middle.

**Sunday 18 October 1914** We generally fight on a Sunday and today was no exception to the rule – we attacked Pont-Rouge with the 2nd Bde. The 9th Lancers got a little bit far, luckily it was during the afternoon and we could withdraw them during the dark.

**Monday 19 October 1914** Still on the river and playing the same game – the 4th Div. are getting a lot of guns up on the ridge behind the chateau. It is only a matter of time that we shall be shelled out of it. This chateau has a tower from which one gets a good view of the country to the east of the Lys River towards Lille. The Germans shell every tower on principle in case it is used as an observing station for Artillery. Nothing of note occurred today except that there was an order for a general attack – the poor Cavalry, they have been holding on to the line of railway west of the river by the skin of their teeth. The Infantry have taken over part of our line and now we have a Brigade in reserve.

**Tuesday 20 October 1914** I knew it would come, the enemy has got more guns up towards Warneton and started shelling our chateau at 8.00 am, I am out of luck today, a splinter from the first shell hit Radway my groom in the side; he is not badly wounded T.G. We had a rush to get the horses under cover, shells dropping all round the house – I personally believe that it is McCarthy's (32nd Bde RFA) fault, he loves being shelled and they follow him about. Then, as we were getting the motors out, another batch of shells came along, one burst and knocked out poor Lewenden. He is not bad T.G. and will be all right the doctor tells me, but

I am terribly depressed at losing him – he has looked after me so well and has been so faithful. I think personally we ought to have moved earlier, but there was no great reason to think that they would shell us. We got everyone out with four casualties, one very serious and have to be thankful for that. The 12th Inf.Bde are not holding the ground well, consequently rather an anxious day. We repulsed several attacks on Le Gheer and St Yves but there was not much sting in them.

Enemy have no aeroplanes therefore cannot locate our guns behind [Hill] 63 – they have been ludicrously wide of the mark all day. We had a narrow escape of our line being pierced today. It is interesting – the 4th Bde* this time were caught in the flank and retired hurridly – luckily De Lisle was suspicious of that flank and sent up the 1st Cav.Bde to Messines. It arrived there only just in time, found the place deserted and the Germans could have walked through. It was another case of minutes. The usual rumours started, one man came galloping up saying the Germans were in Messines and so on. Messines is a tactical point which will play a great part in the next few days fighting, 1st Bde now hold it T.G. and Briggs will not let it go. De Lisle has been wonderful very quiet and calm during a most critical period of time.

**Wednesday 21 October 1914** Went and saw Briggs at Messines – he is holding on all right – and then went back to La Hutte Château where we made our HQ for the day. Met Hunter-Weston (11th Bde*) and heard that Germans had taken Le Gheer at 5.00 am, our own line (cavalry) had not moved. At once decided [it] must be retaken, and Hunter-Weston sent forward Somersets to do so, two squadrons 9th Lancers helping. Retook it at about 12 noon and about 50 prisoners – all Saxons and not a lively looking lot.

A Gunner Subaltern had a funny experience – he was in Le Gheer at the telephone observing the fire of our batteries – he looked out of the windows and saw the place full of Germans, so he sent his last message 'Don't believe any message after this' – and was promptly taken prisoner. He said the Officers treated him with the greatest courtesy and put him in a cellar with a guard over him, so that he should be out of shell fire – the next thing he knew was that the guard over him were taken prisoners by our own people who had retaken the village. It was a critical day but the situation eased a little towards evening, they spared us two columns of the Essex Regiment† to help and hold Messines. On our left the 2nd Cav.Div.‡ are having a bad time of it. Bob Grundy arrived at 10.00 pm asking for a Regiment to help Chetwode [5th Cav.Bde], the 9th Lancers were at once ordered up – and the 2nd Bde ordered to a position of readiness north of Messines by 5.00 am.

**Thursday 22 October 1914** Motored to Wulvergem and found the 1st Connaught Rangers had been brought up in motors, they are very welcome reinforcements. The General* made them dig a trench to show them how it ought to be done properly and then took some of the Officers round in a motor to Messines which was being **shelled to show them what war is like!!!** I bet they saw it all right. Went round to see Gough he was fit and well, but was not satisfied with the situation in front of him at all and I agreed with him. Then came back and saw Briggs and Hutch in Messines, they were quite comfortable. I think we are all right at Messines now and can hold it but it has been a ticklish time – we always fight on a thin line with no reserves. Yesterday the only reserve on a front of about 20 miles was about 2,000 men at the outside – the French and Germans refuse to do this. For the last four or five days the Cavalry Corps have been fighting on a front of six miles with no reserve at all – no other nation could do it, it is a game of pure bluff that is all.

Heavy gun fire all day to the south and north but all reports good, that we are holding our own. It was a quiet day in front of us: a few half-hearted attacks easily repulsed, we are not strong enough to follow them up worst luck. Hear Vaughan fighting hard all day, but held his own well – they are still shelling the chateau, but have not touched one of our guns. McCarthy will be pleased. Hear 1st Inf.Bde Indian Army coming to support Cavalry Corps so all will be well. We want a rest, the men have been at it day and night all for five days now – they cannot go on forever. Hope we shall get it – the situation has eased now I think. Just heard officially of important Russian success on the Vistula†, hope it is a real big one.

**Friday 23 October 1914** Have got McKellar as second servant instead of Radway, am very grateful to Regiment for sending him to me. German losses yesterday must have been very heavy, 800 to 1,000 dead reported in front of 11th Inf.Bde, a battery of 1st Corps fired 600 rounds at a range of 1,000 yards with a good target. Everyone knows what this means – three new Corps reported yesterday 22, 23, 24! I wonder what they are?. Went and saw the trenches at Messines and were at once shot at by snipers. Must not let General do this, not fair on men, it draws fire and gives away position of trenches. He is very fond of doing it and hates sitting in rear which is proper place. All quiet this morning, does this mean a storm later!!

The Indian Divisions* have the Indian mule cart with a native driver, it was quite funny seeing them squatting. Had a long talk to the old padre who came with the Connaughts, he said that the worst enemy of the Indian troops was the damp. I quite agree. They don't mind the dry cold, they cannot stand the wet. Today 57th Wildes' Rifles† were in action, the first Black troops – they lost one man killed and two wounded, they are amongst the best Regiments, they don't understand trench work yet, all they wanted to know was why they were not going forward – a fine spirit. Our aeroplanes are doing fine work now, directing the fire of batteries, that is what is wanted, we missed them on the Aisne in our part of the show. Only one German aeroplane has been over us in three days, hope it is the result of our planes being there. Armoured motor cars with Maxims and 3pr high explosive shells are being much used, one came to Messines last night – tonight we have a 13pr Horse Artillery gun waiting for it – hope we shall catch it all right. Good looking Belgian flapper‡ had very deteriorizing effect on bachelor section of the Staff today.

**Saturday 24 October 1914** Went to Ploegsteert and there saw Hunter-Weston – Archie Montgomery came up from the 4th Div. – learned that [a] heavy attack had been ordered by Germans all along the line, so rushed back to our HQ and met George Marshall with same message from Cavalry Corps. So we all waited for this attack and of course things were more quiet than they had been for days it is always this way. I suppose some secret service agent at the GHQ was trying to earn a good reward and chanced it. Allenby promoted temporary Lieutenant General, and De Lisle a temporary Major General, a niggardly way of doing things. Why not promote them properly at once?

**Sunday 25 October 1914** Woken up during the night with orders – probable advance. Hurley came in at 6.30 and explained matters – no advance is possible at present nor will be until our left has got on. They treat us as if we were Infantry always forgetting that we have not got the **gun** power which Infantry have. Went with Chief* to see Allenby – advance all bosh at present. 1st Corps doing very well up north and it is their success which will enable us to get on – we are running short of 13pr ammunition this is bad, I suppose no one calculated that our 7th Div.† would have horse guns instead of field!!!

Went out shooting from 12-1, missed two pheasants, the gunnery was rotten. There are a lot of partridges, hares and pheasants about and if one only had a dog one would not do so badly. They are still shelling Messines, but I think we have only Cavalry in front of us here. Just heard a story about the German attack on 1st Corps: they made five attacks, each attack about a Regiment advanced in close order singing *Die Wacht am Rhein*‡ and we of course practically annihilated them – they are fine **men** these Germans and fine fighters. These Regiments belonged to a Reserve Corps – as a nation they have a fine patriotism to drive them on in this way.

**Monday 26 October 1914** The 2nd Bde has been ordered south to help the 2nd Corps, they have evidently been having a bad time of it, they are said to have had 8,000 casualties in the last five days. A forward movement was ordered for 3.00 pm after a conference at Goffy's HQ – 3rd Cav.Div. on the left under Byng*, then the 2nd next under Gough and we were to hold Messines as the pivot. But nothing happened at all as the right of the 7th Div. were driven in and the 3rd Cav.Div. had to swing northwards to meet the counter attack of the Germans. We were not informed that anything had happened on the left and it was slow work waiting – the Connaughts† went forward at 4.00 pm and got into the German advanced trenches capturing an Officer, but that was all. In the evening the German shells set fire to the convent church in Messines, it is a fine eleventh century building but I am afraid that it will be gutted, it was burning fiercely tonight. Heavy firing broke out at about 10.00 pm, so went to bed in my clothes as a precaution, but the night was a quiet one on the whole.

**Tuesday 27 October 1914** Went for a joy ride today down to the 2nd Corps. First went upto Messines and heard a curious story about the Church there which was burning — when they went into it this morning the whole place was gutted except one thing and that was the crucifix with the figure of Christ on it — it was absolutely untouched by fire or anything else. If one wrote it in a novel or paper the world would scoff but here is a fact. The 7th Div. have been having a rocky time of it, they have been withdrawn temporarily and the 1st Corps take their place. It is a curious thing how troops vary, a matter of discipline I think. Tonight our line is very thin, too thin I think for safety, but in war risks have to be taken.

Another point today they tried to bring men out of trenches in the day, the result is unnecessary casualties. When will we learn that in war you cannot organise a big attack in five minutes — two or three hours spent in organisation is never wasted? We start organising our attacks at 9.00 am — this should be done at night and the troops got into position under cover of darkness, then when you are ready let it go and it goes with a bang. Time is certainly a great factor, but when you are punching at a line it is not so great as in a turning movement. I think this is the critical time, Joffre is pouring troops up towards Ypres, the trains are coming in at the rate of one every 11 or 12 minutes. If we can really get going here we may do something — it is an anxious time however. Tomorrow we get a heavy battery and some 6in. Howitzers to help us — fine things for a Cavalry Division!! Nice and mobile!! The French official account makes out the Russian victory on the Vistula greater than we thought, but there is no official confirmation. Heavy firing tonight again towards the east of Ypres, hope 1st Corps are taking the Germans on all right.

**Wednesday 28 October 1914** Went to Messines myself and saw the cross, it is a wonderful thing — there is only one small piece of damage to the figure of Christ, a small hole on the left side of the body. As a friend of mine* put it 'It is the only thing amidst a scene of desolation which is whole — not one other bit is there which is not touched.' I shall not forget it. Still at Neuve Eglise — I wish we would move on — this place is beginning to stink: troops are always passing through it. Rumours of great French offensive north of Ypres to the sea, hope it will mature.

**Thursday 29 October 1914** I think that the Germans are making every possible effort to break our line — this is the critical period their attacks are persistent. This morning they attacked and drove in a small portion of our line east of Ypres — the last message we got in was that Douglas Haig was making a counter attack with a Division — that is what is required, it is no good putting troops in piecemeal, the only way if you are going to counter attack is to do so with a large force. The 2nd Bde returned tonight, things are very unsatisfactory down here and once again we have been used to stiffen other troops. The [47th] Sikhs have had a bad time — they most gallantly attacked, but were unsupported — bad Staff work. 2nd Bde [had] about 60 casualties — one does not mind casualties, these things must happen in war, it is all right if troops are pulling their weight, but casualties through mistakes are quite a different thing and leave one cold. Heavy firing heard towards Hill 63 and Le Touquet at about 6.00 pm but has now died down.

**Friday 30 October to Monday 2 November 1914** Have had no time to write for this has been the most anxious time we have had since the retreat — Messines itself has meant everything and the 1st Cav.Div. have had to defend it. The Cavalry have had to do most things but street fighting with bayonets is quite new. We had a Brigade of Cavalry and some Native Infantry (½ Brigade 61st Wilde's Rifles) for the defence. We held our original line round the south and east of the town. The Germans then made up their minds that they would take Messines and commenced the attack quite systematically in their usual way.

The point which will be raised by Historians and Military Critics (sic) after the war will be:

34

The Ypres Salient area.

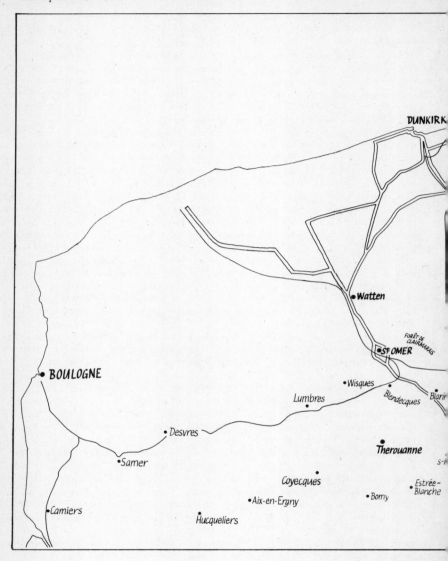

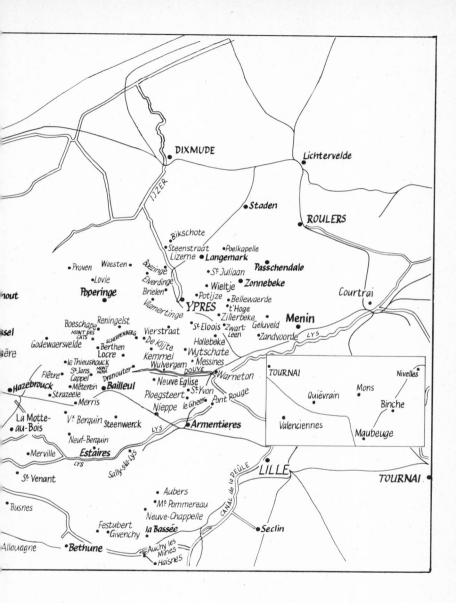

why did we hang onto the place, what use was it to us? Would it not have been better to have retired and made it a piece of neutral ground? The reason to my mind is a plain one – there were two phases. The first [was] where we held Messines and the 1st Corps was advancing on Menin – the advance could not take place unless we held the place. The second was that our troops could not reach Menin and if you look at a map this [phase], a defensive one temporarily, did not need us to hold the ridge as long as we did not allow the Germans to advance much beyond it. It is curious that a thing which is right one minute is wrong the next.

Well the 1st Bde under Briggs held it against enormous odds, it was a wanderful defence by Cavalry with the bayonet, fighting from house to house and street to street to street for two days, defending a corner here and another there. All this time the place was being very heavily shelled, shells dropping about 50 a minute into the town – I went up into the town every day and on the Sunday the bullets flying about all over the place. Hutch had a narrow squeak, he had to get up early luckily for him – half an hour after he got up a shell went into his room and blew everything into bits. Briggs was just splendid he ought to get everything he can be given – his defence of Messines was one of the things which will make history.

We made our HQ at a little *estaminet* about half a mile east of Wulvergem. On the 31st the fight was going on in Messines and the shells were dropping all along the road. Hambro and I were in the room of the inn, looking at the map when a shell hit the house. It was a curious sensation, it felt rather like the earthquake scene in a Drury Lane Drama* – the whole thing came down like a house of cards. It was pitch dark and we got out through the window thinking every minute another was coming in the same place. The President's* car was standing outside and was hit but luckily not in the engine, he is rather proud of the holes – we went to a safer place at Wulvergem. We retired out of Messines on the morning of the 1st to a position about one mile to the west of it and have held on there ever since suffering very heavy casualties. We held on to this position until November 3rd when we were relieved by the 2nd Cav.Div. under Gough. I think personally that this has been the hardest fighting of the war we have had about two Corps against us. We are told that the German Emperor was up here on the 2nd and our aviators dropped 130 bombs that day in the hope of finding them a good billet – our casualties have been enormous: 50 Officers and 450 men out of probably 900 – 50 per cent? The Oxford Hussars‡ joined us, they are very keen and stood the shell fire well – we hope now for 48 hours rest perhaps 72 hours. We want it badly because men are physically tired from want of sleep, not because they have no fight left in them. The London Scottish§ came in for a bad time too on the Messines ridge, they did right well however, but will have to be rested. Our HQ is now in a house near St Jans Cappel.

**Sunday 8 November 1914** The Battle of Messines still goes on. Rumours every day that Germans are retiring, but they still hold the Messines ridge, although on the 5th the number of guns against us were appreciably less. On the 5th the 1st Cav.Div. went back into the trenches again, but the French have sent up a large number of troops and we found Conneau's Cavalry Corps alongside us. They are fine fellows these French Cavalry men, but their training for war has been hopeless and they are therefore useless. They are armed with a small carbine, a pop gun, and carry about 20 rounds of ammunition. I believe they would charge anything if you asked them to do so, but to see a man with a cuirass* on in a trench or trying to skirmish across a field is too funny for anything, only it is very serious as they are then wasted – fine men too, the pick of the people. They are getting short of horses and so they form them into battalions of foot horse – they are no help to us in the trenches.

The French are to my mind bad neighbours to fight with. They never seem to mind retiring three, four or five miles and then advancing again and retaking their positions. It seems to me that they would rather do this and lose 100 men doing it, than stick it out and lose 25 men. I think that it is a matter of numbers. The French fight in depth and can do it, we fight in a thin line and cannot afford to give an inch because we have not enough men to retake a position once it is lost. Therefore when alongside the French the matter is one of continual anxiety, they keep on laying our flank open by these temporary retirements and we loose a lot of men unnecessarily. Just heard Kavanagh's Bde† had a terrible doing and lost many Officers. They had to go into a hole thus made by our allies – have not had full detail yet.

French attacked Messines again yesterday, I went forward to the trenches with De Lisle and we had made about a mile of ground Germans will probably counter attack today. I also went up to La Hutte – the place is one mass of holes where they have been shelling McCarthy's Batteries. They have been using the big gun here, some of the holes were enormous. Our losses have been terrific in this Battle of the Lys – but I think they have given their full value to the war. The enemy's losses must have been colossal. General Foch is now up here commanding the French – he is an optimist and a great thruster, he thinks the Germans are weakening and that Joffre is preparing a great blow somewhere.

The situation at this moment may be summed up as follows. In the east Germany has 19½ Corps all told against the Russian 32‡, Austria is becoming more and more a negligible quantity and will soon be ripe for Italy to deal with§. Here in the West it is difficult to say, but the point is that Germany has not been strong enough to break through and bring about a decisive result. The situation thus would appear to face Germany with the following problem. She must either hold Russia and break through here or hold us here and break through the Russians. It would appear looking back now that, when things were blackest for us at the beginning of September, Germany made a miscalculation and did not have sufficient troops to carry on her successful march on Paris; she must have sent too many troops to the east. Secondly Austria's fighting qualities were overstated and Russia's understated. Now the result of these appear. She cannot hope to hold Russia without very dangerously weakening herself here and thus giving Joffre the chance he is looking for.

It will be interesting to see what happens. The whole of Europe is now at war and there is no other factor namely weight of numbers that can step in that will make much difference. I personally think that Germany's last throw will be her Fleet, when that comes out to fight we shall be nearing the end. We want to refit now, our men and Officers have lost many comrades and dear friends. The black shadow is over Europe – we live from minute to minute and hour to hour – who knows except Providence what is in store for each individual man? The French are still attacking the ridge and progressing slowly – I hope they will get it today.

**Monday 9 November** 1914 Back into the trenches today although things have been much quieter. The French have received strong reinforcements and are by way of taking the offensive against Wytschaete and Messines, they certainly have made some ground against the latter place and dug themselves in but otherwise things go slowly. They have been having a go at the 11th Inf.Bde at Ploegsteert Wood and turned them out of a couple of trenches and hold a house or two, but that is all. The General has again been out under the shell fire – the car was hit in two places, luckily they were not in it. 1st Bde are in the trenches tonight.

**Tuesday 10 November** 1914 Established our HQ at the old place in Neuve Eglise and De Lisle went forward in a car to Wulvergem. As he came round the old corner a shell burst just above them, killed a French soldier just behind and broke the glass screen. The President (Coleman) was hit in the chest with a lump but not wounded – so we returned him as 'wounded but fit for duty'; he was awfully pleased. The car had its radiator smashed and he is taking it back to St Omer to get it mended. How he will buck – he started as soon as he got to Bailleul and Ludlow came up howling with laughter. I went for L.* for always going into the shell area, not right on part of Divisional General except when actually fighting the Division. Otherwise it was a dull day – the Germans still hold the houses at Le Gheer – we are sapping up to these and propose blowing them up. 2nd Bde relieved 1st and so home at 6.00 pm.

**Wednesday 11 November** 1914 We are to be relieved by Gough today and have been promised 72 hours' rest. During dinner we got a wire saying Sir John [French] would present the French decorations, this is the third attempt, every time he has tried to do this there has been an awful battle. Well sure enough half an hour afterwards we got an order to be ready to move to 1st Corps at Ypres – we left at 11.00 pm – a nasty cold and wet night. I motored on to the 1st Corps HQ with De Lisle and there we learnt that we were to form the only reserve D. Haig had got. So back we went to Byng's (3rd Cav. Div.) HQ and and I got the General to lie down while I went on to meet our Staff on the Ypres-Locre road. I found them all in a room and we waited for the Division to come along. Luckily it had stopped raining, but it was very cold – so got half an hour's sleep in the motor. Sent the Division on to their positions and lay down on a mattress and got some more sleep.

At 6.30 got up to fetch the General and motored on to Potijze. Saw General Monro (2nd Div.) and established our HQ for the day just east of that place. It is only now after arrival here that one can realize what this 1st Corps under Douglas Haig have done – they have held Ypres against the attacks of six German Corps and many Brigades exist no longer. I saw Watson of the West Kents*, all there is left of them is himself, a Second Lieutenant and 120 men. The Guards Brigade† numbers 300 all told – this has been fighting if you like. Our losses of 50 per cent look small after these. But it is the **man** one must think of – Douglas Haig – who has taken all this responsibility – who when the French on his right and left retired held on, who ordered the counter attacks, who set his personal feelings aside and became a machine for the good of his country. This is **the man** who has done all this and no one knows the iron resolution and the great personality required to not only give the orders but to inspire the confidence required by the men to fight like they have. These things are read of but no one probes into the circumstances which build them up.

Here you can see the results on men of 19 days' fighting against hopeless odds, continual fighting and who have not yielded their ground – you see some of them coming in for a rest – their faces tell the story. Some look tired, you cannot interest them, they have reached the stage where men hope they will be wounded, killed, captured anything so that they can lie down and sleep, sleep for days, sleep for ever. Others have a half mad look in their eyes – difficult to describe but it is there. A few only are cheerful, these are the men with that great asset – personality – they have each probably kept 20, 40, 50 men in the trenches fighting where otherwise they would have gone back. But to my mind no pen can write a tribute fitting the work of the 1st Corps or its commander in the defence of Ypres. The Germans set their heart on it – the 1st Corps foiled them. The German Guard was the last to attack, they were brought up specially for that purpose; the prisoners tell us that their failure was a great disappointment to them. They are fine men and fought most gallantly.

All Thursday (12th) we awaited the attack, it did not come, our two Brigades are in Reserve. We got quarters in a house just north-west of Ypres and are quite comfortable, having turned a French General‡ out of it. The French Cavalry still wander about all day and fill all the billets at night, I only hope that they will have a chance to pursue, they may be good at that – they have done nothing else at present. A bitterly cold day.

**Friday 13 November 1914** A very dull day except a little shelling, but they were quite harmless – the Germans did not make a move, but the French are very active on the north and a good deal of firing heard there all day. I hope they are getting on, but the day did not pass without an attack – at about 2.00 pm they started south of the Menin road and at 3.00 pm we were told to be ready, but the attack was beaten off without any help being required. We had to put the 2nd Bde (Mullins) into the trenches tonight to relieve the London Scottish – they are fine men but like all volunteers need the discipline which is what makes the men stick it out.

**Saturday 14 November 1914** Great rumours of a reconstitution of the line and that French are going to take over the defence of Ypres; this will mean that the 1st Corps will be pulled out. It will be a great thing to give them a rest.

Very heavy shelling of our lines south of the Menin road all day with a strong attack on the 9th* and 15th Bdes†. The Germans got into the chateau and took one of our trenches. We were ordered at 1.00 pm to be ready to assist and support a counter attack to retake it. Rode round with the General to the 3rd Div.‡ and 3rd Cav. Div. and 1st Cav. Bde and Guards Bde. Going along the Menin road they were Black Mariaring a battery and we thought we could gallop through as they always like some minutes between the shots – but we made a bit of a miscalculation. As the General was reaching the place we heard them coming, four of them. One pitched in the middle of the road and the General's horse whipped round and went down a 10ft bank with a ditch at the bottom. I thought he was certain for a nasty fall, but the horse got over all right – old Mary Antoinette‖ never turned a hair although she jumped a bit at the explosion. We came back another way, that road was a bit unhealthy. As we left they were preparing a counter attack to retake the trench lost.

On the way to our night quarters I spent two hours extricating a block of carts on the road. The roads in Belgium are generally made as follows – about 15ft in the centre there is the pavé – on each side about another 10ft of mud often bottomless. If you get one wheel on the pavé and one in the mud you will probably turn over. Last night the block consisted of two waggons with their wheels locked in the centre and a Brigade of Cuirassiers¶, motor cars and other things helping. We got one wagon moving and it promptly turned over – at the same moment French oaths on one side and shouts of English laughter. Two cuirassiers had fallen into the ditch at the roadside – then a French supply column came along and the picture was complete. It was pitch dark and one was only thankful that no shells came along that road. It took much cursing but at last we got the columns moving and I went home. One thing, it warmed me, I was bitterly cold before.

**Sunday 15 November 1914** Last night we retook our original position the Germans got into a farm and we could not get them out, so they brought up a few guns by hand through the mud and blew holes in the place and then took it at the point of the bayonet. The 1st Bde had a Regiment in support but it was not needed and took no part in it. Today is the first day of real winter, it has been snowing and is very cold. A wretched day for the men in the trenches. The French are relieving the 2nd Div. today. The news from the Russians* continues to be satisfactory. The roads are terrible – one sea of mud. The British Army is the nearest approach to rabbits as possible, they all live underground in dug-outs, there are no billets available. Back to Reigerburg[?] for the night.**Monday 16 November 1914** Our 2nd Cavalry got out of the trenches at 2.00 am and were very dirty but very cheerful. They were in a wood, with the German trenches 50 yards away – the trees between them had been levelled down by the shells which had burst and formed an impenetrable abattis. We are keeping them out tonight and they go back tomorrow. Allenby came up this morning – he brought a story that the Kaiser and the German General Staff recognise that they made miscalculations, one of them being the value of the British Army as a fighting machine – they are now fighting for terms of peace. I only hope we shall not stop until the terms are such as will make Germany harmless for many years to come if not for ever. On the other hand the Germans are not fools and they are not likely to risk absolute extermination by fighting on to the bitter end. I personally think that this war will be over sooner than people think – but whatever happens Germany must be crushed. The French relieved the northern position of our line successfully last night, so we all hope the 1st Corps will be pulled out to rest.

**Tuesday 17 November 1914** Went up to 1st Corps and found them all very sleepy. They had been up all night because the French had not carried out their promise and relieved part of our line as promised – it is hoped that they will do so tonight. There is a certain amount of friction as regards billets – I think we are rather high-handed regarding them, but on the other hand the French spread themselves a great deal; they put 50 men where we would put a Regiment. The reason is that the French Officers carry no bedding and expect a bed – one room, one Officer – with us we put 10 Officers into a room. Today we move the 1st Bde Batteries and Divisional troops back to the old Bailleul area and go back ourselves to our chateau at St Jans Cappel. The men badly want a rest and clean and new boots and so on. The Staff has had little or nothing to do lately – but one is never free from thinking and one's brain is always working. Hope to ride back this afternoon as am short of exercise, but whenever I propose riding I have generally to go off somewhere in a motor. Quite fine today but cold.

# 3. Stalemate

**Wednesday 18 November 1914** We left Ypres at 4.30 pm yesterday for St Jans Cappel. We pulled out the 1st Cav.Bde last night and retreated to our area here, the 2nd Cav.Bde being left up there to do trench work. Had an awful journey back: the roads were choc-a-bloc with troops and transport, but on the whole the Staff work was good and we got on fairly fast considering everything. We got to Corps HQ at 7.00 pm and home here at 8.00 pm. We were glad to get away from Ypres, it is an awful place now.

The condition of things there was described by Toby Lakin as follows this morning: 'We went into the trenches which were partly blown in and there lay the dead in and around the trenches, it was impossible to bury them as the Germans were within 200 yards and every movement drew their fire – the stench was awful, but we just had to stick it out.' He describes the mortar as follows: 'You saw the great shell come lobbing along like a bottle that is thrown into the air – unless it landed in a trench it did not damage beyond making a great noise. The worst of it was that in a narrow trench you could not run away from it.'

Heard today that the Prince of Wales has come out, I only hope he will show himself to the troops; it will be a great thing. We hear that the French at Ypres want more reinforcements, the place is already stiff with troops and Joffre says he cannot spare any more – I only hope that the French will hold on, I shall never forgive them if they allow the Germans to get the place after all the blood we have spilled there.

**Thursday 19 November 1914** A snowstorm and bitterly cold and here we get war at its worst, when climatic conditions proceed to multiply the horrors already existing. It has been snowing on and off all day. I went out this morning with De Lisle to try and get some pheasants. We saw a few but only got one and a couple of rabbits. I hate this snow: the men are all under cover but the poor horses stand out in the open, they have all got long coats but they did not look too happy as we passed them tonight and it will be worse before the morning. Our 2nd Bde comes out of the trenches and marches back here tonight; they will have a bad time but **anything** is better than the trenches and they will have a rest when they return.

How a night like this brings war with a capital 'W' home to one. Although on the Staff we are in a comfortable house with a fire, yet one knows the whole time that the men are in the trenches – wet, cold and tired – there is nothing one can do to help them. I am afraid that with this weather we shall have another enemy and that is sickness, the health of the troops up to the present has been wonderful but standing in the wet trenches for 48 hours at a time will take its toll, let us hope it will not be too big a one. This is a doleful note which I have struck, but to look on and see others suffer is always a difficult thing and in the case of dumb animals doubly difficult. This **battle** still continues, the Germans keep on attacking and losing men, but they don't gain much ground. Hope the weather will improve.

**Friday 20 November 1914** A very hard frost last night and all the snow frozen, but a lovely day today, fine keen air. In the morning went round to see the Regiment and took some photos – then discussed our situation with Barrow and Henley. In the afternoon drove out with General in a car to see our new billeting area. Went up to the Mont des Cats which is a Trappist Monastery on the highest hill round here – you get a very fine view to all sides but it was very cold up there. The new area did not produce a house into which we could go, so we have asked to be allowed to remain on here or else go into Mont Noir if it is vacated by Corps HQ. Everyone asking if it is true about leave – some of the 1st Corps have got 72 hours from shore to shore. I doubt if it is a good thing to take it – but I suppose one will if given the chance – it is only human nature. Freezing very hard again tonight – just heard that our 1st Bde has to relieve part of the 2nd Cav.Div. tomorrow. I hoped that they would have a longer rest, let us hope they will not have too bad a time.*

**Sunday 22 November 1914** Relieved 2nd Cav.Div. in the trenches just east of Kemmel – very little activity on the part of the Germans. We are to be relieved by the 1st Corps on Monday.

**Monday 23 November 1914** Had a quiet night. Our HQ was at the school at La Glytte [De Klijte]. Quite a quiet day but at 10.00 am the Germans began shelling the cross roads. They only put five shells on to the crossroads, they were wonderfully accurate. They then put one into the next house but one to our HQ and killed a man and woman and then another on to a road on the other side – this was all, about half a dozen shells fired and yet a great loss of life. The Germans systematically shell all crossroads. We were relieved at 3.00 pm by the 1st Div. and went to Corps HQ at La Motte-au-Bois with the General. We had a conference there and returned to our chateau at St Jans Cappel. Am off home for 72 hours tomorrow. We start at 5.30 am for the Calais boat.

**Saturday 27 November 1914** A journey home during war time is a thing which must be actually carried out to realize what it means. We started on Tuesday and our troubles began at once. It had thawed a little in the early part of the night and frozen again later. The roads were just ice and having non-skids* on we thought we should be in the ditch every minute. The result was that we did not get to St Omer till about 7.30 am. Most of the time the motor was going sideways and we had to push her up on one or two hills. At St Omer we met Dalmeny and Shea and they passed us just after we left that place going very fast. Our next trouble was a burst tyre and we had to put on a spare wheel. Then we made the driver let her out and I do not think he had ever driven a high powered car going fast – it was quite a dangerous drive expecially to people on the road. We were continually stopped by French soldiers who wanted to see our passes. As they were in English and they could not read them, it seemed rather unnecessary.

We got to the basin side at Calais at 9.30 am, just in time to see the boat cast off. We shouted but it was no good – it started punctually for the first time for a week as a sympathetic Frenchman told us – so there was nothing to be done but to go on to Boulogne and catch the 11.30 boat from there. The journey was without incident, the country in this part is full of Belgian soldiers – resting I suppose. We got into Boulogne in plenty of time and went to report ourselves. There was a fearful crush, only a small room and only one door. We got our tickets and on to the boat, many friends on board. We started fairly up to time; everyone impatient to be off and to get home. Many wives on board who had come over to meet their men and travel with them. We had quite a smooth crossing and met a floating mine on which fire with rifles was opened and it was sunk in about 10 minutes. Nothing further happened and we got to London at last.

To the student of expressions, the faces one saw as the train slowed into Victoria would have been interesting at any other time except the present. Here was joy as brother, son or husband was spotted by those waiting, there doubt and anxiety – never indifference. Such a crowd is un-English to the callous observer; to those who know what is behind it, one's heart goes out with joy to the joyful ones and with sympathy to those who are in doubt and who perhaps may be disappointed. But this is not the London we are used to, and it brings one to the reality of things, those who remain behind have the hardest burden to bear. They have none of the excitement, to sit and wait patiently is the hardest of all roles to play – they do it well in London – this is the first impression on landing. They are very afraid of Zeppelin raids at home – in the trains when travelling at night all blinds are drawn and so on. Everyone afraid of a German landing on east coast. I cannot think why – I should think the Germans are so fully occupied in Europe that they could not spare troops for any sort of a raid. Left England at 1.00 pm on Friday 27th and got back to harness at our new HQ Château at Le Nieppe at 8.00 pm. Found everything very quiet and heard great news of a Russian success†.

**Saturday 28 November 1914** The General, the President, Pat [Armstrong] and Brooks Hambro left at 8.00 am this morning for their leave. There has been nothing doing all day – we are rather far from our Division here but there is no room anywhere else, so we have to make the best of it. We are on duty for the next 48 hours. Everything is quite quiet at present.

**Sunday 29 November 1914** Another quiet day. I went and saw Briggs who is temporarily commanding the Division – I had a long talk to him, he was very kind and open with me and I heard many things which officially I should never have known. It helps one a great deal especially in the way of keeping things running smoothly.

There seems to be a good deal of mistrust about – it has ever been thus in our army. It is the natural result of small wars, where personal ambition may be satisfied by some feat of arms – South Africa was the worst case, a lot of small columns each operating on its own and the reputation of the commander depending on those operations. This must lead to jealousy and the situation of the personal factor when put in contradistinction to the whole. Here we get quite a different thing; every unit forms part of a long line. The qualities which are required are a stout heart and an eye for ground and a personality for command. The individual is eliminated – I think this is apt to be forgotten – to fight for the good of the whole. A commander is a pawn in this game – there is but one King and that is **Joffre** – there are no Queens, Knights, castles in this game. The weather is very bad again, south-west gales and cold rain – it must be bad in the trenches, but the men have many comforts now, braziers and so on, which make a great difference.

**Monday 30 November 1914** Very cold and wet. The Channel crossing must be awful. Smythe just been here, he has very little news – the Russians are getting on well but they won't let us know how well. There are signs of the Germans weakening towards St Eloois. We shall know today if they have really gone back or not. I should not wonder if we are told to go forward sooner than we expect. Allenby was here to say that the King was coming over to see the troops. What an excellent thing it will be – I think it will be a very popular visit and will do an enormous amount of good. He sees our Division on Thursday.

**Tuesday 1 December 1914** The fourth month of the war and winter really on us, very cold gales and rain with them. It must be very bad in the trenches. Our lines run peacefully now but how long it will last no one knows. The King is visiting the Indians today. I went over the ground we are to hold and then went to Corps HQ and had lunch there. Everyone has been home and looks all the better for it, but I have never seen so many new hats, such a blaze of gold peaks. Allenby really distinguished himself when he said at dinner that every idiot in the army was being made a Brigadier General!!!

**Wednesday 2 December 1914** Was woken up in the middle of the night with a wire to say Sir John [French] was going round billets. Of course thought that plans had been changed and it was the King – I wish when people write these messages they would think of the people who have to act on them. So I compromised and at 8.30 went off to Corps HQ. The King was to present French decorations at 10.30 am. Found the place full of brass hats and the gravel being raked and so on. It was like a Lord Mayor's Show. Goffy was there and chaffed me unmercifully as if he thought I was going to be a recipient – got my own back a little later when I sympathised with him getting knees dirty while being knighted. I did not wait to see the presentation but slipped off to my work. Saw Briggs [who] had just had his holiday – he took his Staff to Dunkirk to look at the sea!!! The men are wonderfully keen to see the King, I wish he could be told [of] the enthusiasm it has aroused, I am certain he will never know. This visit of his will make history. No news of Russia, am certain the Germans had got out of the trap at Lodz, they are too good soldiers and fighters to be caught.

**Thursday 3 December 1914** The King's visit. A cold day with heavy squalls of rain but it cleared towards midday and the afternoon was beautifully fine. All the arrangements worked well and I motored out with the General. The Division was formed up on both sides of the road facing inwards, in single rank. The men looked well and the horses, though very woolly, are in good condition. We received the King with swords and lances at the carry. Staffs on the right of formations and the Div. Staff at the Messines end of the road. As the King passed each unit cheers were called for and given. It was well done. The King arrived in a motor and walked down the line, he was accompanied by Wigram and a few others, the only representative of GHQ being one of the Chief's ADCs.

Now I am going to be disloyal – I expected great things of this visit. I tried to see the King stopping here and talKing to this Officer and there talKing to that man. Giving a word of praise here and there and above all showing that he appreciated the hardships the men had suffered – this was the picture I made out in my mind, the picture I hoped to see reproduced in real life. On the part of the men, I knew they had looked forward to seeing their King, they have talked and argued about it for days ever since it was whispered abroad that he was coming out to the Army. To the men he is a real King, their King and they expect many things – a word to them is a decoration to the snob. I pictured a scene which was to live for a long time in these modern days of callousness and selfishness: a real thing in a modern world of sham. But the picture never matured. On the side of the men the cheers were real, given to their King – he walked up through the line, hardly waiting for Brigadiers to be presented to him – there was no picture, but the framing was there, real live gold.

This has, to me at all events, been a disappointing day – a sense of failure only remains. Perhaps I am years behind the times, have too much sentiment, but war with all its ups and downs brings out sentiment, this is probably the reason. But we finish the day and blot out our hopes and dreams and mark it as a red letter day and say that 'The King was with the 1st Cavalry Division in the field today'. The Prince of Wales was with him, a slight boyish figure – he is very like his father, walks in much the same way.

**Friday 4 December 1914** A howling gale blowing today with very cold showers. I went and saw Briggs and Mullins with the General today and settled the question of DSOs. It is a hateful job as one feels that there are so many who deserve them and it is very difficult to pick the most deserving ones out, but it is now done for the present thank God and I will forget about it till the next time. I wish we could get more news of Russia, but it is all going to be a slow business so it is no good being impatient. There are rumours of Italy and Rumania joining in, but they cannot be believed until the thing is an accomplished fact.

What a funny nation we are, just because we are doing nothing for the moment, the 9th Lancers are making a point to point course and have already begun schooling their horses – football is played daily by those not on duty in the trenches and so we make war. Everything is **too quiet**; in front they say that Austrian troops are being sent to this side – it is quite possible and more than probable. How the Germans hate us and quite naturally too – they would have had quite a walkover if they could have used the sea as they liked.

**Saturday 5 December 1914** Another wet and nasty day – very cold wind and a good deal of sleet. Smythe came early but had no news to give us. Talked very wildly about a Cavalry Raid – what's on I wonder? The Kiel Canal* and the German Fleet?? We are an extraordinary nation – times are quiet so men at once commence casting about and some one remembers the word 'raid' having probably read the American Civil War. So at once they say what a good thing it would be – they forget the essential of a 'raid': quick movement, secrecy, surprise. Take our present position – the Germans are probably in 15 mile depth opposite to us – it is

Casualties by units of 1st Cavalry Division from commencement of campaign to December 1st 1914.

|  | Total Casualties | Percentage to War Strength |
|---|---|---|
| Headquarters 1st Cavalry Division | 5 | 5.1 |
| Headquarters 1st Cavalry Brigade | 5 | 10.6 |
| 2nd Dragoon Guards | 205 | 37.7 |
| 5th Dragoon Guards | 202 | 37.2 |
| 11th Hussars | 245 | 45.1 |
| Headquarters 2nd Cavalry Brigade | 4 | 8.5 |
| 4th Dragoon Guards | 323 | 59.4 |
| 9th Lancers | 288 | 53.0 |
| 18th Hussars | 203 | 37.3 |
| Royal Horse Artillery (H and I Batteries) | 27 | 4.2 |
| 1st Field Squadron | 18 | 9.4 |
| 1st Signal Squadron | 17 | 19.1 |
| Field Ambulances | 2 | 1.0 |

no use making a raid against anything except that which lies behind the Germans. How are you going to get through 15 miles of Germans? Such talk is childish, it shows an absolute lack of knowledge. Let the Infantry burst a hole in the German lines first so as to let the Cavalry through, then something might be done. It is really rather amusing if it were not war that we are playing at.

**Monday 7 December 1914** Another vile day, wind, rain and storms – but we went out shooting – the General, Tommy Pitman, Mullins, Phipps-Hornby and so on. At the first covert an irate Frenchman came up and asked us who had given us leave to shoot. On these occasions it is not a good thing to understand French, he came up to me and I played the village idiot until the drive was finished. He turned out to be the mayor and owned the land, but he told us that the next wood was outside the Pas de Calais District and that we could shoot there if we liked. So we went on to it and had a jolly shoot.

There is a rumour that the Russians have had a reverse at Lodz* – also another rumour that things are not as they should be in Berlin – that people put up placards saying 'Stop the War' during the night. If the Lodz rumour is true we shall have to make a push here to prevent troops being taken away from here to reinforce the east. I shall be sorry to leave these comfortable quarters, but the more we push the sooner the war will be over and that is the only way to look at it. I only hope the advance will be properly planned and carried through by the proper people and in depth, no more long thin lines.

**Tuesday 8 December 1914** The French have been making progress at La Bassée and Bethune and also in the north towards a point midway between Dixmude and Ypres. On our front all is quiet. The news from Russia does not seem so good, but it is impossible to say until we get definite and official reports. The Russians are very truthful in their communiques. There is every sign of a push on this side being contemplated. I think everything points to the Germans having weakened here, but how much no one can tell. I cannot imagine the Germans giving up one yard of Belgian territory unless forced to but the fighting in the Eastern Theatre is so much nearer to Berlin that they may have had to weaken themselves pretty considerably. I saw one of the hand grenades used by the Germans in the trenches today. It is evidently improvised in the field and quite a rough contrivance but like all German war materiel very effective. It is funny to think that we are close on Christmas and nearing the shortest day of the year. I have been out here nearly four months and into that the events of a lifetime seem to have been crammed. We all wish the war was going to finish soon, but there is not one of us who feels that the war must not be finished until Germany is crushed. German arrogance must be a thing of the past.

**Thursday 10 December 1914** Another vile day. The Germans have taken Lodz. It is no good to them; in that country the further they get in, the worse their plight becomes. On the other hand the Russians seem to be progressing towards Cracow. It is rather curious how the main theatre of war has changed from the west to the east. I think that they will have to send more troops still to stop the Russians. The Servians* are doing good work, we heard this officially. It is curious how the Austrians can do no good anywhere, history repeats itself, they never have been able to wage successful wars.

**Friday 11 December 1914** Attended a conference at Corps HQ on the question of an advance. We must keep as many Germans in front of us here as possible. The Russians want to keep their freedom of manoeuvre, they do not want to come to the stalemate that we have here. This is quite right — we are going to push a bit. In this part our objective is first the Messines—Wytschaete—Hollebeke ridge — the French attack the line Hollebeke—Wytschaete, Smith—Dorrien with the 2nd Corps attacks Wytschaete and, if this is successful, Pulteney pushes forward east of Messines. The 3rd, 4th and Indian Corps stand fast and the 1st Corps is notched for work in the south. The Cavalry will be used as follows: Gough's (2nd) Div. in close support of Smith—Dorrien; Brigg's (3rd) Div. as a mobile reserve; De Lisle's (1st) as a Corps Reserve. I think either we shall get the ridge quite easily, the Germans having prepared a position further back, or we shall have a very stiff fight for it.

I do not agree with the use of the Cavalry — it must be remembered that a Cavalry Division dismounted produces 1,500 rifles or two weak battalions of Infantry. On the other hand 1,500 rifles plus the mobility of the horse (ie put in quickly at the most favourable place) are equal to 4—5,000 Infantry put into that place 24 hours later. But let it pass, I am not in possession of the whole facts and therefore cannot criticise. Wytschaete is the key — let us take and really hold it in force with plenty of depth and Messines must go. I am afraid once more we shall be fighting in a thin line and the only reserve will be the Cavalry Corps. I must confess that we have done so successfully up till now — ie on the Aisne and here at Messines and again at Ypres — but the habit is a bad one; with one Corps in Reserve all would be well. The country is simply under water — they tell me it is the usual thing here, but they generally get frost at Christmas, I hope we shall have a change soon.

**Saturday 12 December 1914** We have been innoculated against enteric*, it ought to have been done before, but I have never had time. It is funny how the men hate anything of this kind, they will go to any length to avoid it; some man spreads a yarn and they all think that they are going to be awfully ill. Saw the new clothes that are being issued out to the men — they consist of a British warm coat and a mackintosh. They are of splendid material and ought to keep them warm and dry — they could not be better. The latest thing we hear is that the French Cavalry is already going into winter quarters about St Pol but one cannot believe that. All the troops are fit and well and up to the present there has been very little sickness and I hope this will continue.

**Sunday 13 December 1914** Woke up feeling fairly fit after the innoculation. It has been a beastly day today, cold and rainy. The operations for the straightening out of the Messines—Wytschaete line commences tomorrow; it will be quite a pleasant Christmas present if we straighten it out without too much loss. All the same I shall be surprised if they give up one yard of territory which they have gained in Belgium without a struggle. These are peaceful days for the Cavalry, but unsatisfactory ones, we certainly have done our share in the war up to the present.

**Tuesday 15 December 1914** Yesterday the attack on Le Petit Bois east of Wytschaete was launched in the early morning and everything went according to order. The first German trench was taken with a run and an Officer and 50 men captured. A farm just south of the wood was also taken. The French on our left also made progress. We had collected an enormous number of guns and the woods just east of Wytschaete was bombarded till one would think that nothing could live in it. As a sum total of a day's work it must be considered as satisfactory. We took no part.

Now to the attack. We hoped for great things and what actually resulted was nil. The whole failure can be summed up as follows: a Corps was ordered to attack, the Corps ordered a Division to attack, the Division ordered a Brigade to attack keeping two in reserve, the Brigade ordered two Battalions to attack keeping two in reserve. Now this attack was not a small thing — we know that the Germans sent five Corps against our 1st Corps at Ypres. What chance had we of success? A Battalion took the farm, it was driven out by a counter attack. Why was it not at once supported and the place made secure against counter attack? All these points have to be elucidated. People say the French on our left did not attack but we had 12 Battalions and only used two.

Let us hope that we are not beginning to be afraid of losses — in this war there must be losses if we want to win and thus prevent greater loss in the future. The attack is going on tomorrow, let us hope with better results. If we are going to take the Messines—Wytschaete ridge, we shall have considerable losses. Our failure these last two days will increase these losses because we have alarmed the enemy and he will be ready. I hope we shall push tomorrow for all we are worth and support our attacks with every means available — if not we shall not get on.

**Wednesday 16 December 1914** The whole offensive has fizzled out, I cannot understand, have we been so long on the defensive that we have forgotten how to attack? Or are we forgetting the losses which our allies are suffering and think that we can make a hole in the German trenches without loss? We lost 400 men in the attacks of the last two days and these losses are for no good purpose unless we get on. I think we are all rather dispirited as a result of this offensive movement — one hates to fail in a thing. We went up to the Scherpenberg and saw our old friends Messines and Wytschaete, there were a few shells bursting but that was all.

There was no news in Bailleul — so finding nothing doing we went down to the 8th Div. and saw many old friends. I did not enjoy it as much as I might have as I had a bad head, but it was very nice seeing them all again, they were very comfortable at Estaires. Their men they told me suffer from foot trouble, most of them came from India and had Indian—made boots, good for that country but useless here. These trenches are very wet, many have water in them and I think the German knee boot is better than any either the French or ourselves possess — but a man must be trained to walk in them otherwise he does not get very far. A rumour today that the French Cavalry have got across the Ijzer at Nieuwport and are working along the sand dunes, this will of course require confirming, one comes to the point here when one believes nothing one hears. No more news, I think we shall sit here for Christmas!!! Awful!

**Thursday 17 December 1914** Heard news of the bombardment of Scarborough* and so on. Hope our people will catch some of the ships before they get back to port. I suppose this is the revenge talked of in the German papers and they will be full of the uselessness of the British Fleet — this attack must be political it can have no military effect except perhaps to raise our recruiting. My sympathies are with the poor women and children who always suffer most.

**Friday 18 December 1914** It has been a beastly day, wet, cold and raw. The attack has been made all along the line so as to help a big French push which is being made about Arras. Have had no news of the result yet, but hope progress has been made all along the line – we must push and keep on pushing so as to keep the Germans from moving troops as they wish. The C-in-C had a conference in Bailleul but what the result of it was I have not heard.

**Saturday 19 December 1914** We are still attacking but progress is slow. Inspected the Brigades today. Allenby brought Squires the American attaché round and he dined with us tonight. A very nice man and very wide awake I should think. The Inspection of Brigades was satisfactory but it was cold work – the horses are looking very well considering all things.

**Monday 21 December 1914** The shortest day in the year. Cold, wind, snow and sleet and rain are fitting accompaniments to this day. Hear that the Indians were driven out of their trenches and came back rather fast and a good deal further than necessary. The rumour is that they came back two miles, I don't believe it myself and will wait and hear the truth – this war has made me believe nothing. Anyhow the 1st Div. have been sent down to help them regain their ground. People now at once shake their head and say 'I knew these troops would be no good.' I do not agree with this: if native troops do come back it is because they have lost all their white Officers – only about 10 a Battalion – we have no reserve at all. It stands to reason that the native unless he is well led does not fight as well as the white man, or else how could we have conquered, much less held, India! Also our small wars on the frontier have been bad training for this war – it is the same with all black troops.

We went on towards Armentieres to Nieppe to see the General's old Regiment, the Durhams*. I found McMahon, who was musketry man† at Aldershot, in command of the Durhams. He told us that the trenches on the Ploegsteert front are in a very bad way – Germans worse than ours. Of course when we started the country was fairly dry and the ditches then existing were used to make the communicating trenches – but when the wet weather came these ditches all filled with water, being the natural drainage of a low lying country. The result is that there is three feet of water in some of them. Saw a good many Infantry, the men looked well in spite of the work. The Special Reserve men lack discipline I am told but extra digging in the trenches has had a wonderfully sobering effect on them.

**Tuesday 22 December 1914** Went down to Corps in the morning to see if I could get some news. The main news was that 1st Corps was relieving the Indian Corps. I am sorry as I think that it was a great feature of strength to have such a Corps as this in Reserve – now the Indian Corps has been in places badly hammered and has probably lost a large percentage of white Officers and again it gets no reinforcements as far as I know. But the trenches which the Germans took have nearly all been retaken and if they knock their heads up against the 1st Corps; well, all the better for us.

The latest news today is that the last two Divisions before K's Army* are arriving in this country. I suppose our ultimate position will be on the left of the French up towards the sea – this is quite natural as it will simplify the question of supply. De Frisson (our new Liaison Officer) dined with us last night. He speaks English very well and looks like an Englishman. He reported that the French are making progress although slow all along the line, but it is very steady progress. I was innoculated (second dose) much stronger than first, has got hold of my arm fine.

**Friday 25 December 1914** A white Christmas – it began with a fine bright sunny morning but at about 11 am a fog came down and so spoilt the weather. Went with the General to the 9th Lancers' service – that parson ought to be sacked, he talked badly for a sermon and I could not understand what he was driving at. I am certain the men did not. It was very cold standing out there – then came back here and had lunch and went out to shoot. We beat the wood out to two guns and got two brace of pheasants and a hare – the beating was really scientific. We had a regular Christmas dinner – the servants had decorated the table – we had three bottles of champagne and a dozen crackers. It was as merry as could be and we all drank to those at home and abroad. Also to those who spent a Christmas in the trenches. The 1st Div. was on duty and we fully expected that the Germans would celebrate the day by one of their attacks and we might have to go out – but all passed quietly for which we were thankful. The Royal presents arrived. Each soldier got a Christmas card from the King and Queen, a metal box and pipe from Princess Mary or a metal box and a writing case if a non-smoker. I became a non-smoker for the time and chose the latter. The men appreciate this very much, the box making a very nice memento. Hope this is the last Christmas I spend on service, but one never knows one's luck.

**Sunday 27 December 1914** Went to Cavalry Corps. They had no news except a rumour that Russia is short of ammunition too. This is rather serious, if Russia stops Germany will be at liberty to concentrate either east or west as she wishes — but on the other hand Russia has plenty of men and the news is good from that side. Here we are slowly progressing but it is siege warfare: nothing more or less.

**Monday 28 December 1914** I do not think that the Russians mean pushing very much further; it looks like a halt till the spring and then the campaign will be resumed. I heard a rumour that the Indian troops are going to be sent to Egypt\*; it is the best place for them as this climate does not suit them at all. They are excellent in the attack, but do not like sitting in the trenches under shell fire.

**Tuesday 29 December 1914** Good news from Russia today\*, they are doing well over there now. A story reaches us that the Austrian Financiers are telling the Government that they had better make peace before it is too late, and so cut their losses. If this is true, things are worse in Austria than one imagined. Went round Divisional troops today — Sandys' horses† looking very well. We had an awful gale last night, a regular hurricane — it blew down the ammunition column stables but the others stood well.

**Wednesday 30 December 1914** A fine day with a cold wind. Inspected all the squadrons of the 1st Cav.Bde — the Bays' horses are looking a long way the best. Rather disappointed with my own Regiment. The whole country is one sea of mud. Most Squadrons have built shelters for their horses and some are very good. Shelter from the prevailing wind is what is most required. Am off home on Monday for a week if all goes well.

**Thursday 31 December 1914** The last day of the year, spent it inspecting the billets of the 2nd Cav.Bde. They were mostly good, with dryer stables than the 1st. It was a nasty cold wet day and we did not get home till late. Have come to the conclusion that I don't like an open car in winter — but as long as Coleman is with us I suppose that we shall use his car. The American Note is a serious matter. Of course this war is affecting American trade and when it comes to a loss of dollars there always will be trouble. I think that this is partly German made and will blow over, but we shall have to give way a little so as to smooth things over.

What a year this has been! The prophets were right in which they said that there would be an Armageddon — but it is really the law of balance, in past history you find the parallel. Great soldiers and great statesmen arise and they raise their countries until it seems that they must dominate the world. For one man or one nation to dominate the world is against the law of nature. In this world everything is balanced — to have 'Good' and all that is implied in the word you must have 'bad' as well. Therefore when a nation strives to place itself over all other nations, the other nations combine against it to overthrow it. It has happened all through history and, if Germany is humbled and Russia is raised to a position of great strength, it will be Russia's turn next — no one can claim that Germany has worked for good. Her very way of working for self-aggrandizement is patent to all the world. Thus she has brought on herself the punishment which all countries in parallel cases have incurred all through the world.

To my mind there is no doubt; the law of balance must bring things to a level. Call it what you like — superior numbers, better soldiers, Right — at the bottom it is the natural law — that on which every religion in the world is based, the just law: ie Balance. It is a simple trust in a power indefinable, incomprehensible, real, always with us, the 'right' as opposed to the wrong. So we pass into a new year believing that our cause is right, hoping and praying that the coming year will make one a better man, striving to do what is right as opposed to what is wrong. For us and ours, we hope and pray for peace with honour (that is with Right).

**Saturday 2 January 1915** Another miserable day, the papers published a list of honours but no DSOs for anyone in this Division, although seven have been recommended for Messines. It looks as if F.\* was venting his dislike of L.† on the Division. He must be a small man if this is the case and it is very hard on the Division. Every one of these DSOs have been earned several times over and yet they are not awarded. Is this a war where we are fighting for our country or is it a means of venting personal dislikes? Officers and men will not fight if they are not encouraged and this is poor encouragement after a show like Messines. I personally cannot understand it. To me it is criminal — no personal feeling can come in.

**Monday 4 to Monday 11 January 1915** A week at home and spent it at Bylaugh* with the family, it came to an end much too soon. But perhaps this war will be over and then all will be well. Came back on 11th via Calais.

**Tuesday 12 January 1915** Cavalry Corps temporarily placed under orders of 2nd Army (Smith Dorrien) this morning so went to Hazebrouck to find out what it was all about. Nothing and no chance of doing anything. Heard a rumour that Hungary has broken away from Austria, wonder if it true, it is within the bounds of possibility. Went to the 27th Div.* to find out the line of their trenches. General Snow was not in but saw Reed his Chief [of Staff]. On our way into Boeschepe we saw some of this Division coming out of the trenches, they looked bad. The few we saw looked as if they had been there a month instead of a few days. Yet they are not holding a long line and there is no apparent reason why the men should look so bad. It seems to me that such things should not occur, it is part of the work of the Staff to see that they do not occur. On the other hand we are a curious race, we don't like taking advice and are inclined to think that individually we know best. With all our experience of trench work lately there should be nothing that we do not know about it and knowledge should be freely disseminated. There is something wrong somewhere.

**Wednesday 13 January 1915** Interesting report from Russia from one of our attachés there — he says there is a small shortage of rifles and ammunitions. This is a pity as the Russians have taken 1,200 Austrian guns and should have a marked advantage in this respect. The Russians also do not consider the Germans as good fighting men as the Japanese, this is interesting. The Russians are not good at rearguard work, but the Austrians are excellent at it. Rumours of Italy and Rumania joining in, won't there be a great squabble amongst the Allies when it comes to sharing the spoil? I think that that is the German hope.

**Thursday 14 January 1915** A sad fatality happened today — the 5th Dragoon Guards were doing a scouting scheme and one of the men who were hiding went into the top of a farm thinking he would make it as difficult as possible to find him. The people in the house thinking he was a German spy sent and told the 18th Hussars who sent out a squadron and, owing to a mistake, the man was shot as soon as he put his head out of the window. This is to my mind a really incredible story, but it is a true one and we shall have the full details later. It is very bad luck on the poor man who was doing his best for his country.

There is a howling gale tonight and it is raining hard. Gough has moved back with his whole Division, he was billeted in very low ground and was practically flooded out. The country is absolutely waterlogged. The men are really wonderfully well. Our sick last week in the Division were only 1.35 per cent which is less than the peace average.

**Friday 15 January 1915** A visit to Vermelles [south-west of Bethune]. This village held out for three weeks against the French attacks and forms an interesting study of the kind of siege warfare that is now going on along the whole Western Front. We went and had *dejeuner* with the Brigade Commander* who actually took the place. He was a fine man to look at with a strong face, about 55 years of age and a Marine. He had seen service in Indo-China and was a fine type of soldier. We walked down the zig-zag approaches and saw each line of trenches as the French slowly advanced: these trenches were well dug and dry on the whole, the soil being chalky, very different to the heavy land further north. The approaches gave good cover from hostile fire, in fact the young Officer showing us round told us that reliefs were carried out in broad daylight without casualties which speaks well for the design. Another point was that machine guns were always used on the flanks and never frontally.

The chateau was the point of attack and regular siege warfare was carried out before it was taken. The village was an absolute ruin — not one roof or a pane of glass was left. It looked just as if an earthquake had taken place: shot and shell holes everywhere. The French showed us how the Germans had made themselves comfortable in the cellars, they had brought down pictures, sofas and a piano — but I never have seen such desolation. I wish some people in England could see it. I took several photos but, the light being bad, I shall be surprised if they came out at all.

50

**Saturday 16 January 1915** Another vile day with a cold wind and rain. Went to 1st Cav.Bde and saw Osborne and had a long talk to him. Then went on to Corps and had a buck to Curly Birch. He says that a list is coming out so I hope that 1st Cav.Div. will get its share in the way of rewards. A day's coffee housing with no news.

**Sunday 17 January 1915** No news today. We cease to be attached to the 2nd Army, so I suppose that Sir John [French] is back again. There was talk of doing away with the 3rd grade GSO, Corps have quashed it. I don't think one is necessary but it is better to have too many than too few in war.

**Monday 18 January 1915** Many rumours of changes: Ludlow* has been offered another job, but as usual they are trying to do him down, won't say what pay or rank it carries. I hope for his sake it is a good one, but shall hate his going – he is one of the best and will be very hard to replace. Little or no Russians news – does this mean that they are getting on or are the Germans making another desperate attempt to reach Warsaw? Another question is are we doing enough? Personally I don't think so. I think it a great mistake allowing hounds and so on to be brought out – our Allies don't understand that we would have all these things and go out and fight like billy-oh, they think we are losing interest and so on! We are engaged in a serious war and the feelings of the Allies must be considered – we cannot ride roughshod over them. Enough moralizing and so to bed.

**Tuesday 19 January 1915** Wind had dropped a good deal during the night and it was warmer today. The General left early this morning on a week's leave. Briggs commands the Division pro tem. I went in the car to see him. He was very cheery and asked me to lunch tomorrow and hunt with the long dogs. Alas the order has come out tonight to say that the Field Marshal regrets but he must stop all shooting and hunting, it is a pity but it was bound to come. A good deal of gun fire heard towards Ypres, but no attack reported at present. I think they will probably have another go in that direction, a success from a military point of view in that direction will not do much good.

**Wednesday 20 January 1915** Got a note asking me to stay the night at Corps HQ. Went over and discussed Audregnies with Allenby and so am getting a story of the battle out for him with maps. I think that there will be a lot of argument about this fight and so it is best to get a clear history on paper and, as I saw it all, I think that I ought to do it. Allenby very cheerful and well and jolly and was quite amusing during dinner. Ludlow has decided to leave us and I think he is quite right and has got a better job than the present one. I am sorry there is no better fellow in the world. I only hope Brooks Hambro will get his job and then we shall know where we are.

**Thursday 21 January 1915** Accompanied Allenby to see some bomb throwing by the 3rd Cav.Div. and watched some very interesting experiments. To throw a bomb from a trench requires a good deal of knack especially if the trench is a narrow one – they do a good deal of damage. A pound of gun cotton on a slab of wood also makes a good bomb. On my return I found that they are trying to hoist a GHQ man on us instead of giving us Hambro, so I went to the Military Secretary's office and hope that I have squared things all right. Luckily I found an old friend there and saw the papers – of course everyone has a friend they want and mean to push on regardless, but fairness should come in in all cases. A nasty wet day but warmer thank God for the poor fellows in the trenches.

**Friday 22 January 1915** Went to see Briggs and found him and all his Staff out, will have to pull his leg about leaving me to command his Division for him.

**Saturday 23 January 1915** A very fine day at last, a hard frost during the night. Sounds of heavy guns heard towards the north of Ypres. Heard news of German air raid on Dunkirk not much damage done and our fellows got one of their aeroplanes, another one got near Bailleul – two in one day is a good bag.

The 28th Div. has arrived – I hope that they will go easy with them until they are a bit salted and not make the same old error of pushing them at once into the trenches. I think that it would be a good idea to have all the senior Officers in K's new Army out here in batches and let them see the conditions existing, it would do no harm and would probably do a lot of good. Have been noticing the country lately, it is of course all cultivated and the crops are beginning to show already. It is extraordinary how much new sowing there is. It does not look as if the people round here will starve at present.

**Sunday 24 January 1915** The frost has gone and it has been a very raw cold day – in the morning motored over to the 3rd Cav.Bde*. I got the position of the Brigade at Audregnies out of them and then went on to the 4th Hussars. Great mourning at the hunting being stopped, they had had good sport down there.

America is giving some anxiety I fancy as regards the trade position, but this is bound to be. What nation who is coining money out of a war does not want to make more? This is the long and short of it and when the cry of votes is raised then the administrations tremble in their shoes. It does not matter if a thing is just or right. One thing I am certain is that America does not want to fight Japan at present† and this will be a peaceful factor in the situation at present.

**Monday 25 January 1915** Heard news of the naval action – this is good – it shows that the heavy gun wins and our guns are heavier than the German ones in every case. Germany will have to do some thing now as a counter irritant for public opinion, will probably be an attack on land. They attacked Givenchy today and fighting has been going on all day. They took some of our trenches but the counter attack restored the line all right – the place is simply stiff with troops down here. They also shelled Bethune, but did not do much harm.

**Tuesday 26 January 1915** Went to see Briggs. He was down in Bethune yesterday and was very caustic as regards the attack. He thinks that our counter attacks are too elaborate and take too long to organise and that we do not counter attack enough with our local reserves. If this is the case, I quite agree with him – a counter attack against a trench that is taken must come at once before the enemy has time to organise the defence and make himself secure. The French appear to be much quicker at it than we are. Had a long discussion as regards the distribution of honours and awards; they have treated this Division disgracefully and I quite agree with his complaints. Got a wire from Corps that the Division was to saddle up at midnight and remain saddled up until further orders and ready to move at the shortest notice. So arranged for report centre to be established at Meteren by midnight. Arrived at Meteren at 11.30 pm. All quiet in front – a little rifle fire to be heard.

**Wednesday 27 January 1915** The Kaiser's birthday – I wonder with what sort of an attack they are going to celebrate it. Spent the night on a stone floor in my flea bag. A fairly quiet night, some gun fire but not much. We went home at 5.00 pm after a very dull day, the Kaiser's birthday attack evidently did not mature.

**Thursday 28 January 1915** Went to Cavalry Corps with the General to attend a conference but the conference was for Generals only and so sat and talked to Rosy Weir instead. Hear we are to go in the trenches for about 10 days to relieve the French 9th Corps which have been there about two months. Each Division goes in for 10 days: we are last and will go in about 23 or 24 February. I think it will be a good thing for all and will keep them up to the mark. Heard of the French attack near Vermelles and it was very well carried out. Far better than ours. Came straight back here, it was freezing hard. Went for a walk in the afternoon with the President who told me bits of his youth, he is a very fine fellow really, if he did not talk so much. At all events his heart is in the right place.

**Friday 29 January 1915** Went round Brigades, the President driving me. The car stuck going up Cassel hill. He loves scorching up the hill making a beastly row – so chaffed him unmercifully. Heard about the French fighting – they claim 20,000 Germans between 25-27 January. Their repulse of the German attack north-east of Ypres was a fine thing – all gun work well carried out and beautifully conceived. As soon as the first German line attacked, they turned all their guns on to the German trenches out of which the second line must come to support the first. The result being that the first line was isolated and simply wiped out with rifle and machine gun fire. The Artillery observers were in the front trenches. Am going to dine with Gough and the 2nd Cav.Div. tonight and it ought to be great fun going into the camp of the enemy. I shall hear a lot of gossip.

**Saturday 30 January** 1915 Read a letter today from Vandeleur who recently escaped from Germany. I don't think escaping is quite playing the game as the Germans give the others who are left behind hell. He tells a most awful story of the way in which the Germans treated the prisoners – the Prussians and Bavarians seem to be the worst. They kept them for 30 hours in a truck full of dung – then they pulled them out and people spat at them and kicked them on wounded places and so on. He has told his story to the King and to K. and I only hope that strong action will be taken by them. We treat the German prisoners too well and they think that we are afraid of them. The letter made one perfectly sick.

We have been standing to all day and will probably do so for some days to come. I think that the Germans will attack in force. I don't see how they can allow our new Armies to come out without making an attempt to break through before they arrive. No actual news of any push today, but the neighbourhood of La Bassée would appear to be the spot. Hutchison returned, he went all along the French line and says that the French are in excellent spirits and full of confidence so we may hope of great things – he also says that the Soissons business* was the result of jealousy between two Commanders – how the human element reaches far even in times such as these!

**Monday 31 January** 1915 A change in the weather. Snow fell quite hard for a couple of hours this morning, but did not lie. It is a good deal warmer tonight. We are still standing to – this I take is a precautionary measure. As long as we only stand to no harm is done – but it is very hard on the horses if we have to saddle up and stand to. That is a very different thing – it means unnecessary wear and tear. Coleman got a whole set of photos out, they are very interesting and I hope to get a complete set if I am alive. He has the artistic touch and there are no bad ones among them.

**Monday 1 February** 1915 Six months of war gone past and what has Germany gained? She is in occupation of nearly the whole Belgium and Luxembourg. What has she lost? The whole of her oversea trade, a very large number of men on land, all her friends, several battleships of all sorts of sizes. She is practically ringed in by a steel band – what has she to gain now? Nothing. I think that she is fighting for terms, but she will fight very hard and we shall see many fierce attacks still on our line. As regards the Allies we are stronger than ever, the French are gaining confidence every day. Today we got a report of the operation for the last 10 days, this may be written by an optimist but it certainly showed progress all along the line – very little gun fire today. Kaiser Bill is reported to have returned to Berlin, perhaps that is the reason. He must however have been disappointed at the La Bassée business, it was an awful failure – I wonder what the Germans really think. The 3rd Cav.Div. go into the trenches tomorrow to relieve the French.

**Tuesday 2 February** 1915 Blair M.P. who is our Field Cashier is taking 3/1 that the war is finished by 12 April. He is evidently an optimist or else has got a lot of money to waste. Orders have come out forbidding us any more joy rides to the French and Belgian trenches and so we have to sit here at present. Went round and saw the Brigades and also the Field Squadron – they had all kinds of bombs ready. Briggs with his usual humour suggested that the Field Squadron should be allowed three days in which to blow themselves up before they started teaching other people to do so and this has been arranged. Cavan's [4th Guards] Bde took two machine guns and 40 prisoners yesterday, quite a nice morning's work. These guns had been annoying the French a good deal so they were very pleased.

**Thursday 4 February** 1915 Germans reported very active. Great activity east of Armentieres – again we think that the Germans have more guns here than they had. I think that this is but a prelude to the spring campaign. Went into GHQ and saw Tavish Davidson, he told me that the Germans have lost very heavily in their attacks on Givenchy. Hambro has got HQMG; I am glad for his sake although I shall miss him. He has played the game by me, where being senior he was yet under, and I owe him a debt of gratitude. Fine day today and fairly warm, the first for a very long time and much appreciated.

**Friday 5 February 1915** A gloriously fine day. The 28th Div.* were shelled out of their trenches [south-east of Ypres] but occupied them again – this always happens with new troops. But if they are ordered to retake them, this generally puts a stop to men going back. The one reason why our men stayed in the trenches at Messines was that they knew that we had no reserves – that they must stick to them. More activity and shelling also reported towards Armentieres, but no attack to speak of.

Bertie Paget and Dalmeny came to tea – the former had just come from Macdonough who runs the Intelligence. The opinion at GHQ apparently was that no great concentration was taking place opposite our line and that although units of five Corps were about, only one Corps was about Lille. It was also thought that an attack on a large scale would take place before K's armies arrived, but that it would be in the direction of Arras rather than Ypres – this I agree with. I think that all the small attacks are only the reconnaissances which must take place first. I don't think the attack will succeed, but there will be heavy fighting all the same.

Jebb and Lloyd returned from leave today, they say that the betting in London is 3/1 on the war being ended by June. Of course the money markets are great factors in war but in this case I think that the men are optimistic. We had a French lawyer lunching here and asked him if the people of France would be satisfied to make peace supposing that Germany offered them Alsace and Lorraine. His answer came pat out without a moment's hesitation 'No – there are still too many Germans alive' – this is the feeling of the bourgoisie. Yet Germany is putting out feelers. As Brooks rightly remarks, the political side is beginning to pull some strings. Does Austria want peace? If so Germany must recognise the end is in sight.

**Saturday 6 February 1915** Went up to Ypres to see Byng (3rd Cav.Div.) and if possible go round the line of trenches which we shall have to take over later. Horne drove us up in his car and we met the usual obstruction – two motor lorries trying to pass and one stuck in the mud. After some time we had to bring up another lorry to pull it out. We saw a civilian there and it turned out to be Bonar Law, who was I suppose going up to Ypres on a joy ride. He was an interested spectator at the block.

We went out to Briggs' day HQ just outside the town on the Menin road. He showed us all his plans and we found that we going to be loaned to the French and are under command of General D'Urbal (9th Corps). You cannot get to the trenches by day and are really at the mercy of the telephone communication. There was not very much to see – they kept on shelling the railway crossing all the time. All along the road the ground is pitted with shell holes and they must have given it an awful doing.

**Sunday 7 February 1915** Heard that Fitzgerald (11th Hussars) is going to succeed Percy Hambro as my [GSO]2. It is always my luck to have senior men under me, but I suppose that he has only accepted it so as to get a footing out here and then go on to something better. Heard that the King of the Belgians* is coming tomorrow, so arranged to turn out two Regiments for him.

Good show at La Bassée by 4th Guards Brigade (Cavan). They turned the Germans out of a brickfield down there and captured a machine gun, a trench mortar, 18 unwounded Germans and an Officer. It was a good show, **well and thoroughly** prepared, with a definite objective. We are learning a lot from the French now in this war. Russians news shows very heavy fighting and the Germans are pushing again at the centre, I think that if it fails the Germans will cut back after it – but no one can tell.

**Monday 8 February 1915** Clive arrived at GHQ from Joffre's HQ and says that they are pleased there with the Russian news. 28th Div. lost two machine guns which is not so good, but they are new at it and will learn. The Bays and 9th Lancers turned out for the King of the Belgians and lined the road just west of Meteren. He is a very tall man with a pleasant expression. He played the King well, had Commanding Officers presented to him and appeared very interested – so very different from our last Royal visit. It was a good show. Tom Bridges and Teck came round with him and Mick Harper was the cicerone*. It was a lovely day but with a cold wind and we hacked back to our chateau.

**Wednesday 10 February 1915** Lyon came as Liaison Officer. He told us about Rumania and said that they had some good Generals, but the other Officers were not much good. Went to see Gough about the occupation of the trenches at Ypres. There is a lack of support trenches which I don't like.

**Thursday 11 February 1915** We got out trench mortar this morning and arranged a display. I brought Sandys back from the Field Squadron and we had great fun. The first two bombs did not go off at all – we thought that the detonator fell out so we tied it in the third time and still nothing happened. So we examined the beastly thing and found that the bursting charge was gun cotton and that the detonator was too short and not in touch with the primer. It would have been a fine thing to have fired at the Germans – how they would have laughed. So we had an explosion of our own and it made a real good bang. In war we are always improvising and here is a very bad case – a bomb made for an old pattern of detonator, whilst they issue the new pattern. Pat and the President took photos, some of them ought to be very funny.

**Friday 12 February 1915** The Russian news is most encouraging*. There is a distinct tendency towards peace talks – where does it come from? Not from the Entente powers – the speeches in the Russian Duma and the French Chamber of Deputies clearly show this. On the other hand the socialists in the Reichstag are raising their voices for peace – Germany has most to gain by a peace now. What must be the view of peace from a British point of view? Our policy must be the maintenance of the Balance of Power in Europe. Germany has threatened this and hence this war. If we see Germany wiped off the map and the Latin and Slav Races predominant, one of these will threaten to overrun us – which will it be? I don't think France. We clash only in the matter of colonies, not very much in the case of trade, in fact there is room enough for both of us on this globe. On the other hand what about Russia? We are fighting as Allies now, but in the past her methods have not been to our liking especially in Asia – she will get a free exit in the Dardanelles – will this satisfy her? I cannot think so. I see a man or a set of men in Russia whose one idea will be a Russian Empire which will reach from the Atlantic to the Pacific and the Arctic to the Indian Ocean. This is only a matter of Evolution, you may call it patriotism, the Russian Bismark who is bound to be born and who will work to this end.

Founded on past history, what are the most favourable conditions of peace which will keep the balance of power in Europe for the longest possible time? I say the longest possible time, because I believe that another war must come and that it will be against Russia – a coalition of Latin and Teuton Races against the Slav Races. The problem resolves itself into the solution of the following questions – Germany must be humbled to such an extent that she will not be able to raise herself to such a power in Europe that she would single-handed threaten the peace of Europe – but she must not, on the other hand, be ruined to such an extent that she would be unable to offer a stout resistance to Russia if Russian expansion westwards threatened the British Empire.

The danger lies in Russia – she is showing her power in an unmistakable manner. Provided that Power is working for good, all is well – but if it is working for self and self-aggrandizement it will lead to trouble. On the other hand people may say how will this affect Russian expansion in Asia – the answer is that India forms only a part of the British Empire. If the hub (ie England) is beaten, the foundations are shaken; should we lose India – we lose prestige and country but we do not lose all. What will the actual conditions of peace be? What is the minimum Britain can take? That is the question for politicians.

**Monday 15 and Tuesday 16 February 1915** Things do not seem to be going as well as they might be with the 28th Div. We continually hear that a trench is lost here and there and then retaken with considerable casualties. The French Corps which they relieved was not a good one. The trenches were not good, but of course the country just here is very difficult, it is low lying and water very near the surface.

**Wednesday 17 February 1915** Went up to Ypres to pay our respects to General Dubois commanding the [French] 9th Corps and General Le Fevre the [French] 18th Div. — both of them charming men. We shall be under them when we take over the trenches. Dubois is an oldish man and Le Fevre looked much younger. What wonderful manners these Frenchmen have — was very much struck with them. They went on to see the 2nd Cav.Div. from whom we take over. We saw Bob Greenly and talked all things over. They were very perturbed about the 28th Div. on their right — these had been driven out of a trench near Zwarte—leen and then the Germans could fire on Zillebeke. This made communication with Cavan's House* very uncertain. Something wrong here. Bob full of French Artillery, they are wonders and no praise is too high for them — the French very complimentary as regards the British Cavalry — nothing too good for them. Hope that 28th Div. will regain their trenches, otherwise things will be uncomfortable. A perfectly vile day — pouring with rain and very cold. It must be awful in the trenches.

**Thursday 18 February 1915** Hear 28th Div. have recovered all lost trenches which is good. Sent Sandys and Macfarlane to arrange Signals and Sappers.

**Friday 19 February 1915** All my arrangements for the move to Ypres spoilt because the buses will not turn — was very angry but had to readjust everything: an awful waste of time. Hear 28th Div. are being relieved, that they have had a good many casualties. This is the old story — new troops, new Officers, new everything and people expect it to work like a wound—up machine — the thing is absolutely impossible. Today Despatches came out, will cause a good deal of heart burning. It is the old story, private influence is paramount. The Division has been very badly served.

**Saturday 20 February 1915** A most exciting day — the Honours Gazette has come out — De Lisle and Briggs made Major Generals, Allenby KCB, Tommy Pitman a CB, and so on many friends honoured. have got DSO and am delighted and was greatly surprised — the result is that most people happy. Am delighted about De Lisle and Briggs, they thoroughly deserve it. Completed the arrangements about the Ypres trenches. Bob Greenly came down and saw me this morning, he has a CMG*. I hope that everything will work quite smoothly now.

A rather anxious thing happened — an Alsatian deserted near Ypres some days ago and said that the Germans meditated an attack between the 16th and 20th. Well on the 18th they attacked the French on the Menin road with five Battalions. Prisoners say that the reason for the attack is to find out where the left of the British rested. Alsatians are always deserting, it is funny that in 45 years the Germans have not Germanised Alsace, the province is still French and all her sympathies are French. The French seem to have great faith in the Russians and do not seem to be worried at the German advance. I only hope that it will not precipitate an attack here before we are ready. A push here must be prepared with the utmost patience and must not be premature.

**Sunday 21 February 1915** Another lovely spring day and quite warm in the sun. Very little news from the Russians — their official despatch is rather naive!! It says 'Our troops are gradually leaving the sphere of fighting'!!!* The 28th Div. have been split up — the three Brigades forming this Division have been replaced by Brigades from the 5th and 3rd Divs. The Germans will probably get a nice surprise if they try and attack these seasoned troops. The list of honours and despatches is raising the usual howl. I am a sympathetic listener on these occasions. It is the only thing to do — you cannot always please everyone.

# 4. The Second Battle of Ypres

**Monday 22 February** 1915 Very foggy all day. The 1st Cav.Bde moved to Ypres and went into billets there prior to taking over the trenches from Chetwode's [5th] Bde. Went to Flêtre to see them off – all went smoothly. Just heard that 16th Lancers have suffered a great many casualties. The Germans mined under one of their trenches and blew it up. The 16th at once counter attacked to recover it but came under a very heavy Maxim* fire from the Germans' original trench. They lost five Officers in a few minutes. It is especially hard as they informed the French that they thought that the Germans were mining, but the French would not have it at all and said that the line had been quite quiet and would continue to be so – the result was they were blown up themselves as part of their trench also went.

**Tuesday 23 February** 1915 Went up to Ypres in the car at 2.00 pm and saw Gough from whom we took over and then went on to see General Lefebre (French 18th Div.). He is a very polite man, full of compliments, a great talker and inclined to give one lectures on tactics. Bridges (1st Bde) took over from Chetwode and all passed quite quietly. Went out to the trenches with the General and saw all the dug-outs. The mud is very bad in places and some of the communication trenches are full of water. We were not shelled either going or coming which was lucky. The 2nd Bde got up all right and went into reserve at Ypres. Had a terrible shock on arrival, always thought that the French battalion was there to support our line; now the French say that it is there to occupy the second line. This upsets the whole system of defence, making it purely passive which is always wrong.

**Wednesday 24 February** 1915 A cold day with some snow. The General went to visit the trenches and had a very narrow escape. A German sniper had got into a position from which he could enfilade a piece of the communication trench. He missed the General's head by inches and hit Bell Irving in the thigh. There was considerable trouble in getting the latter away, but we have great hopes that he will be all right. I rode down in the afternoon and saw General Briggs and then went with Sewell [4th Guards Bde] and selected a position for the supporting Squadron and trenches which will cover the right of the line. It is very muddy down there and there are continual snowstorms. The dug-outs where Briggs is are quite comfortable and fairly dry, the men have plenty of straw. It is a curious situation: in some places the Germans are only 25 yards away and yet one can walk about behind our trenches in perfect safety from rifle fire. In other places one cannot poke one's nose anywhere without getting a bullet somewhere near one's head. Generals Allenby and Plumer both came to see how we were getting on, the former very unsympathetic as regards our troubles with the French as he always is. Lots of new troops coming out, many Canadians all over the country now. I suppose we shall be taking over the line from here to the sea later on, but I hope not. Sitting still is always very difficult.

**Thursday 25 February** 1915 A very cold day after a hard frost and a good deal of snow. In the afternoon walked out to the trenches and went round the ground in rear of them with the General. Found the trench made by the 4th Dragoon Guards and completed during the night: a good one. Whilst we were with General Briggs, the Germans continually shelled Cavan's House and a ruined farm to the right of it, they must have put 50 shells into it during the day. They have not shelled this part for a very long time, but they do not neglect a single corner of the ground and quarter it all quite regularly. It was a very dirty and tiring walk, but we got round it at last. We have had a few casualties each day, mostly due to a thin parapet. I don't think that the other Divisions could have done much. The French especially must have sat there and done nothing, not even fired a shot. The 5th Dragoon Guards have got nearly all the water out of their trenches in about two days.

**Friday 26 February** 1915 Did not go down to the trenches today but had a talk with Nicholson [new GSO3] regarding the partition of the work and taught him the different cyphers in use. Had many visitors, the Bull* came up in a beastly bad temper and started bullying me, but I just took no notice. Then General Plumer and Jeudwine also came in. The General was out so we had to entertain them all.

**Saturday 27 February** 1915 Took Nicholson down to the trenches and left him to go round with Balfour; I went across to the left of the line to see Wilberforce (The Bays) and inform him that he was to take over command of the 2nd Cav.Bde as General Mullins has gone sick. He has already had five days in the trenches and did not seem to relish the idea of another five but, as Briggs put it, it was an opportunity not to be lost. They were full of the usual grumbles. They seem to think that the Staff do nothing, that is the idea of the Regimental Officer, he keeps it till he is put on the Staff and then grumbles because he has too much to do. But I smoothed matters over.

This part of the line reminds one of the pictures of the wood fighting in the American Civil War – there is no difference at all as far as I can see. They all however seemed cheerful and well. Walked back with Briggs. He is a fearless man, but when he has anyone with him, he looks after them to the utmost. He was most careful to make me run across two places where they do a lot of sniping. Mouse Tomkinson* is getting up a spy hunt in Zillebeke, but I personally do not think that there is any spy there. Men are continually being shot there but I think it is from stray bullets from the lines.

**Sunday 28 February** 1915 A very quiet night for once in a way. Went down to see the German saps*, also to see the ground in front of the trenches on the right. Had to look through a periscope as it is bad to put one's head over the parapet. Saw where Curran crawled out to, it took him 1½ hours to get 25 yards. We came to the conclusion that we could only watch it very carefully. He sank a shaft to begin a counter mine but it had six foot of water in it so that was not much good. I do not think that much can be done for this reason. The 5th Dragoon Guards have improved their trenches no end. They shelled the dug-outs on the right of the line very heavily while I was there – there were several casualties. The men will not stay in the dug-outs, they will walk out to see how·their cooking is going on; they are always cooking something and this is how they get hit. There has been more shelling but less sniping.

**Monday 1 March** 1915 The 2nd Bde relieved the 1st Bde in the trenches last night and the relief was carried out smoothly and was without casualties. Very satisfactory, especially as it was full moon and very bright at that. Today we hear definitely that we are to be relieved by the French. This is a nuisance as we shall have to take away a lot of stuff from the trenches which otherwise would have been left for the unit coming after us. The Russian news continues to be good*. It is something to hear of the capture of the German prisoners on that side, especially any large number of them. I think that the German offensive there has reached the limit. A very nasty day, cold and dark – I think it will snow.

**Tuesday 2 March** 1915 Aviators report 60 German trains in Menin, we are all wondering if this means an arrival or a departure. Had a visit from the French, they are relieving us on the

4/5th instead of the 5/6th. The shelling has increased today but I think that it does not mean anything.

**Wednesday 3 March 1915** Had a very busy day arranging for our move back. The French down in the South are making wonderful progress and are full of fight*. The Russian news is also good. In fact for the first time it seems as if we are fighting on equal terms with Germany, she has had the advantage so far in numbers, arms and equipment and preparation, but it seems now as if the tables are being turned. The question of the Dardanelles is also interesting. If we can open that passage, it will free the route for Russian wheat and will stop the Yankees trying to corner it.

**Thursday 4 March 1915** This is practically our last full day in the trenches but what a day it has been. The first thing has been the trouble as regards the relief of our men by the French: the French say all is right, we understand everything but when the time comes difficulties invariably arise. So spent the morning making certain as regards the relief — how they panned out we will see later.

All this week we have been digging a mine under the German trenches. The idea was that the Germans were mining towards us and we were going to counter mine so as to prevent them. On the left the French also had a mine. The orders were that the French and English mines were to be exploded one five minutes after the other. The 18th Hussars held the trenches, a squadron of the Bays under Sloane formed the storming party. At 7.40 pm up went our mine, the storming party advanced and occupied the crater and the old 10th Lancers' trench for 70 yards beyond the crater and barricaded the trenches communicating with the main German lines. So far so good but what did the French do? Nothing — their mine did not go off, the result being that our left was exposed. The Germans, as soon as they recovered, proceeded to bomb the Bays out of the trench gained — so it ended. Many point of military interest arise:

 a. The futility of such operations if half French, half English.
 b. Mines must be exploded simultaneously by order of an Officer who is named.
 c. Reconnaissance by day and night.

The work was well done on our part and, if the French had co-operated, we might have reoccupied the trench lost by the 2nd Div. Was up all night as French relief of 18th Hussars four hours late.

**Friday 5 March 1915** We have finished our 10 days in the trenches. I think we have had luck — but it is wonderful how casualties mount up. Ours are: 11 Officers wounded (none seriously), 11 men killed and 70 wounded. This shows how trench work saps an Army, it is one here and one there that mount up in a week. It has however done us good I think. It has certainly made the men good and we have had little or no sickness. It has taught us many things.*

**Sunday 7 to Thursday 11 March 1915** Was at home on Urgent Private Affairs. On the 9th the first real offensive of our Army started*. The special order issued by General D. Haig is of great interest as it shows the conditions under which we have been fighting up to now, how slowly and gradually we have had to make up leeway. At 8.20 am on the 10th the 23rd† and 25th‡ Bdes and the Gharwal Bde§ took the front line of the enemy's entrenchment. The idea of this offensive was not to capture a trench here and there but to carry the operation right through and push forward to the Aubers-Mont Pommereau ridge — there to push forward mounted troops through the gap there made. To assist this the 1st Cav. Div. was to be ready to concentrate at the Mont des Cats within one hour, the 2nd north-west of Estaires, the 3rd in the Bois d'Aval.

The first attack was very successful. By night we had gone forward 1,000 yards and captured 700 prisoners, the prisoners saying that the attack was a complete surprise. A mist came down over the land and it was not possible to get any observation of Artillery fire, so the operations were greatly hampered with the result that not as much progress as could be desired was made. But positions were consolidated against counter attack.

**Friday 12 March 1915** Morning report says that all the positions captured held. The Germans counter attacked against that position held by the Black Watch at 5.50 am, but were beaten back by 6.25 am. German artillery very active – about 60 prisoners taken here – the Germans then heavily shelled our trenches east of Neuve Chapelle at 6.00 am, this was followed by an Infantry attack which was easily repulsed by the Rifle Bde*. The 2nd Cav.Div. and a Brigade of the North Midland Div.† were formed into a temporary detachment under General Gough and put under GOC 1st Army. Many piecemeal attacks by the Germans reported along our new front between 5.30 am and 6.30 am east of Neuve Chapelle. Germans reached our trench in one place but were counter attacked by West Yorks who followed up and drove them back, inflicting heavy losses on the Germans. The weather has cleared at 2.00 pm and so we may expect further developments. The present operations promise some success. Germany is making every effort on her eastern frontier, what we want is to have her going back on both frontiers at the same time, that will bring war home to them.

**Saturday 13 March 1915** The attack is finished – GHQ are disappointed. The reason is that it was **nearly** a very big thing. It seems that we nearly broke the line and the idea was to push through the five Divisions of Cavalry. But war is full of if's and nearlys. On the other hand it was considered that it would take three days to capture Neuve Chapelle, it took us three hours. Why did we stop? Jocy D.* has been stellenboshed† for not pushing enough. He stopped to consolidate his position. he would have been right nine times out of 10. In this case in the eyes of the judges he was wrong. **That is war.**

It appears from gossip that the first part was properly prepared and beautifully carried out it was in the second part that we failed. What was the result? On a front of 3,000 yards we made a bow in the enemy's line of nearly a mile in the centre. Our casualties were 13,000, we captured 1,700 prisoners and the enemy's casualties were very heavy. Was it a profit or a loss? A profit certainly; you cannot attack without casualties, and if you don't attack the men lose all spirit and dash. Another consideration: is this attack one of a series all along the line to weaken him and tire him out? We know the Germans had to bring a Division by train to repel this attack, prisoners say it came from Roulers. Are we going to attack opposite Roulers? If this is part of a general scheme – it may have some far-reaching results; if alone its success is somewhat discounted.

**Sunday 14 March 1915** A quiet morning and after that the deluge. The Germans started shelling part of our line at St Eloois and it was the heaviest shelling experienced during the war. At 5.30 they attacked and drove our 27th Div. out of its trenches. Now this is a curious coincidence. We know that the Neuve Chapelle attack drew German reserves from Roulers – and yet what do we see? Two days afterwards a heavy attack opposite that place. Here we see the theory of attack: they are weakened in a certain place, they don't sit quiet they attack to prevent us attacking. Here you have the German creed of war and a good one too. At 10.00 pm two Cavalry Divisions ordered to be ready to move by 6.00 am. At 1.00 am we get orders to concentrate at 6.00 am. At 2.30 am a counter attack is launched; it retakes all the trenches except a small mound just south of St Eloois. Thus we arrive at 6.00 am – no sleep for me – I have a beastly cold and I hate all Germans.

**Monday 15 March 1915** Established advanced report centre at Gudewaersvelde and got there at 7.15 am. News not good – people a bit jumpy. Casualties in counter attack very heavy. Sat there till 2.00 pm. News better during afternoon. They decide to plaster mound with shell and take it tonight. At 2.00 pm, order Brigade back to billets and ready to move at two hours' notice. Very cold today and my cold boiling up finely. I only got two hours' sleep last night, so am fairly tired.

**Tuesday 16 March 1915** Have got a vile cold in the head, the worst I can remember. It is so violent that I do not think it can last very long. It has been a very quiet day. They have not as yet retaken the St Eloois mound, but they seem determined to do so, I wonder they don't turn Grandmother, Mother and the Twins on to it (Grandmother is a 15in. gun, Mother 9.2in. and the Twins 6in. guns). Went over to Corps and tried to get some idea as regards how they proposed using the Cavalry at the Neuve Chapelle show. Could not get any ideas and I do not believe that they know themselves. Everyone says that someone else said something else – no truth, no one will give an opinion. I asked them to let us know beforehand when we are to gallop to the Kiel Canal and capture the German Fleet – so I hope that in future there will be a definite plan known beforehand to the Staffs concerned. Secrecy carried to the extreme in Cavalry work or rather the preparation for it, is the worst possible thing; the reason being that when launched it is difficult for the big commander to control it and the Cavalry has to act on its own initiative very often. Evidently all is going to be quiet for a day or two – we are back to four hours notice.

**Wednesday 17 March 1915** A very quiet day – the GHQ advanced report centre has moved back to St Omer and so I suppose that for the present the effort has stopped. We are trying to move our Brigades out of their present areas, they have been there a long time and the areas are getting pretty foul – whether we shall be able to or not remains to be seen.

**Thursday 18 March 1915** Colonel Budworth RHA arrived today and joined the Staff. They have gone back to the old Gunner Staff – why I cannot make out. Especially as senior Gunner Officers are badly required with the new Armies. I suppose they don't want the Gunner Staff appointments to be reduced, but they mix up peace and war once again. These Staffs are required for instruction in peace but not for war.

There is still a good deal of mystery as regards the Neuve Chapelle show. They now say that it was only a local show. But Haig's special order points to something further. It is no good breaking the line unless **everyone** is ready to take advantage of it and go forward – not only ourselves but also the French. Everything must be arranged and thought out beforehand and all informed. This was not the case. It must therefore have only been meant as a side show. This sort of thing does not give one a great deal of confidence. In Cavalry work the carrying out of orders intelligently means making decisions on the spot without being able to refer to higher formations for orders. In the case of cavalry ordered forward this applies specially. Hence this screed. Weather has turned very funny and looks like a bad spell again. The Dardanelles news is good – I think the taking of the Dardanelles* will have a very great influence on the war.

**Friday 19 March 1915** My cold much better and so hope to have shaken it off. Snowing hard last night and a bitter cold north wind today. Germans have of course got hold of Haig's special order and are bolstering everyone up with the cry that three German Battalions have held up 48 British ones. All this is very annoying – the British papers are also going in for the staring headline business. They might take a page out of other countries as regards this question.

**Sunday 21 March 1915** Went to church at the 1st Bde service. Then had a conference on the question of honours. Very difficult, of course no one satisfied. Heard of the loss of three ships in the Dardanelles*. It is lucky that we have not lost more. It is rather funny to think how war changes the tenets of peace. The teaching has always been that a ship is such a valuable thing that is was never worthwhile risking it within the reach of fortress defences – yet in war all these things are changed and we find the Fleet taking on forts at close range. War is the master, and necessity dictates the actual use. So much for peace theories!

**Monday 22 March 1915** Great news tonight. Przemysl* has fallen, this will release a good many Russian troops. But the garrison have done well – they have put up a very gallant defence and deserve all honours for it. It will have a great morale effect and might buck everyone up no end. We are now hearing details and criticism of the Neuve Chapelle attack. Of course everyone is criticising – but it was very nearly a big thing. The summing up of the whole situation is that everyone judging after the event thinks more might have been done.

**Tuesday 23 March 1915** The first warm day of the year and all the buds are shooting out very fast now. Hear rumours of changes. Byng to get a Corps, Kavanagh some other job and Bingham to get the 3rd Cav.Div. I can hardly credit that Briggs is going to be passed over for

Bingham – to my mind there is no comparison between the two. I am afraid it looks like a case of influence. Let us hope that rumour will once more be a lying jade.

**Wednesday 24 to Saturday 27 March 1915** Had no time to write the Diary. Been busy with work and entertaining. Arranged for a personally conducted tour round the second line of trenches. Went round three of the 2nd Corps today. We walked solidly for three hours and took Brigadiers of 1st and 2nd Cav.Bdes with us. It was very good value. Found second line well dug and very strong between Neuve Eglise and Vierstraat but north of that very bad and behind St Eloois probably nil. This is bad. St Eloois to my mind is our present storm centre – it certainly is the weakest part of our line and it is to be hoped that the matter will be taken in hand at once.

Generals Lowe and Osbert Lumley who are Inspectors of Cavalry came here and stayed with us for a couple of days. On Thursday they went and saw billets. On Friday I took them to see the trenches in Ploegsteert wood and Osbert Lumley went to see his boy's grave* in Ploegsteert cemetary. I took them up on to Hill 63 and we looked at our old Messines Ridge and spent quite a profitable day. We have more ammunitions to burn for the moment than the Germans – they think that the Germans are massing troops opposite Arras, but this has always been a storm centre. We are extending our line to the Menin road. This looks as if we are going to do the holding part of the business and the French the attacking – I do not like this. I do not think we ought to extend too much especially towards Ypres, the line round that place should be **very strong** and in great depth. At all costs the Germans must not be allowed to get Ypres, it would add two months on to the war.

All cameras must be sent home – the result of the *Daily Mail* offering prizes for war photographs, what a nuisance these papers are. I wander if I can evade the law, shall have a good try. Went to a show got up by the Corps Signals. It was very topical and there was a tremendous amount of talent got together. It is curious how and what Officers are made from in war. At this gaff† one Officer in the 15th Hussars got up and sang a couple of songs – anyone could see he was a professional‡. Inquired and found out that he had been earning £60 a week on the music hall stage, yet he is a very good Officer. We came back to the old saying that war makes men. Many men say that this procedure should be followed in peace; it practically comes to Officers being chosen from the ranks – but peace and war are as far apart as the poles. What is good in war is not always good in peace, on the other hand what is good in peace helps towards war – that is the difference. It was an amusing evening.

**Tuesday 30 March 1915** Still fine and colder than ever. Hardress Lloyd saw Cyril Hankey in St Omer who told him officially that Italy is coming in*. What a nation the Germans are – they are fighting the whole of Europe practically single handed. What would have happened if they had fought either France or Russia single handed? They have just missed a great coup – I suppose now all the smaller dogs will chip in – Bulgaria, Rumania and Greece. What are they going to get out of it? I suppose all these questions are settled before they come in – otherwise the squabbling and growling over the dead meat will be terrible. History will show what Italy's game really was, it is quite interesting to conjecture at present.

A Taube† came over Cassel and dropped six bombs over that place yesterday morning but they did no damage to speak of and no one was hurt. There is a persistent rumour that another push is to be made at or near Neuve Chapelle. Again the Cavalry are going to be pushed through the gap. Officially we know nothing about it – this question of secrecy has become a terrible one. If Major X in a Battalion knows that a push is to be made, the thing cannot be called a very secret thing; yet the Cavalry know nothing, but are expected to carry out a manoeuvre, the success of which depends on forethought and rapidity. The one condition necessary to accomplish these is that subordinates should know a good deal. The question of secrecy of plans is always a difficult one but if secrecy is going to destroy the plan, either the plan is a bad one for this reason or else the plan forms a bold throw to carry out which successfully secrecy must go to the wall. I only hope that if they want the Cavalry to do quick

62

work, they will take the Divisional Commanders into their confidence and then we may hope of some degree of success.

**Wednesday 31 March 1915** Another fine day but not nearly so cold. Visit [to] second line trenches of the 3rd Corps*. The country south and east of Armentieres is very flat — the trenches seemed very broad and in some cases wet — but it is a curious soil: a sort of crumbling clay. They had only one line of wire in front of them, I don't like this but this could be quickly improved. The line was well furnished with good supporting points. Armentieres, although within two miles of the front line, was very little knocked about. Things seemed very quiet along that part of the front. Got back about 4.00 pm. Most of the Staff, chaperoned by Brooks Hambro, went to Dunkirk and brought back some excellent lobsters which we had for dinner.

**Thursday 1 April 1915** Went up to Brigades this morning and lunched with Mullins at the 2nd Cav.Bde HQ. They thought that they had caught a man tapping one of our telephone lines — so they arrested him. They found a wire keyed on to our wire and running into the garden of his house. The owner turned out to be a Curé and was very angry and indignant at being arrested. He was liberated the next day, but it did a lot of good as it shows the people that we will not stand any nonsense. He also made a great mistake in getting angry, he could easily have explained it all.

**Friday 2 April 1915** Good Friday. Went for a ride early in the morning and then went to see Rowland Anderson and lunched with the Regiment. They made a splendid April Fool of Luke White — sending him a puppy in a parcel as if from home. He has no sense of humour and buried it in the back garden, remarking that some people had no idea of the proper fitness of things.

**Saturday 3 April 1915** Freddy Guest came in to lunch, he has just returned from the Dardanelles. He was very interesting: he says that he considers the whole thing a very difficult job and that Constantinople will not be reached in a day. Also that a good many troops will be required. He was on board the *Queen Elizabeth* and described the shooting of the big guns*. Got news that we have blown up a trench near Givenchy but do not seem to have occupied it.

[Sir John] French had a conference with Cav.Div. Commanders today and there was some straight talking as regards the use of Cavalry — there have been too many wild rumours about lately. He stopped and had a talk with L. after it so I hope that the gap has been safely bridged over at last, it will be a good thing for the Divisions. Anderson very well, but I did not like his description of the training of the Reserve Cavalry Regiments at home. They are not up to date and don't seem to understand what is wanted.

**Sunday 11 April 1915** The week has been an eventful one as both the French and Russians have been making very marked progress. It would appear that, unless the German and Austrian Forces make some great counter move, the Russians will invade Hungary in real earnest and that would be the end as far as Austria is concerned. But Austria has come up to the scratch time after time in a most wonderful way and it is dangerous to be too certain on the point. Germany seems to be reinforcing Austria. This is unlike them — a counter offensive from Cracow would be more in keeping with German methods and teaching. But of course it may be a political move — the bolstering up of Austria so as to allay public feeling.

The French have been making great progress in the Woevre and will now probably close the St Mihiel gap*. Today's official information is interesting. It reads: 'Three counter attacks have been repulsed at Bois Monthare.' This shows how hard put the Germans are at this part to hold the line. We have relieved the French 9th Corps east of Ypres and they have passed south and will be relieving the 20th shortly. We shall there join up with the Belgians who hold the line to the sea. Yesterday (Saturday) the 1st Bde had a horse show and jumping competitions. It was a beautiful afternoon and went off very well. Saw many old friends there.

Much gossip flying about as regards who is to get command of the Bays. Also rumours that Briggs is moving on, but I had no news for them. The 9th Bde is being formed and comes to the Division at last. Bob Greenly is to command and I thought Cecil Howard would be

Brigade Major, but I hear that someone out of the 2nd Div. is to get the job – yet Allenby recommended Cecil. We are getting back to the old system of personal jobbery which is a pity, it is the result of sitting still. It is high time to leave the army when this war is over unless one is prepared to compete in the intrigues for advancement. It is a pity, I thought this war would finish it.

**Wednesday 14 April 1915** Went up to the 1st Bde and had lunch with Briggs. We blew some German trenches in at Givenchy and the Germans did the same to us at St Eloois. But nothing to matter occurred. I went up to the 5th Corps* at Poperinge, all was quiet up there. A Taube dropped a bomb in Poperinge – it would appear that we are short of anti-aircraft guns, also that the planes they have there climb very slowly. This should be remembered. Did not like the state of the Poperinge-Ypres road. Too much transport on it altogether in the daytime, Staff work required here.

**Friday 16 April 1915** Went out for a ride in the Clairmarais Forest. It is a lovely day and the wood was full of primroses. It seems such a pity to be at war at this time of the year, trying to kill when everything is growing.

**Saturday 17 April 1915** A lovely fine day. Went to the 2nd Cav.Div. Horse show which was held at Vieux Berquin. It was one of the best shows that I have seen. Very well run and people collected for miles round. I saw a whole host of old friends.

**Sunday 18 April 1915** Last night we blew up three metres under a hill to [the] south-east of Ypres. It was a very important piece of the line as it formed the operation post for Artillery fire on to the road between Ypres and Vlamertinge. The Germans counter attacked four times in great numbers but were beaten back. They at one time got a footing in one place – but at about 6.00 pm were pushed out of it. I believe that we had 19 Maxims at work there, they came from one of the new motor Maxim Batteries. It is the first time I knew of their use, it will be interesting to know how they were brought up and used and so on. We hold on to the ground gained – our casualties have been heavy, mostly from the attacks with bombs. I believe about 1,200, but the actual taking of the trench only cost three men. I think the country will probably object to these casualties, but the point is that every place we carry makes us stronger and the enemy more hopeless. I hope we shall hold on to it all right.

**Monday 19 April 1915** Inspected the 18th and 19th Hussars during the morning – they have been doing Divisional Cavalry up till now and now form our 9th Cav.Bde. Went to lunch with Jeffrey Lockett and Camperdown Yates and attended their Squadron sports. It was a peaceful afternoon although the growling of the guns could be heard towards Ypres. Went and had tea with Bobbery Anderson at Regimental HQ and then home. Heard a lot of gossip – that Hubert Gough had got an Infantry Div. – am very glad as he will do it well and it will get him on. Also a good thing to let him leave the Bull as things were getting too hot*. Hear Kavanagh has got the 2nd Cav.Div., he ought to do it well.

**Tuesday 20 April 1915** We still hold on to what we have gained and that is good. 2nd Cav.Bde had a Field Day, the General and I went and looked on. It is funny to think of white cap bands* and blank ammunition in war. We then went on to Poperinge to 5th Corps HQ – they had not much detail to give us. The road behind here and that place is bad; like most Belgian things, the foundations are bad – and it nearly shook one's teeth loose coming home.

**Thursday 22 April 1915** As far as one can hear we hold Hill 60 but it is nearly flat now, having been bombarded by both sides and practically knocked to bits. But all events we have clung on to it although the casualties have been heavy. Dined with the 7th Cav.Bde and then went on to a gaff given by the 1st Life Guards. They had a lot of talent and it was very good although they started pretty near the wind and the censor of plays would never have passed the Revue from London. At midnight got a message to say that French line had been driven back near Langemark* and that the Division was to be warned to turn out at an hour's notice – so got out orders and tried to get some sleep.

**Friday 23 April 1915** Got orders to concentrate Division about Godewaersvelde and this was completed by 8 am. We then learned that the Germans had attacked the French line with asphyxiating gases* and that the French had given a good deal of ground and carried the left of the Canadians† with it there. This is the first time that gases had been used on this side although it has been rumoured in the east. At 9.00 am we got orders to move up to the south of Poperinge and this move was completed by 12.30 pm. Here we began to hear details. The French had only a Territorial Div. backed up by an active one‡ – it appears that the line had given from Langemark-Bikschote to Boezinge-Steenstraat – about two miles. At about 1.00 pm we were placed under orders of the 2nd Army and at 2.00 pm got orders to move up to the line Elverdinge-Woesten with orders to cover the left flank of the 2nd Army.

We got up to the line at about 4.30 pm, sending the 1st Bde to the latter and the 2nd Bde to the former place and getting Officers out in touch with the neighbouring forces. It was rather a curious position to be in. On our right were the British, in front the French under General Putz and on the left the Belgian 6th Div. Here we soon got a hang of the situation. The Germans were across the Canal at Lizerne and the line bulged back south of Pilkem and St Juliaan. In fact the Germans had bulged our line on a front of seven miles and a depth of three miles. The situation was pretty serious. The French were pouring up troops and so were we, the 2nd and 3rd Cav.Divs and the Northumbrian Div.§ were moved up. We went back to Poperinge for the night holding the same line.

**Saturday 24 April 1915** Up at 5.00 am and back to our HQ at the 4th kilometer stone on the Poperinge-Elverdinge road. Moved the 9th Cav.Bde behind the 1st Bde south-west of Woesten. Arranged for the defence of the line and improved the trenches. On the east of Canal very heavy firing heard and the Canadians have been ordered to counter attack and try and regain the lost ground. French attach on Lizerne had been carried and [I] report the same, but as usual the French report is not accurate and [I] find out that Germans still hold Lizerne and that the French attack never got near it. The latter are now moving in more guns and the roads are simply blocked with them, Battery after Battery is seen coming up from the south. Went to 5th Corps HQ in the evening, they have no definite news. It is extraordinary how in modern battle you cannot get news, telephone wires get cut by shells and bullets and [the] man on the spot has to go on fighting without getting any orders.

**Sunday 25 April 1915** Our orders for the day were that the Divisions were to be ready to come into action between the French and Belgian forces and to concentrate to the north of Woesten. Moved our HQ to a little inn at cross-roads south west of Woesten. News from our front not good. On the east of the Canal [we] were driven out of St Juliaan – the question now is one whether we are going to retire on Ypres and thus cut off the salient east of that place or else stick it out. It is a difficult question to answer – the Russians would have shortened their line at once, but we as a nation hate giving up an inch of ground – especially ground that we had to fight so hard to keep in November. It will be an important decision. The French organised an attack on Lizerne and at last really turned the Germans out of it. This has been and is one of the greatest battles of the war. I have seldom heard so many guns firing, there must have been over 600 guns on both sides. Division placed under orders of General Putz.

**Monday 26 April 1915** Moved to our old inn at crossroads at 6.00 am. The attack on Lizerne is going to be once again organised and a counter attack on a large scale to east of the Canal. In the latter place the French, Lahore Div.* and other units are attacking. It is a day of thunder, the guns heavier than yesterday if anything. The French attack failed owing to the gas, the Indians got into the German trenches in one place and the Northumbrian Bde took St Juliaan – a good performance for a Territorial Brigade, but these troops are very good now. The situation in the evening was obscure, but we had not lost any ground – that was the main thing. We had evidently made ground in the centre of our line west of St Juliaan.

Today they shelled Poperinge with the big 17in. Austrian Howitzers and they dropped one in the garden of our night quarters. It had a tremendous effect – smashed every window in the place and made a hole 20ft deep and 30ft across. In the middle of the night they began again but did not get nearer than 200 yards, but the explosions were terrific and in consequence we passed a restless night.

A troop train with the 11th Hussars aboard, halted at Rouen on the way to the front, early August 1914

An 11th Hussars' Squadron billet at Barbonval, 1914

French troops during the Retreat from Mons, August 1914

An 18pdr crew at Chavonne, c10 September 1914

Horses of the 11th Hussars taking cover between River Aisne and the road, September 1914

French and Algerian Cavalry near Braisne[?] during the Battle of the Aisne, c11 September 1914

9th Lancers just before their charge at Moncel, 13 September 1914

The HQ of Colonel Serocold (60th Rifles) just behind Sugar Mill trench during the Battle of the Aisne, c29 September 1914

The XIth Hussars on march from Aisne to Flanders, early October 1914

16th Lancers on the march, late September 1914

First Battle of Ypres: First line transport of the 2nd Cav. Div. in reserve behind Hollebeke Château, 2 October 1914

5th Lancers near Wytschaete, October 1914

The estaminet between Messines and Wulverghern which received a direct shell hit while A.F. Home and Percy Hambro were inside; they had to escape out of the window, 31 October 1914

The Crucifix in the church at Messines, 28 October 1914

1st Cav.Div. Staff outside their temporary HQ near Messines, November 1914 (from left: 'Mouse' Tompkinson (APM); General De Lisle; Percy Hambro (GSO2); Hutchinson (BM. 1st Cav.Bde); AFH (GSO1))

Improvised stalls by the 1st Cav. Div.'s Field Squadron, probably December 1914

1st Cavalry Division staff (Coleman's) car after being hit by debris from a shell between Messines and Wulvergem, 31 October 1914

AFH (looking left) and De Lisle (facing right) waiting for George V to inspect the 1st Cav. Div. 3 December 1914

A corner of the chateau yard at Vermelles, 15 January 1915

A typical Flemish farmyard used for billeting a regiment, probably early 1915.

Lt Pat Armstrong (ADC to de Lisle); AFH; Captain Hardress Lloyd (ADC); taken by Frederic Coleman, early 1915.

A trench at Zillebeke, probably late February 1915

An 11th Hussars' machine-gun trench, probably late February 1915

P.D. Fitzgerald examining German prisoners on 5 March 1915. They were captured as a result of the mine explosion at Hooge.

The Menin gate at Ypres, looking west towards the town over the canal moat, March 1915

1st Cav. Div. Staff having lunch, probably 28 April 1915 (from left: 'Babe' Nicholson; AFH; Percy Fitzgerald; Hardress Lloyd; De Lisle; Pat Armstrong)

Cook huts of the 11th Hussars at Vlamertinge, 16 May 1915

**Tuesday 27 April 1915** Position still the same. Our Batteries are supporting the French attacks on the Canal and so Budworth, our C.RHA*, is having the time of his life and is quite happy. We decided that we would give Poperinge a wide berth tonight if we are still here — the French orders are to continue the attack. The Germans now hold a bridgehead on the Canal south of Steenstraat. Heavy firing again on the east of the Canal. The fighting there has been terrific, the Canadians have fought most gallantly but have lost about 60 per cent in casualties — other units have been practically wiped out. Towards the evening things quiet down a little. At 6.00 pm we get a message from General Putz that we are no longer required and so the troops bivouac in their position.

**Wednesday 28 April 1915** Ordered to concentrate south of the Proven-Poperinge road. A beautifully fine warm day and we did nothing. A conference was held at Poperinge but the result was not known. Today was the worst day for Staff work I can remember since the retreat [from Mons]. At 12 noon we were given a billeting area, it was changed three times during the day and at 7.00 pm we had no area — then we were sent back to the original area.

**Thursday 29 April 1915** The Germans today bombarded Dunkirk from the sea. I suppose one of their light cruisers was out on a raiding expedition. Hear that the 7th Div. under Gough are moving up to Ypres.

**Friday 30 April 1915** There appears to be little or no change in the situation. We are still attacking alongside the French. We have made some headway but not very much. One can draw certain deductions from the fighting in the 2nd Battle of Ypres, if one compares it with Neuve Chapelle. In both cases there is the element of surprise and in both cases surprise has made success. Secondly in both cases it has been said that the attacking side had the one opportunity of breaking the line in the war if they had pushed on. Thirdly in both cases there was a delay and this enabled the defenders to dig in and hold the line on to which they were thrown back. It would therefore appear that for absolute success, surprise and sufficient forces (large ones) to exploit the success are necessary to break the line in this kind of warfare. From the latter it follows that not only depth but breadth is required. If you have only depth, the time necessary to develop the forces required gives the defence time to strengthen itself; also too many casualties on a narrow front are not a good thing.

How then is one to gain a real success in the trench warfare? Such an attack would appear to divide into two phases. The first consists in the actual breaking of the trench line and supports; second masses to go forward behind this line. We must therefore mass men close up and be prepared for **great losses** during the initial stages of the fight. The thing that stands out is that any body of troops given 12 hours can so dig themselves in that any but an organised attack cannot possibly turn them out. So much for tactics. Dunkirk has again been bombarded. They must be firing at a range of over 20 miles — probably with a gun that they intended to use against Dover when they reached Calais. The only bag they will make is one of wounded men in the Duke of Sutherland's Hospital, but that I suppose is according to their tenets. We get very little news here, I don't like the look of Corps — they seem sad, I wonder if P.H.* is to blame. They certainly have not got the information they ought to have.

**Saturday 1 May 1915** We have been at war nearly nine months — it seems years and yet only like yesterday. Another fine warm day and the French and ourselves have once again been attacking north of Ypres. I have heard ugly rumours as regards the French and ourselves at the junction of the lines and that there is a certain amount of friction. I sincerely hope that there is nothing of the kind — but with heavy fighting going on, men's nerves and tempers get strained and often friction will result. This is one of the advantages of attacking at a point where Allied forces join — the Germans have probably taken full advantage of it. Progress is reported all along the line — I only hope it is true, but it is a French report and their news is not always accurate.

De Lisle has heard from home that he may go on to an Infantry Div. — he does not like the idea of it at all and I think got Hardress Lloyd to sound me if I would go with him. Am very happy where I am but if I can help him by going with him, I will certainly do so.

66

**Sunday 2 May 1915** The 2nd Cav.Div. which has been in the support trenches east of Ypres, is being pulled out tonight. They have had a bad time, over 150 casualties and have never fired a shot themselves. They come into billets east of us. There has been a general post today – Indian Cavalry Corps has moved south to the area Staple-Noordpeene, we have moved west bringing the 1st and 9th Cav.Bdes to Wormhout and Esquelbecq so as to make room for the 2nd Div. It would appear that the situation east of Ypres is pretty well in hand now, but it has been an expensive business.

There has also been some friction with the French which is a great pity – but combined attacks of two nations seldom go smoothly and this has been no exception to the rule. The French on the east of the Canal are pretty well tired out. They have been fighting now for 10 days without being relieved at all and Norrie, who was doing Liaison Officer yesterday, told me that the Officers could not get the men to go forward. It is not very surprising. I don't think that the French mean to do much more up there and therefore the line will remain as it is now for the present. The result will be that we have lost ground and the Deutsch will crow accordingly.

**Monday 3 May 1915** Today we returned to our old areas and to the chateau at Le Nieppe. Ten days has made a wonderful change; all the trees are out and the chateau looks very different to the bleak place it looked in winter. I was glad to get back, I love my fleshpots. We are going to shorten our line east of Ypres. I don't like giving up ground but in this case I think it is wise . We have a regular bottle neck up there; a strong attack with these gases would probably close it and we should lose a Division which we could ill spare. Casualties at Ypres still growing, but can only hope that the Germans have suffered heavier ones.

**Tuesday 4 May 1915** The Germans are very active all along the front. Tonight got news of a Russian reverse east of Cracow* – the news is from German and Austrian sources. It may be exaggerated to make Italy hold her hand. An attack eastwards from Cracow is so obviously the best way to counter the Russian offensive across the Carpathians that I cannot see how the Russians could allow themselves to be surprised at this particular point. I can only think that it is a local success and one that will not affect the campaign as a whole.

**Wednesday 5 May 1915** Just heard we are going to dig round Ypres tomorrow night. Also heard that Germans had taken Hill 60, attacking it with gases. They drove our men back and got as far as the village of Zillerbeke. A counter attacke [was] launched at 5.00 pm but it failed, and there has been no more information. There is no doubt that the gas has a most demoralizing effect on the troops, they feel powerless to fight it. The only answer to it is a strong offensive on some other part of the line. There is no Russian confirmation of the German successes claimed on the Duna Jets.

**Thursday 6 May 1915** Went up to Ypres at 7.00 pm and spent the night in a farm just west of that place – all our men digging. They shelled Ypres hard the whole night and have practically razed it to the ground. At 3.00 am a fearful row commenced – guns, machine guns and rifles all spat out together. We learnt afterwards that the Germans had attacked but that the attack was driven back with great loss. Great changes have taken place: Allenby has gone to the 5th Corps, Plumer gets the 2nd Army vice Smith Dorrien who goes home, Byng gets the Cavalry Corps and Briggs the 3rd Cav.Div. I am very sorry for S.D.* – he has had bad luck and been badly served I think.

**Friday 7 May 1915** Went round to Advanced GHQ at Hazebrouck. There is going to be a big attack tomorrow – the French about Arras and the 1st Army at Givenchy. We are digging again tonight but Fisher is going up instead of me. We hear rumours that the German success in the Carpathians is not as great as claimed and that the Dardanelles show is going well* – but they are only rumours. All men now have respirators and we hope to combat the gas question. We retook one of the trenches on Hill 60 today and I hope will get the whole back soon. The German offensive at Ypres has now stopped I think.

**Saturday 8 May 1915** The Division has been placed under the orders of the 2nd Army – this will probably mean shepherding that Army. It always means trouble and we shall be out of any advance that may be possible towards the south.

**Sunday 9 May 1915** Always the way on a Sunday, got orders at midnight to move at 4.30 am – as I said 2nd Army in trouble – again off to Ypres. Ordered Bdes to Vlamertinge and started off in a motor car to see 2nd Army and 5th Corps – the latter just taken over by Allenby. Heard a terrible tale of woe, Germans attacking everywhere and our fellows being blown to bits by the Germans' big guns. The 28th Div. has had to give ground. The Bull was full of heart; he said he would not budge back an inch and that the troops were to hold on to the line they then held, which is called the Switch and runs from t'Hoge to St Juliaan. The 2nd Cav.Bde was was at once sent forward east of Ypres to support the 28th Div. and we made our HQ just south of Vlamertinge. Went on to HQ of 28th Div. – things not right there; everyone looks very tired. The men have been in the trenches fighting for 18 days.

The General went forward to see Brigadiers – his report not very encouraging. Hear the French and English attacks started this morning between Givenchy and Arras – French doing very well. Reports received during the day mostly bad – the Boches are once more fighting with their heavy guns. They simply blow our trenches to pieces and the men with them. Most of our heavy guns have been sent south to help 1st Army in their attack – the result is that we are at a very grave disadvantage. Shelling has been incessant all day. General Allenby came to see us and the result is that we have to send the 9th Cav.Bde forward; this makes two Brigades out of our hands and only one left.

**Monday 10 May 1915** Went out at 8.00 am and visited the 2nd and 9th Bdes. I drove through Ypres – the place is an absolute ruin. Left Coleman about half a mile west of Potijze and went out to look for Mullins – found him having breakfast. They all looked tired and spoke of the shelling the previous afternoon as some of the worst of the war – the ground on this side is terrible, shell holes everywhere and the stench from the dead horses nearly made me sick. Went back and found Coleman in a beautiful dug-out where he had gone to ground – don't blame him*.

Our APM† was sent out to get and collect saddles and harness from dead horses – he tried to cut the harness off one horse and was promptly sick. We are all very sorry for him, but the natural remedy is to go out every day until he gets used to it!!! Very much quieter today – the French have made good progress at Arras and that will affect us here. If the Germans are strong, they will go on attacking us here; if weak, they will stop and send reinforcements from here to Arras.

**Tuesday 11 May 1915** We have now been ordered to be ready to put the whole Division into the trenches. They are going to pull out the 28th Div. and give them a rest. We hate the work but feel that we must help the others and so on doing Infantry work quite cheerfully. Had a lot of casualties in 11th Hussars. We occupy a front line tonight and so went off to see things all right, escaped a shelling but things are much quieter today. We all think that the French attack has drawn troops southwards and that there will be a lull here for a bit.

**Wednesday 12 May 1915** Last night Ypres was a wonderful sight – half of it was burning and the ruins against the light of the fires looked like a staged piece. Spent a very hard day – the 3rd Cav.Div. (Briggs) was put under our orders and we take over the whole line of the 28th Div. This means an awful lot of work – the General was wonderful, he tackled the problem and had all things going in next to no time. I think that we have the whole thing organised by now – and hope it will work all right. The signalling and communication is a difficulty as lines get cut by shells.

**Thursday 13 May 1915** This has been one of the worst days of the war as far as the Cavalry is concerned. The 3rd Div. under Briggs took over the line of trenches last night between the Bellewaerde Lake and Verbranden[?]-Potijze road successfully during the night. At 4.00 am the Germans began bombarding that piece of the line with their heavy guns. It was a terrible bombardment; it laid everything flat, the shells fell like rain. The result was that the 7th Bde very soon did not exist at all – out of 750 about 200 came back and that was all. It meant that that part of our line was broken – the 6th Cav.Bde* on the right and the 1st Cav.Div. on the left stuck it out, the fire not being so heavy. So the day did not begin too well. The 18th Hussars on the left were also badly hammered but the Infantry supports behind came up and reoccupied the trenches.

General Allenby ordered us to retake the line of trenches and Briggs, who was in command of the right section, was ordered to carry it out – the 9th Bde under Greenly being placed at his disposal if he required it. The counter attack was ordered for 2.30 pm and was brilliantly carried out by Bulkeley Johnston's 8th Cav.Bde† being helped by one squadron of the Royals from Campbell's 6th Bde. They reached the old line and got into the old trenches but were shelled out of them once again – only about 200 out of 750 coming back again. At night we held a line about 700 yards in rear of the original line. The casualties have been heavy – 500 in the 1st Div.; about 1,300 in the 3rd.

**Friday 14 May 1915** A quiet day after the storm, the Germans suffered pretty heavily yesterday which is a consolation. The 2nd Cav.Div. came up last night to take over to give us a little rest.

**Sunday 16 May 1915** Back again into the trenches tomorrow night, this time to relieve the 80th Bde* of the 27th Div. Spent a long day making the preliminary arrangements and then went back to Esquelbecq. It is a lovely old fifteenth century castle with a large moat round it, a drawbridge and all fittings correct. Heard a lot of criticism of counter attacks on 13th, most of it nonsense. The Germans were on the ridge and had to be turned out and there was nothing more to be said about it.

**Monday 17 May 1915** Spent the day at our advanced report centre just south of Vlamertinge. Made all arrangements for our relief tonight. 1st Cav.Bde takes our line from Menin road just near t'Hoge to the Railway line where we join on to the 2nd Cav.Div. It is not a very satisfactory line, none of these Infantry lines are. Our HQ goes back to the old friendly Menin road. I hope that we shall have a peaceful time. At 9.00 pm went down to our Advanced Report Centre on the Menin road – it is a beastly place in a cellar and very stuffy but they shell the road so we shall probably be very glad of the shelter later on. Relief commenced at 9.00 pm and finished at 2.00 am and then I had a few hours' sleep. No casualties but trenches bad – many of them full of water.

**Tuesday 18 May 1915** Tonight the 9th Bde take over another piece of line from the 81st Inf.Bde*. No news of any kind, it is dull and cold.

**Wednesday 19 May 1915** A very cold raw day, even the cellar feels nice and warm, raining hard most of the day. A good deal of shelling on both sides. We started it in the morning. An old Terrier* battery near here must have annoyed the Boche as they turned a lot of small fry loose and peppered the countryside but did no harm to anyone. In the afternoon walked over our section of the Canal line – it runs along the eastern fortifications of Ypres and is a strong line, only the biggest guns could hurt this. There are large cellars under parts of the wall and these form good places to put the men into. Emplacement for machine guns and rifles have been dug along the outside of the old wall and with a little improvement will do very well. We have three armoured motors now, each with a machine gun; they are Rolls Royces very heavily armoured and are proof against anything except a direct hit by a shell. We use them to run up the Menin road in and also going backwards and forwards through Ypres.

**Thursday 20 May 1915** Walked up this morning to the trenches and saw the 9th Bde and the 1st Bde – everything fairly quiet although a good deal of sniping going on. We relieve the 1st by the 2nd Bde tonight and have pulled out the 4th Dragoon Guards for one night. Still living in the cellar but today the atmosphere is pretty bad. They dropped a 6in. about 30 yards from our house just across the road, but it seemed to be only a shell fired at random and no others followed. The GHQ line has been well shelled today, but only with 'wizz bangs' as we call them.

**Friday 21 May 1915** We come out tonight for a couple of days and go in again till 27/28 when we are relieved by the Infantry. The relief began at 9.00 pm and was completed at about 1 am. There were several bursts of heavy fire during the night, but no attack at all.

**Saturday 22 May 1915** Got up for 7.00 am breakfast with a feeling of relief that two days' rest were coming. One does not realise the strain of trench work until it is over. All day and night one's brain is really working – one is never at rest. We all show signs of it – the old man* is very irritable. At 8.00 am we went to see General Byng at Corps HQ at Lovie chateau and got him to give us the Goldfish chateau for our HQ. Then came on to our chateau at Esquelbecq – it is really a lovely place and very peaceful and quiet. There are a lot of Belgians round here, loafing about doing nothing – no wonder the French hate them like poison.

The news is better today – Italy seems certain to come in and she may bring in some of the Balkan states as well. But the worry at the end of the war will be worse than ever. Heard through a fellow at the Foreign Office that they are much more optimistic now and think that the war will be over before next winter, I sincerely hope so. The Russians seem to be standing again now. Our own operations have come temporarily to a standstill but hope they will go on again now. K's Army is coming out – a fine body of men I am told, but I have not as yet seen them.

**Monday 24 May 1915** A real bad day today. Woken up at 3.00 am by a smell of gas and the wind being in the north-east we knew that we were in for it. At about 4 am, the first lot of Infantrymen who had been gassed came by. We promptly put men across the road and herded them into the field close by so that we could see those really bad and those who were panicky. Shortly afterwards we got a report from General Mullins (2nd Cav.Bde) that they had been gassed along the front on both sides of the Lake at Bellewaerde and that he had been forced to put his HQ at the Menin bridge on the east of Ypres. The number of men we collected soon grew to about 300 and we began sorting them out and sending them back. A great many were very bad; they were very sick and suffered from violent fits of coughing and were a pitiable sight. Then a great many absolutely collapsed, the doctors soon grew very busy.

At about 5.00 am we began to get news. Hardress Lloyd and Nicholson had gone forward in an armoured car, then returned and reported a regular belt of gas vapour sweeping over the country on the Menin road. As far as we could make out then, only a bit of the line at Bellewarde Lake had given. Soon Mullins was brought back in a state of collapse and Bertie Paget his Brigade Major shortly afterwards, he was very bad. Nicholson was also bad – the matter was serious as the 2nd Cav.Bde were without Commander or Staff. We then heard that Greenly (9th Cav.Bde) had moved his two Regiments forward (15th and 19th Hussars) to support his front line and was bringing on the 4th Dragoon Guards who were temporarily attached to him. The General then sent me forward to get to Greenly and tell him he was in command of the 2nd and 9th Bdes and to straighten out things on the north side of the Menin road.

I got into an armoured motor car and went down to the Ecole de Bieufaisance. They were shelling the road pretty hard, men and horses had been hit and gassed and were lying about the road. I went into the Ecole de Bieufaisance and saw Makin (1st Cav.Bde) in the cellar, all his lines had been cut and the cellar was pretty full of gas. I asked his situation and having got it, saw Phipps-Hornby (9th Lancers), Mullins' ADC, who was going to and knew where Greenly was. We walked up the railway and saw Greenly under the bridge and I joined him there. We discussed the situation and agreed to rally any of the 2nd Cav.Bde who had been gassed behind the GHQ line; to hold the GHQ line with one squadron of each of the 15th and 19th Hussars; and bring the 4th Dragoon Guards into the GHQ line north of the Menin road.This was I think wrong as they found Infantry occupying it and had several casualties from shell fire getting there and returning. Later a Battalion of the Cheshire Regiment also came up and got into the cutting.

The shelling was now very severe – they had got the railway crossing to a yard and were using shells filled with the gas which came flooding down the cutting. They were also shelling the Menin road very heavily. News was scarce, all wires being cut, but from our position the whole country up to t'Hoge could be seen and I saw no retirement from the south of the road. This meant that our fellows were hanging on and was very comforting indeed. By midday the 1st Cav.Div. was all out and nothing more could be done. The Infantry were organising a counter attack north of the Menin road.

At midday, Nicholson came out and as the General wanted me back, I took his place. I went and saw Makin, the shelling was not so heavy as I went back. I came to the conclusion that with the effects of gas and fighting, the Division ought to be relieved that night. I got back and made my report and was sent on to Byng commanding the Cavalry Corps. I told him the situation and also expressed my opinion as regards the state of the troops – he was very kind, said he would do what he could. I went back and the news continued about the same. A small part of the front was broken but the Germans showed no disposition to advance; we used the armoured motor cars to locate the exact position of the German left. They were the greatest use and got us information that could not have been got otherwise without great loss of life. They went down the road and the Germans fairly peppered them with every sort and kind of shot and shell. All three were hit in their petrol tanks, but they have reserve tanks which were armoured and ran on them.

At about 2.00 pm, things became a little quieter and an Infantry counter attack was launched by Bols' (84th) Bde*. This got about half way and was stopped; it could not have had much go about it. All this time the 9th Lancers were hanging on to their trench in a very exposed position and continued to do so all day – a very fine performance. Things quieted down and the 2nd Cav.Div. relieved ours in the front line – the relief being finished about 3 am. This was a heavy day's fighting: casualties about 530 out of 1,800 and besides that about another 300 suffering from the effects of gas who stuck it out. The situation to my mind is thoroughly unsatisfactory – the troops up here are tired out. We want fresh troops to give the others a rest. The Infantry attack has no sting in it.

**Tuesday 25 May 1915** Moved HQ to Reningelst. Many officers and men feeling the effects of gas – in fact Division reduced to half its strength. Got a great surprise at 9.30 pm: was sent for to the telephone and given a message that De Lisle had specially been asked for to command the 29th Div.* at the Dardanelles. He was very sad about it and said he wanted to finish his soldiering in the Cavalry. I cheered him up and told him that it was promotion. I am sorry he is going – he has been a very good chief to me, kind and considerate – he is a great fighter, quick at a decision and his worth will be found after he has gone. I wish him the best of luck in the world.

# 5. The Dismounted Division

**Thursday 27 May** 1915 Another disappointment, we stay here another day. Have just got the casualties for the 24th – 650 killed wounded and missing out of about 2,000 are pretty heavy. Cis Bingham took over command today*. I hear that Tommy Pitman gets his Brigade – the 4th. I am very glad as Tommy has done wonderfully well and I think that he ought to have had a Brigade before. All GHQ fussing about the gas and issuing strange orders and instructions – the only remedy is for us to use gas and jolly poisonous gas too. People just sit in offices and write reams of stuff that no one reads.

**Friday 28 May** 1915 A quiet day with little or no shooting – they are reorganising the defences round Ypres and making a 6th Corps. I hear Lock is going as Chief of the Staff – it is a good thing to be a Lord. I only hope that they have a definite policy on which to work. The buses came at 5.00 pm, the General and I saw the 8th Bde embuss and then we drove on to Esquelbecq. I was quite glad to get back as now I feel that the men will have a bit of a rest; we shall get our reinforcements out and once again become a **Cavalry** Division instead of trench dismounted horse.

**Saturday 29 May** 1915 Rode round billets this morning with the General and saw the 11th and 19th Hussars, they are very comfortable in nice farms and are glad to get back to their horses again. We hear Germany is sending 10 Corps against Italy*. Where they are going to get them from I don't know. We seem short of ammunition for guns; otherwise we could walk through the Germans here. You cannot improvise armies – you can get the men all right but not the arms and munitions. The French are still very confident and are making good progress – I only hope that it will continue. Am going in to Hazebrouck with the General† and hope to get my hair cut as I am getting very woolly.‡

**Monday 31 May** 1915 Went home on three days' leave quite unexpectedly and found all well. I think we thoroughly deserved this leave after our fighting in the beastly Ypres salient and I hope we shall not see it again unless it is to attack and to push through.

Went into the Club* and saw Irwin and Puff Gore: it really reminded me of all the pictures of the old men who sit in clubs and say that 'The service is going to the dogs'. Only the question was: when are they going to use the Cavalry at their proper job? Every job is a Cavalry job if the Cavalry are wanted to do it and are pulling their weight. We are armed with the rifle and bayonet, men are wanted quickly to a certain spot – why not the Cavalry? It is certainly not what we train for, but we can do it as well as or better than the Infantry. Being wanted, should we sit behind and say 'No, it is not Cavalry work and so we cannot do it'? That is the attitude of some people – it is a bad and rotten attitude! On the other hand the policy is not a good one as there must be heavy casualties and the Cavalry man takes time to train and is difficult to replace. All well at home but everyone depressed at the fall of Przemysl† and the quarrel of the Cabinet‡. Fisher at logger heads with Churchill, J.F.§ and R.‖ not at all friends. It is not a cheerful outlook, especially if you throw in a Zeppelin raid on London. On the other hand Przemysl is no longer a fortress.

**Saturday 5 June 1915** Bertie Fisher is leaving us. Went in the afternoon to see Sir Philip Chetwode and try and get Howard-Vyse to come in his place. Was successful and then off to GHQ to pull the strings. Think all will be well and hope so as GSO(2) is an important person.

**Tuesday 8 June 1915** One of the hottest mornings I can remember. Rode over to see Makin who is temporarily commanding the Division. Discussed the question of machine guns. As usual we shall have to improvise as they will not increase the establishments at all. All reported quiet along the line, but the French are still pushing on*. Drafts are slowly coming out to replace casualties and by degrees we are filling up our depleted ranks. A patient at one of the volunteer hospitals describes his treatment rather pithily: 'I was supposed to be washed by a very pretty girl – the result was that I was a mass of dried soapsuds and my bed a pool of water!!'

**Thursday 10 June 1915** Went to GHQ in the morning. Makin was called to a conference at Sir John [French]'s house, so left him there and went on to see Hutch who was well and flourishing. The conference turned out to be one of wiggings: I do not know what some of these young fellows in the Cavalry think they are. One wrote a long criticism of the general situation to a Cabinet Minister who was a relation of his, and the Cabinet Minister of course showed it to K.* and K. sent it back out here and so the fat was fairly in the fire. I think that the Cabinet Minister, who ever he is, should have put it into the fire if it came from a very young Officer; if from a responsible Officer, the Officer should be court-martialled. It is rather drastic but no one can criticise a policy such as whether to hold the Ypres salient or not unless they have full knowledge of the whole situation – Belgian, French and English. Wrote to De Lisle. Persistant rumours of a success in the Dardanelles† but nothing official at present. Bedford Yeomanry join the 9th Cav.Bde – don't think 'Bob' will be very happy.

**Friday 11 June 1915** Went out for a ride before breakfast. Met Sir Julian Byng and had a talk to him on various military matters, mostly connected with the Cavalry – trouble about hiring land for training of our troops. This country is so highly cultivated that the only ground available is pasture – of course the inhabitant wants this for his cows and so one has to pay through the nose.

**Saturday 12 June 1915** General Cis Bingham and Hambro returned from England last night. Rode round and saw the bomb practice – the small egg grenades are quite good – easy to throw and very effective. I like what is called the hair brush grenade best of all. We then saw some of the new gas bombs – did not think much of them, we let eight off in a narrow length of trench. It made an awful smell and would have driven anyone out of it but they are not strong enough at present as one in a trench should be sufficient to clear it. A frog in the trench seemed to enjoy it immensely. Motored down to Hazebrouck to meet HQ of Bedford Yeomanry who complete the 9th Bde – the Division is now complete as regards troops.

**Monday 14 June 1915** Inspected the 1st Cav.Bde – a very good show, but am sorry to say men out of my Regiment compare badly with that of the 2nd and 5th Dragoon Guards who were very smart indeed. Hope they will alter that and that Bobbery will buck them up. It was not up to the standard of the 11th Hussars. Fine day but cold north-east wind too strong for gas (1.9) as this is a favourable wind for the Boches. Went out in motor car in the evening and saw arrangements for C-in-C's* visit. Hope all will go off all right and that it won't rain. The country is now looking lovely. Strawberries are all ripe and we live on the fat of the land.

**Tuesday 15 June 1915** Sir John French came today to say a few words to the Brigades – he was received in a hollow square by the troops who presented arms. It was very smartly done, rather to my surprise, by all the Brigades. He spoke very nicely – told the men how he personally appreciated their work in the trenches and patted them on the back generally. I think that the men appreciated it greatly – but of course the one person to whom a great deal of it was due was De Lisle and he has gone.

During the day we got orders that from 6.00 am tomorrow we are to be ready to move at three hours' notice. The 1st Army are attacking towards La Bassée – the Highland Div.*, 7th Div. and Canadians doing the push. The 2nd Army are making a push in the Ypres salient – the French are also attacking from Arras. It is a slow business, we know nothing except that we are to be ready to move. I don't see any chance of our being able to do anything.

**Wednesday 16 June 1915** Have sat in all day – last night the 1st Army took a redoubt and some trenches near Ocully[?] east of Festubert but we heard later they were forced to evacuate them. On the Ypres salient we advanced towards the t'Hoge Château and took 100 prisoners. The French took the first line of enemy trenches opposite Arras and the village of Souchez – another step towards the high ground east of that place which is what is badly wanted. But reports are yet vague – we hear that the French have been gassed out of part of the trenches taken – we ought to hear more later. A very fine day; played some tennis this afternoon to shake my liver up on an asphalt court here. Mons. Bergereux our kind host* lent me a racquet.

**Thursday 17 June 1915** The French are still progressing well, the Russian news is about the same. We are now standing to at four hours' notice, but at present I see no chance of our doing anything. Tonight I went to a show given by the 15th Hussars – it was excellent. The performers were mostly from the Artists Rifles and there was a lot of talent.

**Friday 18 June 1915** I wonder how far the Russians will be forced to go back*; I do not think that things are looking any too well over there. Have taken to tennis here as was getting very fat.

**Monday 21 June 1915** The longest day of the year and beautifully fine. Attended a conference at Cavalry Corps on the subject of Cavalry operating through a gap. We have heard a great deal about this gap – but it has not yet been made – the conference was very dull. Hugo Montgomery represented GHQ and beyond having a dig at him there was nothing. He has, as usual, original views. He says we should make peace now – Germany has lost all her best men, let us keep ours. Such a peace will force conscription on England and we shall have to fight Germany again in 10 years time – and shall be very much better prepared. The theory has some points – but who wants another war in 10 years time? Lunched at Corps – the French appear to be troubled over their losses*, but one hopes that they will go on. Our attacks seem to have made little or no progress. I cannot understand it – after every attack one hears that something went wrong – are we really such amateurs?

**Tuesday 22 June 1915** Rode out with the General and watched 2nd Cav.Bde route marching. Quite an exciting morning as they again started shelling Dunkirk, Berques and Canal with their heavy guns. The Germans certainly seem to have plenty of ammunition to spare. Their organisation is wonderful. We captured a soldier with a letter on him which points to the fact that the Germans have taken away every man they dare from this front and are using them against the Russians. I do not think they will attack here just yet except with gas, but they mean to hold on to the line for all they are worth. Just heard that our attack on t'Hoge was driven in because our own guns did not stop shooting in time. This is very bad and one can see no reason for it.

**Wednesday 23 June 1915** Rode in the morning with General to see troops. In the afternoon went into GHQ to see if we can get some 18pdrs for the Warwick Battery. Saw Hutchinson and had discussion on the use of Cavalry – from what I heard I don't think they are quite sane on the subject themselves. Also saw Hugo Montgomery and tried to get him to see the usefulness of training men on the sands; he seemed hopeful but that is always their attitude.

**Thursday 24 June 1915** Saw 9th Cav.Bde route marching in the morning – it was a good show, the 19th Hussars being especially good. In the afternoon we went to the horse show of Indian Cavalry Corps. A wonderful sight – but was it war? I don't think so. A French Cav.Div. was close there and many Officers came over. It was a brave sight – but yet men were fighting not 20 miles away. If men are not fighting, the best thing for them is to keep their minds free from it – on the other hand people say it is not right.

The show was held at Estrée-Blanche, in a sort of amphitheatre – it was very well done. A French band of a Regiment near played and the trumpeters of a Dragoon Regiment. Three French Officers performed on hunting horns – the place was of course full of old friends – many one had not seen for years. Douglas Haig came for a short time. It was a lovely fine day, but I wished all the time we were in 'the piping time of peace *. Lemberg has fallen† but that was a foregone conclusion. I wonder if the Germans will try and make peace after their thrust at the Russians. Heard the Germans can turn out 250,000 shells a day – the French 120,000 – we turn out? Despatches published – find I am in them again. Brooks Hambro got a Brevet‡, I am very glad – he thoroughly deserves it.

**Friday 25 June 1915** Have been warned that we shall be required to dig again. I suppose in the Ypres salient once again.

**Saturday 26 June 1915** Dined with the 1st Cav.Bde and saw some experiments in signalling. The idea is to reduce the light of the lamp to so small a radius that it cannot be seen by any enemy. A long tube is fixed to the lamp and the result is that, at a distance of 1,200 yards, the light can only be seen in a rectangle of 4ft height and 10ft broad. This will be quite invaluable in the trenches to supplement telephone wires which are generally cut by shells. Worked out a scheme for hiding from aeroplanes for next week. The Russians are still going back – it is difficult to foresee the result but as long as they are not broken all will be well. If they can only scrape together some ammunition. We are doing nothing here, why? Want of ammunition I suppose and the Dardanelles show takes up a great deal of that.

**Monday 28 June to Friday 2 July** Caught the 10.30 boat from Boulogne – a cold dull day in the morning. Got to London and had my hair cut and went straight down to Stanmore*. Sent in an application to get my DSO from the King. Found England depressed, they are only just beginning to realize what war is. Saw fewer men about in London which is good.

On Thursday 1st went to Buckingham Palace at 10.30 am. There was very little ceremony – just walked into a room and the King hung the order on a hook and out again. Clive Wigram was in attendance†. Went to Cox's afterwards and invested some more money in the war loan – then straight back to Stanmore. Played tennis and forgot about war and work. Returned by the 2.00 pm train from Victoria.

**Saturday 3 July 1915** Cis Bingham and Wombat* left for England this morning. At 9.00 am went up to Ypres where we have 1,000 men digging under Pilkington (15th Hussars). A very hot day. Found the men working like beavers – they are making enclosed works running northwards from Vlamertinge and doing it very well too. Saw Grandmother (the 15in. gun) up there; had been firing and the concussion had taken all the tiles of the roof of a farmhouse near by.

**Monday 5 July 1915** Rode out in the morning and watched the bomb practice. It was quite good. The trench mortar is just an old bit of iron piping but it throws a bomb weighting 4lbs and containing 3lbs of gun cotton – it makes a real good explosion.

Got a letter from Hardress Lloyd from the Dardanelles. He says he and General De Lisle are living in a dug–out by the sea and soldiering there is very different from the comfortable chateau in France. He says it is very hot and the flies very bad – also if the Turks had as many guns as the Boches, they could blow us to smithereens.

**Tuesday 6 July 1915** A very slack day. Visit from General Makin commanding the Division in Bingham's absence, but nothing doing. The 6th Corps [are] very active in the Ypres salient near Boezinge and took a trench and 80 prisoners – what is more it was held.

**Wednesday 7 July 1915** Today Lord Kitchener went round and inspected part of the defences in the rear of the Ypres salient. He went to see an all–round work which the 1st Cav.Bde (Bays and 5th Dragoon Guards) are making – there was the usual procession. They had walked him round the rampart defences of Ypres previously, so they will kill the old gentleman if not careful. Asquith looked like a first class clown – wearing old clothes and old hat – no one would have accused him of looking the part of the Prime Minister. Lord K.

looked well but has aged a good deal since I saw him last, and hard tired eyes. I was told that the reason of the inspection was that people at home said there were no defences of Ypres!!!

**Thursday 8 July 1915** Went with the General to Vlamertinge to meet Sir Julian Byng and walked round our line of works. There was little or no news except about the attack mentioned on the 6th. We heard that 300 casualties had occurred; not in the Regiment who took the trench, (there were very few casualties in the actual taking) but in the Regiment next door who exposed themselves on the parapet to cheer the others on – so like a fool of a Tommy. Saw a prisoner today, a fine looking fellow, looked well and well fed but his clothes were dirty as if he had been in the trenches a long time.

**Friday 9 July 1915** Attended a conference at Cavalry Corps HQ and Sir Julian Byng gave us the situation as told him by Sir John [French]. There was a conference of the Cabinet Ministers at Calais and Joffre and all the big wigs attended it. It appears that Joffre took charge of the meeting at which France, England, Russia, India and Italy were all represented. He told them that Germany had a million bayonets still in Germany; there were three courses evident – either to continue to push the Russians, to turn against Italy or to turn against the West. Which they would do, no one could tell at present. He said he considered the situation satisfactory and had proved himself far greater than anyone thought possible, his grasp of the situation was wonderful. Then K. got up and said what England could do, so Joffre touched a button and in came a secretary to take it down in writing!!! K. said that the second Kitchener army was starting at once, the third would be out here in September, the fourth at the end of the year and the sixth in the spring. That is good news if it is true and can be carried out.

The next conference was between Sir John and Joffre – Joffre was meditating another offensive and he wanted us to take over more line. Sir John said that he also wanted to take the offensive himself; so Joffre asked him how much ammunition he had*. The result is not yet known, but I think we shall probably take over more line. It was a very interesting conference and put us *au fait* with the situation as it stands.

**Saturday 10 July 1915** Went up to Vlamertinge with Heydeman of the Bays; went over our forts and sited the place where we wanted the machine guns placed. Got back at 5.30 pm and arranged for the Batteries to go and swim the Canal at La Motte-au-Bois. Got a cheery letter from De Lisle at the Dardanelles. Things seem to be going slowly but well there.

**Monday 12 July 1915** Another day amongst the diggers and more machine guns questions. I think we have fairly settled the question now. Then came back and played tennis. Heard the Boches have retaken the cemetery and Suchey, it is a nuisance but does not affect the line at all.

**Tuesday 13 July 1915** Went to Wisques to the Machine Gun School there and had a very interesting day. Also met many old friends in the Indian Cav.Div. – some of whom I had not seen since Sandhurst.

**Wednesday 14 July 1915** Went up to Ypres and saw our men working on the new line, walked round the whole and they are making very good progress and doing very well. Got back here for a late lunch. In the evening dined with 15th Hussars and went to a Squadron concert afterwards. Most of the performers were Artists Rifles, but the plum of the whole evening was Kennedy Rumford who came and sang five songs to us. The first was *The Two Grenadiers* which is a great favourite of mine. I am told he has been down here since October working with the Red Cross (more power to him). His puttees were the envy of all, they were beautifully put on. A wet night, but rain badly wanted so must not grumble.

**Thursday 15 July 1915** Went down to La Motte-au-Bois to see I Battery crossing the Canal. It was a moderate show, but I think all that sort of work eyewash.

**Friday 16 July 1915** Spent a second day at the Machine Gun School at Wisques. Had a very interesting day especially as a lot of Officers of the Indian Cavalry Corps were there. They did not help much and their training is a long way behind ours. I suppose that the climate affects them, but they did not impress one at all. The Germans appear to be having another go at

Warsaw from the north, but the Russians appear to have the matter well in hand*. The Boche has been quite active this side too, but I think it means little although all the inspired reports point to another attack here some time soon.

**Saturday 17 July 1915** A perfectly beastly day – a south-west gale blowing and pouring rain. The Babe [Nicholson] has returned from leave, he always bucked about being a good sailor but he was the colour of pea soup. He said they had an awful dusting* and had three shots at Boulogne Harbour before they really got in. Spent the day with the diggers and then went to the 2nd Army at Oxelaëre and saw Glubb the CRL. Also heard that Bruce Williams had been appointed CGS† of the 2nd Army, vice Milne who gets the 27th Div. No news except that the French had rather a bigger knock in the Argonne [Champagne] than they admit.

**Sunday 18 July 1915** A fine day. Went to Corps in the morning and saw Anthony Henley on affairs of state. The Babe brought back some very interesting news. Firstly that Spain as a mass was anti-French and pro-Boche – the minority was the King and the Anarchists. As a result of this, some of our Statesmen were of the opinion that we should exchange Gibralter for Ceuta* which is opposite, because Gib was not defensible from the land side. Secondly that a German and Turkish Division were in Afghanistan and bribing the Amir for all they were worth to declare a holy war and pass into India. Thirdly Aden† was being attacked and they had had to send a Brigade there from Egypt. Lastly that within a month the Dardanelles would be open as the Turks were running short of ammunition.

**Monday 19 July 1915** The General and Wombat went up to see the digging but I stayed behind to finish some work. A very fine day but no news.

**Tuesday 20 July 1915** Went down to see the Warwick Battery swimming in the Canal. It was quite a good show I thought, considering that they are Terriers. Sir Julian Byng also came down – White T. also there full of importance – at last the Cavalry Corps have found something to do to keep them employed. We blew up and occupied about 100 yds of enemy trench near t'Hoge and still hold it. Quite an event in these days of siege warfare. How small the mind grows under these conditions – 100 yards in a front of 50 miles or more! As far as one can hear ammunition on this side has improved a good deal, but the reserves which have been accumulated are still insufficient for our needs. In Russia the question must be acute – I am informed that she only produces 25,000 rounds a day, but I think that this figure is too low – the front she is fighting on being close on 1,000 miles.

On this side the French must be meditating another big offensive. We are taking over more of the line towards Amiens – this means that the French force, or rather the French offensive*, will have British troops on either flank. It is a curious arrangement, I do not like it. All K2 will go into the trenches – but Joffre considers that the French troops are best for this offensive, that they have more guns and better ones, and of course more ammunition. On the other hand our 3rd Army will be separated from the 1st and the 2nd by a long gap and this gap is filled with French troops. The only thing one can say is that it serves one right for not being ready.

**Wednesday 21 July 1915** Went down to our ammunition railhead at Strazeele and had an interesting enquiry into the question of hand grenades and other death-dealing machines. Then went on to Cavalry Corps at La Motte-au-Bois and attended a conference on our digging operations. I have never wasted more time in all my life. The Corps are trying to interfere with things which belong to the Division and putting forward their views without knowing the situation. I was glad to get away. The Russians are still retiring – I think they will retire still further, but that does not matter.

**Thursday 22 July 1915** Went up to Vlamertinge and saw the diggers. No news up there at all, everything very quiet. Saw Solly-Flood who commands our show up there. The news tonight on the Russian side is the same – it looks to me as if Warsaw is bound to fall. I hope not, but it will not make a great deal of difference to the attack issue, although it may delay it.

**Friday 23 July 1915** The Russian news is that they are still retiring – the point is retiring or driven back. To my mind this is a very anxious time for on Russia's existance a great deal depends. If she resists on a place of her own, the Germans are no nearer their goal which is the decisive defeat of Russia. The humble student of Military History must therefore wait until the end of the war before he can know the why, the wherefore and the when. Went for a ride to the ammunition park bent on the question of grenades and bombs.

Leslie Rome (my best man) came to lunch, I was very glad to see him again. He was as keen as mustard – he wanted to know when we were going to fight again. Every newcomer asks the same question – if it were not for the fact that the one idea is to beat these Germans, the man who has been here would say 'I don't want to see another fight.' But I expect we shall have plenty of it later on.

**Saturday 24 July 1915** The Russian news is a bit better this evening and they seem to be holding on to Warsaw, but it is by no means over yet. This morning rode out with the General and inspected Echelon 'A' of the 2nd Brigade arranged for the 'G' in GAP and found as usual that theory and practice do not always coincide. Our front is very quiet except now and again we or the Germans take a trench or blow up a mine – at present honours are about even. We go on digging in the Ypres salient and that place should be soon strong enough to withstand any attack, provided we have enough guns and plenty of ammunition. It ought to have been done long ago and would have stopped us going back as far as we had to go – gas or no gas – and would have saved a lot of casualties.

**Monday 26 July 1915** Went up to Vlamertinge and saw the works. Solly-Flood in command up there and full of fuss and imaginary worries. A Belgian mission were visiting our works so I saw Tom Bridges – his arm and shoulder are still very stiff. His report on the Belgians is none too good – they are very lazy and do not like digging so he brought them along to show them what we could do. We asked him about the whole situation and he said that we should have to sweeten the French up next winter and take over a lot more line, but on the whole they were quite satisfied with what we had done. The Belgians are the difficulty; he said that the question of the inundations* was not at present anything to worry about, but of course we must hold the sluices on the coast. Decided to go home tomorrow till Saturday as nothing doing here.

**Tuesday 27 to Saturday 31 July 1915** Had a good trip home and enjoyed the sea immensely. The news of the impending occupation of Warsaw came while I was home – from a military point of view it is a matter of no great moment – but the Boches will make much of it and one will hate that. Wasted a day at the dentist but will be thankful for it later.

**Sunday 1 August 1915** Heard of German attack on 14th Div. at t'Hoge. Pretty heavy losses in the counter attack which failed. Situation well in hand now – it appears a case of panic and rather an unnecessary one. As far as one can find out, hardly anyone was burned by the flame projectors* and if they had only stuck it out, they might have made a good bag of Boches. It is curious how in war the best troops become at times panicky – the reason is always that they are surprised either mentally or by the use of some new and unexpected implement of war such as this flame projector. Saw Harry Dalmeny on the way back, he was reported wounded but it was only a graze in two places from a wizzy bang. He had no news to give one except that the Germans had evacuated Warsaw two days ago and had laid waste to all the country behind them, but I do not suppose that they burnt Warsaw.

**Monday 2 August 1915** 9th Cav.Bde under Bob Greenly started on their Scheme to Mardecque and bivouac by the sea tonight. Tomorrow bathe, drill and return. GHQ vetoed this trip two months ago, so this time we have not asked. It was simply killed by ridicule – Wallie* said 'If the Cavalry want to go to the seaside, let them go to Ostend!!!' and so everyone laughed and leave was refused. I expect they will be furious if they hear about it, but it won't hurt very much.

Heard a curious story which I believe true. A Russian Liaison Officer from the Grand Duke is said to have brought a message to Joffre that the Russians were all right and, though retiring now, would be ready to advance later. That they did not wish their Allies in the west to make a hurried attack in order to help them in the east, that they wished us to move along according to the plans made and thought right. If true, what a Staff and people Russia has! Any other nation would be squealing for help. It takes a big man at the head of a nation to keep calm and collected in such times as these, especially when your country is being invaded. Also it takes a nation used to autocratic rule to have faith in leaders. If such a thing happened in our country, every politician would have his say. Questions in Parliament! What is the army going to do? Sack the Generals! and so on. It is a lesson of patriotism, of faith in a cause, of patience which modern nations do not possess.

**Tuesday 3 August 1915** A dull day with heavy rainstorms and I should think a rough sea. Poor Wombat will be very seasick. The 9th Cav.Bde have not had much luck as regards weather for their seaside trips. Today we heard that we are to take over the work of defence of Elverdinge from the 3rd Cav.Div. This will mean that we have 2,000 men digging; once more we are immobilised and we become mining cavalry engineers. Moreton Gage came over today and we had a long talk; he considers and I agree that the GSO(1) should be given the substantive rank of Lieutenant Colonel and so enable us to qualify for £420 pension. At present they will not appoint us to command Regiments and so we are done.

**Thursday 5 August 1915** Went up to see the diggers at Vlamertinge and at 1.00 pm got wire to say we are to take over Elverdinge tomorrow. So went on to that place and met Philip Howell and Sir Julian Byng. I told Howell what I thought of things and so we all adjourned to 6th Corps at Loire Chateau. On the way met Bruce Williams also full of complaints. In fact the whole of his digging has been grossly mismanaged, the people to blame are the 2nd Army. They had no plan to begin with and now they try and cover their shortcomings by bluster. Have known Bruce Williams too long to let him annoy me, but he and Howell are of the same kidney and it was rather amusing to hear each blame the other for the same fault.

Got back at about 5.00 pm and heard of the tragic death of poor Hamilton Grace\*. It was all very sad, especially as I had to attend a concert given by the Supply Column that evening. How I hated it all, but one has to show a bold front these days and nothing matters. The show was good – if it had been held on any other day I should have loved it. Poor Raymond, the best of good fellows and a first rate soldier and gentleman – no man can have a better epitaph.

**Friday 6 August 1915** Spent a day up at Elverdinge with Sandys looking round the place and siting some new trenches and machine gun emplacements. The works are going on well and I think we should be clear of the place within a month with any luck. Dined with Bob Greenly and went on to a gaff. It was the usual show, but Tommy loves it and it keeps him contented.

**Saturday 7 August 1915** Gen's birthday\*: he is 14 years old. In another five years I suppose he will want to go in the Army. Let us hope a lasting peace will have been made by that time. The outlook at present is none too good – the Boche has taken Warsaw† – will he now try to make a separate peace with Russia? From all things one hears, the Russians will not listen to such a thing for the moment. I think however it will be one of the events of the autumn. Everyone who ought to know is optimistic about the Dardanelles, but there is nothing to show any weakening on the part of the Turks at the present minute. I again went up to Vlamertinge. The Germans are pretty active at the junction of our line with the French at Boezinge but otherwise all is fairly quiet.

**Monday 9 August 1915** Very heavy firing heard from 4.00 am and this was the prelude of the attack of the 6th Div. to retake the trenches south and west of t'Hoge. Went up to Elverdinge and at about 12 noon, heard heavy firing again. The reports we received said that everything was going well and the first trenches had been taken at very little cost and that the attack was proceeding. The 10th and 18th\* Bdes carried out the attack which was made from the south and the west. Three Officers and 120 men were made prisoners and also two machine guns taken. As we came back through Vlamertinge, we saw a batch of about 30 of these, dirty looking underbred brutes they were. The German Infantryman does not impress at all. The only question that now remains is will they be able to hold these trenches against the German counter attacks which are bound to come — I don't see why not. Our losses up to the time we heard were small.

**Tuesday 10 August 1915** Went up again to the digging with the General — started with Anderson and then went on to Elverdinge. Everything going on well. Heard a few more details about the t'Hoge attack — our losses about 1,600. We only lost 100 in the actual attack but were very heavily shelled as soon as we got the German trenches. This is always the way. There seems to be a general opinion that the 14th Div. did not come very well out of the t'Hoge affair. It is a pity as they were supposed to be one of the best of [the] Ks but I hope that they will find their feet all right. Heard that we have to complete the Brielen defences now and that Vlamertinge is to be left at present.

**Wednesday 11 August 1915** Went up to inspect the new works which the French have been constructing and which we have to take over. They are enormous with great concreted dug-outs which look like ice houses. The trenches are very bad — too wide, parapets not thick enough — in fact every fault which we are taught to avoid. Then went on to Douglas Lock at the 6th Corps HQ to arrange details. The result is we send up another 500 men: 250 from each of the 1st and 2nd Cav.Bdes: this makes about 2,300 of the Division. In fact it leaves about one man to four horses and these will naturally suffer*, but the powers-that-be say we must dig and so there is nothing more to be said. News from Gallipoli says that fresh landings† have been effected under cover of the fleet, but with what troops one does not know. Frankly I do not understand the game but I suppose at least hope it is all right. Heard the Germans shell the crater at t'Hoge very heavily. As we only hold it lightly at night, I hope they will go on expending as many shells as they like.

**Thursday 12 August 1915** Went up to Brielen and met Sandys, Marindin and Hill (both of 6th Corps). Went round the site of the proposed work which we are to take on at once. Things were very quiet in front of us but they were lobbing 17in. shells into Ypres and trying to knock down the church tower which has been used as an observation station. They also put two into the Cloth Hall and buried a lot of men who were in the cellars of it. This does not look like making much of a fortress of the place.

**Saturday 14 August 1915** Went up and saw the digging. The 2nd Cav.Bde camp was heavily shelled on Friday night and young Tom Hankey had a narrow escape, a big bit of shell going through his bivouac. He was very cheerful and rather pleased at being under fire for the first time. I hope it will be the last.

**Sunday 15 August 1915** Was going to have a Europe morning but was wired for the digging, so spent the morning up there. In the afternoon went to 2nd Cav.Bde for their private gymkhana — Ladies present — events all sorts and kinds.

**Monday 16 August 1915** Went up to the digging and saw the new work which had been started in 23 — they had a good many men digging there in the daytime. We are taking over the work from the French and such a thing is always most unsatisfactory. We don't agree with the French views and it is difficult to adapt the work completed by the French to our methods. I don't think that B.* is quite happy and I wonder what is wrong — something is worrying the old man and I only wish he would let one know straight out as perhaps one could help him. But I shall find out sooner or later. No news here at all — the Dardanelles show is worrying me a good deal, I don't think we are getting on nearly fast enough. If we are going to do any good there, we ought to make certain of doing so by sending enough men — once it is through the men will come in useful in other places.

**Tuesday 17 August 1915** Went up to the digging in the morning. In the afternoon the General had a tennis party and some of the nurses from the D. of S.* Hospital came over and played. They were rather good.

**Wednesday 18 August 1915** Up to the work in the 23. For some reason or other the Boche started to shell the wood. There were no casualties and they did no damage. They have to work at night and so the work progresses but slowly. Heard Germans have taken Kovno* by

80

storm – the situation looks none too good, but all those who know Russia say she is not beaten in any way – hope so most sincerely.

**Thursday 19 August 1915** Sir Julian Byng has gone to the Dardanelles to command a Corps there and Fanshawe has got command of our Corps. Hear awful mess made of the last Dardanelles show – Stopford, Mahon and Hammersely all sent home*: the story is that [the] landing was quite successful – not a shot fired and the covering party got to its position and everything. For some reason the main disembarking body did not move up to the covering party but started to entrench itself on cliffs just close to the shore. Am told that thing was an assured success and now the Turks will have to be kicked out and there will be heavy casualties.

How can one blame a commander who has not been a soldier for years but has been Keeper of the Crown Jewels? Hammersely was found wanting years ago. There are many Brigadiers here who would command a Division well – then why oh why don't they promote them? Our older men have never studied war: they have fought the savage in many lands but 'War' has had no meaning for them. Few such men have done well, Cavan is a brilliant exception. Twenty-five years' service in our Army is very different to 25 years in the German army and there you have the crux of the whole matter – the professional versus the amateur.

**Saturday 21 August 1915** Had the surprise of my life. Was rung up at lunchtime by Philip Howell and he told me that he was going to the 10th Corps and that I was to succeed him as Brigadier General at the Cavalry Corps. It is of course a great step for me as it gives me the temporary rank of General. It is rather curious how one may go up in war. In peace time I had no hope of ever reaching that rank and now I find myself suddenly pushed up into it – a Captain in June 1914!! Everyone congratulating me and very kind. I shall be sorry to leave the Div. as all my friends are in it and I have been in it since the commencement of the war. Played tennis in the evening.

# 6. The Battle of Loos

**Monday 23 August 1915** Got my orders this morning and joined Cavalry Corps this afternoon — I am very sorry to leave all my old friends but shall not be very far away from them. I only hope that I shall not make too many enemies as I go over the heads of a good many people one way and another. Met Fanshawe and made my bow. Our HQs are now in Therouanne village, a great difference from the chateau at Esquelbecq; but I think it is good for one to change as we were too comfortable at the latter place. General Cis Bingham has been awfully good to me all the time he has commanded the Division.

**Tuesday 24 August 1915** First day at Corps. Went with Fanshawe to see 2nd Army to settle questions of training and digging. Found Bruce Williams difficult at first, but all was serene before we left. Heard news of naval fight near Riga and a good many German vessels damaged. It is the best news we have heard for a long time as it means that the Russian right is still intact. Do not like Corps nearly as much as the Div., but I suppose that I have been with the Div. too long — hope that I shall settle down all right.

**Wednesday 25 August 1915** Spent a very quiet day mostly doing office work. Very different to this day last year (1914)*. The weather is simply glorious, but I am afraid that I shall get fat at this job. Have been absolutely overwhelmed with letters of congratulations on my new job. People are very kind to me.

**Thursday 26 August 1915** Went with the General* to Armentieres and saw the works which the 3rd Div. are doing there — it was very interesting, but most people are trying to be too clever and there is a good deal of eyewash in some places. Drove through places we were fighting in last October — the country changes very little and the country people go on farming the land as if there was perfect peace everywhere. In Armentieres most of the good houses are shut, but in the poorer quarters women stand gossiping in the doorways and children play in the gutters. It is a curious sidelight on war — poverty I suppose produces absolute apathy. Saw Bertie Fisher who succeeds me in the 1st Div. — he was very pleased with the appointment.

**Friday 27 August 1915** Went up with General to see the works at Kemmel village. Got back and found message waiting for me that Freddy Maurice wanted to see me. So went and dined with him. Maurice wanted to see me about the contemplated offensive. Big French attack in the Champagne district by about 35 Divs — 10th French Army to attack near Arras. We are to co-operate between the Bethune Canal and Lens — the Cavalry Corps to work with Conneau's Cavalry Corps. Got orders to get into touch with Conneau and find out his views. Played bridge and lost a franc — a Jonah as usual!!!

**Saturday 28 August 1915** Spent the morning in the office thinking out operations. In the afternoon went with the General to see Conneau and talk things over. Discussed question of the use of Cavalry if the gap is ever made and found him in agreement with our views, but of course we do not agree with the majority of the French views. Had half an hour's interview and then returned. Nothing can be kept secret in our Army – everything seems to get out one way or another. It is a great pity that people cannot stop themselves gossiping.

**Monday 30 August** 1915 Got out for a long ride in the morning for a wonder. It is a lovely country for riding over – now the crops are cut one can gallop for miles. Saw a good many partridges but alas the most stringent orders exist against shooting so one has to watch them and do nothing else. Went up to see the 2nd Army. Very fine and hot.

**Tuesday 31 August** 1915 Went into GHQ, the Chief had an interview with Wallie R. Went to lunch with Capel to meet de Grandry who is sub-chief of Conneau's Staff – he has been with them the whole time and was very interesting. It is rather a tough job having to carry on a French conversation all through lunch. No news at all but making all preparations we can in case of a move.

**Wednesday 1 September** 1915 Why am I not shooting partridges? Went to see the 1st Army and had lunch with Tavish Davidson – afterwards a short interview with Sir Douglas Haig who was very nice and kind. Then was taken by a Staff Officer to an observing station and had a good look over the ground between the Bethune to La Bassée Canal and Lens. It was a fairly clear day and one could see a good bit of the trenches, both ours and the Germans. It is a desolate sight: all the houses in ruins and the terrain simply honeycombed with trenches of all sorts and kinds. Yet people still live in the shell area. I suppose they get used to it.

**Sunday 5 September** 1915 A fine day but still cold. Went to lunch with the old Division and found them all cheery and well. In the afternoon went to see the RFC at St Omer and saw Festing (5th Fusiliers). They are very busy in that quarter always. No news to speak of – the Russian news is decidedly good, but of course this will not shorten the war. I believe the Germans will now try and play the same game as the Japanese did in '05! Against such a country as Russia a short sharp war and a decisive victory is the only thing. The Germans must realize this. I believe that the show on 15 September is going to succeed and that we shall spend the winter nearer the German frontier than we now are. Who knows! I should like to feel that I am going to cross the German frontier. It is a step in the right direction – peace for one's children, they won't see a war like this one hopes.

**Monday 6 to Friday 10 September** 1915 Have not been able to write my Diary daily. All preparations for the big push are going on, although know no dates at present. Cavendish (9th Lancers) came and had lunch with me, he is Liaison with French GHQ. He tells me that the French are very optimistic indeed and hope to drive the Boche out of France. We can also do our share, but what is going to happen no one knows. The French views on the use of Cavalry also differ from ours – the French Cavalry with no dismounted training has little power of resistance, whilst ours has great powers of resistance. Hence the French Cavalry can only be used in one way to effect a purpose whilst ours can be used in several.

There can be no question putting our Cavalry through the gap and then allowing it to be pinched. An advance through the gap should be a systematic operation of war: ie unless there is a debacle and that may sometimes happen. Have also had many interesting talks with the flying people and found Trenchard in the Royal Scots Fusiliers, he and I were subalterns together at Sialkot in '95. In case of an advance we have great hope of aeroplanes being of the utmost use to us. The Dardanelles casualties have been very severe, but I don't see how we can give it up without the loss of all our prestige and so will have to carry it through.

**Saturday 11 September** 1915 Went out to watch a scheme by the 3rd Div. As I was going out, I saw several horsemen galloping about on a hill and also a man carrying the Chief's flag. I found the Chief* and his two ADCs hunting partridges on horseback. They caught one too – I joined in the next hunt and we had a good gallop. There is a very strict order against shooting and the place simply crawls with birds, so it is rather tantalizing. It is a lovely day and it was difficult to believe that we were at war except one could hear the distant thunder of the guns.

**Sunday 12 September 1915** Sir W. Robertson (CGS) came over to see the General this morning. We had a long interview and he was very interesting on the whole situation. I wish I could record here what he told us, but I am under the seal*. The Russian news is better – they seem to be holding the Germans fairly well and I should say that the German programme is at least six weeks behind its time.

**Monday 13 September 1915** This day last year we began the Battle of the Aisne – which has gone on ever since. Hear that Sandy Ruthven is back from the Dardanelles wounded, he says all is well there if they only stick it out and they can do so. Rumour has it that De Lisle has got a Corps – I hope so.

**Wednesday 15 September 1915** Had a visit from Louis Spiers who is the Liaison Officer with the 18th French Army (General D'Urbal). Had a long and interesting talk with him especially on the employment of Cavalry. His views are the written French views, those they held before the war and the war has proved them to be wrong. Their ideas are superb but fail in execution.

**Thursday 16 September 1915** Took the General down to St Pol-sur-Tenoise to visit the French lines near Arras – unluckily General D'Urbal had been called away and so did not meet him but met his Chief of the Staff*. He is a typical Frenchman, I should say from the south, a delightful man to meet and I had a long talk with him. We motored to Mont-St-Eloi and here had a good view of the country from Ecurie to the northern end of the Bois de Folie on the Vimy Ridge. All was desolation and trenches running in all directions. Here also we saw dug-outs made for the Corps Commander and his Staff for the direction of the next attack – 20ft under the earth and lit by electric light. We went on to another new point of view which formed the observing station of the commander of a group of about 100 heavy guns. Here we got another view of the same ground. The Colonel was most charming and took an enormous amount of trouble to show us everything. We then went to the village of Villers-au-Bois and had a look down the valley to Auchey-les-Mines and Givenchy. The place is full of French soldiers and guns. We came to the conclusion that a position of readiness for a large force of Cavalry must be west of the Mont-St-Eloi ridge; also that no advance could take place until the enemy had been turned out of Folie Wood. I saw the new French steel helmet. The men like it and it saves their heads from shrapnel and splinters.

**Friday 17 September 1915** Was sent for to GHQ and had an interview with Sir William Robertson who gave me his views on the use of our Cavalry during an advance. He was very interesting and evidently thought or feared that we might lack push after all our trench work. As he put it he thought it a good opportunity 'to comb out our brains'.

**Saturday 18 September 1915** Went and saw Hugo Montgomery with reference to the movements of the 11th Corps and spent the day getting out orders.

**Sunday 19 September 1915** Went down to St Pol-sur-Ternoise at 2.00 pm and had an interview with General D'Urbal, General Conneau being present. It is a pity my Chief cannot speak French. We discussed the question of the co-operation of the British and French Cavalries in the case of a successful break in the line in front of us. It was very interesting. D'Urbal's views were those of Foch and therefore agreed with ours. The only difference appears to be regarding the question of who is to give the order to the Cavalry. In our case it is the C-in-C and in the French D'Urbal himself. It is extraordinary how many big Frenchmen there are, both D'Urbal and Conneau are well over 6ft. Conneau is interesting because he was Tutor to the late Prince Imperial* when the latter was at Woolwich.

**Monday 20 September 1915** A very busy day indeed; ended up with attending a conference at GHQ held by the Chief of the General Staff*. The Chief was quite optimistic in a way – spoke of the coming operations as having a great chance to succeed: everything being in our favour on this side, men, guns and so on. This is going to be one of the biggest battles of the war. All Chief Staff Officers of Armies and Cavalry Corps there, amongst them many old friends.

We have no letters as Folkestone has been mined and I suppose they are not letting the boat sail. Lucky for the fellows on leave – but the other day they made them stay at Folkestone instead of allowing them to return to London and did not even pay their hotel expenses!!! Have been trying to find a job for Prince Arthur [of Connaught], so shall probably have to take him temporarily – he is rather a responsibility but he brings Bonham his equerry with him, so Bonham will have to look after him, that is all. Conneau came at 4.00 pm and gave us his plan – I think if there is a break in the line and our Cavalries get through, we shall be able to push through and work together with any luck.

**Tuesday 21 to Friday 24 September 1915** No time to write up my diary as I have been very busy getting things ready for the operations. Went to see Louis Spiers at the French 8th Army HQ at St Pol-sur-Ternoise. I think that he is suffering from a swollen head and wants sitting on badly. Arrangements going on apace, the French are very confident, but this is practically fortress warfare and one does not seem to have enough troops to carry it through.

**Saturday 25 September 1915** The first day of the fighting* and I must confess that I am a bit disappointed. The plan was as follows: about 35 Divs of the French attacked east and west of Rheims in Champagne country; the 10th French Army (19 Divs) were attacking south of Arras with the [British] 1st Army (1st and 4th Corps†); and Cavalry and Indian Cavalry Corps in reserve. I had great hopes of these attacks and that especially here, opposite Arras, things would go with a run – we also used gas for the first time. The attack of the 1st Army began at 6.30 am and they made about a mile or so of ground. In the south they took Loos and Hill 70 – the centre reached Hulluch and in the north the outskirts of Haisnes. Here however a check occurred and it may be said that no further advance was made. The French in front of Arras attacked all along the line commencing at 12.30 pm. They made a little progress at points along the line, but as a whole they were not very successful.

The Cavalry Corps (less the 3rd Div.) was disposed ready to move at two hours' notice from 5.00 am, from Estrée-Blanche in the north to St Pol-sur-Ternoise in the south, so as to move through either the French or the British line should a gap be made. At about 10.00 am it was thought that things were going well, the 1st Div. was ordered up to the Bois de Dames which lies south-west of Bethune and later the 2nd Div. was ordered to follow it. The HQ moved up into a chateau at Labuissiere. It rained all the day and the Divs did not have a pleasant day. In addition all sorts of troops were moving up and so the congestion on the roads was pretty bad. This must occur in this sort of warfare where a large crowd of troops are massed on a narrow front and roads are few. A disappointing day on the whole although our troops have done very well, but the French not having got on makes a lot of difference.

**Sunday 26 September 1915** A day of very heavy fighting – of attacks and counter attacks. During the night we lost the Quarries north-east of Hulluch – we were driven back from Hulluch and so things did not look any too rosy, especially as the French attack which was to commence south of Lens at 8.20 am was put off till 12 noon owing to the fog. Rumour as usual was busy. Attacks were ordered by the 1st and 4th and 11th* Corps on the Quarries, Hulluch and Hill 70. The fighting then became very confused and at 2.00 pm we heard that the first of the 3rd Cav.Div. had been ordered into Loos. At about the same time we heard the boom of the French guns south of Lens and knew that the French had started to attack.

At about 5.00 pm the situation was as follows: the Worcesters† had practically retaken the Quarries, Hulluch was not taken, the 21st‡ and 24th§ Divs were in the blue and the Cavalry were holding Loos whilst the Germans were digging on the face of Hill 70. South of Lens, the French had surrounded Souchez and had made a good progress all along the line. If it is realised that this is one of the biggest battles of the war, the situation here may be said to be satisfactory. In the Champagne country where the main French attack takes place, the result of the 100 days fighting is quite satisfactory: a good advance – 12,800 prisoners, 200 Officers and 20 guns. The day was fine and the roads are drying up for which everyone will be thankful. At 10.30 pm the gun fire is still heavy all along the line.

**Monday 27 September 1915** Last night Capel brought in a report that the French had broken through near Thelus and, although I did not credit it, I had to sent it on to GHQ. The result was that we were ordered to move at 5.00 am. Of course the report was wrong. The Boche heavily counter attacked and drove back the French. During the day Briggs with two Cav.Bdes of the 3rd Cav.Div. was sent in to hold Loos. In the afternoon the Guards Div. attacked the Quarry, Pit 14 and Hill 70 – they reached their first and third objectives, but did not get the second. The French have progressed a little south of Lens but are not in any way in line with us yet; until this happens we cannot do much good pushing on as we only form a small salient which we could not hold.

In the evening the fun started owing to an intercepted German message – at 10.00 pm we got a message to say that the English had pierced the line and the post at Haisnes was retiring on Wingles[?]. The 4th Corps there I think went mad. They gave orders that the whole line will advance and that Briggs' Cavalry was to be in Pont-a-Vendin by 5.00 am next morning. We got orders to be ready to move at 5.00 am and so on. Now a bright idea struck someone and that was that the post mentioned in the message referred to the wireless telegraph station which we knew was there. This must have been the right solution as there was no question of an advance this morning. It just shows how people will go mad, their horizon narrows.

I am convinced that the front we are attacking on is too small to make if broken any appreciable effect on the German line as a whole – if they break the front and push the Cavalry through too far, they will lose it. On the other hand if we on the north of Lens and the French on the south break the line, then the Cavalry will have the opportunity of the war. Casualties are very heavy I believe, about 20,000, but not excessive considering the numbers engaged.

**Tuesday 28 September 1915** A quiet night. The French have made a little progress near Givenchy – we heard this morning that Fosse 8 was in German hands and so were the quarries. This is a setback – the programme for the day is to retake Fosse 8 and Pit 14, otherwise to consolidate the line. The bag at present of prisoners consists as follows: 53 Officers, 2,800 men, 21 guns and 35 machine guns. The news in Champagne is still good and the bag there is 20,000 prisoners. We are going on attacking here, they are bringing up three fresh Divisions: the 12th*, 28th and 47th†. The French are attacking Lens from the west and we may do something.

**Wednesday 29 September 1915** A very wet day and cold. There is a lull in the fighting north of Lens. The French on the other hand are on the Vimy Ridge and in Champagne we hear that they are through the German defences with three Divs. This is all good news. Again prisoners have been taken who have come straight from the Russian front. This shows that the line is not very strong.

Had a long account from Briggs how he held Loos. He said it was a perfect hell, the Germans put every sort of shell into the place: gas shells, shells small and big. He gave a very good account of the fighting and told us that the German machine guns took a very heavy toll of us. It appears that the new troops did not do very well, they got out of hand in the attack and so went too far and of course were heavily counter attacked and came back a good deal faster than they went forward. This seems to be the difficulty. They do not know how to meet a counter attack – this is simple lack of training and I think they will be alright now after their first fight. Of course there is the usual amount of chat about what might have been done but they all judge after the event. A good story is told by Briggs – a batch of prisoners were being marched along and a Officer standing by said 'They look a scruffy lot.' A voice in perfect English answered 'So would you if you had had gas for breakfast.' Changed HQ to Allouagne. A beastly wet night – I am sorry for the men who are out in the open.

**Thursday 30 September 1915** A quiet day with nothing doing. The front gained is being consolidated with a view to making it a jumping off place for further attacks on Hulluch and Hill 70. Heavy fighting is still going on round Fosse 8 and the Hohenzollern Redoubt. The former is the chief observation post of the Germans and they will not let it go without a great

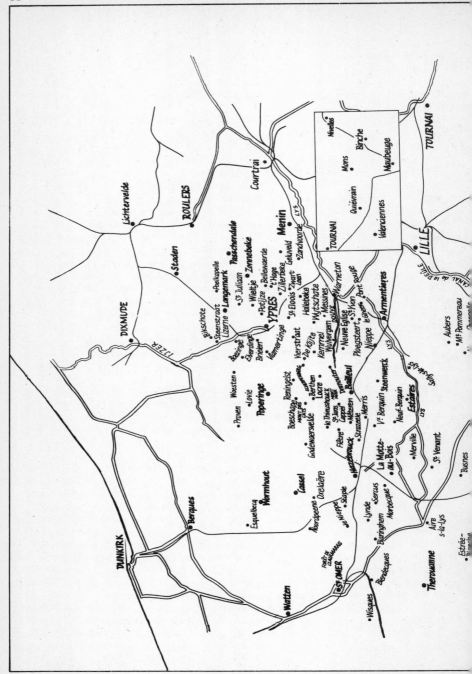

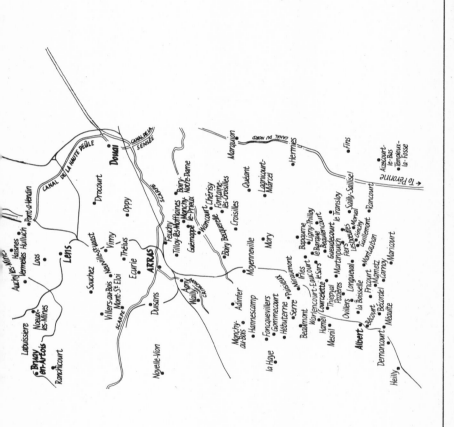

The Battle of Loos area.

struggle. The 28th Div. are now having a go at it, and I hope will succeed in taking it, but it will be costly and mostly grenade fighting. The French 9th Corps is taking over the southern end of our line from the 47th Div. and will attack Hill 70, why I don't know at all.

The French news is still good – they are getting on in Champagne and have got within inches of the railway north of La Tahure. I don't think we shall get on very fast here. If the French are successful in the south, the Boches must hold on here to get the Soissons lot away and I think therefore that there will be very heavy fighting here. We shall, by our attacks, contain a lot of troops which would be very useful down in Champagne and so we shall be helping the whole – but will get all the hard knocks and none of the plums.

**Saturday 2 October 1915** Things are fairly quiet on our front, with the exception of the Hohenzollern Redoubt just south of Fosse 8. Had a very long talk with Capel on the question of the French attacks on our right, between Lens and Arras. I have thought all along that they were only making faces and that there was no real ginger in their attacks. He said he thought the same and he put it down to the fact that we do not, and never shall, really understand the French. We interpret orders differently and fight differently. If an Englishman gets an order to attack a place, he does so and goes on until he can no longer move. The Frenchman getting the same orders meets some machine guns in a house and at once sits down until his guns come up to blow the house to pieces. Again the Frenchman wants more ginger to start him – if you really want him to go all out you have to talk to him of the glory of dying on the battlefield and so on. To sum up I think that the French mistrusted us and so did not do their best. On the other hand their failure to come up on our right has made all the difference to these operations.

Today we got orders to send 2,000 men to clear up the battlefield and put the German trenches into a state of defence. It is a beastly job – especially that of clearing the battlefield as there are many unburied dead lying about. But of course one must do all one can to help. Bulgaria is coming in against us. I wonder where this war will stop, the whole of Europe will soon be fighting. I suppose Greece and Rumania will also take a hand now – on our side I hope.

**Sunday 3 October 1915** We made two attacks on the Hohenzollern Redoubt which both failed. Moved the 1st Cav.Div. right back today towards Estrée-Blanche.

**Monday 4 October 1915** Heard this morning that Scrubbs Wormald was killed by a shell last night. He was down commanding the working party of the 2nd Div. It was a chance shot. It is extraordinary how in the last day or two the chance shots have hit the mark. What it means is that if a shell comes along with one's name on it, there is no avoiding it.

As regards the general situation, personally I don't like it. We have prepared for this offensive with a flourish of trumpets, the whole world has known of it – it is on a par with the German cry of Calais last October. I hope it will succeed better. Tonight I am not optimistic. We have lost the Hohenzollern Redoubt, in fact have been bombed out of it. This ought not to be. Are we man for man not better than the Germans? I think we are and therefore we ought to have been able to hold on to it. I have a feeling that we shall not get on much further; it means another winter campaign. The danger is peace parties and peace rumours, they keep on cropping up – peace intrigues – these are bad signs. Germany would make peace tomorrow on certain terms but those terms could not be accepted by us. One can only hope for the best and fight – that is the true solution.

**Tuesday 5 October 1915** A cold wet day – there is a lull in the fighting although the guns are still going it hard. German prisoners who were sent straight across from Russia say that the Artillery fire on this side is appalling. They have never experienced anything like it on the other side. This goes to show the shortage of ammunition on the Russian side. Reports show a landing of Allied troops (French and English) at Salonika* and that Bulgaria has stated that she would consider such a landing as a hostile act. So the fat is probably in the fire in the Balkans once more. It seems highly probable however that the Csar of Bulgaria† will be murdered; such things are common over there. The world will really be at war and Armageddon as a name will be justified.

**Wednesday 6 October 1915** There is a French report that they have taken La Tahure which is good. We are still re-organizing here as far as I can make out. Gough's 1st Corps is being pulled out to rest. Haking's 11th Corps are preparing for an attack at Fosse 8, Hulluch and Haisnes, whilst the French attack Hill 70 north of Lens and carry on their attack south of the place. I hear tonight that Cavan says he won't be ready for a week. It is a pity that we have to delay because the winter is coming and, if we could really push them back a bit, it would be everything. I hope that our attack and the French one will be simultaneous, otherwise there will be the usual trouble and neither will get on.

**Thursday 7 October 1915** A good deal more Artillery fire than yesterday, but no attacks. Had a long talk with Bob Greenly on the question of Cavalry and we came to the conclusion that, if we are to sit here for the winter, it would be best to hand over part of the line to the Cavalry Corps and let us hold it permanently. We should feel then that at all events we are doing our bit. The German wireless today reports that Austrian and German forces have crossed the Denia and the Lave. However Servia has had eight months to recoup and they licked the Austrians last time, so we hope they will give a good account of themselves.

**Friday 8 October 1915** A fine day with an east wind. Heavy firing all day – we have consolidated our position well as far as one can find out. We heard the Germans were making a big attack with gas but no details yet. Now at 8.00 pm the firing has stopped, so I hope that the attack has been beaten off and the Boches killed. News from Champagne of heavy attacks by Germans against La Tahure and all have been repulsed with great losses to the Boches – I think one can consider the news good.

**Saturday 9 October 1915** A very strong attack last night. The French put it at 27 Battalions and we at 17 which is much more like it. They attacked all along the line and specially at the Double Crassier where they took and kept a length of French trench; against the chalk pit held by our 12th Div. where nine Battalions attacked and were hurled back; against the Guards opposite the Quarries and Hohenzollern Redoubt. They got into a trench called 'Big Willy' at the latter place but were bombed out by the Coldstreams. The Germans suffered heavily and their casualties are estimated at 4-5,000. I don't think the Germans will leave us in our present position and I hope they will attack again. It is the only way to kill the brutes. In Champagne they made four strong counter attacks in mass formation and were again beaten back – all this looks good, if we can only force them to use their Infantry that is what we want.

**Sunday 10 to Tuesday 12 October 1915** We are preparing for an attack on Fosse 8, the Quarries and Hill 70 – this is due to take place at 12 noon tomorrow. It is purely local and I suppose we shall look on as usual. The French attacked Givenchy again yesterday. The attack started at 4.15 and was not successful, they took a trench or two and that was all. Had a long talk to our Liaison Officer with the French today. They seem to take things very lightheartedly. The inexplicable thing to me is that they seem to be satisfied. An attack fails and they don't worry – this is not the spirit which is going to drive the Germans into Germany. I am afraid they will make peace and what a peace it will be!!! Our only chance is to go on fighting – for two years more if necessary – but we must show the Germans that they cannot ride roughshod over the world.

I hope that our attack and the French one will be simultaneous, otherwise there will be the usual trouble and neither will get on. We must keep on attacking if we want to do any good at all and simply wear the Boche out. The Servian job is still a puzzle* – I don't know what we are going to do – if we weaken here, we are playing into German hands. Is Germany trying to get some more territory to bargain with or what? I personally think that there is a good deal of bluff about. Anyhow the Servians will give a good account of themselves, of that I am certain. I believe we shall go into winter quarters on this line.

**Wednesday 13 October 1915** A fine day for an attack. It rained a bit in the morning and at one time it looked like being not good for gas. The object of the attack was primarily to straighten out the line and to take Fosse 8 and the Quarries – so as to get a comfortable line to hold and, if successful, a jumping off place for a fresh effort against the Boche second line. It is interesting to note that the objective is now a limited one, no more wild cries of getting to the Canal de la Deûle: a proper operation of war, to get a certain line and to make certain of holding it against the inevitable counter attack. The 11th Corps were to attack Fosse 8 and the Quarries, the 4th Corps to make good the line of the Lens-Haisnes road up to the trench known as the 'Duck's Bill'.

The operation started with an intense bombardment at 12 noon and at 12.10 the first letting off of gas and smoke. The wind at this time was south-west – good for the 11th Corps' objectives but not good for the 4th Corps' one. The gas and smoke were very successful and for once luck was on our side. At 12.30 the wind went to the west and so took the gas and smoke over the 4th Corps' objective. The General watched it from a fosse near Noeux-les-Mines. He describes the gas and smoke advancing like a wall. The bombardment of Fosse 8 was terrific. The Germans began by answering against our front trenches, but did not keep it up and their shooting was a bit wild. They however gave Vermelles a very good doing and they devoted much shelling to Loos. The attack at the first rush was quite successful. We took two-thirds of our objective on the Lens-Haisnes road – retook Gun Trench and the Quarries and also the Hohenzollern Redoubt – and are now at 8.00 pm attacking round the sides of Fosse 8. This may be called a good day's work and I can hear the guns still firing. It won't be finished yet – we have lots of fresh troops and should attain our object.

Lawrence came in from the French 10th Army. His report is none too good – they say that their offensive is finished, their troops are tired and they have no fresh ones. The spirit is not good at all – it is heartbreaking. Capel came back from Chantilly – his report is none too good either. The French think, as far as he could make out, that the main theatre is now the Balkans, that here and on the Russian frontier it is a matter of stalemate. If they think so what are we to do? It means that they are going to sit down and say Kismet. We shall have to finish this war ourselves. I firmly believe this war will be finished by the Russians, French and ourselves – that the Balkan show is only a red herring put across our noses by very clever people and it looks like succeeding. I think we have a great chance still here and would pin my faith in a spring campaign.

For the winter, I would worry the Germans in the trenches all I could. I would at once bring out the K. armies and Territorials and **train them out here**, put them in the trenches and get them shot over. Train the officers and in the spring make a combined effort with the French and Russians – the Balkans is a by-show. We ought to take over the line now held by the French 10th Army. I hear Foch won't hear of it – pure selfishness as he thinks he would lose his job. If we arrange another offensive it must be in our line – not at the junction with French troops. They do not fight when alongside us – we knew this on the Aisne a year ago and yet we go on in the same way. Everyone is discussing the Balkans and everyone agrees our diplomacy is bad. Money would have bought the Balkans – we bought Italy why not the Balkans? Briggs has gone to command the 28th Div. and John Vaughan takes up the 3rd Cav. Div. – a most unpopular appointment, but there is nothing against the man officially*.

**Thursday 14 to Sunday 17 October 1915** I am afraid our attack has not been very successful as we have failed to take Fosse 8. As far as I can make out, we shall make another attempt to take Fosse 8 and then settle down for the winter. What an outlook! We have been given our winter areas and shall move into them shortly. I only hope that they will give us something to do – a piece of the line to look after and so on. Otherwise we all get restless, young Officers feel that they are not pulling their weight and want to go where there is more fighting. It is only natural – yet one does not want to lose the best Cavalry soldiers we have got.

On Sunday Corps HQ moved to Therouanne for a couple of days before going back to our winter quarters at Lumbres. On Friday we walked the country between Sercus and the Forest of Clairmarais with a view of digging a defensive line at that point and Sunday we did the same east of Watten for the same purpose. It was interesting work, but of course whichever line is selected someone always comes along and says that there is a better one. Part of the 1st Div. came back to Allouagne to rest. The men looked a bit tired, but next day when they had washed and cleaned there was a wonderful difference. Not much news from the Balkans, but I fancy things are pretty serious out there. Whatever is done will have to be done quickly. It is a clever move on the part of the Boches, but should have been foreseen.

**Monday 18 October 1915** Orders and counter orders has been the order of the day. If only the higher commands thought for a minute, they would be more careful. I hate to change my orders, but was forced to today.

**Tuesday 19 October 1915** Went out to reconnoitre a line of trenches for a back line at Le Nieppe. It was a lovely day and although we walked miles it was very pleasant. The woods are just turning and were lovely. Went to GHQ on the return journey and then came back to our new quarters at Lumbres. Quite a nice chateau but badly furnished and very cold; we shall get it warmed up in time. This is going to be our winter quarters – a hateful term as it means another winter of war. The chips are on the green*, Sir John is at home fighting – I only hope that if troops are going to Servia, they will send a lot of them and do the thing properly. If we could gain a success there and bring in Greece and Rumania, we should have the troops we need out back here in four months' time.

**Wednesday 20 October 1915** Ordered by GHQ to make out establishments for a Division (Inf) from our Corps and Indian Cavalry Corps. I suppose England threatens to have the Cavalry home and we have to show we are doing something.

**Thursday 21 October 1915** A quiet day. My Chief leaves us to command the 5th Corps vice Allenby who goes to the 3rd Army. I am very sorry. I do not know who succeeds him, I suppose it will be either Cis Bingham or Philip Chetwode. Hear we are sending eight Divs to Serbia. The King comes out here, but I am told he is not seeing the Cavalry this time.*

# 7. Waiting for a Chance

**Monday 1 November 1915** Returned from a week's leave at home. Had a very rough crossing. Everyone at home seemed rather depressed – London looked as if they had forgotten to light the lamps. The Servian situation looks none too good – strong action is needed to prevent 'Tino'* joining the Boches. I think that Greece should be made to choose as soon as we have troops enough to enforce our arguments. We are a funny nation – here we have been at war for 15 months and yet we use 'peace methods' – no one else does!

What is the best way to coerce Greece? Why to land a large force to help the Servians and then to turn round to Greece and say – what about it!!! We have up to now dealt mostly with natives – the Germans have shown us that they can be as bad and worse and more treacherous than any native. Other nations are following the German lead and repudiating their honourable guarantees – therefore we must take off the gloves and treat them the same as the others. All our people are now digging on the Le Nieppe line – poor work for Cavalry, but then we are doing something to help. Cis Bingham [the new Commander of the Cavalry Corps] has gone home for a week.

**Tuesday 2 November 1915** Went into GHQ to interview Sir John [French]. Dropped in and saw Vesey; he had no news at all. It seems to me that we are fairly set down for the winter and so there is little or no prospect of any real work in the near future. It has been very wet indeed and the country is all waterlogged and so there is little or no work to be done.

**Wednesday 3 November 1915** A fine day and no news. P.A.* has joined [us] again. What we are to do with him I don't know at all, but I suppose it is his proper place.

**Thursday 4 November 1915** A fine day at last and I hope the poor fellows in the trenches will get a bit of sun. Went and had lunch with the 1st Div. and combined business with pleasure.

**Friday 5 November 1915** Hill Whitson ordered off to rejoin his Regiment which is moving from India, destination quite unknown. I wonder if it is Servia or what our plans are – today I see that the Greek Government has been defeated and that means Venezelos* will come into power. I hope that this will bring in Greece – this flouting of treaties is a very serious thing for the world in general. No one will trust anyone else and the whole morale will be lowered – I should drown Tino. I suppose he will now once more retire to his bed. It would help us a lot if Greece came in – their troops are not worth a kick, but we should then know how we stand which we don't now. I believe that things will go all right now and am prepared to take 2/1 that by 1 January 1916 the Turks will have stopped fighting. If we can only settle the Balkans and Turkey temporarily and get those troops back here for the spring campaign, the war should soon be over. But it is here that the war will be decided.

**Saturday 6 November 1915** Went out to gallop the horses on a piece of land about two miles from here and of course found the 9th Lancers having a race meeting. Had a good gallop and so home after watching the first race – a match over five furlongs.

**Monday 8 November 1915** Have got to send 750 men up to dig for the 2nd Army* – they say that their trenches have fallen in through the wet and are in a bad way. The men just hate that Ypres salient like poison and I don't wonder at it at all. Had to go into GHQ, so had tea with Whigham. Sir Wallie was in very good form and chaffed me about the Cavalry – he loves people to think that he is a Cavalry Soldier – of course he kept off vital subjects so I did not get any news.

**Tuesday 9 November 1915** It is a poor heart that never rejoices so they say – but a pouring day with a south-west gale does not cheer one up very much, especially when one thinks of the poor fellows in the trenches. One can only hope that the Boche is having a worse time of it than we are. Winter has really set in and we are in for the usual bad time.

**Wednesday 10 November 1915** We have been ordered to change our billeting area to go further west. So I spent the day with O.K. Chance in a motor having a look round our new bit – it was a nice day but cold. The reason we have to move is that the 1st* and 2nd Armies want a training ground behind their zones to train the Divisions which are resting. Also new Divisions coming out are at once allotted to Armies – this is what I have advocated all along as then it will be possible to salt† the new troops and get them shot over without breaking their hearts. Of course the poor Cavalry will never be now comfortable, but that cannot be helped.

**Thursday 11 November 1915** Went into a conference at GHQ reference our new billeting areas and won all along the line. This Staff is getting too much Royalty attached to it. P.A. is treated by the Chief* as a Prince instead of a brother Officer – it creates a beastly atmosphere and I don't like it at all! Hope things improve.

**Friday 12 to Sunday 14 November 1915** A certain amount of excitement caused by two boats being blown up by mines outside Boulogne and so we got no mails. Friday and Saturday one of the worst gales I have known and it rained in torrents. It breaks one's heart to think of our poor chaps in the trenches.

Everyone discussing Winston Churchill's resignation*. We got a wire on Sunday asking if he could come back to the Oxfordshire Hussars, of which he is second in command. Life is full of changes – a Cabinet Minister one day and then a few days after a soldier living in a dirty farm. Anyhow it was the only thing for him to do. It is some years since I have seen him to speak to, but we crammed and were at Sandhurst together and I knew him better than most men in those days. His dreams have most of them come true, but whether he will ever be Prime Minister the future alone can show†. Whatever may be said of him, no one can doubt his physical courage. The Russians seem to be pulling along a bit and if they conduct a winter campaign, the Boches will not like it and will suffer a good deal.

**Monday 15 November 1915** Nothing of interest except that P.A. has a letter from his sister* the Crown Princess of Sweden – she said that the question of peace was being openly discussed in Germany and that people wanted peace very badly. This is news indeed. I only hope that we won't make peace until we get what we want. Another letter from a Swiss banker says that Germany is absolutely broke – the same man said six months ago that she could go on for a long time, so evidently things are moving quickly. Poor Tom Gurney was tried by General Court Martial for writing forbidden things to his wife – I am awfully sorry for him, but there has been too much talk in our Army altogether and he broke every rule of the game.

**Tuesday 16 to Friday 19 November 1915** Have been very lazy about the Diary. The main bit of news has been Winston Churchill's speech and his joining his Regiment. The general opinion is that had he not attacked anyone, his speech would have made a hit but I personally think it lacked dignity. There is no doubt in my mind that he has rendered us great service – that he made mistakes and that History can only show where he was right or wrong. Anyhow now he is a Major and second in command of a Yeomanry Regiment. I don't think he will remain there long. We have had a long spell of frost and it has been quite cold, but anything is better than rain. On the high ground where some of our Bdes are, there is six inches of snow.

Lord St David's speech has caused much comment especially out here. The attack on the HQ Staff is as unjust as it is as untrue. He has made the mistake of attacking it as a whole, where an attack on a very small part of it might have been justified and done some good – not as regards operations but as regards the personal Staff. The worst of it is that if you throw pitch some of it will stick. This attack is bound to affect new formations and may give them lack of confidence in their own Staff which would be deplorable. It must do more harm than good and therefore a very grave crime is laid at Lord St David's door. However one may have suffered and whatever personal losses one may have experienced, the time for these attacks is not yet.

The situation at Salonika is not at all to my liking – I firmly believe that the Greeks will turn against us. The story is that only one French and one English transport is allowed in daily; that a Greek Army Corps surrounds the place and that three German Officers sit on the quay counting the number of British and French troops landed: a decidedly humourous situation if we were not at war. Lord K. may be able to tackle the situation but at present it does not look very hopeful – on the other hand here we have got the upper hand in this trench war. Having enough ammunition and plenty of guns if the Germans annoy us we can and keep on trouncing them. If we are only not soft-hearted the Boche troops will not be much use after such a winter in the trenches.

**Saturday 20 November 1915** Went for a ride with the General round the 4th Bde area. A very raw day. Our Artillery is very active – the Boches called out the other day to our fellows in the trenches 'What is the matter with your Artillery? Why is it shooting such a lot?' I only hope it will go on doing so. Motored out to see the 1st Cav.Div. They are just outside Samer. Everyone feels they ought to be doing more. But I tell them all that unless the war finishes on this line, there is plenty of work in store for them.

**Monday 22 November 1915** Went to Amiens to visit the *Ecole de Camouflage* – the best translation is the schoolboy word – a suck in. In this School, nature is copied and the copy is placed during the night instead of the real thing, except that the copy contains a man for such purposes as observing the enemy. For instance a dead horse or man is lying in a certain place from which the enemy trenches can be observed. An exact copy of the dead horse is made, only it is hollow, lined with steel bulletproof plates, and a small slit for observation purposes is left – during the night the dead horse is taken away and the copy put in its place. The copies were most clever, done and painted at the school which is under the Head Scene-painter of the Opera in Paris. I saw a marvellous reproduction of a tree inside which was a periscope. Every sort of ingenious device was seen there*.

**Tuesday 23 November 1915** We have started to play hockey so as to keep fit – today was the first day and we played only 20 minutes each way – it was a case of bellows to mend* with most of us. Hope however we shall improve with practice.

**Thursday 25 November 1915** A long conference in the morning on the question of the Dismounted Division. Everyone went away quite happy I think – it is a big question. Played hockey to straf the lumbago. Went to bed very stiff, but bellows worked much better.

**Friday 26 November 1915** Walked round the line which is being dug by the 1st Div. in Clairmarais Forest. It was very wet and muddy. It is slow work making defences in a forest. A very fine day but cold.

**Saturday 27 November 1915** Motored down to Aix-en-Ergny to attend the review of the 5th Dragoon Guards by the King of the Belgians on his appointment as Honorary Colonel. It was a lovely day but had been freezing hard. The Regiment put up a very good show for him and marched past well. He then made them a speech in very slow English and we went back to lunch – about eight courses – Lucky Barry represented the C-in-C and Prince Arthur came with us. Prince Algy of Teck was with the King of the Belgians. The lunch took place in the house of the Mayor of the village – as we rode up the Mayor and the Mayoress were on the steps ready to receive him: the Mayor in evening clothes and his lady in black. The latter presented him with a laurel bush (which had white flowers) on arrival and another bush with pink flowers on departure. She also made a speech but all I could catch was France. The Mayor stood by with his top hat and evening clothes. As soon as this ceremony was over, he popped into the house and appeared in a billy-cock set at a rakish angle over one eye and I think forgot to change it when the King went away.

**Tuesday 30 November 1915** Walked round the diggers in the morning. The Channel is full of mines so we get no letters which is very annoying. Heard about the expedition to German East Africa – Smith-Dorrien is to command; Tom Bridges is to command a Division and the other to come from India. I suppose it is a political necessity so as to say that we have got all the Boche colonies. If it is finished before April it will be a good side show, if not a bad one – I hope that they are sending sufficient troops to make certain it is a good one.

**Thursday 2 December 1915** Today arrangements had been made for Prince Arthur to present French decorations to the Officers and men of the Cavalry Corps. The arrangements were made by the 7th Cav.Bde. Troops were drawn up in three sides of a square in the village of Hucqueliers and a band had been borrowed from the Blues. It was a pretty scene in an old-world village lying in a pretty valley. The French inhabitants had hung out flags as they always make a great show when they present medals.

**Friday 3 December 1915** P.A. went in to see Sir John [French] and found Winston Churchill as aide-de-camp on duty!!! It is rather funny. He will end by commanding the British Army.

**Saturday 4 December 1915** Prince A. has been wired for by the Monarch. We are all rather curious to know why. He did not know himself – it is probably a mission and he thought either to Sweden or Rumania. I don't think he wanted to go a bit. A beastly day, pouring with rain and a howling gale blowing.

**Sunday 5 December 1915** We believe that Germany is beginning to fly peace kites, but of course they will fly very high to begin with. Germany will try and protect Turkey at all costs so that at the end of the war she will have a footing in Asia Minor. I think that is her game and the peace terms will be based on these lines. For us the position would be intolerable with her well settled between India and Egypt. Heard today that K. thinks the Senussi* are certain to rise and this is the reason why he wants troops in Egypt – they never rose even in the blackest days in the Soudan†. If they rise now Germany will have done her work thoroughly. Rumours that Sir J.F. is going home: differences with the Government – *Quien Sabe?* I wonder will D.H.‡ succeed him?

**Sunday 12 December 1915** Have not written my Diary for a whole week and on the whole have been very busy, what with inspections of the Dismounted Division and visits to our digging parties. All reports show great activity along our front and we are giving the Boches what for with our guns. We hear that the big East African show is off. K. stopped it as soon as he got home – rather a sell for some of them I fancy. The Bulgar news is not good – I fancy that we shall have some difficulty in holding Salonika*. Poor Greece, what is she to do? Austria will take Salonika if she can. The latest news is that the next thrust will be at Egypt: Turks from the east with a rising of the Senussi on the west. All sorts of rumours regarding sending more troops to Egypt. This is a world war with a vengeance – where will it end? I still believe when we force a war into Germany and not before – that is the only end to the war that I can see. A very bad week as regards weather – very heavy rains and south-west gales.

**Monday 13 to Thursday 16 December 1915** On Wednesday went down to the 18th Div. which is commanded by Ivor Masse to have a look at a piece of ground with a view to offensive operations in the future. This Division is armed with the Lewis gun only – as they wanted to borrow some of our Maxims*, I thought it just as well to see the ground and how it lent itself to this kind of work. They hold a line due east of Amiens just at the bend of the Boche line.

On going through St Pol-sur-Ternoise, I was stopped by a French post and asked if I could give a lift to a French airman as far as Amiens. He had been working just south of Lens and was a great enthusiast. He told me he had two planes: a biplane in which he observed for the Artillery and had a companion who worked the wireless, and a monoplane on which a machine gun was mounted and in which he went hunting. He was a cheery little fellow and talked the whole way. Luckily having a big coat on he never discovered my rank, otherwise being only a Sous Officier†, he would not have been so talkative.

I got to Heilly late and met Baker Carr and Pigot Moodie just starting for the trenches. We motored due east for about eight miles and ran the gauntlet of an exposed road which has an artificial screen of bushes to hide it from the view of the Boches and reached a very battered little village called Becourt [north of] Becordal. Here live a Pioneer Battalion of the Northumberland Fusiliers – they are shelled every day but very happy. We walked to the trenches which are about 800 yards away. The soil is chalk and the trenches on the whole are good: 7-8ft deep with deep dug-outs. In some places they had fallen in owing to the frost but were being repaired. The Germans here have a very pronounced salient and we went on to an observing point where we could see into the German first line trenches, which did not appear very good, but the second line trenches were very heavily wired and very strong. I made a good reconnaissance of this side of the salient.

The Germans were very quiet, quite different to the old Ypres salient days and except for an occasional shot where a sniper was at work and an occasional shell they were silent. On our side however machine guns were continually at work and we saw some pretty shooting with a light Howitzer at a Boche trench. We came back and Lewenden told me that in our absence a shell had caught a platoon passing our house and knocked out six men. After that I went back to Heilly and saw Maxse and then started home.

Today Thursday brings historical news. Sir John French goes home and he is succeeded by Sir Douglas Haig. Sir John has done great things – on the other hand he has a great many enemies. Has he been too great an optimist? That he was one everyone knew – has this led him to make mistakes of judgement, advising the government at home as regards the war? History will show. To the Cavalry he has ever been a staunch friend. One Cavalry man goes – he is succeeded by another. Perhaps Douglas Haig will be succeeded by Hubert Gough in command of the 1st Army – I think it would be the best appointment possible – Infantry and others will probably disagree. These changes are we hope for the good. We have reached what will be considered a phase in the war.

**Friday 17 December** 1915 Two good little attacks in which they killed about 80 Germans took place in the 1st Army sector. I hope that they will go on being successful as the Boches hate being worried.

**Saturday 18 December** 1915 In the afternoon went to see some trials with the Hotchkiss gun* and decided that, if we can get it, we will adopt it for the Cavalry and issue it eventually at one per troop. Also saw some firing with a luminous bullet for shooting out of aeroplanes; it was a very ingenious thing as one can see the course of the bullet in the air quite plainly, a very good device for aeroplanes.

**Sunday 19 December** 1915 Sir John left for Paris on his way home – he passed down the St Omer-Aire[-sur-la-Lys] road and we turned out the 3rd Cav.Bde to line the route. It is a sad thing always and we hated it. Sir John got out of his car and shook hands with all of us and said goodbye. He has had an uphill task in his 17 months of command.

**Monday 20 to Friday 31 December** 1915 The end of a year of war – got leave on the 22nd and went home. There was an awful crush on the boat trains and it was not pleasant travelling. Sir William Robertson, Freddie Maurice and Bob Whigham were also there. It was a case of the old regime leaving in a body – they all go into new posts at the War Office under the CIGS*. Had a splendid time at home with the family and forgot about the war altogether.

Got back on the 30th and found that the Dismounted Division had been ordered into the trenches under Gough (1st Corps). Cecil Howard issued all orders in my absence and did it well. Everything is working smoothly – about 8,200 bayonets form this Division and a very fine one it is – I only hope they will not have too many casualties as the Cavalry man is hard to replace and we have little or no reserves behind us. They will do well I know, but their usefulness lies in the future and so they will cause me a good deal of anxiety. A Cavalry soldier is not made in a day, a good one in about a year. I am proud to think that our men are taking their share and I wish I were with them instead of sitting here at a desk.

Here we are on the last day of a year full of hopes and of disappointments. A year of lost friends and also one in which friends have advanced towards their ambitions. Who would have thought 12 months ago that we should now be in the same line as before? There was not a man who would have given such a thought voice. Some dreamt of the Rhine – the French probably of revenge of 1870 – some of an honourable peace and so home at last. Yet what is the real situation? The Germans are in Russia miles further east than last year – they hold Servia and bombastically threaten Egypt. On paper they certainly have had a successful year's campaign. On the other hand they are no nearer their object; their victories are barren of decisive results. They must feel that they are up against a stronger power than their own – their war of success must be a quick one and having failed in the commencement, they must see ultimate defeat before them.

How can this be reconciled with the fact that they have conquered territories? The reason is that of resources. Last year the Germans fired 100 shells in the west to one of the Allies, this year the Allies fire more than the Germans. The Germans through superior peace preparation were in their prime for the first year. Now other nations are commencing. England is her greatest enemy and is now commencing to fight a real fight with all the necessary concomitants. Germany's cast was not for France or Russia – to take the place of England was the aim of *Kultur*† and *Weldpolitik*‡. She is no nearer this aim today than she was on the day she determined to embroil Europe in a colossal war.

What of the future? Greater battles are yet to be fought, both east and west, and no man can say that he will see another sun – but I am convinced the end will be that Germany will be forced to conclude a peace – not on his own terms but on those of the Allies. I may be optimistic, but if everyone is so, the result is beyond a doubt. Before this end is attained many dark hours are before us and many sorrows – but there is one thing that should always guide us – let us fight it out so as not to leave a war such as this as a possible heritage for our children. Exit therefore 1915 – it reminds of one of gas, the Ypres salient and the disappointments of September but 1916 may see us plant our feet on German soil – D.V.§

**Saturday 1 January 1916** The new year ushered in by a gale and torrents of rain. Our Dismounted Division takes over the trenches between the Quarries and Fosse 8 – not the best part of our line. They are under the 1st Corps (Gough) so they will be looked after.

**Sunday 2 January 1916** Went to Bethune to the HQ of the Dismounted Division and saw Philip Chetwode who is commanding it – they are getting on well and all arrangements are working smoothly. All the men are fresh and keen and we ought to hold the line and improve it a good deal.

**Monday 3 to Saturday 8 January 1916** A busy week and forgot the Diary. Up to now we have been fairly lucky as the toll of casualties have not been very great. There has been lots of room for improvement and our men have been working well – but not all of them – it is funny that good Regiments in peace are good in war. The worst of it is that the Boche have got the start of us in mining and we think that they will certainly blow up another bit of our trench line. This is bad but it is the fault of our predecessors (the London people). It will take us all our time to get the upper hand again.

On Friday I went and gave a lecture to the Staff Course at GHQ. I think it went all right – but of course I was talking about things at the beginning of the war which I had seen and which they had not, so I suppose it was fairly interesting to them. We are all very pleased at the vote in the house for compulsion*. Seely made quite a decent speech and John Ward was splendid. I hear that the Russians won't be ready to advance until summer – I only hope that the effort when it comes will be a continued one, not an offensive here and then one in the east. It seems as if Germany were afraid of an offensive here first as she has certainly brought troops here from the Russian front – or she may contemplate an offensive on this side herself, but I don't think it, it would be too good to be true.

**Sunday 9 to Tuesday 18 January 1916** Am getting worse and worse and the Diary has been very neglected. The Dismounted Division are having casualties at about 18 a day. This cannot be looked on as heavy if one considers that there has been a great deal of work to be done. If you sit quiet and do nothing the Boche does the same, except that he mines and blows you up when the time comes. John Vaughan now commands with Moreton Gage as his GSO1. It is not a happy combination – the former is oversugared, the latter a soured man.

Have been thinking over the strategic situation lately. We know that the Boche have taken heavy guns out of Metz and Strasbourg. They have reinforced their western front. What can they do? An offensive against Russia will not produce any decisive result. They must do something to keep public opinion up to mark – on the western front they have a chance of a decisive campaign or probably they think they have. The French morale barometer is very sensitive – it goes up and down with success or failure. Now what are the portents? To my mind as follows: the Boche are fighting in the Balkans with Balkan and Austrian troops – they threaten Egypt with Turkish troops and oppose us in Mesopotamia with the same; in central Europe are Germans. The war will be decided in central Europe. Germany is therefore very clever: the Egyptian threat is forcing us to take troops away from the vital point (ie France), but no German troops are detached – Salonika is the same.

This game is therefore the best that Germany can play if she meditates an offensive in the West – it will be her last throw. Russia may be ready by July – therefore this offensive must succeed before that date. If it comes, it will be big, magnificently directed, but we ought to be able to hold it – if we can, then I think the end is near.

Today I met Captain Macaw (3rd Hussars) who has been with the British Mission at the Russian GHQ since the commencement of the war. He said the Russians were very short of rifles and might be ready in June – that the German line was very thin and that the Austrians opposite them were practically kept in their places by Germans. He said that the Austrians surrendered on every possible occasion and were finished, but that Germany practically ran the Austrian Army. He told some amusing stories. One was that the Russians will not take single Austrian prisoners unless they pay a rouble or bring in a batch with them. He witnessed the following event: an Austrian Officer advanced with hands up to give himself up. After a parley with the Russians the latter agreed to take him. The Austrian then whistled to his line and out came his sergeant carrying his portmanteau. The German Cavalry raid on the east of Vilna* was carried out by a Cavalry Corps† and had an important effect on the evacuation of Vilna.

**Wednesday 19 January 1916** Went down to see the Dismounted Division. They are getting on all right and doing a great deal of work to the line.. It was a lovely day and fairly quiet, although the Boche blew up a mine. It was 30 yards short of our parapet, so did not do much harm and we had no casualties.

**Thursday 20 January 1916** Went in and saw Tavish Davidson at GHQ on how long we should be in the line. Heard to about the middle of February, but that he was watching our casualties very closely and once they touched the 400 mark, he would pull us out at once. Tried to find out something of the future plans, but nothing as yet settled. General Joffre was paying a visit to Douglas Haig in St Omer today; he was going on to see the 1st Army and to present some French decorations.

**Friday 21 January 1916** Went up to see the Dismounted Division. Saw Beale Brown, who was very indignant at the idea of being kept there for a month. The British Officer is a very funny person: if he likes and trusts a man he will condone practically any mistake; but if the reversal is the case, every act is looked on as underhand and for self-glorification and so on. I think this war has shown me that more than anything else. The casualties still keep up, but I am in hopes that they will soon drop again. The GHQ idea is now that the Boche is preparing another eastern campaign. I cannot see what they are going to gain by it, at least not a separate peace which is what they are working for.

**Saturday 22 January 1916** My General returned from leave and so did Prince Arthur both looking better for it. They had a very rough crossing. We are supplying Russia with 300 Howitzers and the ammunition for them which they badly want.

**Sunday 23 January 1916** Went up to the Dismounted Division with the General. They blew up a mine just south of the Hog's Back crater and hope they did in some Boches – at all events they got some of them with machine gun fire. On the way back called on Goughy*, now Sir Hubert, and got well told off for calling him by his proper name. We went on to Busnes with him and listened to the Artillery band for half an hour. I saw several old friends. It was a treat to hear a good band.

**Tuesday 25 to Thursday 27 January 1916** There was a general sign of greater Artillery activity all along the line. This is interpreted as a preparation for an attack on the Kaiser's birthday. In fact they did have a try at the kink in front of the Royals and 3rd Dragoon Guards. The Boche shelled our trenches very heavily and then 18 men started to walk into them. I suppose they thought that the trenches must no longer exist. But every bay was manned and only one Boche got away. We had about 50 casualties all along the line, which was not heavy considering the intensity of the bombardment.

Arthur Capel came back from Paris – I had a long talk with him and he was most interesting. The French insisted on holding Salonika for a political reason: to give an appointment to General Sarrail – who is a power in the Socialist Radical group. Also Poincaré*, Briand and Co now run the Army – that Joffre, Foch and Co are merely servants of the political people. It is rather curious because at the Battle of the Marne, Joffre was King of France, the Government were at Bosteaux and did as they were told. The result of this trench warfare is that political factions have had time to recoup and so have got the reins into their hands again. There is also an idea that the French cannot afford to lose many more men. They are a curious race: I think we shall probably have to give them a lead. If we could only start making a hole, the French would very soon have their tails up and come in too. There is no doubt a good deal of jealousy between the French higher command and the British Forces – what the French say is 'We are the older army, our Staffs are better trained, now your men are better than ours in the attack – the British Army should be under Joffre (ie Poincaré Briand and Co).' Briand is a **very clever** man, I think cleverer than Asquith and Grey† – he seems to have got round Asquith and the result is that the strategy is made subservient to **Politics**, not even to Policy. The greatest catch phrase of the embryo strategist is '**Policy** and strategy should go hand in hand.' **Policy** here looks like party politics and vote catching, Politicians and not Statesmen. Clemenceau seems the great hope. As regards England, have we any statesmen who are in their prime?? Just heard of an attack by Boches on Loos, which was very roughly handled. More enthusiasts for the Kaiser's birthday.

**Saturday 29 January 1916** Went up to the Dismounted Division and found things very much quieter. Cannot quite make out what the Boche is up to. He has been very active lately and yet we know of no great concentration of troops opposite us. It may be that he is withdrawing troops as it is a favourite trick of his to attack on such occasions, but his attacks have not been co-ordinated – they have been just here and there as it were with no special object. They attacked the 15th Div. on our right on the 27th on about a mile of front and got it from five machine guns and so did not get very far. There was no very apparant reason for it except that it was the Kaiser's Birthday. We are giving the Boche no rest, but are at him the whole time with our guns and machine guns.

**Sunday 30 January to Friday 4 February 1916** We have had several excitements with the Dismounted Division, such as the blowing up of a mine or two, but that is all. On Thursday I went to dine with Vesey at GHQ and met Colonel des Vallieres who is the head of the French Mission now that Huguet has gone. I corresponded with him when I was at the Staff College as he was my opposite number at the Ecole de Guerre in Paris, but had never met him before. He speaks English quite well.

F.E. Smith* and Lloyd George have been out here joy-riding and a good story is told of the former. It appears he came out here without authority and started wandering about on his own. Macready the Adjutant General told him to stay at GHQ. At any rate he disappeared and an order was sent out 'A gentleman named F.E. Smith in a Lieutenant Colonel's uniform was to be found and arrested at once and sent into GHQ.' F.E. was unearthed in Winston's dug-out and without any ceremony bundled into a motor and sent into GHQ. On arrival there the Provost Marshal† asked him for his parole that he would not leave GHQ – this F.E. refused and so a guard was put in his room. The story goes that L. George was very indignant that such an indignity should be put on a Cabinet Minister!!! But where the soldier rules Cabinet Ministers are small cheese. It is a good story and probably has a grain of truth in it.

Prince Arthur went down to the 3rd Army to find out about the German attack on the French at Frise [on the] Somme. They certainly drove the French back some 1000 yards and captured a good many prisoners. General Dubois is sending the Colonial Division to retake the line, but it seems to be [a] waste of men as the loss of Frise does not appear to hurt the situation much. However if the French always give way like that, a big offensive would have some chance of success. The Dismounted Division will be out of the line by the 16th and I shall be glad to see them with their horses.

**Saturday 5 February 1916** Conneau who commands the French Cavalry Corps with the 10th Army came today to inspect Jacco's signallers. He brought one of his Divisional and one of his Brigade Commanders. They were given a splendid show by Jacco: wireless, cable, visual signalling were all shown. They were much struck with the competence of the Signal service and also the quiet way in which the men worked. They told me that the French would have been chattering like monkeys. Luckily it was a very fine day. The Air people showed us also a wireless telephone working with an aeroplane, it was wonderful how you could hear the observer talking quite plainly*.

**Tuesday 8 February 1916** Went up to see the Dismounted Division. The Boche have got another mine under our trenches which may go up at any time, so we are quite prepared for it. We exploded a mine at 10.15 pm under the Boche trench in front of Gap 8. The result was a furious bomb fight but we have got a loop hole looking into the crater so the Boche cannot occupy it. I don't think that we shall get away under 800 casualties. It is the worst bit of line and we have improved it out of all recognition.

**Thursday 10 February 1916** Went down to the Indian Cavalry Corps to lecture on Cavalry during the early stages of the war. I had a large audience and was well received. I saw many old friends. I enjoyed the trip, but I hate lecturing the more I have to do it. Bingham went into St Omer to dine with D. Haig and to meet K. who is out here. He says that the latter was very optimistic, and the whole tone there was cheerful. I am glad to hear that someone is optimistic.

**Friday 11 February 1916** Went up to see the Dismounted Division. They are beginning to hand over part of the line to the 12th Div. On my return I heard over the telephone that the Boche had given them a good bombardment. It started opposite Fosse 8 and then went the whole way down the line to Loos. No harm was done except the trenches were a good deal knocked about. They began by blowing bugles and sounding gongs. This may have been done to make us man our trenches, or else they may have panicked and thought that we were going to make a gas attack. As I went up I saw K. and the Staff of the 1st Army reviewing the Bantam Div. The men are of course very small – and some of them I am afraid very young – but they swing along well.

**Thursday 24 February 1916** A week's leave home from the 14th-22nd was most pleasant and I found all well. I went and saw Bob Whigham at the War Office and also went up to Grantham and saw the HQ of the new Machine Gun Corps. They have got a good show up there and ought to make it a success.

Came out on 22nd and found a big German attack going on against the French north-east of Verdun*. The Boche has had a small success there. Of course we and the French knew that the Boche was moving troops but it was not quite known where it would take place. He moved four Corps down to the vicinity of Verdun. I suppose this is a sort of set off to the Russian success at Eserom†, but it must have cost the Boche a good few men. The country is covered in snow and it is freezing hard.

The casualties of the Dismounted Division work out at about 1,000 all told; this is heavy for seven weeks' trench work. On the other hand the fact that they have been in the trenches has done a lot of good. The Officers and men feel that they have done their share, and there is not that restless feeling in the Corps. We are all busy training now in real Cavalry work in the hope that if the day comes we may be ready.

**Monday 28 February 1916** The Boche have been putting in a very strong attack against Verdun and have pushed the French back about three miles, but nothing to hurt and they have had very heavy losses. They seemed to have massed a great many heavy guns there and given the line a proper doing. We calculated that they had 17 or 18 Divisions in the attack but I think we shall find it was more. According to the German wireless the Kaiser was there in person, I suppose they hoped to take Verdun and then offer France peace. The French seem to be holding their own all right. We are taking over the line held by the French 10th Army from Lens to Arras and the famous Vimy Ridge. We now hold a line about 85½ miles long and this gives us no troops for an offensive, so what is going to happen I don't know.

As regards the Cavalry the Corps formation has been done away with, so we are all out of jobs. I believe I am going to be retained so that a Corps can be formed quickly if required, but I am heartbroken over their decision. We have all worked hard for this old Corps and hoped one day it would be used in open warfare, but that of course is now no longer possible. Each of the four Armies is to have a Cav.Div. attached to it with one Cav.Div. as GHQ reserve. It looks as if the powers-that-be had given up all hope of breaking the line. Is the war going to end in a compromise, a drawn war? If it does, it will be the French that have let us down, for they will be the people who will make peace first. It will be a bad day for us because we are the people who stand in Germany's way, not France or Russia. I shall be very sorry to lose my General − he has been very good to me and it is hard luck on him being suddenly put out of his command through no fault of his own.

**Tuesday 7 March 1916** A very full week − most of the time spent in giving a decent burial to the poor old Corps. The 3rd Div. sent us a wreath, so we sent it on to the Cavalry Club as a souvenir. As regards the future, I am going to be Chief of Staff to an army which may be used for attack, defence or pursuit. The thing has great possibilities in it of course as it may turn into a big command at any minute, so I must consider myself lucky.

The attack on Verdun appears to have come to a standstill for the moment. They were grave moments of anxiety when it started as the French, although they had plenty of warning, did not do very much in the way of preparation and the black troops which were there did not stand*. However we hear that the French have not as yet used their main reserves at all. The French up to two days ago estimated their losses at 30,000 and those of the enemy at 70-100,000. The Germans must have lost pretty heavily. There are persistent rumours of Turkey wanting to make peace. Of course it is her best time now and so break once and for all with the German influence. The American Embassy in London has it that the Dardanelles are being cleared of mines. Is there going to be a great debacle in the Balkans I wonder, it is the region of volte faces.

**Wednesday 8 March 1916** Woke up this morning to find four inches of snow on the ground. Truly the laws of compensation are wonderful − a mild winter and everything very forward and so down comes snow and frost in the middle of March. It is freezing hard again tonight.

Today the Corps Commander* left for England and tonight it is brought home to me that the Corps 'non est'. The Corps Commander felt it very deeply. He is a lucky or an unfortunate man. It is a question of degree and of mind − he has been out the whole war and has commanded successfully in succession a Cavalry Brigade, a Cavalry Division, a Cavalry Corps; only the first of these in real active operations. He goes home regretted by everyone for he was universally loved − he ought to be a fairly contented man. He may not think so at the present moment. The rest of us are left to struggle on, our hour of trial is not in reality begun – we go from one task to another, each more difficult. We do our best, as in the *Happy Warrior*†: 'He comprehends his trust and to the same is faithful with a singleness of aim.' I believe Kavanagh is to be my new Chief – we are to have charge of the reserve – this may consist of anything up to four Divs and five Cav.Divs. We are to form a force ready for offence or defence. I shall hear more later.

**Monday 13 March** 1916 We are a very small party here and may become smaller any minute. The General went home on the 8th and some of the Regiments turned out on the Boulogne road to give him a farewell. We are all very sorry that he has gone. I went down on the 10th and stayed the night with the 1st Cav.Div. (Mullens) and the next morning saw the whole of the Division file past. The men looked clean, healthy, smart and alert and went past well. The horses looked well on the whole – the 19th Hussars being easily the best.

The German attacks on Verdun have stopped for the moment, but whether they will commence again or not it is difficult to say. As far as we can judge, they have only two Divisions left which are not accounted for. Everyone is wondering what this attack means – it is rather hard to find a reason for losing about 150,000 men at a place like Verdun. Of course they may attack at another place – say the British line about Vimy – but where are the troops coming from? Have they brought more from Germany, if so one ought to have heard of any big concentration for this means railway movements. Perhaps they thought that they could take Verdun and make a separate peace with France, who knows? D.H. has been at Chantilly and Paris and I believe there has been a conference at which all the Entente powers were represented, so something may come of it. The snow has gone and we are having lovely warm weather, which is a comfort after all the cold. *

# 8. The Infantry on the Somme

**Saturday 8 April 1916** Left England, having accepted an offer of GSO(1). Arrived at GHQ, which had moved to Montreuil and was informed that I had been appointed as GSO(1) to the 46th Div. which is commanded by Stuart-Wortley. Luckily I know him as he is Cis Bingham's brother-in-law. My new quarters are near the Vimy Ridge. There is no news; the French are doing well at Verdun and have got their tails up. Wondering what an Infantry Division is like, luckily a Sahib commands it.

**Sunday 9 April 1916** Went down and had breakfast with the Reserve Corps. I picked up my kit, and Lewenden, and made for Camblain l'Abbé. Arrived at 12 noon and met my new General. Luckily I have Gervase Thorpe as my GSO(2) and he is a very good man and an old hand. Went out in the afternoon and reconnoitred the ground between Mont St Eloi and the Vimy Ridge.

**Monday 10 April 1916** Went in the morning to inspect the Divisional School with the General, then went on to 17th Corps HQ, but Byng was out. Met Kemp, one of the Brigadiers, and we went round the left sector of the trenches – they are not good and the French left them in a very bad state. Walked solidly from 1.00 to 6.00 pm and was quite footsore.

**Tuesday 11 April 1916** Went round the right sector of the trenches, met Campbell who was in the Seaforths and commands the left Brigade of the 51st Div. Then went and inspected the Neuville-St-Vaast defences. Started at 9.00 am and got back at 5.00 pm and walked the whole time, pouring with rain and a beastly day – trenches are bad, but improving.

**Wednesday 12 April 1916** Stayed in and did office work. At 4.00 pm, went out with the General and saw a demonstration with a *flammenwerfer** captured from the Boches at Ypres – a most terrifying thing to look at, but really very harmless. An Infantry Division is quite hard work when it is in the line.

**Thursday 13 April 1916** Went round a sector of the trenches – the French certainly left us a bad legacy and we have had practically to redig the whole line of trenches. Started at 9.30 am and got back at 5.00 pm – walking all the time. Found the young Officers not goo; they are very young and don't seem to be able to take hold of the men and make them do what they want. The trench discipline also is not good and will have to be taken in hand. Very wet in the morning and the trenches rather muddy, but a very drying wind will soon alter that.

**Friday 14 April 1916** Another poisonous day, very cold and wet. After lunch, rode out to Mont St Eloi and then walked over to the Ouvrage Blanc to find a position for a forward Observing Officer of the Division during a big attack on the line. Found a place from which an excellent view of the whole line could be obtained, but if there is a big fight it will be a regular shell trap and I think that most of the communications will be cut. We move back into reserve billets on the 23rd for a month. I am sorry as we have not yet got the line in perfect order. We are told that we shall come into the same bit of line on our return which is a good thing – I only hope it will be true.

**Saturday 15 April 1916** A fine day in the afternoon. Went round the right sector in the morning and started off in a snowstorm. The trenches were very clean and are improving every day. The Boche fairly active on the left of our line – walked back towards Mont St Eloi and had a look at the country behind the line. In the evening Dunford, the mining expert, came and told us we should have to explode two mines or else the Boche will do it. So will have to make the necessary arrangements. No news here, although papers report an advance on the part of the Kut relief force*, hope Townsend will hold out.

**Sunday 16 April 1916** A real fine spring day but cold out of the sun. Sir Julian Byng came to HQ and was very nice and kind to me. Found we have to blow up our own mines tonight, so have arranged to fire them at midnight and to make two small raids on the enemy trenches at the same time. Mines went off beautifully and I hope that they killed some Boches, but one went off too soon owing to the French Officer's watch having gained seven minutes between 7.00 pm and midnight! Luckily nothing untoward occurred, but the French are helplessly unreliable the more I see of them. We occupied both craters but had a loss of an Officer killed, four men killed, two Officers and 14 other ranks wounded. The show was well arranged and well carried out, but we did not get a German prisoner for which I am very sorry.

**Tuesday 18 April 1916** Last night at midnight, the Boches blew up a mine on the north of the centre sector. They blew in a small portion of our observation trench. We had a good many casualties – about 50 – from the German bombers who attacked our working party consolidating our lip of the mine. It does not appear that the situation was as well handled as it might have been. The excuse given is that the Lewis guns, which should have covered the crater from the north, jammed owing to the wet and the earth thrown up by the explosion. Again the weather is vile. It has been raining hard and it makes digging in the clay soil very difficult. We must do better in future.

**Wednesday 19 April 1916** The rain has made the trenches very bad and one cannot work at them at all. News comes that the Russians have taken Trebizon*: they are progressing very fast in the quarter and it is bound to have a very demoralizing effect on Turkey. I only wish we could relieve Kut as well. Germans blew up a mine in our right sector at midnight – no damage done.

**Thursday 20 April 1916** Last night we blew up a mine in our left sector. We charged it with four tons of explosive and believe that we exploded a German mine as well. We occupied the near lip and crater and got into some Germans with a Lewis gun as they came over the other side, and hope to get an identification* tonight.

**Friday 21 April 1916** Last night the Germans did pay us back; they blew up a mine close to ours and buried 15 of our men, out of which we have recovered eight alive. In the afternoon went down to inspect the place with Thorpe and found two great holes with high walls on our side of the mine, so crawled round the back of them and had a look at the posts of bombers which we placed there. It was a very dirty crawl as the mud and water were awful. Talked to one of the bombers, he was a topper: told me how he had shot a German Officer who had come out to reconnoitre and was very pleased with himself. A fine type of man who, I think, loves fighting for its own sake.

**Saturday 22 April 1916** Our last day before we go into reserve. Trouble about our new HQ, so went with GoC* and settled the matter.

**Sunday 23 April 1916** (Easter) A quiet night, but relief of our last Battalion very slow and was rather worried when relief was not reported by 5.00 am. Kemp commanding 138th Bde* came to see me at 6.00 am and explained matters so was rather relieved to find all was well. At 11.00 am motored back to our new HQ at Roëllecourt which lies about two miles east of St Pol-sur-Ternoise on the Arras road. Motored out in the afternoon and visited Brigades and talked about training. I don't think that I know very much about Infantry!!! So I have to look wise.

**Wednesday 26 April 1916** The Boche has been a pig again – he blew up two mines in our old left sector and got into one of our trenches, but we kicked him out again. There was some fighting there one way and another. Walked round the Corps line or part of it with Gervase Thorpe. It has been a lovely day and the enemy planes were very busy – we watched our anti-plane guns at work for some time, but did not see a hit. Have got to make a smoke attack with a Brigade for the benefit of 3rd Army and Brass Hats* from GHQ. Don't like the idea at all – as I hate all this show.

**Friday 28 April 1916** The Boche was very active last night. He blew up five mines on a front of 600 yards opposite the 51st Div., but did not do any harm. Went this morning to the 5th Army School at Auxi-le-Château. Saw an attack through smoke, also a competition and bayonet fighting. Hear we may move south, hope so as motion is better than sitting still. Had a long talk with Berkely Vincent – he seems pretty discontented. He wants a command, but he got a nomination for the Staff College and so ought to be content to work on the Staff. Self is still rampant in the BEF, I am afraid.

**Saturday 29 April 1916** Another fine day but a strong east wind. Enemy have been very active about Hohenzollern [Redoubt] and Loos. They used gas and smoke. In one place the wind changed and the gas went back over their own lines – aeroplanes report area 1,500 by 1,000 yards affected. I hope it caught a good many of them.

I am afraid our fate is sealed and we go to the 7th Corps* – I hate changing Corps because they generally run things a little differently and one has to get into new ways. I don't know when we really move but it will be very shortly. The French think that the battle of Verdun is finished†. I wonder if the Boche is meditating a further attack on our front so as to stop our offensive and paralyze it before the Russians are ready? That ought to be his game if he has enough men and munitions to do it with. If the offensive of the Allies is made simultaneously on all sides, it is bound to have a great effect on the Germans. If we break the line it will, I think, finish the war – if we don't I am afraid some of the Allies will want to stop. I hope not but that is the sort of feeling I have.

**Sunday 30 April 1916** Went down and had lunch with 7th Corps. Frank Lyon is BG.GS and Snow commands it. The latter is a fusser I should say. Went and had a look at Gommecourt. We shall have to attack it later on. It is very extraordinary how quiet that bit of the line is – they say that the Germans and French lived there in absolute peace for months. I think that is one of the reasons of the German success – the line has not been active enough. Anyhow whenever the British get there, they make things hum; so I suppose we shall do the same*.

**Monday 1 May 1916** Took Abadie[?] and Raymer of the 137th Bde down to our new line and walked round the trenches. I don't think much of the trenches but the wire is good. One comfort is the lines are too far apart for mining. The village of Foncquevillers, only 1,000 yards from our trenches, is in a very good state and does not show much signs, although they shell it at times. It is very funny to compare it to Neuville-St-Vaast which is just a heap of bricks and stones. Had a good look at the German wire which is thick and strong. Gommecourt itself is a ruin but strongly held.

**Wednesday 3 May 1916** Had a gas alarm last night – it is thought that one of our shells hit a gas cylinder in the enemy front trench. Anyhow, it points to the fact that enemy may be contemplating some devilment on our front. Wind today west and north-west; as long as it stops there he cannot do very much. Had to put off smoke attack as too much cloud for observation from kite balloon, so hope to get it over tomorrow. Went and made special preparations for the movement of Reserves in case of gas attack and got out orders for our move.

**Friday 5 May 1916** Had our smoke demonstration and made an Infantry attack through it. It went off very well and was quite interesting. In the afternoon went and said goodbye to Sir

Julian Byng and had tea with him. He told me that they were skimming his front terribly so as to have every man possible for the attack. This is the right principle, but it seems to me that extra precautions should be taken on the Vimy Ridge. The French lost a great many men there and it would produce a very bad effect if we had a reverse there. But I suppose the powers-that-be recognise this.

**Saturday 6 May 1916** Moved down to Pas-en-Artois and into 7th Corps' area. In the afternoon went out to La Haye Farm – the HQ of the Brigade in the trenches which we hold opposite Gommecourt. All very quiet and I am told we have the Prussian Guard opposite, I suppose they are **resting** there as it is a very quiet bit of the line! It is extraordinary how quiet it is after the Vimy Ridge. Had a long talk to Raymer and Abadie[?] and consider it very necessary to have patrols well out at night, as the Boche is sure to make a raid as soon as he thinks that the units have been changed. This has been the hottest day of the year.

The General* came back from England with Berkley Sheffield. They said that England was very pessimistic – that there was bad news from Russia and that they were afraid that Riga† would fall. This is very curious as there has been no mention of any sort of activity in that direction; I suppose that they have kept it pretty quiet. How the Boche manages all this is a marvel – he must have many more men in Reserve than we think.

**Sunday 7 May 1916** Had a conference at Corps HQ. We may have to attack Gommecourt in conjunction with 56th [Div]*. In the afternoon went to see the 137th [Bde]† at La Haye Château and then went into Foncquevillers and studied the Boche trenches for a good long time. Things were very quiet. Here and there one saw the top of a spade appear and earth being thrown out. The wire in front of the Boche trenches is very strong and thick, but all the easier to cut with trench mortars and artillery. It was a lovely clear night after the rain and one could see very well. There was no shelling and, except for an occasional ricochet from a sniper, there was no sound. We extend our trenches northwards and take over a further bit of line.

**Monday 8 May 1916** Went to 37th Div.* (Gleichen) and saw Berkeley Vincent on the subject of taking over new trenches. It is bitterly cold today and we have gone back to winter. Then went on to the 137th Bde – met General† and discussed questions on attack and defence on our line. Everything very quiet and although fairly close to the line not a sound could be heard. Had a conference in the afternoon on military matters and cleared the air a good deal. There is no news here; it is very different to being with the old Cavalry Corps. We used to get outside news through our wireless, but now we do not get so much and of course we have no wireless.

**Tuesday 9 May 1916** A very wet and nasty day. Went in the morning to Foncquevillers with the General and examined the enemy line and wire from one of our Artillery observation posts. It is in an old house which has been half knocked down by shell fire. They have built a brick square tower inside it. They told me that they shell it daily but at present have not done any harm.

The tales that are told of Fonquevillers during the French occupation are wonderful. When the first British Officer went round to take over, he found the French sentry sitting on the top of the parapet reading the paper. The German and French Officers were said to dine together – I don't believe the last story. But it is quite certain that the French either fight like devils or else there is a sort of truce. We inspected the medical arrangements and then I went to the 139th Bde*. In the afternoon I walked round the back area and looked at the ground from the point of view of making communication trenches for use during offensive operations.

**Wednesday 10 May 1916** Wind changed to north-west and a fine sunny day. In the morning went to a demonstration of cutting wire and making saps with a pipe fitted with sap wires. It was very interesting and carried out what was claimed for it. Saw many old friends. Germans seem to be attacking again at Verdun, cannot make out with what object. I suppose it must be to stop a French offensive. Things seem to be boiling up in the Riga direction but no definite news.

**Thursday 11 May 1916** A very busy day – spent morning in looking over ground for the purpose of making a model of the Boche trenches. In the afternoon went down to the 137th Bde and spent more time studying the Boche line from the edge of Foncquevillers. Things were very quiet, a bit of sniping only going on. It was a clear day but no sun, so the Boche wire did not show up as clear as it might have done. I think we must attack on a two Brigade front, the General wishes to do so on a single Brigade front. I think this must be unsound as there will not be enough depth.

**Friday 12 to Sunday 14 May 1916** Have not had time to write daily. On Saturday afternoon met Brind who is GSO(1) of the 56th Div. and settled the right boundary of the Division, which wanted doing badly. At last we are getting a move on with reference to the Gommecourt business. We got objectives settled and Hull, commanding the 56th [Div.], had a talk with the General.

On Sunday morning there was a more or less futile conference at Corps HQ. It would appear that we make the Scheme* and Corps sit and look on − this is quite wrong. The Corps wants ginger badly − it ought to take the thing in hand and issue quite definite **orders** as to what it wants. They will not take the responsibility − but the only thing left is to do it oneself.

**Monday 15 May 1916** Last night the Boche suddenly woke up and strafed* the 56th Div. on our right. They had several casualties and the shelling worked up to us − we were attacked with gas shells this morning. The gas was still lying about and one could smell it quite distinctly.

Had a great morning studying the Boche lines with Thorpe. He climbed up a tree and found a splendid place to see from and and I went up too and learnt a lot. It is very curious how one learns by studying the ground. A project of an attack seems hopeless when first mooted. After careful study of the line through glasses, one gets all sorts of ideas − the points which are easy and those which are difficult begin to stand out. Thus the ridge between Gommecourt Wood and Pigeon Wood will be probably easy to take, but difficult to hold against counter attack; on the other hand Gommecourt Wood itself will probably prove a difficult nut to crack, but will be more easy to hold on to. The whole attack will depend on the Artillery preparation; if that is sufficient and adequate, I think we shall succeed. It has been a lovely day, real summer at last, and I hope it will continue.

**Tuesday 16 to Thursday 18 May 1916** Went round with the General to inspect the rear lines on Tuesday. On Wednesday went round and watched the Infantry training. That is the worst of being a Cavalry soldier, one can take very little interest in Infantry, it all seems so slow. A man has a pack weighing 56lbs on his back and how he gets along at all is a marvel to me. The men look well now.

On Thursday went round and settled the rear lines for an attack with Thorpe − the weather is simply glorious but there is a gas wind, so one never knows what devilment the Boche will be up to. It is a constant source of anxiety − which is not good for Generals. Germany is once more flying peace kites, but that does not mean she is beaten. The sooner she can make peace on anything approaching her own terms, the better it will be for her. Have met Snow several times; he is always very nice and charming to me but is a bit of a bully really if he gets going.

**Friday 19 May 1916** Have come to the conclusion that Territorials do not work as well as the Regular or the Kitchener [armies]. The whole of this Division wants ginger putting into it from top to bottom!

**Saturday 20 May 1916** Went down to the Bde HQ holding the line. They shelled one of our Batteries very badly and knocked out one of our guns. The Battery is badly placed and it is a wonder that they have not had a go at it before.

**Sunday 21 May 1916** Had to take Sir E. Allenby commanding the Army round our line − I am afraid he got very hot. It was a lovely day but the hottest of the year at present. He was quite pleasant and, beyond strafing a corporal for being improperly dressed, was quite tame. Last night a white terrier came over to our lines from the Boche lines, he has often been seen on their parapet. The men of course say he is thin and therefore the Boches are starving.

**Tuesday 23 May 1916** Took Egerton out and went over training ground near Lucheux. Got the digging shield successfully and hope all will be well. Heard account of the attack on the Vimy Ridge. The Boche massed over 40 Batteries against the northern end of the ridge which we held – they fairly blew our trenches to blazes and then attacked and got our support trenches. We, of course, heard that they had taken the Talus des Zouaves which would have been a misfortune, but things were not nearly as bad as reported. All the same they have made a fair advance and their attack was successfully organised.

**Wednesday 24 May 1916** Had a conference at Corps HQ. Old Snow very fussy and making points of things we had already done, but he must be humoured. In the afternoon, went to meet the C-in-C (Sir D.H.) who came to see our Brigade at Lucheux. 5th Army are evidently afraid of an attack on Arras or in that direction.

**Friday 26 May 1916** Spent the afternoon looking at enemy's line from the hill just east of Hannescamps. It was a lovely clear evening and the Boche trenches stood out clearly – I saw two Boches and a black dog come out of their second line trench just above the Little Z. The view of the enemy wire was good and, although strong in places, is not very strong the whole way through. They say that the Boche has lost very heavily at Verdun and the French are full of fight – even talk of a winter campaign. This is good hearing as I have always been very frightened of them. I have often thought that Germany might offer them such terms that they could not resist.

**Saturday 27 May 1916** Went in the morning and inspected our trenches for burying cables. In the afternoon had a conference on the proposed attack on Gommecourt. The 137th Bde will attack on the right and the 139th on the left. Got a good many details settled I am glad to say and am now beginning to see a little bit of daylight.

**Monday 29 May 1915** Had conference at 7th Corps HQ in the morning and it was not of great interest. Then went on to Lucheux to watch the training. This is progressing quite satisfactorily – a good deal of improvement in the way the attack is carried out. In the afternoon went to see young Burton of the Robin Hoods*, who is preparing to carry out a raid against the enemy lines. He is a good boy and has the right jaw for such things.

**Tuesday 30 May 1916** Went round some of the trenches with the General – the work is not yet satisfactory. The reason is that the Brigade Staffs do not supervise nearly enough – also the tasks are not allotted to the men and labour is wasted.

**Wednesday 31 May 1916** Got up at 4.30 am to watch a practice smoke attack but the wind was wrong and so it did not come off. Hear Beauchamp Doran has been sent home over the Vimy Ridge business. The Artillery work was bad and he stuck up for his BG.RA*, the result was bad for him. Heard that the French losses at Verdun are about 200,000 and the German 350,000 – pretty tall figures. The Italian situation is rather worrying†, the last thing that is wanted is for the Italians to get a real knock – they are as a whole bad soldiers.

**Thursday 1 June 1916** Spent the day in the trenches – walked the whole line and saw the new trench which we had dug. Watched the Monmouths* making Russian saps†; they are getting on well and these saps will be very useful some day.

**Friday 2 June 1916** Took the General down to Foncquevillers and looked at our communication trenches. They are getting on very rapidly now and work as a whole is being pushed on. Just heard a German report that there has been an action at sea* and we have lost the *Queen Mary, Inflexible* and *War Spite* and that the Germans have lost the *Pommern* and two light cruisers. I wonder if it is true. I hope that they have not scored to this extent.

**Saturday 3 to Wednesday 7 June 1916** There has been no time to write a diary these days. The air has been full of alarm – the French, Italians and Russians howling for us to attack – then that the Russians were to attack first and so on. Great excitement and much bustle! It is a good thing however, as our preparations are not as far forward as I could wish for, and it hurries everyone up.

Our first news of the naval fight off Jutland was through the German wireless who put their losses at three and ours at eight* – then our own official reports read as if the action was a defeat for our fleet. At last the truth leaks out – a victory announced in the first place would have had a great morale effect. John Bull is often called 'stupidly honest' quite correctly. Today we got news of Lord Kitchener being drowned† – what can one say? Nothing – words fail: a great brain and a successful career – a builder of the Empire. What an end – being a soldier the battlefields would have been the best. 'But he died in harness' and what better epitaph can man want?

Attacking these trenches has become an exact science – with the troops here it is possible to estimate how far you can get and what you can do. The heavy gun is everything – if they shoot straight we shall have no difficulty, if not our troubles may be very great. S.W.‡ is very excitable just now. Today our fellows dig a new line on our left – may Providence watch over them.

**Thursday 8 June 1916** Last night we extended our line to the north in conjunction with the 37th Div. The lines did not meet as the 37th Div. joined up to the wrong spot. This was very bad as it left our left flank in the air. So had to trot out this morning with Vincent and Barnes who is commanding the [37th] Div. in Gleichen's absence. It was the old story of putting the operation into the hands of a sapper – I was very angry as we had done a good night's work. Had a long walk round the trenches. Things were pretty quiet although there was a bit of 'daily hate'* flying about. Tonight we join up and I hope that things will be all right.

**Friday 9 June 1916** Another cold day. Went down to Foncquevillers with the General this morning and had a look at some of the communication trenches. They are getting on but it is stiff work. The Russians seem to be driving the Austrians back a good deal and the news tonight is that they have done in three Austrian Armies*. Hope it is true as this will relieve the pressure on Italy and help them considerably. The naval battle is turning out well and the Germans are beginning to acknowledge their losses. The Kaiser has been making the usual speeches, I wonder if he was misinformed of the real situation – it looks very like it. Our preparations go on apace, but it looks as if one would never be ready, there is so much to do.

**Saturday 10 June 1916** Another beastly day – wet and cold. The worst of it is that it stops our work for our offensive – it is practically impossible to dig in this soil if it is wet. Saw Butler who is ADC to Snow – just out from leave. Beatty had told him that he put the German losses at five battleships, five cruisers and 22 destroyers. If this is true, it was a victory indeed. But one cannot get over the fact that the Boche got his news out first and led the world to believe that we had suffered a heavy defeat. It may do good in the long run as it may open the eyes of the world to German methods – but for the time being they certainly have been clever.

The Boche is very quiet opposite here. Our great difficulty will be the civil population who live in places within 1,500 yards of the trench line. If you try and move them they say 'All was quiet until the English came – are they never going?' This is the peasant mind. They have sons fighting at Verdun but their horizon is limited to the few acres they cultivate and live on.

**Sunday 11 June 1916** The whole morning was taken up with conferences and this afternoon I had to take Lyon round our trenches and a nice muddy dance I led him. After this rain the bottom of a good many trenches are just liquid mud. Our guns were registering on the Big Z and on Pigeon Wood and making quite good shooting, although there were a good many duds. The Boche was quite quiet beyond a sniper or two who were active. They were also dropping some 4.2in. west of Foncquevillers. The men are working well and preparations are going on apace. If we could only give them a real knock, it would probably end the war.

**Monday 12 June 1916** We had a smoke demonstration this morning, all the big whigs were there. Heard today was to be made a Brigadier General again and going to the 5th Corps. I wonder if it is really true. If so, I was right to sink my rank temporarily and come out as a GSO(1). A filthy cold day and more like winter than summer.

**Thursday 22 June 1916** Many changes to report since I last wrote. I have been home for four days and found all well. My new appointment is not to the 5th Corps after all, but to a new Corps: the 9th. My General is one Hamilton-Gordon – who has been at Aldershot all the war

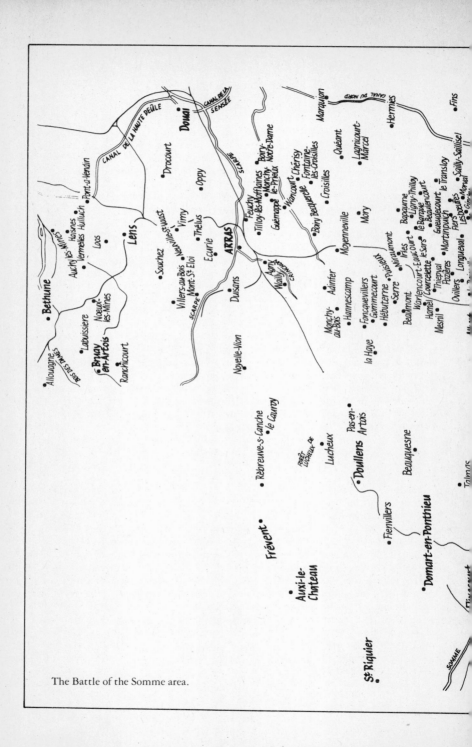

The Battle of the Somme area.

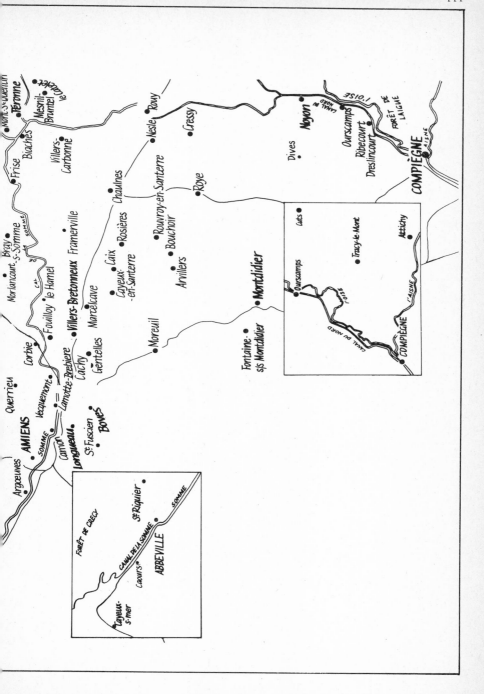

in an administrative capacity. However, in war one has to do one's best and not air one's opinions. I am now in Bailleul and our HQ will probably be in the chateau at Mont Noir where the Cavalry Corps were during the fighting on the Messines ridge on October 1914. I have always said I should like to see the other side of the Messines ridge again and who knows one may do so.

Preparations are now going on apace and I think that there may be a great surprise in store for all of us. Of course no one knows what will happen down in the south, but things may go much quicker there than anyone can expect and with us it is generally the unexpected that happens. I wonder what the French are playing at – from the little I hear I think they are at their old game, they do not want us to pull the chestnuts out of the fire. They growl when we do not attack and growl still more when they think we are going to be successful – that may be exaggerated, but certainly the date was put forward to please them and now it is delayed again. I have not as yet got any of my Staff. Went up to Kemmel today to study the ground – it was very interesting but we have a hard job as the Boche lines are a bird cage*.

**Monday 26 June 1916** Went down to stay with Sir Hubert Gough for the night on the 24th and saw the 15th Corps' preparations for the attack. Most of the heavy guns were registering and it was extraordinary how little the Boche replied. The idea is that, if this push is successful, Gough with the Reserve Army will move on Bapaume. From there the thrust is going to be northwards – if this is successful no one knows what may happen. Today I went on to Hill 60 behind Ploegsteert. It was quite curious revisiting the old place. It was very interesting to see where the Boche has been using gas – the whole of the ground is yellow and the grass killed, but it is beginning to grow up again now. Went and interviewed Cupper (24th Div.). He was interesting on the subject of our attack.

**Tuesday 27 June 1916** Had a good walk round our future line of trenches so as to know them when we take over – it was very funny to be creeping along places where in 1914 one used to ride about. Our trenches are certainly not good but, as we hope to transfer our line to the east of the Messines-Wytschaete ridge, it is not worth worrying about. There is very little news – we have got a new bomb for destroying the Boche kite balloons – it just sets them alight and we have downed seven of them in the last two days which is good. I think H-G* will do; he has a mind of his own I am thankful to say. Humph is a pearl and very cheery – I think I am lucky in our Staff.

**Wednesday 28 June 1916** Attended a conference at Army HQ – Met many old friends there. The whole situation was discussed. Tomorrow morning at 9.30 am our offensive* is being launched by the 4th Army and may good luck attend it. The French are putting in four Corps of four Divisions each and with one Corps in Reserve, so the offensive is going to be a fairly big one. Very hard work getting out the plans for our attack on the old Messines-Wytschaete ridge as I have no Staff to help me.

**Thursday 29 June 1916** Heard today that our offensive has been put off for two days, I wonder why? It may of course be the wet weather, but on the other hand it looks like the French once more* – we always come up to the scratch at the time given, our Allies on the other hand never do. This is a severe indictment but a true one. Spent the day working out problems, and went to Dranouter to look at gun positions for the heavies. There is going to be some trouble but I hope to get round it – these old 8in. guns are very clumsy and heavy. Castlerosse just arrived and reported himself as a GSO(3). He has had no previous Staff experience, but that must be expected now.

**Friday 30 June 1916** Took the General round the land on the east of Kemmel Hill and saw the old farm where a Bde HQ used to be. The country which used to be highly cultivated is very rank with grass and weeds. They were shelling a Battery and, as my General is new to the game out here, he was very interested. Got back and found that things are going wrong a bit. I think B.H.* is inclined not to get on with his superiors, but he is an excellent man and will do well. I think it is another case of P.H.† – I hope not as it makes a lot of trouble.

**Saturday 1 July 1916** The offensive in the south* began today and has been partially successful. The 13th Corps† with Congreve have done well and so have the 15th Corps‡ under Horne. Hunter-Weston [8th Corps]§ and Morland [10th Corps]‖ have not got on so well¶. It is however the beginning and perhaps it is as well not to start with too great a rush. We have always done so before and always come back; perhaps this time we shall be able to go forward and stay there. I hear the Gommecourt attack has not succeeded, I wonder why? If it was the flanking fire from the edge of the village, that was the place we were always afraid of. I am sorry as I should liked to have seen it succeed. They were too ambitious, I think, and the original plan would probably have been the best. I am sorry for E.S.W.†

**Sunday 2 July 1916** Went up to the Army for a conference – it would appear that the attack up here may not come off as they may want the troops in the south. Hear the French have done well south of the Somme – the bag up to date is 7,500 prisoners which is a good start*. There is no news of Verdun today but I fancy the Boche is pausing in that part of the world. The Russians are supposed to be starting their big push against Hindenberg in the north today†. It may be a great success, they are doing very well in the south. On the whole one may say the result is fair, but of course one would like things to go a bit faster.

**Monday 3 July 1916** It has been definitely settled that for the present we do not go south, so our preparations should go forward up here. Went up to Mont Noir this morning and saw that the work on our new HQ was going on quite satisfactorily. It will be miles better than Bailleul which is very stuffy this hot weather. The Australian Corps* are on our right and they are fine men, tanned and straight and first class fighters.

**Tuesday 4 July 1916** Went round the ground east of Kemmel today with Cupper who commands the 24th Div. and we settled on some battle HQ for the attack of the right Division.

**Wednesday 5 July 1916** Got into our new HQ at Mont Noir and have got Allenby's old room as my office – how little one realised at that time that one would still be here nearly two years afterwards. I hear that they have sent Stuart Wortley home – I suppose it is as a result of the failure of the Gommecourt attack. The failure has been a great blow to me as I helped in the preparations and was responsible for the preliminary work. It was purely a case of Artillery preparation as the place was very strong – if that did not succeed, there was little or no hope of taking the place. I am very sorry for him as they meant getting rid of him and I suppose this was the opportunity. He was very good to me.

**Thursday 6 July 1916** In the afternoon I went up to Kemmel Hill and sat in an observation post for an hour. It just cleared up for a bit and I got a good view of the Wytschaete-Messines ridge, so I had a good study of it. Not much news from the south, it would appear as if there was a pause before the Boche second system of defences. I hope that they are going on pushing down there as I believe that the Boche may be forced back a good deal.

**Friday 7 July 1916** Was called up to a conference at Army HQ – more changes. The Anzac Corps are moving south and we have to extend our line to the Douve River – what memories of October 1914 that brings out! Then we were holding a thin line with the 1st Cav.Div. and now we hold the same line with a fat Infantry Division or more – it shows how we have grown. The battle in the south appears satisfactory. The fighting is very heavy but it is a case of hammer and tongs and who can last out the longest. At any rate they seem to be putting troops into the point where they are winning and that is always the best game to play. I heard today the 16th Div.* is out of the line and has had tremendous losses; some of the others are just as bad.

**Sunday 9 July 1916** For once Sunday has been a quiet day. I spent the afternoon on Mount Kemmel with glasses studying the Boche lines. It was a lovely clear day and one could see a very long way. The Boche was kind and left the hill in peace, although he shelled some Batteries just south of it. The news continues good – I hope that the French will come along north of the Somme. The Russians still seem to be advancing. I don't fancy that they take many German prisoners, as the feeling is pretty bitter. Had a letter from Thorpe and he told me of the attack on Gommecourt. It was a pity the right was held up – it was always the danger point*.

**Monday 10 July 1916** Had a morning on a horse inspecting the construction of emplacements for heavy guns. The men seemed to be working well. Things are very behindhand east of Kemmel but without men one can do nothing.

**Friday 14 July 1916** Have had no time to write. The 36th (Ulster) Div.* have been given us – I went over to see them yesterday. They had a real gruelling in the south, their casualties came to 5,500† which is over 50 per cent. I am told nothing would stop them and that, although very fine, is a danger in war. They are being given a fortnight's rest and will then have to come and give us a hand. The news today is very good, we have penetrated the enemy second system of defences in four places on a fairly broad front. It is not broad enough yet to do much good, but if the French come on on our right, the gap may be made fairly wide. A Cavalry patrol was used during the morning for the first time for about 18 months. The Germans still hammer at Verdun. I suppose they hope to keep the French there. They are certainly thinning their line everywhere else; we know that much.

**Sunday 16 July 1916** Got orders on the 15th that we were to move to 4th Army at once – so got busy to move HQ to Talmas today. We went on to 4th Army HQ at Querrieu – there I saw a whole host of old friends. They had several captured guns outside their HQ.– most of those taken have already been sent home. They told us that there were several 5.9 and 8in. guns yet to come in; this is the first time we have taken any of these. As far as I can make out, our present job here is to mother Divisions that have been pulled out of the line – we hoped we were going to be given fighting Divisions, but our time may come yet. At all events the Boche is very tired and we may have a great success. Tomorrow I hope to go joy riding and see some of the ground won.

**Monday 17 July 1916** A pig of a day – the Corps Commander* and I had intended to go and study the ground north of Mametz and had hoped for a fine clear day, but we were disappointed as it was hazy the whole afternoon. Anyhow we drove through Amiens and Albert to Fricourt. It was very interesting to be able to drive through No Man's Land and past the trenches so lately held by the Boche. We walked up to Mametz and then on to Montauban. Our guns had played great havoc in these places, there was hardly a square yard which had not been hit by a shell.

The German dug-outs were very interesting, very deep and although the entrances had been blocked up by the bombardment, a great many of them had held good. I went into one at Montauban which had evidently been the HQ and found a lot of maps of the country around Verdun. The German trenches were deep but, with the exception of the deep dug-outs under the parapet, there was no special feature. At Montauban the only thing that stood up was a small side chapel of the Church. The figure of the Virgin was there practically untouched: the single thing in such a mass of desolation. The German guns were active, there did not seem to be very many of them, but people who had been there the whole time told me their numbers had increased.

**Wednesday 19 July 1916** The Boche heavily counter attacked Delville Wood* last night and got into the northern portion of it. This is disappointing as the Wood is essential to us to cover our flank if we are going to attack eastwards towards Ginchy and Guillemont. Tonight the news is that we have got half of it back.

This afternoon I went with the Corps Commander through Albert on the Bapaume road and had a good look at La Boisselle and Ovillers – these villages are simply pulp but it is a strange thing how long the latter held out†. Then we went on to the high ground between Mesnil and Hamel and had a look at the Thiepval front. We got a very good view of Thiepval Wood – the Boche and our trenches. Thiepval is a very strong place and will need a lot of taking. There were alas! still signs of the struggle which took place there as, in certain areas, bodies could be seen lying in No Man's Land. We heard heavy fighting towards Longueval, but this evening's wire shows this to be German bombardment, but no Infantry attacks.

Today we have been appointed the mother of about seven Divisions – but most of these appointments have been cancelled, I am thankful to say. The Russians are getting on well – without being optimistic I think the Boche General Staff will have a great problem before them by next winter – I hope the gods of war will be on our side.

**Thursday 20 July 1916** Went to see David Campbell who commands 21st Div. and had a talk with him with reference to his attack on the north of Fricourt village. He had over 5,000 casualties in his Division. He was very interesting on the subject of whether Fricourt should have been attacked or not. His view was that it could have been taken in the first rush before the Boche had time to get his machine guns out of the dug-outs. Later it cost us a Battalion or more. Then went to see Mullens and the old [1st] Cav. Div. They considered that there was a great opportunity of using Cavalry on the day High Wood* was taken. On my way home saw my old Chief de Lisle, who has the 29th Div. He told me that his men were put up against a very hard nut and, although they attacked gallantly, were driven back by machine gun fire from the village of Beaumont and the attack failed.

**Saturday 22 July 1916** Went for a ride in the morning to see our Corps Cavalry. Do not think that Walters is any good. He is much too old-fashioned – we want young men in this war. The Australians* were attacking Pozieres whilst an attack on a big scale was being put forward by the 4th Army. I hope the Australian attack will succeed – I have seen a good many of them and they are a very fine body of men – what they need is good officers and discipline. Their NCO's are good and they all fight like tigers. However they drink a lot and are a nuisance in billets. I am told they get 6 shillings a day and are paid every fortnight – the result is a fortnightly bust when they can get it.

**Sunday 23 July 1916** Moved our HQ from Talmas to Villers-Bocage. The latter place is much more convenient in every way. So as to escape rush, went to see the Regiment. The Australians took most of Pozieres last night, but the remainder of the attack failed as far as I can make out; we may hear more news later. I hope so as we want to get the ridge whatever we do. Good news from Russia, they have taken another 12,000 prisoners* and, I hope, have killed a good many more.

**Monday 24 July 1916** Had a rotten day. Went into Amiens and saw an eye doctor who gave me a pair of specs. The first thing that I have got out of Government for nothing in my life. He says my eyes are quite sound but just want help at night and so on. Saw Caviare Cavendish who had just come back from French HQ. He said they were full of heart and very pleased and had lots of troops. I am glad to hear it and hope that they will attack soon and so help us. I wish we could go into the line, as it is very dull work administering troops, especially tired ones in the back areas.

**Tuesday 25 July 1916** Continued my voyages in search of information and lessons. Drew the Reserve Army first and saw Moses [Beddington]. The Australians hold the whole of Pozieres and this morning the Boche counter attack against the place was beaten back. Then went on to the 3rd Corps and saw Romer – they were not so happy as, although they had taken Munster Trench, they were once more turned out of it. The 15th Corps were quite happy and full of heart – I had lunch with Vaughan and an interesting talk on the subject of attacks. The Boche attack on Verdun has stopped at present. Our offensive was a good excuse to stop it. Hear the 14th* and the 8th Corps are changing places – I expect that the 14th will be glad to get out of the Ypres salient.

**Thursday 27 July 1916** Not very much news except that very hard fighting has been the rule – today we took Delville Wood and established ourselves in Munster Trench which will be a great help. Just now we are fighting very hard for the ridge which commands Courcelette, Martinpuich and Flers – when we have got that ridge we shall be able to prepare for a fresh advance. The French have not yet really moved on the north of the Somme – I hope that they will be able to push on a little. The weather is fine at last and we can use our planes. The cloudy weather of the last few days has been a disaster, as the Boche has been able to bring up and dig in new heavy guns without being observed.

**Friday 28 July 1916** Another fine day and we have retaken the whole of Longueval village. The Australians are attacking Windmill Ridge either today or tomorrow. Saw Dillon who is with the French Army — he says that they have lots of troops but will not move until their aeroplanes can work.

**Saturday 29 July 1916** Another fine day and good news from the Russian side that they have taken Brody and a goodly number of prisoners. The Boche has made no serious effort to recover Delville Wood — if we can only get the ridge, we shall have a good start for further operations. There is still the usual story that Rumania is coming in at once, but one cannot credit it as it has been said so often before. We have got a good few fresh Divisions coming down and I suppose we shall see some more attacks on a large scale. The Boche certainly shows some signs of weakening in front here as his counter attacks lack sting. Hope it is true. Tomorrow we attack Guillemont and the French are also putting in a big show. Hope it will be successful.

**Sunday 30 July 1916** Another glorious fine day but rather misty and therefore bad for aeroplane observation. I think that we hold Delville Wood securely now and the Boche does not attempt to recapture. A slight advance made today towards Guillemont and Ginchy — it is not very much but gives us a jumping-off place for a further attack. Saw aeroplane photos of Delville Wood before and after the fighting — there were no leaves left on the trees at all. At the last attack, Sir Henry Rawlinson told me that he had 386 guns on it. Hope that we shall get the ridge all right as then we can go on. The Russian news continues to be good and the Austrians and Germans towards Lemberg* are having a good knock, I only hope it will last.

**Monday 31 July 1916** Another change — we are now going to be under the Reserve Army (Gough) instead of the 10th Corps who take our place. Rode over in the morning to Beauquesne where the advanced GHQ are, to try and find out the reason for this. Got no change at all except guessed it was a personal matter between Goughie and Morland*. It is such a pity that G.† is so quarrelsome and feel I should keep him in better order. They seem to be fairly satisfied as to the general situation there and agreed that we must keep hammering away here. They seem to think that the Boche have had pretty heavy losses.

**Tuesday 1 August 1916** Moved today from Villers-Bocage to Domart-en-Ponthieu and are now under the Reserve Army. I don't like this place nearly so much as the last. It is in a hollow and rather smelly. We have the 48th Div.* — Fanshawe commanding and Hanway Cumming as GSO(1) — and the 3rd Cav.Div. under us. It is a poor game this sitting at the back, but they are quite right not to change Corps HQ in the fighting line unless absolutely necessary.

Had a long talk with Morris who has been examining Boche prisoners. He is of course pessimistic; he says their morale is good and they still think that they are going to win the war. There is a very large concentration of German troops and guns opposite us here but that to my mind is a good thing, because if a crack does occur, it will not merely be a rift but a chasm. The French ought now to be able to make themselves felt. As far as one can tell, they ought to be able to put in 15 to 20 Divisions at any given point. This has great possibilities. If the Boche has every available gun between the Aisne and the Somme, then a thrust about 15 miles south should be of some use and would be successful: it would come as a surprise and there would be few guns to oppose it. I do not know if this is contemplated but, given the necessary force and a **fair** amount of guns, it should be quite possible.

**Wednesday 2 August 1916** Another boiling hot day. The Reserve Army are issuing armsfull of paper — most of it is stale news — but it takes a lot of time reading it all through. Went for a good walk after tea. Wish they would put us into the line and then we would be busy — but I am afraid they won't as we are too new.

**Saturday 5 August 1916** Have not had much time to write up my Diary the last two days. Slow but good progress has been made on our front. Today we have heard that the Australians have got the windmill which lies north of Pozieres and that gives them a footing on the main ridge, which is a decided step forward. The French have also been very active. We hear that one Division has gone east to fight against the Russians, but I don't think that the Germans can afford to send many more provided we keep up the pressure here.

Went to Reserve Army HQ last night and saw Neil Malcolm. He said there was a strong rumour that Bulgaria had had enough of it and was now seeing what she could make out of the Entente powers* – it would be very like her, but I shall not believe it until it is a fait accompli. These Balkan races are treacherous brutes. Goughie is full of energy and keeps his Staff very busy – rather too busy as of late we have been having some rather ill-considered masses of paper.

**Monday 7 August 1916** Things seem to be going well, if slowly, and everyone seems to be very satisfied. We are continually making ground and also killing Boches, that is the main thing. Just heard of the Turkish attack on the Suez Canal*. They ought to mop up the whole crowd with any luck – that is the place to be with Cavalry and they ought to have the chance of a lifetime in rounding them up. It is a German plan of course. How it ever could hope to succeed I don't know and how they got heavy guns across the desert is another question. But the Turks are getting left now, as will all the Boche Allies – they have made a good bid for the mastery of the world and have been beaten by the sea.

Went out and watched our Cavalry working this morning and then went over and lunched with Cavan (14th Corps). I have to inspect their Corps Cavalry this week. It is a beastly job as the commanders have been pitchforked out from home. They are mostly old men who have influence – I am told that as soon as it was known that there were to be Corps Cavalry Regiments out here, the wire pulling began. The result will be that a good many of them will have to be sent home again.

**Tuesday 8 August 1916** Spent the morning watching the Corps Cavalry doing a Scheme. Good news from the Russians again today, they have got another batch of 8,000 prisoners. Of this number 2,000 are said to be Germans, which looks as if Germany was once more trying to bolster up the Austrian Armies without much success. Weather here is still fine and we are getting on slowly – the French appear to be gaining ground at Verdun* too. We are in for another winter campaign but next year should see the end of it.

**Wednesday 9 August 1916** The Italians seem to be going forward and taking some prisoners*; this is really the first time they have done anything. The news on our right is not so satisfactory – we do not seem to be able to take Guillemont village – there must be some special reason for this and I will send to find it out. We have met with greater difficulty in this quarter than everywhere else. Of course there is a large concentration of guns behind the enemy line in this direction, but we can also mass a larger number of guns and so we ought to be able to take it. It means a great deal to us, I think, and it is a necessary step for a further advance.

Have been out all day with the Corps Cavalry Regiment working out a Scheme – am getting very tired of being back here with no particular job except inspecting Corps Cavalry. I should like to be given a chance in the line so that one can see if one is any good as a BG.GS of a Corps and if one's ideas are right, but no such luck at present.

**Friday 11 August 1916** Spent the last two days inspecting the Corps Cavalry Regiment of the 14th Corps and am glad that it is over. I hate inspecting work, but it had some interesat to get back to the Cavalry again. They were not up to much and had some very old men in them. We have established ourselves on the Pozieres ridge, which is a good thing. I think that a big attack on the whole front might now do some good and we might get well forward by means of it. Have just heard that the French have again got on just north of the Somme, the Boche seems to trust more and more to his machine guns opposite the French and he seems to put the men in opposite our front. I think that he is losing pretty heavily.

**Monday 14 August 1916** A great many changes in the last three days. We are back to Bailleul again and in the line. I am thankful as one is doing something instead of shepherding tired Divisions which was no catch at all. Here we are holding a front of 15 miles with three Divisions – from the Lys River to the Vierstraat road. We are getting the 4th Canadian Div.*

shortly and so then we shall have some Reserves. At present the line is pretty thin, but I don't think there is very much of a chance of attack as things stand at present. I am glad to get out of the Reserve Army, I think that they worry one unnecessarily.

The King has been here today and has been inspecting some men of the 19th† and 36th [Ulster] Divs. They all lunched in our HQ and so things have been pretty upside down. Saw Tiny Ironside who is now GSO(1) of the 4th Canadian Div. – he says that they are a splendid body of men and much better disciplined than the first lot that came out. He has been training them for the last four months.

**Friday 18 August 1916** Have been very busy. We are holding a very long front and, as far as I can see, we shall continue holding it. It makes the work very much more difficult as it takes a long time to cover the front. We are still sending Divisions south. The Canadians are being pulled out of the line and will relieve the Australians on the Somme. I wonder if they are going to put in a push on a large scale both north and south of the Aisne? It might succeed and make a real good hole in the line, as a surprise might be effected north of the Ancre.

The situation here is very quiet. The Germans seem to be very much on the qui vive, but are not at all active – we have taken several prisoners in No Man's Land, but do not get much information out of them. Their morale is quite good, but they now say that the war will be a drawn war and we shall never turn them out of their present lines. It is a significant change as before they always said that they must win. The weather continues to be fine and that helps us a good deal – we are half preparing for a winter here already; our lines are not good and want a lot of work on them. Have not yet had an opportunity of walking round them.

**Monday 21 August 1916** Too busy to keep a daily Diary. Went round trenches of 23rd Div.* on 19th, they are good and the Division is lucky to get them. On Sunday attended a music Mass at the old Church at Bailleul and there was a collection for the poor families of French soldiers in the occupied area. The collection was made by young ladies of Bailleul and each young lady was accompanied by a British Officer – no Generals allowed! The Staff sat on one side of the chancel and the Mayor and local authorities on the other. It was very peaceful in the old church and it is one of the few quiet moments one has had for a long time. Went back to war and walked round the 56th Div. trenches today – they are a bad line of trenches and have not had time to get them right.

**Wednesday 23 August 1916** Cecil Howard came in from GHQ – he said that GHQ were satisfied with the progress. I asked how long we were going on, he intimated we could not stop as long as the Russians were pushing – so that gives a clear idea of the situation and a right one to my mind. The Boche has sent away about 1½ Divisions to the Russian front and we must stop him from sending any more. The talk is once more that Rumania comes in, the date given being the 28th*. Our front is very quiet just now and I think the Boche is hard put to it with all the fighting on the Somme and Verdun. I don't think the line will snap as people at home think, but the war is steadily going in our favour.

**Friday 25 August 1916** Nearly had some excitement yesterday morning. We have very little luck as the Boche found one of our shafts under Petite Douve Farm, which is 20 feet below the surface, and we thought we should have to blow our mine. Anyhow, something will have to be done and I am in favour of blowing it up, if we can induce the Boche to thicken up his parapet at that point. It is not an easy thing to do – on the other hand it is no good wasting the mine if we are not going to catch any Boches. Personally I am in favour of blowing the mine on the first possible opportunity as the Boche is now bound to find it and it will be wasted. In the afternoon went up to Kemmel with the General to watch a straff with some heavy guns and trench mortars. It was a lovely clear afternoon. The shooting appeared to be fairly good, but it was difficult to judge.

Today walked round the subsidiary line. Drove out to Hyde Park Corner in the Ploegsteert Wood – Lewenden did not recognise the place which was within 200 yards of where he was hit nearly two years ago*. He was much interested when I told him. Inspected the defences of Hill 63 and Wulvergem and went up to the old estaminet on the Wulvergem-Messines road where we had our HQ with the 1st Cav. Div. in October 1914 and out of which I was blown†. The walls were still standing on one side and that is all one can say about it.

**Friday 1 September 1916** Have had no time to write up the Diary as I have been very busy. Have got round a good bit of the line and know it more or less now. Had two gas attacks, one on the night of the 30th and the second last night. The former was I think quite successful, the latter a great failure. The gas came back, owing to a change of wind, and we had over a hundred casualties. I think there must have been gross neglect on the part of the officers in the trenches, especially as the men were allowed to walk [back?] with their packs on*. The gas has evidently great power and the action comes on after 12 hours sometimes. It is horrible to think of this war and all these beastly things.

Yesterday Kavanagh commanding the 1st Corps came up to see me – I could not make out why [he was coming]. He told me that GHQ were very sanguine of success and that they thought a big attack or two might succeed – they were therefore going to put the five Cavalry Divisions under a commander; he was going to be given command and I was to do Chief of the Staff to him. It is only a temporary thing – they are going to resuscitate the old Cavalry Corps, but it will be five Divisions instead of three. It is, of course, the chance of a lifetime and, if one can only get on the move, it is the one thing one has dreamt of but never thought possible. I wonder if the old Cavalry will come into its own at last. To be with it if it does, will be stupendous. I am glad Kavanagh is going to command as he is a real leader of men and knows his job, has a mind of his own. Today he wired me it is all settled and we collect on Monday. Longmore comes as DA.QMG† – he is an old friend. Chance, Heydeman are also well known to me.

**Saturday 2 September 1916** Our gas casualties have now mounted to 200 – it is very sickening as the wind changed only for a matter of a few seconds – it shows the potency of the gas. Saw Harrington today and heard that it is settled that I go down to the Cavalry for the proposed operations.

# 9. The Cavalry Corps Revived

**Friday 8 September 1916** Back to the Cavalry Corps once more and was much touched by the greetings of many old friends – it is very nice to be amongst the old Cavalry once more. We are going to have all five Divisions and it will be a great day for us when we get going. Full of work getting things ready. Saw the new tanks* today; they are wonderful machines – real ironclads on land – they ought to be a success.

**Friday 15 September 1916** The last week has been full of work and last night our Divisions moved into position: 1st Cav. Div. at Carnoy; 2nd Indian Cav. Div. near Mametz; 2nd Cav. Div. about Bray-sur-Somme; the 1st Indians south of Dernancourt; and the 3rd Cav. Div. north-east of Corbie. We came up to our advanced report centre just south of Carnoy at 6.00 pm last night. The attack was timed to reach its final objective about mid-day, but the 6th Div. were held up east of Ginchy and the Boche in High Wood held out well. We have made good progress but I don't think there is much chance of the Cavalry being used today. Of course, everyone in high places was very optimistic and they thought that the chance would come. It may still come tomorrow, but today it is getting a little bit late for a large forward movement.

It would appear that if the Cavalry does not get a chance this time it will be the end of them. I suppose that people at home are howling about expense and so on. Today we used the tanks for the first time: these are armoured cars carrying 6pdrs and machine guns. They appear to have been very successful in some places especially towards Flers. High Wood has been a hard nut but we have got it at last. We now hold most of the ridge – I shall be very sorry if we don't get a chance this time, but it may come later when we least expect it.

**Saturday 16 September 1916** Yesterday we had a fair day. We made a big advance all along our front and took the villages of Courcelette, Martinpuich and Flers. It was however not quite good enough from the Cavalry point of view and we had no chance of doing anything. We took over 2,500 prisoners and the losses must have been pretty heavy. This morning we attacked again the villages of Lesboeufs and Gueudecourt, but I am afraid we shall not have much chance as we are to all practical purposes attacking with the same troops as before and one day's work often takes the sting out of them. Our men have done splendidly and the Boche has fought well. The reason why our success was not greater yesterday was owing to the failure of the 6th Div. to take the Quadrilateral*. They say that the Artillery failed them and that the 6th Div. Artillery was taken to support the attack of the Guards Div., but that is only gup†. I saw a kite balloon brought down yesterday and the man came down in the  parachute which was very interesting. He got down quite safely.

**Monday 18 September 1916** Today my spirits are down to zero. The glass fell very rapidly last night and it has been pouring with rain since the early morning. The 6th Div. attacked the

Quadrilateral and took it quite easily with a lot of prisoners as well. Then came the news that Morval was unoccupied and so two squadrons of Cavalry were sent up. Of course when they got up there they found it was occupied. I think the Germans were surprised, they did not expect an attack on such a filthy morning, and so the line south of Morval may have been temporarily unheld. But it raised a great flutter in the Dovecots.

I cannot help thinking that we want more fresh troops here before we can break the line, also we must make an attack as the same time as the French so as to drive the Boche back on a broad front. I am afraid that the French are very difficult to deal with. I certainly think they are very jealous especially in the higher command. If we can only bring off a combined effort it might succeed. There is no doubt in my mind that the Boche is deteriorating – his counter attacks lack sting and I also think he is tired. Prisoners are not so confident of winning the war now as they were. His whole attitude is chastened.

The country at the rear of the battle line and where our HQ are, is a wonderful sight – just masses of men and horses and vehicles and motors. The land is black with them, yet by organisation they are all fed daily and so on. The railways are being pushed forward and are within two miles of the line of battle; water in pipes is laid, in one place, to within 600 yards of the front trenches. The tanks have as a whole been a success*, the idea will probably be developed and we shall come back to the steel armour on land once more. This time it will be petrol driven, as opposed to the horse of the old days. We must pray for fine weather now – it may rain itself out.

**Tuesday 19 September 1916** Rain in the early morning but it cleared later and, with a north wind, looks like being fine. But the rain has put our attack back 48 hours at the least. ttended a conference of Corps Commanders this morning at 15th Corps HQ at Heilly. I do not think the atmosphere was as optimistic as usual, but of course super optimism reigns there as a rule. I think our next attack will not produce anything for the Cavalry, as the new Transloy line* blocks the way. Of course if the French take Sailly-Saillisel it may help.

**Tuesday 21 September 1916** Yesterday the Boche evidently brought up some reinforcements by train and put in a very strong attack against the French between Rancourt and the Somme – it lasted the whole morning. According to French accounts, it failed everywhere with heavy losses for the Germans. I hope the Boche will go on with their attacks; they are very costly. He also attacked us just north of Flers and was again beaten back.

We are moving back the 1st and 3rd Cav.Divs and later the 2nd and 1st Indians to the area between St Riquier and St Pol-sur-Ternoise. But the Corps is to remain at the present, so I suppose that further operations are contemplated. I hope they are as it is only by hammering away at the Boche that we shall be able to do him some harm. It is sad for the Cavalry having to wait and the men feel it very much, but I am certain that their time will come.

**Friday 22 September 1916** Went out for a walk to reconnoitre the ground towards Flers and walked to the Switch trench between Delville and High Wood. It is from here that one can see the value of the ridge we have gained and the reason that the Boche hung on to it. The ground on the other side lies in front of it like an amphitheatre: Le Sars, Le Barque, Ligny-Thilloy, Beaulencourt could be easily seen and identified. The ground is open and even in its present state of shell holes could be quickly crossed by Cavalry in open order.

Dolly Baird came with me. He was in High Wood at the beginning of the Somme Battle and was very interesting on the defence of the wood. The New Zealand Div.* were holding this part of the line and nice cheery devils they were, only wanting a couple of days' rest before they had another go. One of them told me that the Boche was getting the better of them in a bombing match, so they just fixed bayonets and went at them across the open and the Boche bolted. That is the spirit which will win the war. A good many dead still waiting to be buried† and it is never a nice scene in cold blood.

**Sunday 24 September 1916** The weather has continued fine and we kick off for the attack on the villages of Morval, Lesboeufs and Gueudecourt at 12.35 pm tomorrow. The French attack south of us at the same time. I don't think the Cavalry can have anything but a very small show; it might get a squadron through and do some damage, but I am not very sanguine. The attack will be on a fairly wide front if we include the French attack, so the unexpected may happen as it often does.

**Monday 25 September 1916** Another most disappointing day for the Cavalry – we had the 1st Indian Cav.Div. all up ready with Neil Haig commanding the leading Brigade. The attack went splendidly, except at the point at which we hoped to push through. The Guards took Lesboeufs and the 15th Div. Morval – we got two battalions into Gueudecourt but were beaten back again. The French took Rancourt and advanced towards Fregicourt. It can be looked on as a successful day as a whole except for the Cavalry. My heart bleeds for them. All they want is a chance and yet, as today, the chance was very near but just out of reach. Kavanagh is a brick, he is very disappointed but does not show it at all. I suppose we shall now move backwards until the next big attack. I am certain that Douglas Haig means to go on pushing and if so our chance will come yet.

**Wednesday 27 September 1916** Yesterday we took Gueudecourt village and at last the Reserve Army took Thiepval, it has held out for a long time. Of course all was excitement. The young Observing Officer said he saw Cavalry north of Gueudecourt and the next minute the tale went round that a Brigade of Cavalry had gone through. What a time for excitable people! We took a lot of prisoners yesterday, nearly 3,000 – I do not think the Boche is fighting as well as he usually does, I hope that this means that he is weakening. Of course now we are his equal, or possibly his superior, in guns and he does not like shell fire any more than anyone else.

This morning we walked out to the ridge east of Maricourt – one gets a good view from there as far as Peronne. The French were shelling Mont-St-Quentin hard and I think that they mean having that place. Today we have got orders to go right back for a time, it is only I hope for a time. I heard today from Jock Stuart that my place with the 9th Corps has been filled up. I am very annoyed as I once more become a wanderer.

**Friday 29 September 1916** Moved Corps HQ to Daours and we are all going back again in about 10 days' time for another big attack, I hope. All things point to a successful ending to the Somme Battle, that is a good gain of ground and a heightened morale and a correspondent decrease of the enemy. Aeroplanes have been coming over our camp at night on the plateau and last night one bomb killed 60 horses about 500 yards away. The weather looks like changing for the worse, but I hope it won't.

Moved today to our new HQ at the chateau at Regnière-Ecluse just north of the Forest of Crecy. I got a good bed and sheets which are always good to come back to. Went into GHQ and saw Jock Stuart. They are all working hard to revive the Cavalry Corps. I would rather spend the winter with an Infantry Corps and come back to the Cavalry Corps for the spring offensive, as I don't fancy spending the winter in the back areas.

**Saturday 30 September 1916** Went into advanced GHQ and had lunch with Sir Douglas Haig. Had a very interesting conference after lunch when D.H. explained his views on the possible uses of Cavalry during the big attacks which are to take place this month. They seem to take a very optimistic view of things at GHQ so that is good.

**Sunday 1 October 1916** Rode out to the coast this morning with a view to seeing what the ground was like for training. The sand dunes are all enclosed here with a wire fence and it looks as if they were being used as a rabbit farm!!! But the sands are quite firm and hard. It was a lovely morning for a ride and I enjoyed it very much. I hate being back here and hope we may move forward again soon. There is no news today but we keep on making ground north of Courcelette which is all going to help. The Boche is, I think, concentrating all his effort against Rumania, so as to keep his communications with Turkey open.

**Tuesday 3 October 1916** Went out yesterday to do a reconnaissance of the enemy line between Leer and Hamel. It was a beastly day pouring with rain and became worse instead of better so did not see much although we went forward to an O.P.[Observation Post] just south of Hebuterne. Today motored over and saw 3rd Cav.Div. with reference to future operations.

It cleared up about lunch time – so went for a ride in the Forest of Crecy. It was very nice but rather soft. Saw some deer and the rootings of the wild pig.

**Wednesday 4 October 1916** Had a long day in the car – started out in the morning to see 1st Div. carry out a Scheme, but it was pouring with rain so it was not possible to carry it out. We then went on to the Reserve Army and discussed the possible uses of Cavalry with Goughie, then on to the 4th Army to arrange details in that area. There we got a message to say that Kiggel wanted to see us at GHQ, so we went off again. They are very optimistic at GHQ and still hope to bag the Boche in the Monchy-au-Bois salient this year – it will be a decisive success if we do. The weather at present is however against active operations.

**Monday 8 October 1916** Went to watch a Scheme which was being carried out by the 2nd Indian Cav.Div. yesterday. I think the Cavalry were slow but we can trust Macandrew to speed them up. I do not know what is the cause of it, but the slowness is remarkable. It may be the result of inaction and trench warfare. In the afternoon we had to go and see Trenchard of the R.F.C. at Fienvillers. The Germans have got a new machine* which is very fast and a fast climber so we shall have to look out.

We carried out a biggish attack so as to take Le Sars and establish ourselves on an intermediate line north of Gueudecourt and east of Lesboeufs so as later to take on the Le Transloy line – the French attacked towards Sailly-Saillisel. The weather has been vile and the difficulties of bringing up ammunition enormous. I also think that our Armies are beginning to feel the results of the Somme Battle. No troops in the world could have fought better than ours, but when Divisions go into the attack three or four times in the space of 2½ months, it is bound to affect their spring. The big attack has been put off and we can only pray for fine dry weather.

**Tuesday 10 October 1916** Yesterday motored up to see the 2nd Cav.Div. on the plateau south of Carnoy – I have never seen anything like the mud in all my life; motor lorries stuck in all sorts of places. Philip Chetwode quite cheery and busy taking up gun ammunition on our pack horses. It was impossible to get wagons up even with 10 horses in them. But the guns were firing merrily over in front of Goughie's Army. Today I went to see a Scheme by the 1st Indian Cav.Div. Our Cavalry has got slow, it wants a lot of speeding up. They want ginger and to forget that such things as trenches exist.

**Friday 13 October 1916** Spent the last few days in watching the training of the Divisions. We put in a big attack yesterday in order to get jumping off place for the final attack on the Le Transloy to Ligny-Thilloy line, but I am afraid that it was not a success; in fact we made very little progress indeed and, in these attacks, lack of success means very heavy losses. It looks as if the Boche has had breathing space and has recovered himself somewhat. I am sorry as it puts off the chance of the use of Cavalry. I hear that the Corps is going to be kept on through the winter which is not a pleasant outlook for me as it means doing training the whole time, instead of having a line of trenches to look after. I don't think that we shall break through the line now as it is getting late and we shall have the weather and mud against us. I think that many people little realise how close we have been to it once or twice, but history will show that.

**Sunday 15 October 1916** Had to go into GHQ and so had lunch with Barnett Stuart. He was very interesting on the subject of ammunition and the amount we are using daily. Had a long talk with him as regards the future and it appears that in guns and ammunition we are increasing in strength by leaps and bounds. Let us hope it will end the war soon.

**Monday 16 October 1916** Gough with the Reserve Army is going to attack north and south of the Ancre on the 23rd. We are putting up the 1st Cav.Div. to help if required. I got the idea that this attack was the result of political agitation and that the Boche had been spreading his peace propaganda in southern France – offering France Alsace-Lorraine and the evacuation of Belgium. A clever move as there is no war down there and the terms are, on the face of it, good. It shows, however, a decided weakening on the part of Germany and would not suit some parties in that country.

**Wednesday 18 October 1916** We made an attack this morning from Lesboeufs, Gueude-court and east of Le Sars. Although we made some ground we did not make enough and in some places that attack appears to have failed. There is no getting away from the fact that our last few attacks have not been as successful as they might have been. I can see no reasons for this except that, once again, the Boche has slightly the better of the ground and of course the difficulties of bringing up ammunition are great. It seems that we shall now have to fight for the high ground so as to make the best for winter quarters.

The Cavalry Corps is officially once more in being and I suppose we shall all be confirmed in our appointments. I think that Kavanagh is the one man to carry the job through. It is a big command, consisting of five Divisions of Cavalry or 153 squadrons. It has great possibilities as, if things went well, we might find the Cavalry from Egypt coming here during the spring. The Rumanian fighting is disappointing* – I had hopes that she would be able to do more than she has done as I want to see Turkey severed from the Central Powers, but I am certain that the end will come on this front and on no other.

**Saturday 21 October 1916** The 1st Cav.Div. are moving forward to be under Gough for the 25th when he attacks north and south of the Ancre with a view to pinching the Boche in the valley. He ought to make a good bag if he is successful. Baird came back from home and said a great conference taking place at Boulogne: D.H., Asquith, Balfour, Lloyd George and the whole crowd. Wonder what is up – German peace kites I should think. The weather is very fine again, but I think the cold is affecting the natives in the Indian Cavalry Regiments. It was bitterly cold last night, and a heavy white frost this morning.

**Sunday 22 October 1916** Good news today – Gough got his objective and 800 prisoners. The Germans made many attacks on Sailly-Saillisel and they were all beaten back, so they must have lost heavily. Another white frost last night and a clear day today, but very cold – the men in the trenches must be feeling it a good deal.

**Tuesday 24 October 1916** Had lunch with Gough in order to discuss the use of Cavalry in the next attack – He was very pleased with his last attack.

Today I had to go into GHQ as regards our winter billeting areas. It is the usual story of changes and counter changes, but I hope to get things settled. The attack on the north and south of the Ancre has been put off 48 hours and will now take place on the 28th. We shall hold a watching brief unless everything goes better than the programme – then we may have an opportunity for doing a limited amount of work. I don't think, however, that the weather will allow us to do very much. It has been pouring with rain for the last 36 hours.

**Thursday 26 October 1916** Another two days' rain and the attack of the Reserve Army has been put off till the 30th. The French have made a brilliant attack at Verdun and have retaken Deulemont. I saw Eric Dillon last night at the HQ of the 4th Army – he told me that the French had taken in two hours what it took the Boche two months to take. 4,600 prisoners, including many senior Officers, shows how great the surprise was and it also shows a lowered morale on the Boche side. It would be a great **victory** if only Rumania had been able to hold her own; as it stands now it is counteracted by the Boche success against the Rumanians. Yesterday on our way to the 4th Army at Querrieu our Rolls Royce broke a back axle. Luckily a hospital was near so we continued our journey in a Ford Ambulance: the sublime to the ridiculous – a limousine to an ambulance!

**Sunday 29 October 1916** Went to the Carnoy plateau and saw Philip Chetwode and HQ 2nd Cav.Div. – took four hours getting there. Met a whole Australian Division in French buses and they fairly blocked up the road. Took over three hours getting back. The mud up there is awful – horses simply are over their hocks in it. I saw ammunition going up: eight horses with a limber [for] 58 rounds. But the men were cheerful and looked well in spite of everything. I am sorry to say that I came to the conclusion that the Cavalry as a mass cannot be employed before next spring. I don't believe horses would get through the mud and, if they did, they would be stone cold after a very short time. Who knows that this rain may not be for the best?

The longer the Boche holds out the greater will be the smash. I think the attack projected originally for the 28th would have succeeded and it is hard to be stopped by the weather.

Yesterday went down to inspect part of the Canadian Bde* under Seely. The whole thing [is] a failure, the material is excellent but with such a Brigadier the thing is impossible. We asked him to review the operations and he made a speech which was useless from a military point of view. He ought to go back to politics, that is his proper sphere. Honest downrightness is what is wanted with soldiers, not fine phrasing and verbiage. The weather has been appalling. We go forward over bad ground whilst the Boche retreats on to good ground and we have the worst of it. All day long we must plaster the Boche front trenches and all night the approaches to them so that they cannot get hot food up to them. If that is done, they will surrender in shoals.

**Tuesday 31 October 1916** The weather is still stopping all operations except very minor ones and I fancy is beginning to tell on the troops on both sides. The country is just one sea of mud in places feet deep – horses and men simply get bogged and cannot move. The Rumanians seem to have taken a pull or perhaps the Russians have come down to help them; at all events it does not look as if the Central Powers were going to over-run Rumania in the same way as they did Belgium and Servia, at least let us hope so*.

Gough's attack is now dated for the 5th. If a great and unexpected success is not gained there the Cavalry will be withdrawn to winter areas. The horses are beginning to feel it a good deal and we must look after them if they are to be of use later on. If you think you may want Cavalry, it must be kept in a glass cage till the day arrives, no half measures are of any use. Bad Cavalry will never turn a success into a decisive victory. Young Officers do not understand this.

**Thursday 2 November 1916** The weather is still very bad. Yesterday we went and saw the Canadian Brigade on the march, commanded by Seely. I have never seen such a show, it was very bad. Today we went to see a couple of Brigades of the 1st Indian Cav.Div. They were all right and the horses looked very well. We have all been confirmed as Cavalry Corps Staff, so now we know where we stand. We shall have another winter of training to do.

**Saturday 4 November 1916** Went down with the Corps Commander to see the 2nd Cav.Div. which is out in the open just south of Meaulte. They have been having a pretty bad time as regards weather and a good few casualties* owing to the mud pulling the shoes off. They were all very cheery however and the horses were looking well considering the circumstances. Today I went to see the 1st Cav.Div. and had tea with the Regiment. All was well with them except they hate this waiting. The Italians have made another good push† – the turn of the tide will be slow, but it will be certain.

**Monday 6 November 1916** A couple of days of gales and storms. This morning we made a couple of small attacks – we took the Butte de Warlencourt, but were beaten out of it by a counter attack. The 1st Guards Reserve Div. had been brought in and were fresh.

However unpleasant it is to think about, Napolean's fifth element 'mud' is now victorious and we shall have to go into winter quarters. I don't mean that we are to sit down and do nothing, but that an offensive on a large scale is out of the question. It is now a great labour to get supplies up to the men in the front trenches – to say nothing of ammunition for the guns. Guns cannot be moved at all. Men fall into shell holes full of liquid mud and are drowned – horses stick in the mud and have to be shot. As regards the wounded, it is terrible. They cannot be got back by day in some places and so their sufferings are increased many times. People can have no conception of what this warfare means. We shall win through however in time; this is the one consolation. There is a gale in the Channel with a record low barometer – mines get loose and so no boats are running and we have no letters.

**Thursday 9 November 1916** A couple of days of appalling weather and at last a fine day today. Had a long conference yesterday morning and in the afternoon the Corps Commander addressed the Canadian Bde on the subject of Discipline – they want it badly. It was a good

126

straight talk of a soldier and must have been very different from the political jargon of Seely. I think that it will do a lot of good.

Everything has come to a standstill just now owing to the mud. I think we shall have some very strong counter attacks from the Boche shortly as he is not likely to leave us in undisputed possession of the ground we have won. The situation in Rumania* I do not like at all. I hear that we are sending out another Division to Salonika which looks as if they wanted help out there. I am certain that the Turk will have another go at the Suez Canal in the early part of next year. He will be pushed on by the Boche to do this so as to prevent us taking troops away from Egypt and bringing them to France.

**Friday 10 November 1916** A fine day at last and the country is drying up fine. The Reserve Army attack may come off on the 13th after all. Leave has opened again and we are a very small party.

**Monday 13 November 1916** Gough attacked this morning* and we have heard that he has already got over 2,000 prisoners which is very good – south of the Ancre they appear to have got all their objectives – north of the Ancre the situation is not yet quite clear. It looks like a very successful operation. The Rumanian situation looks a little better and I think they are settling down to it. The Servians have again made ground† and taken 600 prisoners. It is very dull back here with the Cavalry. We have got all our Divisions back now and they are busy settling into their winter quarters – then we shall be able to commence some training. A great deal will be required from the Cavalry next Spring and I hope that they all realise it.

**Tuesday 14 November 1916** Everyone very pleased with the success of Gough's attack – over 4,000 prisoners taken up to the present and the Boche has lost his good deep dug-outs for the winter, a thing which he hates more than anything else.

**Wednesday 15 November 1916** Another fine day and more prisoners reported taken by Gough's Army. Rode round to the 2nd Cav.Div. at Ligescourt in the morning. There is a most persistant talk of intrigues at home to oust D.H. and L.G.* and Lord F.† and W.C.‡ are all mentioned as being in it. I suppose if there is any truth in it, it must be because D.H is too strong a man for them. The successors to D.H. suggested are Ian H.§ and Gough – two men as poles apart. The story of the latter being a favourite is too comic as I don't think they could ever make him do what they wanted. But one hears whispers such as 'a useless waste of life in this offensive with nothing to show for it'!!! Again I must hope that it is pure gossip, such a thing at this period is unthinkable.

**Friday 17 November 1916** Beautifully fine weather but very cold with a bitter east wind. It feels more like snow than anything else. From all accounts the attack of the 13th seems to have struck whilst a relief was being carried out and so they got a double bag of prisoners. It is a great pity that the attack on Serre failed. It is a very strong place, but Bob [Greenly] told me that it could be taken all right. I suppose we are certain to have a go at it later on. Our Pioneer Battalions start going out very soon now – I hope they will not have too many casualties among them.

**Sunday 19 November 1916** Yesterday I went to the HQ of the 4th and 5th Armies to arrange about our Pioneer Battalions which are going to them. It was a beast of a day raining hard. The 5th Army attacked yesterday so as to get the ridge just east of Beaumont to Hamel. South of the Ancre the Canadians took their objective and about 1,000 prisoners, but north of the Ancre not very much progress was made. Today I went to see Macandrew – he has decided that he must get rid of Seely from the Canadian Brigade as he is doing no good. I quite agree with him. One has to go carefully however; he has been told that his proper place is with the Government at home and, if he won't do that, we shall have to say that he is no use. I do not like the Rumanian situation* at all. I do not think we should allow Rumania to be over-run and Russia should help, perhaps she is doing so.†

**Saturday 2 December 1916** Returned from home today after a week's leave. I think that everyone at home is very depressed owing to the German successes in Rumania*. Many rumours are flying about us as to the cause of it – Russians and Rumanians being both accused of not playing the game. Had a good journey out here and a smooth crossing for which I was grateful.

**Wednesday 6 December 1916** Have had a busy time. GHQ and the French are a nuisance as they cannot make up their minds whether we are to move two Divs down to the Le Mans area or not. I hope that they will not send any of them as that will upset everything. All our stables are built and our Schools* are running. People spend a lot of private money to make the men comfortable and that will all be wasted. It will put the training back a good deal.

We have heard today that Asquith has resigned. I am only a soldier, but we want a man at the head of affairs who will make decisions when necessary and will not shake the hand of rebels against King and Country†. I think it must be for the good. At a critical period like this, we cannot be ruled by men who think of votes or the way people will vote after the war. We want a dictatorship, which will give us the means to finish the war quickly. We want men and why not get Irish compulsion? A man who says we can do without the Irish men is a renegade. Enough of politics. Went down and inspected the Fort Garry Horse in marching order. They are Canadians and belong to Seely's Brigade. It was a good turn out and a great improvement.

**Sunday 10 December 1916** Have been busy and so no Diary. On Thursday [7th] rode over to watch some camouflage experiments for Hotchkiss guns. The experiments were a success and I think that there are great possibilities. On Saturday attended a conference at Roëllencourt and saw a lot of old friends. Heard a story of the Grecian show: the French Admiral* evidently made a mess of things, he had an interview with Tino and told him of the arrangements. The result was that there were machine guns firing down all the roads along which the leading parties were going to move and there must have been some casualties. I do not like the Rumanian show as the Boche will certainly turn against the Salonika forces next – it is the best military thing to do.

**Tuesday 12 December 1916** Have been busy, but no news of any importance. Tha chances are that we have to move two, or perhaps three, Divisions south to an area about Le Mans. It will be an awful nuisance, but the reason is the scarcity of rolling stock; it will save about 300 tons daily. I shall probably have togo down and make a reconnaissance of the area. I don't suppose we shall change our HQ, but I don't quite know how we shall get the work done.

Yesterday the CC* and I went to see our men working in the front areas. It was a real pig of a day snowing and very cold. The men forward are none too well off; they have had about 60 casualties which is quite heavy. The mud as usual was awful – the men were quite cheery on the whole: they are wonders.

**Friday 15 December 1916** Started off to the Department of the Orne to carry out a reconnaissance for the moving of two or three Divisions down there. It is a beastly day raining and snowing. We went by Abbeville and Rouen – about 160 miles. From Rouen we went south to Alenc›,on which was our destination. We got there at 4.30 pm having started at 8.00 am. We first visited the General commanding*, who was a dear old gentleman but very voluble. He had done a great deal to help us as regards the billeting areas. This Department of the Orne is very like England; it is grazing country – all grassland and hedges and very unlike the rest of France. It must be very beautiful in summer.

**Saturday 16 December 1916** We went round the area and saw the country generally. It is really a lovely country. I think we shall have difficulty in billeting here as the farms are very small and have no great accommodation. We are accompanied by a very nice French Captain named Huerré, who comes from Paris and is on the Staff to the Ministre de la Guerre.

**Sunday 17 December 1916** Spent another day going round the areas. It was interesting to see the men wearing the old–fashioned smock. I think they are a simple and thrifty race. On my return had to pay a state visit to the Prefect of the Department. His name was Robert Lencone and he was a very charming man and said all the nice things he could in a way only a

Frenchman can. Luckily the great French success at Verdun* gave a topic of conversation which was not too hopelessly technical. They have done very well: capturing 9,000 prisoners and many guns. It is a good answer to the German peace proposals.

**Monday 18 December 1916** I am off home tomorrow. It looked like snow, but I hope that it will hold off till after tomorrow. Went down to Mayenne this morning to see the country round that place — wild and reminds me of Ireland. Went and paid a farewell visit to the General and was glad when it was over; I hate these state visits. I am much struck with the draught horse they breed here, a fine upstanding type and most of them are iron greys. Further south they breed riding horses but I have not seen any.

**Friday 22 December 1916** Returned home on the 19th and had a very cold journey in an open car. We left Alenc›,on at 8.30 am and reached Regnière—Ecluse at 5.15 pm having had two punctures on the way. Next day we took our report to GHQ. On the night of the 20th we had a scare as a beam below the fireplace in Longmore's room had been smouldering for a long time and caught fire. But all was well, and all the fireplaces are being lined with firebricks. We don't want to burn this chateau down and yet the place is like an icehouse without big fires. Today we were going to inspect the 20th Hussars and the Carabiniers, but it was pelting with rain so it was put off. The names of the 1st and 2nd Indian Cav.Divs have been changed to the 4th and 5th Cav.Divs which is a good thing.

**Sunday 24 December 1916** Things are very quiet all along the front. We have got a golf tournament for Christmas day. Today we played the first round; Clayton and I were knocked out by the Corps Commander and Ryan. We had a selling sweep on the result last night and it is worth over 600 francs. We heard last night that we are not going to move any of our Divisions which is a comfort as they would otherwise be so far away; everyone is very pleased.

The Americans are taking too much of a hand in these peace suggestions. I am honestly frightened by them. Any meeting even to discuss terms is full of danger as it takes all the willpower to keep such a war as this going. I am afraid that if they once start talking, the Allies may weaken and Germany will get what she wants: ie time to prepare for another war — also the realisation of a German owned and controlled Berlin-to-Bagdad Railway. We however must be firm and the more the Germans talk about peace, the tighter our blockade should become.

**Monday 25 December 1916** This is the third Christmas I have spent at the war and I hope that it will be the last. The day began badly as it poured with rain, but cleared up in the morning. Sir Douglas Haig and Kiggell came to lunch. The Chief told us that things were much worse in Germany and especially in Austria than people knew, so that was comforting.

**Friday 29 December 1916** Today I had to go to the 1st and 5th Armies. Neil Haig came to see and talk over some questions — he had no news except everyone says that Austria is jibbing pretty hard. Russia has, I see in the papers, stated her war aims — which are Constantinople and the Dardanelles — so there is no getting away from it. Things certainly seem brighter and perhaps this coming year may see great things, but I have so often said the same thing and nothing has happened.

**Sunday 31 December 1916** Another year of war has passed and, on the face of it, not much progress seems to have been made. Verdun and the Somme mark the greatest battles of the world. To the outward eye, the results do not appear to justify the expenditures. But [in] the Somme Battle, to those who watched it carefully, one sees the balance change. Our guns are better and more numerous than the Boche. We make more prisoners — the Boche does not fight as well as he did. It is the gradual weakening of the nations — small at first but I hope it will increase rapidly. As regards our own men, I think the nation is waking up, the fighting quality of the Britisher is coming to the fore and I look forward with great hope to the future.

As regards the general situation, how does that stand? Germany and Austria are both in greater straits as regards food than one realizes. Hence the wish for peace, they will take very liberal terms, so they tell neutrals. I think they are getting very near peace at any [price?]. The

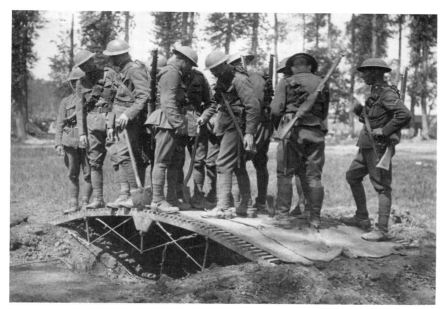

Cavalrymen testing a bridge which they had just thrown across a trench near Vaux-sur-Somme, July 1916

A Cavalry Hotchkiss gun team practising coming into action, near Querrieu (4th Army HQ), 29 July 1916

Battle of Albert, near Courcelles: shell bursting close to 10th Hussars while waiting to go forward, 21 August 1918

Battle of Flers-Courcelette: 2nd Dragoons (The Queen's Bays) on the march approaching Hardecourt Wood, 18 September 1916

The German Retreat to the Hindenburg Line: British Cavalry crossing a wooden bridge over the River Somme at Brie, near Peronne, March 1917

The German Retreat to the Hindenburg Line: British Cycle troops and Cavalry passing through the ruined village of Brie, March 1917

Battle of Vimy Ridge: British cavalry riding through Arras, 11 April 1917

Battle of the Scarpe: British Cavalry resting on the Arras to Cambrai Road, April 1917

German Retreat to the Hindenburg Line: Surrey Yeomanry on the edge of a crater near Vermand, on the Amiens to St Quentin Road, 21 April 1917

Cavalry near Neuve Eglise, crossing a bridge over a communication trench up which some Australian signallers are going, 7 May 1917

British Cavalry awaiting orders to move forward during operations in the Arras region, 26 May 1917

Canadian Cavalry marching past the Cavalry Corps Commander, General Sir Charles Kavanagh KCB near St Pol, 18 August 1917. (AFH is third from right)

Battle of Pilckem Ridge, 31 July 1917. Note the tapes marking the track along which a cavalryman is leading two horses

The German Retreat to the Hindenburg Line: Cavalry officers in the ruined village of Caulaincourt, 29 April 1917

Canadian Cavalry machine gun section during training operations near St Pol, 22 August 1917

Battle of Cambrai: Lancers waiting in Trescault while the guns go forward, 20 November 1917

Battle of Polygon Wood: Cavalry horses tethered behind a line of dug-outs in the ground near Clapham Junction (in front of Zillebeke), 26 September 1917

Royal Horse Artillery Officers with their Christmas mail-bag, December 1917

Actions of the Somme Crossings: Composite force from the 3rd Cav.Div. going forward in support near Nesle, 24 March 1918

The 2nd Dragoon Guards (Royal Scots Greys) resting by the roadside near Montreuil, 8 May 1918

The 2nd Dragoon Guards (Royal Scots Greys) watering their horses at Brimeux, 25 May 1918

The 13th Australian Light Horse near Bray, probably on manoeuvres, August 1918

Battle of Arras: Canadian Cavalry passing a wrecked German tractor near Dury, 2 September 1918

Cavalry on manoeuvres at Auxi-le-Château, 17 September 1918, crossing the Authie River. Note the pack-horse with ammunition boxes.

German Cavalry retreating, September 1918

9th Lancers returning from the front, Fremont on the Aisne, 13 October 1918

General Kavanagh, Commander of the Cavalry Corps, watching the Cavalry passing through Spa, 29
November 1918

poor people are beginning to grumble against the rich, it is the first sign of the storm. Turkey is said to be in a bad way. On our side Rumania is a broken reed*: their prowess as a fighting nation has gone, but Germany has only got three weeks' supplies out of that country. As regards ourselves, we certainly grow stronger and France gets no weaker. Russia is determined to fight to a finish. We want peace but that only on our own terms. Three years of war – that was K's prophecy. Perhaps he was right – things should change a good deal next year. At all events, we start the next year cheerfully and optimistically with the determination to win – so that we may not leave the legacy of another such a war to our children.

# 10. In the Line at Arras

**Thursday 18 January** 1917 Have not had time to write the Diary and was at home on leave from the 6th to 15th. Had a lucky journey both ways and a good crossing each time. Attended a conference at GHQ on the 3rd. Everyone full of confidence and very optimistic.

On the 17th attended a conference at Sir Edmund* Allenby's house at Bryas and saw a good many old friends. We nearly had a bad accident going there. It had been snowing hard all night and the hill into Hesdin on the Abbeville road is very steep. It was just like glass and we performed two perfect circles and finished with our hind wheels over the ditch; luckily the car did not turn over. So we went into Hesdin and got chains, but we were nearly an hour late for our conference. The Greeks look like playing the dirty according to the papers. I hope we shall take a firm stand with them, but it is not nice for our Salonika forces. Went down to inspect the 5th Cav.Div. armoured cars today. They want some brushing up, I think.

**Friday 19 January** 1917 Another snowy day and very cold wind from the east. The Canadians made a fine raid just south of the Double Crasier (Lens) and took one Officer and 99 men. It was done in broad daylight. We have been given another bit of the coast as a billeting area, this will be a help for training. The only comfort of this weather is that, if the Boche is hungry, he will feel it more than we do.

**Tuesday 30 January** 1917 Have had no time to write my Diary. The chief work has been keeping things going and the work for the summer requires a lot of thinking out. On the 27th attended a conference at GHQ and heard Geddes on the Railway question. It was most interesting and shows how necessary it was to take things in hand. All army commanders were there.

We have an Italian Cavalry Officer attached to us a Count Mongheri of the 3rd Dragoons. He is a very nice fellow and speaks English very well. He is supposed to have Anti-British tendencies, but hides them very well at present. We were told to do him well and are carrying out our orders.

We have had 10 days' frost now and the country is as hard as cement. The result is a panic in case the Boche takes it into his head to attack the Belgians. If he does they are certain to bolt and it would be bad if they lost Dunkirk. But at present there is no certain sign to go on. It is quite likely to happen as the Boche is certain to go for the line of least resistance. The news of internal trouble in Germany is pretty insistent and this will not help matters. One cannot help being sorry for the women and children.

**Friday 2 February** 1917 Left Paris for Compiegne which is the HQ of the French Cavalry Corps commanded by Conneau. We drove out in a French car and it had double wheels at the back. It is wonderful what a grip they get and, although the road was very slippery in places, there was never a sign of a skid. After lunch with Conneau, we went to see his armoured cars.

They are decidedly better than ours and have a double steering apparatus – one in front and the other behind – so that they go equally well either way. It is very ingenious and would be of the utmost use in action. He then took us into the forest and we saw them firing on a range. It was very interesting; we must try and get some of the French cars.

We got back to Paris at 4.15 pm. It was very cold so I took the CC for a walk. The CC took a box at the Folies Bergeres, and we were invited to dine at Ciro's*. It was a cheery party and an excellent dinner. Paris is much lighter than London and you can see your way about quite easily. Of course it is a mass of hospitals; big hotels are turned into them, but there is still a cheerful note in Paris. Hear they have made me a Commander of the Légion d'Honneur – why I don't know. 't is a very high honour and I am very lucky to get it.

**Saturday 3 February 1917** Left Paris at 10.30 am. The roads were much better and the car travelled well. Still very cold – most of the Staff have bought skates so it ought to thaw shortly.

**Sunday 4 February 1917** Just heard that America has severed diplomatic relations with the Boche and has mobilized her fleet. She could do nothing else after the German Note*. I wonder if Wilson knew that the German Note was coming out and that was the reason for his peace proposals? At any rate she could not allow Germany to dictate to her. I cannot see Germany's object unless she misjudged American public opinion, just as she did ours at the beginning of the war. At all events Germany will lose all the shipping she now has in American ports – such a loss will be very great as she must depend on her commercial existance as soon as the war ends. Still very cold.

**Friday 9 February 1917** Have not had time to write the Diary. On the 6th went to a conference at the 3rd Army. Yesterday I paid my first visit to Arras. It is one of the few places in our line which I have not seen. It is a fine old town and, although the enemy line is only 1500 yards east of it, it is not so battered as one would think. It was very quiet whilst we were there, only a few small shells being thrown into the place. A good many people still live in Arras but many have left lately.

They were nervous of an attack on the Belgium front, but the story goes that every morning the *'brave Belges'* went out to break the ice and they found the Boche doing the same, so all is tranquil!!!

**Monday 12 February 1917** The 5th Army have made one or two good attacks and in each case the toll of prisoners has been several hundreds. We could not do this a year ago. We also have a preponderance in guns now and are learning how to use them. If this frost only goes slowly, it will leave the trenches in a fairly decent condition and will save a lot of sickness.

**Thursday 15 February 1917** We have made a great many successful raids lately and taken quite a lot of prisoners. Went into GHQ this morning, but there was no news at all. Heard bad news as Baba* has got the flu†, but she seems to be better. It is awful to have to sit out here and not to be able to go home and see how she is getting on.

**Sunday 18 February 1917** Had a conference of Divisional Commanders on the 16th which lasted the whole morning. On the 17th went to 5th Army area to be invested with the Légion d'Honneur by General Nivelle, commanding the French Armies. First he inspected the 7th Div.* under George Barrow. There was a thick mist which spoilt everything and it was pretty cold standing in the mud. Of the Division, a Battery of Howitzers and a Highland Battalion marched past. After this General Nivelle stood under a hanger and presented the orders, etc. It is a quaint custom according to English ideas. First he shook hands, then in hanging the insignia round the neck said 'In the name of the President of the French Republic, I appoint you a Commander of the Légion d'Honneur.' This completed, he kissed you on either cheek. After this ordeal we went and had lunch at Godbert's† where we had a good lunch and paid for it too. Met lots of people at the ceremony that one knew. Today I attended a conference at St Pol-sur-Ternoise. A dull day and nothing doing.

**Monday 19 February 1917** The thaw still continues. This afternoon went to see some tests with the Hotchkiss guns on the sands near Le Touquet golf course. We hear news of 1,900 prisoners taken at Kut* which is good and clears the air a bit in that region. The Boche is very quiet on our front. I think he must try and forestall our offensive. He attacked the French the other day and he may just be feeling his way. I think his attack will be against the French and not against us. As far as we are concerned, we hope that he may not be able to forestall us on anything like a big scale. The French are holding their lines so lightly that an attack at first would be bound to be successful. This year we ought to be prepared to give a little ground rather than be forced to throw our forces in before we are ready. But what would the country say!!!

**Sunday 25 February 1917** Have had not time to write my Diary as I have been very busy with a Staff exercise. Today we hear that the Boche has evacuated Miraumont*. It rather looks as if he intended to evacuate the whole of his forward line and to go back to the Le Transloy-Berre line. He is of course shortening his line a bit, but it is a new phase of Boche work. We also hear that he is blowing up the bridges over the Oise behind his own line. It is difficult to deduce what he is playing at. A reasonable assumption is that he is playing for time. That he thinks this war cannot go on for more than another year and he intends fighting on the defensive and holding on to what he has got so as to have something to bargain with. On the other hand it is not like him to fight on the defensive. It is against his teaching and his policy.

**Tuesday 27 February 1917** Attended a conference at 3rd Army HQ yesterday and again today. The consensus of opinions seems to be that the Boche proposes to withdraw to what is called the Hindenburg Line, which runs from Arras to Soissons. If he does this, he of course shortens his line considerably and it gives him a good many more Divisions for an offensive. Prisoners say that they are going back to the Hindenburg Line and that the retirement will be completed by 25 March. That means that our offensive loses its great weight – which was to pinch the Bapaume salient and thus draw enemy reserves to us so that the French could break through. People may say what they like but this cannot be got away from.

I think the only thing left to us to do is hurry Sir William Robertson's and Joffre's attack of September 15. That is a thrust through the Vimy Ridge and Arras with objectives Cambrai-Douai and working north-east towards the line Valenciennes-Tournai and a French thrust in Champagne. If the Germans go back, this is a true strategical plan having the big thing in view – viz. driving the Boche out of France and Belgium. Whether the French can carry out a thrust in Champagne, I do not know – with our present plans we should be able to do our share. It is one of the most interesting and vital problems of the war. The Boche has been very clever and may have embarrassed us to a great extent – on the other hand his morale must be lowered and he has to explain a big retirement at home. I think he is certain to use the Divisions he gets in hand by shortening his line for an offensive. He has shown signs of activity in Ypres area – he may attack there but I don't think it will be his main push. He will much more likely attack the French; some people think in Alsace – but I have no data to go on. The weather is fine and the country is drying up well.

**Thursday 1 March 1917** The Boche is still giving ground slowly and we have now got the villages of Gommecourt, Puisieux and so on. Again in tonight's wireless he owns to a retirement 'according to plan' and claims to have inflicted heavy losses on us and to have taken prisoners. I only hope it is a retirement to a better position and better trenches, as the morale of his men has certainly suffered in the Ancre valley. If he retires to a line running from Arras through St. Quentin-Laon to near Soissons – he is certainly going to take the wind out of the sails of a carefully prepared offensive. A retirement to a line close behind the present one will do no harm. Spent the day in a car and saw the 6th and 7th Corps. Preparations for our offensive appear to be going on well.

**Monday 5 March 1917** Have been pretty busy flying round. On the 3rd went off to Bailleul to see Bainbridge and the 20th Div. They are having a fairly quiet time up there. It was a long drive and took me three hours. They seem to think in some quarters that the Boche is meditating an attack at Ypres – at all events they are nervous about it. It is, of course, a very likely spot and a threat towards Dunkirk or Calais is quite likely to cause a good deal of chat at home. They are still going back between Monchy-au-Bois and Bapaume. He is only going back as we push him and he leaves machine guns in all sorts of places. We still continue to capture a good few prisoners but we must have a certain amount of losses during our forward movement.

**Friday 9 March 1917** The last three days have been bitterly cold with an east wind. Today it has been snowing all day long. The Germans are still going back. There are various indications of an attack – some think towards Ypres. Other people think Nancy will be the spot. It is difficult to say. A prisoner states their horses only get 5lbs of oats*, they won't get fat or fit on that. Have been very busy getting our arrangements ready and organised. All prisoners seem to pin great faith on the German submarine campaign. At present it does not appear to have had very great success and one hears whispers of a goodly bag of Boche U-boats.

**Sunday 11 March 1917** I do not like this retirement. I think it is spoiling the possible Cavalry work which we were going to do in the coming offensive. If he goes back to the Hindenburg Line, there is no chance of using Cavalry – unless they want to get rid of it – as they will be pushing it into a pocket and it will be opposed to fresh troops of the enemy at the commencement of an offensive. It has been a very warm day today and quite springlike. We took Irles yesterday, our casualties 180 and took over 240 prisoners and eight machine guns.

**Thursday 15 March 1917** Went to see General Allenby on the 13th and had a talk over the effect of the Boche retirement on our plans with special reference to the Cavalry work. Of course it changes everything to my mind and it is most disheartening for the Cavalry. I thought I saw a rosy chance for us, but now we can only be used at a later stage of the offensive or else at some point further north. The French are indicating a push from the south of Roye towards Ham to find out what the Germans are doing. No results as yet so I suppose they put it off.

On this subject of the French, I have heard the following amazing story. Briand put up to Lloyd George that the British Armies should be under the French and that Nivelle will command them. That at the French GHQ there will be a British Chief of Staff who will issue the orders of the French C-in-C to the British C-in-C. Further it is contemplated that the French C-in-C can move any part of the British Armies to any part of the Allied line in the west. It is said that Lloyd George agreed to this!!! Of course D.H. won't stand it and has I believe said so*. Now who is responsible? Nivelle and the French War Minister deny all cognisance. Are there still people in England who are interfering at this time for self? Of course the Staff appointment at the French GHQ would be loved by some. If a soldier were asked, he must at once see the hopelessness of the scheme. Surely D.H. has enough worries and responsibility without being worried by such an intrigue? Went to the coast today and inspected the 4th Cav.Bde under Tommy Pitman.

**Sunday 18 March 1917** Attended a conference yesterday. It was most interesting and yet no real reason was given for the German retirement. Many views were advanced, but the most sound one to my mind was that the Germans found themselves very badly placed in the Bapaume salient and so formed an entrenchment behind it. They hoped that the French and ourselves would follow them up recklessly and then they would be able to deal us a counter blow which, although local, would be fairly serious. I think they have been very disappointed as we do not intend to advance recklessly and we must make good ground as we go along. The French are also advancing between the Somme and the Oise. Our difficulty is the crossing over the bad lands of the Battle of the Somme.

Neil Malcolm told me that the roads on the German side are quite good. They use light railways where we use roads. The Russian crisis* has evidently annoyed the Boche. He accuses us of having stage-managed the affair. I cannot imagine our Foreign Office to be guilty of such a clever and well-prepared intrigue! The weather is still beautiful and springlike and the ground is drying up well.

**Monday 19 March 1917** More night work. Last night at 11.00 pm, we got orders that the

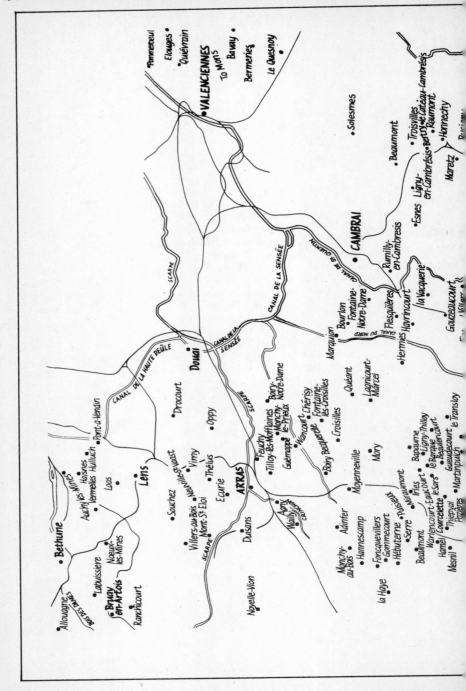

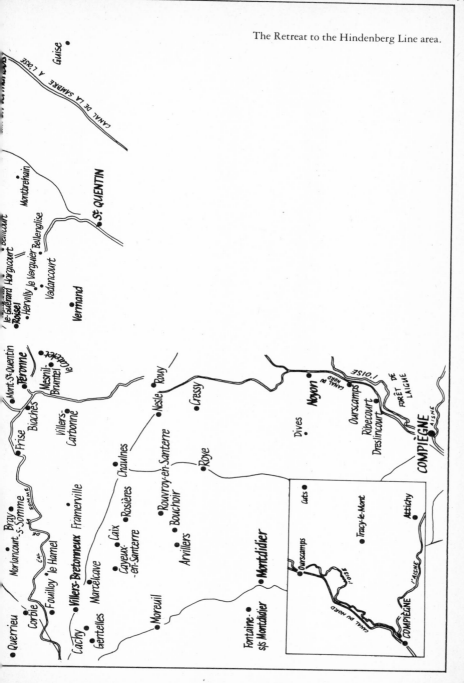

The Retreat to the Hindenberg Line area.

5th Cav.Div. was to go to the 4th Army and the 4th Cav.Div. to the 5th Army. The Germans are going back to the Hindenberg Line very quickly and it is impossible for Infantry to keep touch with them. The possible use of Cavalry in this area was mooted by us 10 days ago. Now all is hurry and bustle, but I think it should have been done before and is now probably too late to have any great effect. A rapid move forward of Infantry is not possible as they could not be fed. The situation from a Cavalry point of view is not cheering as it does not look like a chance of using a large Cavalry mass in the near future.

The Boche is burning villages all over the place* and it seems possible that where he burns there he will retire, otherwise why burn? If he retires behind the burning line, he will go back beyond the Hindenberg Line (Arras-Cambrai-St Quentin-La Fere-Vailly sur Aisne). There seems to be no very good reason to think this. I think he will go back as far as the Hindenberg Line and will either assume the offensive, or be ready to make peace on very reasonable terms. The weather has turned out wet and there is a howling gale blowing. A nice start for our 4th and 5th Divs and it will do the horses no good either.

**Friday 23 March 1917** More cold weather. Our Divisions are having a good time and it will be excellent practice for them advancing over the open country. The French have got on faster than we have but the Boche had been gone 10 days when they did advance, so got clean away. On the 21st the CC and I went and had lunch and a conference with General Allenby and got let in for a ladies' *dejeuner* with the Baroness La Grange. I don't like these things in wartime. German papers here and there snarl at the distance the troops have retired and that may be a sign that they don't like it.

**Saturday 24 March 1917** Had an interesting conference this morning. The situation in Austria is bad as regards food. The reserves for Vienna have been finished. It has been said that Austria may be forced to ask for a separate peace. This is also said so often that I don't believe it. In Germany there seems to be a good deal of discontent. Riots have occurred in Berlin, Hamburg and Hanover. Agents say that parts of Hamburg are in flames and that the soldiers refused to fire on the rioters — that martial law has been proclaimed. This may be an exaggeration, but there is certainly something behind it.

Continual rumours are being circulated that the Germans are preparing an offensive against the Ypres salient. It is very curious as the indications as we see them: ie guns, work and so on, lead one to believe that there is no offensive completed. The main interest at present is: will the Boche hold on opposite Arras and on the Vimy Ridge or does he intend to retire? As far as our information goes at present, it appears to be an even money chance. If he holds on, he is once more forming a salient, the southern line being a single line of trenches and very little behind them. He is laying himself open to a rather big smack there.

Opinion is gaining ground that he does not intend to hold the Hindenberg Line. If this is the case, he intends retiring to the Meuse fighting all the way. Once out of France he will offer her such terms of peace that she will not be able to refuse and that will end the war. Will such an end be a drawn war? I cannot say; but Asquith's claptrap phrase of 'not to sheath the sword etc' cannot be taken literally. I should like to see a fight in the open with large effectives and then a Boche retreat, there would be no question about it then. I believe the Cavalry will have a chance this year. If they don't, it will be a sad thing after two years of waiting.

**Tuesday 27 March 1917** Spent Sunday flying round to try and get some sort of idea on the plan for using the Cavalry either eastwards from Arras or north from the direction of Queant. The result was we put up a Scheme which was approved in principle and it remains to be seem what they will order. Opinion is still divided as to whether he [the Germans] will stay at Arras or else retire.

He has carried out the destruction to a real fine art. Churches are levelled, even those round the crucifixes at the road side. Fruit trees are cut down and left lying in the orchards, even gooseberry bushes are pulled out by the roots and thrown into the trenches. He is laying up a goodly store of trouble for himself in the future, I hope. The Corps Commander visited Bapaume area yesterday and saw the 4th Cav.Div. He says the area is ghastly, hardly a square yard not torn up by shot and shell. The town hall at Bapaume was blown up. I am told that the method they employ is to make a mine and fire it by some acid which is placed in a metal receptacle. As soon as the acid eats its way through the metal, it fires the mine. It is quite conceivable that this may go on for some time, as the time the mine goes off depends on the thickness of the metal. There is also no means of spotting these mines, no wire or anything of that sort. Moral – avoid houses.

**Thursday 29 March** 1917 Went down to Peronne to see the 5th Cav.Div. who are down there. We started at 7.00 am and motored via Amiens, and Biaches. Such a scene of desolation: Biaches just a heap of mud and unless it was marked on a map as a village, no one would know that such a thing had existed. Crossed in[to] Peronne over a pontoon bridge and here again the Germans have wrecked everything they can. Macandrew, commanding the 5th Cav.Div., was in one of the few houses which had a roof over it. They were very cheerful and pleased as their men had had quite a pretty little fight and were all the better for it.

We then got on horses and Howard Vyse took us out to show us the ground that had been fought over. The country is open rolling down and there is no cultivation. This must mean that this retirement is no new thing as the civilians must have been evacuated some time ago. Was our intelligence at fault I wonder? The roads are quite in good condition and that shows that there has not been much traffic. In fact the Germans probably held that sector with two men and a boy. The wanton destruction in the villages was ghastly. The railway was cut, every rail having been destroyed with a charge of explosive; this must have taken a long time. It was very sad and made one's blood boil. Why have they done it? Officially they give out so as to have an open battlefield. This is rubbish as fruit trees don't give any cover. Are they trying to intimidate France? To show what they are going to do if the war goes on, and they are forced to retire? Every Frenchman now wishes to get into Germany and show them what they can do. We shall see.

**Monday 2 April** 1917 On the 31st motored to Adinfer which lies south of Arras in the territory evacuated by the Boche. We lunched in the ruins – the Boche cemetery there had been beautifully kept and the French cemetery had been destroyed by the blowing-up of the church. The whole village was flat as in the rest of the area. Again what struck one was the cleanliness of the country. The Boche must use light railways for everything. No horse standings or cart tracks were to be seen. Up here there were small patches of cultivation.

We went to the top of a rise just east of Boiry-Becquerelle and had a good view of the high ground around Monchy-le-Preux and could also see Boiry-Notre-Dame. The ridge to the east of Croisilles is well marked and is occupied by the Germans. We attack it today, and I hear have made some progress. Yesterday I went to the 3rd Army in the morning and to the 2nd Cav.Div. in the afternoon. All our arrangements are now practically completed* and we can only wait and see what happens. They have changed the bombardment from two to practically seven days†. I should think that this means that Arras will be in flames.

**Friday 6 April** 1917 Moved our HQ from Regnière-Ecluse to Duisans which is about three miles west of Arras. Went down and saw the 5th Army and General Gough at Albert this morning on our way. They have got a good house, but had to put in new glass in all the windows. They were well bombed by the Boche shortly afterwards and all their glass went once more. Got to Duisans at 5.00 pm and held a conference at once. There has been a good deal of rain here, I am sorry to say, which is not good for the projected operations.

**Saturday 7 April** 1917 Spent the day on a horse with the Corps Commander and did the best part of 30 miles. We went towards Queant and had a look at the country from that direction. We went to Mory and here we saw the new craters which blew up by themselves 12 or 14 days after the Boche left. I wonder how many more places will go up in this manner? The day was bitterly cold with a fierce north-east wind, but it is a drying wind, so one cannot complain.

**Sunday 8 April** 1917 (Easter) Spent the day making final preparations for tomorrow, as we attack in the early morning. For the last four days we have been listening to the bombardment, which does not stop day or night. We pray for a success as that will help the

French attack in the south. If that is successful, there may be a great change in the German line shortly. Today is gloriously fine and I only hope we shall have some luck tomorrow and a fine day as well.

**Monday 9 April 1917** One of the best days for the British Armies in the war. The 1st and 3rd Armies attacked the Boche from south of Arras to the northern end of the Vimy Ridge. Everything went according to programme and the result of the day's operation was a bag of about 9,000 prisoners and 90 guns. The day itself was wet and cold – our aeroplanes found it very difficult to observe owing to the low cloud. At 12 noon the 2nd and 3rd Cav.Divs were moved up east of Arras and waited there for a chance to advance. The attacks were going so well that, at about 2.00 pm, they were ordered to move east with the idea of getting on to the Valley of the Sensée.

Up to this point all had gone well, but the Boche lines running through Feuchy Chapel to the River Scarpe proved to be a harder task than was at first thought. The wire was very thick and had not been cut*. This delayed the attack and this line was not taken till about 6.00 pm. The attack of the 7th Corps south of Arras was not so successful and the Hindenberg Line here held out quite successfully. There appeared no chance to use the Cavalry that evening†, so it was brought back: the 2nd Cav.Div. into Bervines between Agny and Wailly, the 3rd Cav.Div. north-west of Arras between the main St Pol road and the Scarpe River. As regards the Cavalry, the day was disappointing, if the Feuchy line had gone, I think the Div.s would have gone through and probably made a bag of guns.

The attack on the Feuchy line was ordered for the next morning and the Cavalry were told to be ready to move after 11.00 am. Many Bavarian prisoners were brought into a cage near here and they were certainly the most miserable specimens of war that anyone ever could wish to see. Of course they were wet and muddy, but their physique was wretched. Pat Shannon of the 10th [Hussars?] who was in charge of the digging parties saw the whole attack on the Harp, south of Tilloy-lès-Mofflaines. He said there the Boche prisoners came running in with their hands up. A couple of soldiers promptly ran out as if to stick them and they (the Boche) at once emptied out their pockets. The men found this such a lucrative practice that they continued it for quite a long time. We did not move our HQ, but stayed at Duisans.

**Tuesday 10 April 1917** The troops north of the Scarpe having attained their objectives consolidated them, and the attacks south of the Scarpe continued. At 12 noon we got the order to move the 2nd and 3rd Divs forward again. It looked again to be a chance of getting through, but nothing happened as the Infantry attacks went slowly. We spent the night where they were. It was bitterly cold and snowed hard during the night, the men and the horses having a bad time owing to the lack of water for the latter. It is curious in the modern battle how hard it is to get information continually during the day. The Army told us that Monchy-le-Preux was captured and they issued orders for a Cavalry advance for the next day. We luckily got the order changed. Our aeroplanes flying low brought us in quite good information, but it is only what the observer can see and must therefore be treated with a certain amount of care.

**Wednesday 11 April 1917** A few Infantry assisted by our 6th and 8th Bdes took Monchy-le-Preux in the morning. We hung on to it all day and at night were relieved by the 12th Div. The 10th Hussars and Essex Yeomanry, both of the 8th Bde, suffered fairly heavy casualties. We practically held Monchy and this will be found of the greatest use later on. We were much worried by machine gun fire from the Valley of the Scarpe which is full of guns. From this point onwards the operation ceased to be one for Cavalry and so we asked for the Divisions to be withdrawn. They spent the night in a blizzard, the 3rd west of Arras, the 2nd in the Crinchon Valley between Agny and Wailly. The weather has been quite appalling and for April, the coldest I can ever remember.

**Thursday 12 April 1917** Moved the Divisions back to their old areas. These three days have done in most of the horses in the 2nd Cav.Div. and they are in a very bad way. There has been something wrong there as it ought not to have done so. There is a lull in the fighting except opposite Lens; here the Boche appears to be getting ready to move back. He is of course burning the place down.

**Friday 13 April 1917** Went to see Bob Greenly in the morning and found him fussed as regards the horses of the [? Cav.]Div. and I don't wonder at it. The 17th and 29th Divs attacked east of Monchy-le-Preux and did no good. The reason is plain — an attack south of the Scarpe will not succeed unless they attack north of it as well. It is time that these piecemeal attacks were stopped; no good can come of them and we only lose men.

**Saturday 14 April 1917** A poisonous day, cold and wet. Today the Boche attacked the 5th Army from Hermies to Lagnicourt-Marcel on a front of 8,000 yards with three Divisions. He had a success at first and drove us back nearly 2,000 yards in places. We counter attacked and drove him back again. Our casualties were 500, but 1,500 dead Boche were counted in the battlefield and we took 400 prisoners. It shows that we are not so bad in the so-called 'open' fighting.

**Thursday 19 April 1917** Things have been very quiet the last few days. There has been a decided lull, and a very good thing too. The attacks will be now co-ordinated and there will be no more piecemeal attacks I hope. We still hold Monchy-le-Preux, but very nearly lost it when the 29th Div. were counter attacked and driven back east of that place. A regular attack is now being organised and will take place on the 23rd. The scope is from Oppy in the north to Croisilles in the south.

I went for a walk today with Muirhead and looked over the ground over which the 2nd Cav.Div. operated on the 11th. We motored as far as the Faubourg St Saveur and then got out and walked as the traffic was very thick. We walked as far as Feuchy Chapel, and then went on to the high ground south of it, overlooking Wancourt and Guemappe in the Valley of the Cojeul. It was very interesting to see the wire on the German second system north and south of the Feuchy Chapel. It was quite recent and the Germans cannot have out us much of a fight on that line. Between Arras and Tilloy-lès-Mofflaines, the country was pulp and shows the efficacy of our bombardment; the nearer one got to Monchy-le-Preux, the less the ground was cut up. It was quite easy to realise the difficulty of an attack against Wancourt and Guemappe, as the ground on the east bank of the Cojeul dominates the whole valley. There were three or four derelict tanks about, but the battlefield was really wonderfully clean.

Between Tilloy and Monchy our Batteries cover the ground and we ought to get up to the Queant-Dury line quite easily. Our horses have suffered much but I think we shall be able to remount them. We move back to Regnière-Ecluse tomorrow and I just hate going back. One can quite realise the bad morale effect it has on the men. On the other hand there is no possible use for Cavalry just now and we must clear the way for other people until our turn comes once again. The French news tonight is good*. They started slowly, but the Boche countered and so they lost in these counters. Now the French are progressing steadily and will, I think, do great things.

**Saturday 21 April 1917** Back at Regnière-Ecluse again. The weather is certainly improving and the country is drying up well. The French are still getting on and, if they only keep it up, there will be the opportunity of something big. Had the most disquieting rumours of political interference and that the French were not going on and so on, but think they are only rumours.

**Sunday 22 April 1918** Inspected the horses of the 4th Cav.Bde today. I think it a very lucky thing that we have had this preliminary canter. The horses except those of the Oxfords* are bad — but a few weeks will put them right again especially if the weather is warm. I don't think that Bob likes people inspecting his Brigades, but he was always like that. We attack tomorrow on a large front† from Oppy in the north to Fontaine-lès-Cròisilles in the south. Both the 1st and 5th Armies take part. I hope it will be successful.

**Monday 23 April 1917** Waited in the whole morning in case anything developed. Our attacks on the line Chérisy-Oppy [were] only partly successful. Guemappe proved a stumbling block. It has been a very heavy day's fighting as the Boche has had orders to hold on. It was a case of attack and counter attack and pretty heavy casualties I expect one way and another. It would appear as if we were hustling the Boche and he is not ready to retire.

The French are evidently boiling up another attack. Caviare [Cavendish] lunched here yesterday and told us that the French were very disappointed at first, but are much happier now. They evidently expected to get right through. There is a lot of 'guf' flying about. One thing is that Austria would break away if the Italians were ready to give up any pretensions to Trieste; that things in Germany and especially in Austria are very bad; that Russia has been very wobbly but now is all right. A Boche aeroplane with three Officers in it was brought down right close to this place. I rode out to see it this afternoon. It was a very big one with two propellors and engines*.

**Sunday 29 April 1917** Have not had time to keep up the Diary. Have spent the week looking at horses and they are not so bad as we thought. Given another fortnight of fine weather and the food that they are getting now, all will be well. The French have not moved at all, I suppose that they are getting their guns forward to prepare another advance. We have been attacking all along our front and in some parts considerable progress has been made. We are preparing another attack on a biggish scale. Everyone is very pessimistic about Russia* – it would be a great triumph for Germany if she would make peace.

There appears to be great dissatisfaction in the 5th Cav.Div. as regards the events of the 9-12th. It is not serious at present, but it is hard to find out what is really at the bottom of the whole thing. I shall have to try. The weather has been lovely and the ground is as dry as a bone – long may it continue.

**Wednesday 2 May 1917** Just returned from a long day with the 5th Cav.Div. which is down in the country west of St Quentin. They live in a sort of godown which is one of the few houses left in the district with a roof on it. Found them all very cheerful and well. The Umbala and Secunderabad Brigades are in the woods east of Tingues. At present the country is deserted but a good place for our horses.*

**Friday 4 May to Friday 11 May 1917** Was at home owing to the death of poor W.K. D['Arcy]* on the 10th. At 10.00 pm, got a wire recalling me and saying it was urgent, so got back to Regnière-Ecluse at 2.00 pm. On arrival found that we were to take over the 3rd Corps's front which runs northwards from St Quentin – a front of about 1,500 yards. We shall be very thin but I don't think the Boche meditates an attack and so shall be able to hold on. We have got the 2nd, 3rd, 4th and 5th Cav.Divs and for a time the 49th Div.

**Sunday 13 May 1917** Started at 7.15 am to go and see the 3rd Corps. They have got a camp in an apple orchard at Le Catelet – it looked comfortable. The Boche have, of course, blown up all the houses. Part of the line runs through Lempire where we spent the night after the battle of Le Cateau in 1914, and along the ridge from there to Ste Emilie. Went to 5th Div. HQ and saw the Wombat who gave me lunch – then to 4th Army HQ and then to the 2nd Div.

**Tuesday 15 May 1917** Went into GHQ to look after the interests of the Cavalry Officer. Had a talk to several of them. The Russian situation does not appear at all good and our own one at home is bad. There seem to be strikes at our munition factories and these seem to be spreading and have got to Woolwich. This is most serious as it may put us back a fortnight or three weeks in our programme. It appears that the Government have a good suspicion as to who the ringleaders are and are afraid to arrest them. I suppose they are thinking of votes. They ought to be put on trial in public and the ringleaders of the movement should be shot as traitors. I suppose it is German money responsible for it. Yet here we are with Germany at the last gasp and we allow strikes: such a thing should be unthinkable.

**Wednesday 16 May 1917** Left Regnière-Ecluse for the second time this year for the front and wonder if we shall go back there again. Went out into our new area and visited the 5th Cav.Div., then the 49th Div. with Romer in command and then Gregory's Brigade and Seely's Canadians. On the way back we called in at [4th] Army HQ. It has been a beastly day – wet and raining hard. We were nearly bogged in one place, but with the help of chains got the car out of the mud. Our new area lies in the zone destroyed by the Boche. The destruction is terrible.

**Saturday 19 May 1917** Moved into our new HQ at Le Catelet and took over the command of the line at 9.00 am. I think we are pulling our weight as we will take the place of a full Infantry Corps and so they will be available for attack elsewhere. Our HQ consists of huts. The chateau and farm are of course in ruins, fruit trees are cut down, but luckily a few are standing and these give good shade and shelter. Stayed in today getting my house in order and of course had the usual procession. Our line seems to be a very quiet one at present.

**Sunday 20 May 1917** In the morning went to see the 2nd Cav.Div. north-east of Roisel. Last night the Boche attacked Guillemout Farm, but was beaten back leaving two prisoners in our hands. The prisoners say that they had just arrived from Arras and it was their first night in the trenches, although they had been in that sector before and knew it well. They got orders to attack, take and hold Guillemout Farm. Two Companies, each about 100 strong, attacked but coming under our gun, rifle and [cross?] fire, they were stopped. We then went on to Epehy to look at the trenches. Had a conference of Divisional commanders in the evening and expelled some hot air, but the CC was very decided. The Canadians took two prisoners on the right of the line.

**Monday 21 May 1917** Went down to Seely's HQ at Vadancourt Château and then walked the intermediate line – some shelling and a heavy rain storm. Got very hot walking, but it did me good.

**Tuesday 22 May 1917** A very wet day. General Mandhui, who commands the French 11th Corps and is on our right, called on the Corps Commander this afternoon. I went out and walked round Lempire and our old battlegrounds – it was very interesting but very hot. The French are attacking again soon* and the Russian situation is decidedly better†. I am told we got 21 submarines‡ last week, which is good. Things are fairly quiet in front of us here, although a good deal of shelling takes place at times. The three Divisions opposed to us have all been in the Arras battle, so they are probably recouping and pretty tired.

**Wednesday 23 May 1917** Walked from Lempire to the left of our sector this morning. The line on the whole was very quiet.

**Friday 25 May 1917** Rode round our second line, which we have as yet to construct. It is a very hot day. The front was very quiet but they wre throwing some shells behind Le Verguier and also on Seely's tumulus[?]. German prisoners say that they are sent down here to rest after the Arras battle as this is supposed to be the quietest part of the line. I think it really is.

**Saturday 26 May 1917** Went to the 5th Cav.Div. and rode forward with the Wombat and examined his second line trenches. The Canadians are having a shunt* tonight and I hope it will be a good one. I saw the defences of the Grand Priel Wood, which are very good, and then rode home.

**Sunday 27 May 1917** The Canadian raid was a great success: 18 prisoners and a lot of Boches killed; our casualties two wounded and one killed. Wires of congratulations from the Chief and Army Commander. In the afternoon went and saw Seely, whose Brigade carried out the operation. It was a very well organised show and the Canadians are fine fellows to fight. The CC and I attended the funeral of the poor fellow who was killed; he was buried in a wood – the guns were firing quite near. It was very impressive.

**Monday 28 May 1917** Walked round the intermediate line of Bob Greenly's sector with the Corps Commander. The men have done some splendid work there. Winston Churchill* has invited himself here tomorrow – of course he wants to see Seely, so we shall send him off there as soon as he arrives.

**Wednesday 30 May 1917** Yesterday I rode over to the 4th Cav.Div. HQ and saw Godewin, there was no news. In the afternoon Lancy (the General commanding the French 15th Corps on our right*) came over and paid us an official visit. It has been very cold all day, but no rain.

Today motored up past Hervilly and then walked over the hill and had a look at the ground between Guillemout Farm and Brusson Fontaine[?]; then walked on to Hargicourt and saw Patterson who commands that sector. It is a bad bit of the line as the Boche is very close and overlooks us everywhere. Winston Churchill has arrived and is staying here the night. It is extraordinary how that man is universally disliked. I have not seen him, but suppose I shall at breakfast tomorrow morning.

**Sunday 3 June 1917** Have not had much time to write the Diary. On the 1st, the CC and I started at 3.00 am to go round the front trenches of our Hargicourt sector which is held by the 4th Cav.Div. A part of this line runs through some old quarries with the Boche very near and overlooking us from Cologne Farm. It is the only part of our sector where we are close up to the Boches and the conditions approximate trench warfare. The Boche has 1 to 4 the best of it in this area and I don't think he will attack as he cannot improve his position much by doing so. Winston Churchill had not got very much news. He said one could expect nothing from Russia except that she would probably not make peace and that we were trying desperately hard to get Austria out of it. We are getting quite a good line here and our fellows are working splendidly.

**Monday 4 June 1917** I went for a walk with the Corps Commander and visited G. Post near Petit Priel Farm and then walked up the hill to Lempire and on to Guillemout Farm. Our men are doing a lot of work and the line is gradually becoming stronger. The bombardment for the attack on the Messines Ridge has commenced*. I hope that we shall be successful in taking it.

**Tuesday 5 June 1917** One of the hottest days we have had. Motored to Epehy and then walked to the left of our line where it joins the Infantry. Things were very quiet, excepting some shelling of the Infantry trenches. Cyril Potter came back from England — the attack on Messines is common talk there. It is very bad the way people gossip — especially those at home and some in the highest quarters.

**Thursday 7 June 1917** A real red letter day of the war as the 2nd Army have taken the Messines Ridge. Everywhere we reached our objectives. Our losses are estimated at 10,000 for the nine Divisions attacking. Of course, we shall have more in holding the position. The prisoners taken amount to 6,000 as at present counted — this will rise to 8,000. It has been a real first class show — well run and well arranged. The Boche in his wireless reports talks of the failure of our attacks. He must be very hard pressed to resort to lies which must be found out. Of course, he may be preparing a big counter attack and hopes to justify his action by a success but we are firmly established on the Ridge and will take a good deal of turning out. I think we must look on these successes as a good omen. Vimy Ridge — Arras — Messines — are all a happy augury for the future.

**Friday 8 June 1917** Rode out to the right of our line and looked at some wire and trenches. No Boche counter attack as yet against the Messines Ridge — all is quiet and we are consolidating. It ought to take some time to kick us off.

**Saturday 9 June 1917** Just heard from Pitt Taylor that the Boche put in a strong counter attack against the positions on the Messines Ridge with large forces and that it failed completely — that is good. Tonight we carry out a small raid on the Boche east of Guillemout Farm. The Greys* are going to do it.

**Sunday 10 June 1917** Walked round the HQs of the subsector commanders of the 4th Cav.Div. in the morning. The raid last night was a great success — we took 12 prisoners and killed a few Boches. Our casualties were about 15 all told. We also discovered a new Division on our front which has just come over from Russia — I don't think it will like the Artillery fire on this side.

**Tuesday 12 June 1917** Yesterday went to Flexicourt and gave a lecture to the 4th Army School. Today spent a quiet day in the office. Hear today that the Boche are moving back towards the Lys River in front of Messines. It is difficult to see what they are playing at. Their strategy may mean that they are going to avoid a big engagement and so avoid losses in men. If they carry this through, they will have to go back along the coast and this will be a great acknowledgement of weakness. I cannot see them doing so at present. They say Ostend

Harbour has no ships in it, but that is explained by our having damaged it recently by a heavy bombardment. It is a very interesting problem.

**Friday 15 June 1917** Walked round part of the intermediate line this morning. It is getting on well, but it was very hot – especially in the tin hat. The Germans are hard at it explaining away the Messines show. The Deccan Horse* had a raid last night and slew several Boches.

**Saturday 16 June 1917** The news on the whole line is good and we are successful wherever we attack. Went and paid a visit to the French Battalion on our right and was offered Champagne at 10.00 [o'clock] in the morning! Luckily escaped drinking it as a long walk in the sun afterwards would have killed one. It is a great pity that the Russian situation is so impossible – a big attack on their part now would help the situation a great deal. In fact the Germans have only tired troops on that front, but it is beyond hope that they will be able to do anything.

**Sunday 17 June 1917** Walked round the right sector intermediate line and went round the Le Verguier defences which are getting on well. We are told that we may go out of this line about the first week in July and then come into GHQ Reserve, somewhere behind the 1st and 5th Armies, but this is only gossip and we know nothing as yet.

**Tuesday 19 June 1917** We had a raid on the Ste Helene Trench last night. It was carried out by the 9th Hodson's Horse. We got about 18 Germans. Unfortunately for us, the garrison had been reduced from 60 to 18 the night before or else our bag might have been greater.

**Friday 22 June 1917** A great change in the weather and it is quite cold today. Last night the Boche had a go at the Birdcage work and at Guillemout Farm. In the former case he never got across our wire, and we know we killed 10 and took three prisoners. At the latter he got into our work, but was kicked out by a counter attack. We had, however, a good few casualties owing to a heavy bombardment of all our posts.

We have two American officers staying with us. They are Colonels Anderson and Walker of the Cavalry. It appears that America intends to profit by other people's mistakes and to undertake the organisations of her Armies on the best possible lines. They don't however propose to bring over the Cavalry, which I think is a mistake. But it is a question of transportation and they must weight all probabilities before starting.

**Sunday 24 June 1917** It has been warmer the last two days – Had a Staff exercise over the ground over which the 5th Cav.Div. worked when the Boche retreated and Vanderbyl gave us an account on the ground of the taking of Villers-Faucon. Things are very quiet, but preparations appear to be going on apace*. What our role will be I am very curious to know. We get little news here, being under an Army. When we are under GHQ, one attends the meetings and knows what is going on. One hears vague rumours of troubles in the French Army; they are mostly political and fostered by the politicians, but they are such a changeable race that go from the depths of despair to the height of optimism in no time. I hope that our successful attacks will ginger them up to another effort later in the year when we have worn the Boche out. That and a Russian blow would end a very good season for us – will this be possible!!!

**Tuesday 26 June 1917** Yesterday went for a walk round the intermediate line of the 4th and 5th Divs. They have done a good deal of work and the situation now is fairly satisfactory. We had our concert last night and it was a great success. There is lots of talent in the Army now and a great many of them are professional. Just heard we come out of here on 10 July. Once more we assume the role of a mobile Reserve. It is a great pity that they cannot use Cavalry in the north. No one can tell the course such an attack will take. I would place two Divisions handy so as to be able to get them forward if the occasion arises – perhaps they are going to use the Belgian Cavalry!!! The pendulum swings too much one way or the other – why cannot we take a safe course in the preparatory arangements?

**Friday 29 June 1917** The day after the last entry I heard that we shall take part in the big battle; we are all delighted that we are not going to be left out of it. We have had a Russian Cavalry General staying here and he has been studying our methods. His name is Baron

Wrangles, he is a very keen soldier and has gone into everything in great detail – an accomplished linguist and a very nice fellow. The Duke of Connaught came and had lunch and presented some decorations after lunch. The Duke seems to have aged very much since I saw him last. The 5th Div. come out today and move north on the 2nd and 3rd.

**Saturday 30 June 1917** It has been a beastly day – a cold east wind and heavy rain. The Boche had a relief on last night, so we shelled him hard – he on the other had raided and captured a post of the French on our right, much to their annoyance. We had quite a success opposite the 1st Army and the Boche owns to losing ground in his communique.

**Sunday 1 July 1917** In the afternoon drove over to see Sir Julian Byng commanding the 3rd Army. It was a most interesting drive as we went via Peronne and Bapaume and passed the places which had formed our objectives during the Somme Battle last September, had it been possible to use the Cavalry. The French must have had heavy losses in the fighting round Sailly-Saillisel as there are many graves about there. They are marked with black wooden crosses with a Tricoleur rosette on it and look very pathetic in the middle of the desolation.

At Pozières, the Australians have put up a monument to those that fell – a simple large wooden cross on a white pedestal. What strikes one most is the desolation of the area. The villages were destroyed by shell fire and razed to the ground; rough coarse grass covers everything. Not a living being is seen except a few soldiers wandering about. When the territory was occupied one did not realise the desolation as there was movement and life – but now it is barren and dreary. It was a very cold day and drizzled most of the time.

**Monday 2 July 1917** Last night we raided the Cologne Farm which lies just east of Hargicourt. The Corps Commander, Joe Seligman and myself went to a hill just south of Templeux-le-Guérard to watch it. It was a very dark night and the bursting shells showed up very clearly. The sudden change from quiet into a pandemonium was quite startling. Beyond the flares, which were being sent up from the Boche lines and lit up the countryside, there was hardly a sound. Suddenly at the given moment guns of all sizes, machine guns opened from all directions and lit up the sky with their flashes, the bursting shells forming a line of fire round the farm. The Boche did not reply much, but he held the farm – there was a stiff fight and many Boches were killed. We had about 50 casualties. This morning at 6.00 am a patrol of ours went into the farm but found it unoccupied. Went out this morning and saw the 5th Cav.Bde moving out preparatory to their march to the 1st Army.

**Thursday 5 July 1917** We are in the process of handing over the line to the 34th* and 55th† Divs. It is not always a very satisfactory job. Of course their men are not as good as ours and they find it difficult to do the same amount of patrolling that we do. Went to 3rd Army HQ yesterday and arranged for our march to the north. Our new HQ will be at Aire-sur-la-Lys. I hate that country but we must go back to it. The Boche had another go at Guillemout Farm last night but did not get in. I hope the Canadians will return the compliment with interest on the 8/9th. The Russians have taken 17,000 prisoners in two days‡ so that ought to buck them up and also the French. The Boche is very persistant in his attacks on the French between ? and Verdun. I suppose he hopes to sicken them, but at present he is getting the worst of it.

**Friday 6 July 1917** Rode round and saw the RFC squadron this morning. Shall be sorry to leave our line, but hope that it will lead to better things.

**Monday 9 July 1917** The Canadians made another excellent raid last night. They took one Officer and 34 others as prisoners and killed a good many others. The Boche did not put up anything of a fight. They had just come from Messines, where they had had very heavy casualties and had been filled up with odd drafts – their morale was not good. The raid was well carried out and these Canadians are very good at that sort of thing.

**Wednesday 11 July 1917** Went into GHQ which is now at Blendecques*, a four hour motor journey from here. It was quite curious to get into civilization after being out here for nearly two months. The crops do not seem to be so good this year as a whole, they are thinner and not so high. Saw Wigram – he is certain the war will finish this year as the Germans will not wait for America to come in. Hope he is right as long as it finishes properly. The Russians are doing great things, over 30,000 prisoners in a fortnight is very good, and their offensive must come as a surprise to the Boche. The latter has given us a nasty knock at Nieuwport and practically scuppered two Battalions. He concentrated a lot of guns and just blew our trenches in the sand dunes to pieces and also broke the bridges over the Yser so that we could not support our troops on the other side.

# 11. Passchendale to Cambrai

**Sunday 15 July 1917** Moved our HQ from Le Catelet to Aire-sur-la-Lys and once more we come under GHQ as Cavalry proper. In the meantime, we have released three Inf.Divs with four Cav.Divs. We have made 10 raids, of which nine have been very successful. We have taken 97 prisoners, one machine gun, and I hope we have accounted for a good many Boches. Our casualties for the seven weeks have been about a thousand. The result has been I think most satisfactory: our men have got their tails right up and are quite contented having been in action. I am sorry to leave the line as one has continual work and continual interest. The weeks simply fly; one loses all count of time and if the work goes towards bringing the war to a successful finish, nothing can be better. Last night I stayed with the 4th Div. It was a cheery party.

**Tuesday 17 July 1917** Went down to Rouen to inspect the Indian Reinforcement Depot. Had three punctures between here and Abbeville and had tea at the Officer's Club at Abbeville, a most comfortable place run by the Expeditionary Force Canteen.

**Wednesday 18 July 1917** Up at 6.00 am and saw the men at work – it is a very good show and well run. Left at 2.00 pm and got back without any further punctures.

**Thursday 19 July 1917** Changed our HQ to La Jumel about a mile out of the town – for which I am thankful. Our last place was very comfortable and a very nice house, but the French family hated open windows and the house was always stuffy and smelly. Went into GHQ and saw Solly-Flood on the subject of training.

**Friday 20 July 1917** Went up to Woesten and had lunch with Goughie at the 5th Army HQ. Saw all the plans for the coming offensive and think we have a good chance of giving the Boche a real hard knock. Our guns are doing great work and have got the best of the Boche guns opposite the salient. They have invented a new type of gas which is very deadly and has a greatly delayed action. They use it in their shells.

**Tuesday 24 July 1917** Have been running round trying to get things a bit settled. Hear they are forming a corps of mounted troops out in Egypt\*; this is the Bull's work, I suppose. The Russians are once more a sore disappointment. They had an excellent start and might have done a great deal to help the side by pushing on, but now we hear of insubordination and cowardice and the refusal to fight. The result of course is that the Boche gets his tail up and even the bad troops which he has on that side are having considerable success.

**Thursday 26 July 1917** Went down to beyond Peronne to see the Horse Show which has been got up by the 4th Div. It was a great success and I have never seen horses looking better in my life. The display by the 2nd Lancers\* was especially good. Old Perturb Singh† was there a very interested spectator; he is a wonderful old man and still hopes to be killed leading his men. He always says 'Me a Rajput and it is a disgrace to die in my bed!' There were a lot of

French Officers from the neighbouring French Army. They were much struck at the turn-outs and said they could never take any interest in equipment and their men would never waste paint on a cart belonging to the government. Did not get back till 9.00 pm having had some punctures. The supply of tyres is rotten at present.

**Friday 27 July 1917** Went into GHQ and had a long talk with Tavish Davidson. They have great hopes of a real success up north and think that there will be really heavy fighting.

**Saturday 28 July 1917** Another Horse Show, this time the 2nd Cav.Div. Motored down to Frevent and they had it in a chateau's grounds just east of there. It was very good but their horses don't compare with those of the 4th Cav.Div. It was very hot as there was not a breath of air. Today would have been a good day for the 3rd Ypres Battle to start, but has been put off.

**Saturday 29 July 1917** Very wet and stormy, but cleared up at midday. Still hope for fine weather.

**Monday 30 July 1917** Spent the day visiting the Corps up in the north. They are all full of heart and think they will certainly succeed tomorrow. The morning broke wet, but the glass is rising and the weather experts report a deep anticyclone and fine weather. All the omens appear favourable. We have more guns than we have ever had before and they have been pounding the Boche for over a fortnight. All we want is fine weather.

**Tuesday 31 July 1917** The 3rd Battle of Ypres* began at 3.50 am and we hope it will develop into a chance for the Cavalry. We are attacking on a front of four Corps, all under Gough, [while] the French attack on our left. By 12 noon we heard that all our attacks were progressing favourably − those of the 14th and 18th Corps and the French were going very well. The two southern Corps had the harder task and their progress will, I think, be slower and entail hard fighting.

Saw Eric Dillon and he told me that the French were mounting an attack which is a comfort as it will keep the Boche occupied at another part of the line. Have heard a bit of gossip that this offensive, which is the biggest we have as yet undertaken, was only approved by the War Council three days ago. They wanted to attack in Timbuctoo and not at the vital point which is here. Wallie and LLG however won the day − we are a really marvellous nation! In England now our politicians think themselves soldiers; in Germany they are soldiers first.

**Wednesday 1 August 1917** Yesterday can only be considered a fairly successful start as we did not get on on the right as we expected to. The country there is very wooded − the woods form a regular [abbatis?] and are very difficult to get through. Owing to this our attack got behind the barrage. I am afraid that our casualties in the 2nd Corps must have been pretty heavy as these unsuccessful attacks always cost a lot. We took over 5,000 prisoners. This is the first stage and they are mounting for the second stage now. As far as I can see, this is going to be a fight to a finish and, if we can wear the German resistance down, there may be a chance for us. At present it is very boring sitting here but I expect we shall have plenty to do later on. Today we have had the first wet day since April. It will delay the preparations I am afraid as the rain on the shell-broken ground forms liquid mud.

**Thursday 2 August 1917** Another wet day, we have no luck at all. The country is just under water and will take some time to dry.

**Friday 3 August 1917** Went up to 5th Army HQ and saw Jack Collins and had a long talk to him. Of course the Ypres salient is a mass of liquid mud* − worse than the Somme Battle at its worst. Nothing is possible at present and I hope that they will realise it and not start nibbling. On the other hand, after 10 days' dry weather they could start again and the Boche may be lulled into a sense of false security. General Wrangles of the Russian Army is again staying with us. He did not think so badly of the Russian situation† as we thought he would, which was a surprise. No work for the Cavalry possible for at least a month. This sitting still is very bad for us, especially for me.

**Monday 6 August 1917** The weather has cleared a bit and we have had two dry days. It is to be·hoped that it will continue. There is no news from our front as no movement has been possible. Poor Wrangles feels the Russian situation very much but he has cheered up considerably since he came.

The front in the south is very quiet. Our 4th Div. goes into [the] line east of Ste Emilie for a few days so as to release the troops for operations against the Knoll. We ought to have taken the Knoll when we were in the line down there. We are having a very dull time just waiting. I only hope that something will develop this autumn or else we go into the line for the winter. Another winter like the last will be beyond anything one can bear.

**Wednesday 8 August 1917** Went out and saw a Signalling Scheme in the morning and also inspected the horses of the Bridging Train. In the evening went and dined with the 1st Corps. After dinner the 'Very Lights' gave a show. They were very good – especially in the part songs. Had one of the worst storms I can remember this year. It poured in buckets from 6 to 8.30 pm and flooded the whole country out. It is very bad luck as it puts off our operations at Ypres.

**Thursday 9 August 1917** Went to the 1st Div. to see if they had been drowned last night. Found the conditions much better than one thought possible, so the storm may have been fairly local – at least I hope so.

**Monday 13 August 1917** Things have been very dull. The 2nd Corps attacked and made good the Zonnebeke[?] Ridge, but did not suceed in taking Inverness Copse* which as far as one can see is nothing but a big abattis now. I don't think they will try again, but work north-east towards Polygon Wood† and then turn south and take Inverness Copse in rear. We took about 500 prisoners and seven guns. The Boche evidently fought well from what I can gather and made five counter attacks to try and regain the ground lost. The weather is still very changeable and I have my old complaint of lumbago

**Monday 20 August 1917** Have not had time to write my Diary. The weather has at last improved and looks as if we were going to have a fine spell. On 14th the 5th Div. held their horse show in the grounds of Bryas Chateau near St Pol. Saw many old friends.

On the 18th went over to Camiers to see a demonstration of machine gun work. All the world was there and saw many friends. The demonstration was especially interesting as one could see the result on the sand, where the bullets struck. I saw General Hamilton Gordon, my old chief in the 9th Corps and we had a long talk, especially over the Messines attack* – he was very pleased with it.

Yesterday went with the Corps Commander to the 5th Army. We first went to the 2nd Corps. It appears that in each attack the 8th Div.† got to its objectives‡, but had to come back because people on their flanks did not get on and allowed the Boche counter attacks to come in. It is hard luck on the men when that happens. They mean however to get Inverness Copse and that will help a good deal. The whole of the offensive depends on getting a real good footing on the ridge west of Geluveld. The general opinion is that the Boche is putting everything in here and fighting very well. If the weather holds we can make him very hard put to hold on to the Staden Ridge; if we get this we shall be well placed for a further offensive with a view to clearing the coast line. Whether we can do it this autumn remains to be seen.

**Wednesday 22 August 1917** The weather has kept very fine the last day or two. We attacked again today in the direction of Inverness Copse but from the information at hand, the attack has not been a success. These concrete dug-outs* of the Boche are holding us up badly and till we find some way of taking them they will continue to do so. It is very disappointing as time is now getting on. We are going to have a Corps horse show – I personally hate these shows in wartime, but they are good for the officers and men and keep up their keenness and interest in their horses. The French have advanced north of Verdun and have taken 7,000 prisoners. The Italians are making another bid for Trieste† and have taken 10,000. If we can only move a little faster things will go on, but I see little opening for the Cavalry at present.

**Friday 7 September 1917** Went home on 23 August and had a real bad crossing but was lucky as next day there was a howling gale and no boats got across. Went to the War Office and saw Hutchinson. He suggested I might go there, but I don't think so. It would kill me I think. He had not got very much news. They seem to think that November will be the crucial month and that the Boche will either offer truce or go in for another winter. Any peace under these conditions will be a rotten one as he will still have an army in being.

Again there are rumours that the War Cabinet wish to hold the Boche on this front and reinforce either Italy, Salonika, Egypt, etc. In fact anywhere where there are no Boches. They do not realise that this war can only be ended successfully by killing Boches and this is the front on which it can be done. They are hopeless and I think Wallie Robertson is a wonder the way he holds them all and keeps the show in the right path. Returned last night.

**Saturday 8 September 1917** A very foggy morning, but it cleared up later. Went and saw Gregory commanding the Secunderabad Bde and than went on and saw the 2nd Div. at Houdain-Houdainville. Seely is betting even fivers that there will be an armistice by 25 December and that the war will be over with favourable terms for us. Germany, of course, has a great chance now – to give France, Alsace and Lorraine and take a quid pro quo in Russia. France must be disgusted with Russia and, with the evacuation of Belgium, would certainly want to make terms – at the expense of Russia, of course. Germany would come out well and the danger is that she will put forward this formula, which would probably be acceptable to the German people as Riga was one of the Hanseatic towns*. I wonder if this will develop – it will be a bad peace for us, but we may be forced into making it.

**Friday 14 September 1917** My birthday and I am 43 today. Went up yesterday to see the 2nd Army* who are attacking south of the Ypres-Roulers railway. They were very confident of success and I hope that they will have it. They have got a lot of troops up there and are in great depth. The General dines with the Chief† tonight and meets Asquith and other politicians – what a bore it must be for a busy man like him having to entertain these Cabinet Ministers who after all are only joy-riding. Winston is out here too – munitions I suppose. Heard this morning that I nearly went to Egypt as Chief of Staff to the Bull – I don't think I should have liked it but of course it would be promotion and a very responsible position. It was a compliment at all events.

The weather is just holding up and nothing else. It is curious now how everything depends on it because one may say that, if there is no flying, there can be no battle. They seem to be sending troops to Egypt. I hope they are carefully weighing the requirements and not sending a man too many. Because here is where a decision can be got and where there are no Boches there will be no decision.

**Saturday 15 September 1917** A fine day and a good deal of air activity. Today's *Times* gives many pointers towards the German wish for peace and things seem to be spreading that way. Of course another winter of war is looming up in front of Germany and she must think as to whether she is going to have another winter of it. I shall not believe it until I see it.

**Monday 17 September 1917** Went down to see the 2nd Cav.Div. and had lunch with Bob Greenly. He holds that the French will never make peace until Germany is broken. He is a great Francophile – I don't agree with him – I think that if offered Alsace-Lorraine with the evacuation of France and Belgium, the French would make peace and thus force a peace on all their Allies. Last night we had a ladies' dinner party – the Corps HQ are breaking out badly!

**Tuesday 18 September 1917** Went down to the 2nd Div. to watch a Scheme being carried out by the 5th Lancers*. The weather looks like breaking but I hope it won't. Nixon went to see the 1st Aussies† today – they are very optimistic.

**Wednesday 19 September 1917** Spent the morning watching the Canadian Cav.Bde in a Scheme under Seely. They were a trifle slow I thought. Went up to the 2nd Army and had a talk with Tim Harrington regarding his attack, which takes place tomorrow at 5.40 am. He is full of confidence and they were all very cheerful up there. He told me that he was very well satisfied with all the preliminary work so I wish them all success. They attack [on the] 20th with the Anzac «Corps] and part of the 9th Corps south of the Ypres-Roulers railway, whilst Gough and the 5th Army attack north of these. Just as I left he had a lot of newspaper correspondents there and he was going to tell them what was going on. He said it is best to be frank with them.

**Friday 21 September 1917** Went out to attend the sports of the 1st Cav.Div. just west of Rincq[?]. It was a good gathering and a great number of the men attended. Saw lots of old friends. The 2nd and 5th Army attacks yesterday were most successful – all the objectives were reached except a small and unimportant bit south of the Menin road. Our casualties were quite light so the day was quite satisfactory.

**Saturday 22 September 1917** We had a Regimental Dinner tonight at Desvres where the Regiment is now stationed. We numbered 43. Got back here at 1.30 a.m.!!!

**Tuesday 25 September 1917** Spent the morning in watching the 1st Cav.Div. at work: 9th versus 2nd Cav.Bde. At 12.30 pm got into the motor and went to Bertrancourt[?] south-west of Arras to see some experiments with tanks*. I was a little disappointed in them. Heard that the Boche had put in a big attack today just north of the Menin road with success, but that our counter attacks had quite restored the situation. It will be bad for the Division concerned, as it cannot be relieved before tomorrow's attack.

**Wednesday 26 September 1917** Spent the day in the office and watched the arrival of the news from the 2nd and 5th Armies. It has been a good day and all our objectives have been gained except that portion between Polygon Wood* and the Ypres-Menin road. I think the reason is that the 33rd Div. were tired. The Boche attacked them all yesterday and they could not be relieved last night so they had to carry on. No harm had been done however.

**Friday 28 September 1917** Got up at 6.30 am and went to attend a field day with the 1st Div. At 10.45 am got a message to say the Chief wished the CC and myself to attend a conference at Cassel at 11.00 am. The Officer on night duty had made a box* of it and allowed me to go off without letting me know and of course the CC could not go, being in Amiens. MacAndrew got there however. I was very angry as there was no reason to make a box of it. They were all very optimistic, so I am told and think the Boche has had a good hammering and so he has locally.

**Saturday 29 September 1917** Up to Loire Chateau with the CC to discuss the situation with Hubert Gough and then back to Cassel to do the same with Sir Herbert Plumer. Rather widely divergent opinions between the two Army commanders. I think we have a chance of a big success and use our Cavalry, but not till we have got the Staden Ridge. We must peg away and get the first, then put in a big attack from the Menin road northwards with a deep objective and use the Cavalry there.

**Sunday 30 September 1917** Rode over to Blendecques with the Corps Commander and had an interview with the Commander-in-Chief and the CGS*. The subject was the possible use of Cavalry in a big attack at Ypres – I think there is a chance. We shall lose very heavily; on the other hand we ought to make a big bag of guns and men. It is for the Chief to decide whether it is worthwhile; if he says then we go through with it. The Boche aeroplanes are very active tonight and the anti-aircraft batteries are hard at it for miles around – the moon is the friend of the aeroplane at night. The fine weather continues – if we have a fine October many things may happen.

**Tuesday 2 October 1917** Attended a conference at Cassel at which Sir D.H presided and Plumer and Gough were present. The show in Mesopotamia has been a very good one and the Turk has had a good set back there*. It is evident that the defeated force was an advance guard of a much larger force and the defeat has checked the advance for the time being. There is no doubt that the Turks will make great efforts to capture Bagdad and will be egged on by the Boche by all sorts of promises. In fact the Boche is now supposed to be forming two Divisions, which are called the Tigris I and II, to help the Turk. I don't think these will mature; but the [Berlin to] Bagdad railway without Bagdad is not much use and therefore one may expect special efforts in that direction.

**Sunday 7 October 1917** Have been too busy to write my Diary. The Germans have, in the opinion of the powers-that-be, shown signs of weakening and so the Cavalry have once more been warned to be ready. As usual have had two Armies and GHQ to deal with, so have been rushing about a good deal. All arrangements have been made and the 1st and 5th Divs well to hand – the weather up till today has been good – but it has poured all day. The result is that we stand fast for the present. It is really hopeless – I think we have the Boche very nervous. We ought to have a success after the next two attacks and down comes the rain. We were to move to Poperinge tomorrow, but now we shall stay here [at Aire].

**Monday 8 October 1917** It has been raining in a perfectly wicked way. The Chief was staying the night at Cassel before tomorrow's attack. They were all cheerful and determined to carry out the attack – rain or no rain. There appears to be no chance for the use of Cavalry until the Staden Ridge is in our hands but we may be ordered forward before that – I hope not as we shall lose much of our value getting there*.

**Tuesday 9 October 1917** In spite of all the rain, our attack has been successful and we have gained our objectives*. The reports say prisoners are coming in. This all points to the fact that the Boche is evidently weakening and feeling the strain. We must get on at all costs with attacks on a big front. The French could help a lot now by pushing their attack on the Aisne on a large front as the Boche has six fresh Divisions there in Reserve and attack would keep them there. I am afraid they will attack too late and get a cheap success which will do no good, in comparison, to the cause.

**Wednesday 12 October** The weather has really broken and the luck is once more on the side of the Boche. I do not now think that there is a chance of using the Cavalry this year. I think if we get the Staden-Passchendale Ridge we shall do well and cannot expect more. Day before yesterday, went up to Ypres and on to Wieltje and there walked over the battlefield. There was very little shelling, but [the] masses of men in the area was wonderful – the Poelkapelle, Passchendale and Zandvoorde roads were packed* and it looked as if there must be enormous casualties should the Boche take it into his head to shell the place.

Today's attack has not succeeded in reaching its final objectives and it is not to be wondered at, considering what the ground must be like. It is not the Boche but sheer physical exhaustion which stops the men. I suppose we shall be moved back and I only hope that they put us into the line soon and so keep us occupied during the winter.

**Tuesday 16 October 1917** Have not had any time to write. They have decided to send us south so as to get our winter area ready. It is very disheartening. If the weather had only held, we should have had a chance of dealing the Boche a real good knockout blow. We leave the 1st and 5th Divs behind in case there is a chance of using mounted men. The 2nd and 3rd move to areas west of Amiens and we move our HQ to Beauquesne and get the 4th Div. back again. There is a regular lull now in the fighting but the Aisne front is livening up and I hope the French will have a real success there. The Boche keeps five fresh Divisions behind that front; I suppose because they do not want to lay the Crown Prince's Army open to a bad knock. The weather has been fine the last three days – long may it last.

**Friday 19 October 1917** Spent the day yesterday at Le Touquet doing Schemes at the Hotchkiss (gun) School there. It was a glorious day and quite warm. This morning motored down to St Pol and inspected the 4th Cav.Bde on the march. The horses looked fairly well, but have not got much to go on. They want to have more flesh on them if they are going to stand exposure and cold.

**Saturday 20 October 1917** Moved from Aire to Beauquesne and now we have the 2nd, 3rd, 4th Divs and are under the 3rd Army. Motored through to Villers-Carbonnel and saw the 4th Div.; then went round and saw the building of the winter quarters for the 4th and 5th Divs. They are doing good work and getting on well. On our way home through the desolated area, saw two women standing at the wayside, so offered them a lift to Amiens. They accepted and said they were waiting to be picked up by a French car. It was then getting dark and quite cold. One was the widow of the French Colonel who had been killed and they had spent all day trying to find his grave with no success. It was very sad. There must be many similar cases and what is worse English people cannot get over at all.

152

**Sunday 21 October 1917** Went this morning with the Corps Commander to have a look at the ground east of the Vimy Ridge. We motored up from Arras along the main Arras-Lens road – then walked along the ridge to just south of Souchez and back to Neuville-St-Vaast. It was a bad day for seeing which was unfortunate, but intensely interesting. On the way back I went and looked at some of the craters which we blew when I was in the line there with the 46th Div. The country is hardly recognisable and very much cut up. How the Canadians managed to attack over it is very wonderful. The Boche must hate this present position as the ridge dominates the whole country as far as Douai. Things are very quiet this morning, probably owing to the haze – one heard a machine gun firing now and again and also a few trench mortars and that was all.

**Tuesday 23 October 1917** The French put in their attack on the Aisne and took 8,000 prisoners and 60 guns – it is a fine performance. It will have a tremendous effect on the morale of the nation and will do a lot of good – I think that once more the Germans underestimated their enemy. They thought the French were bluffing and would not put in a serious attack. In nearly every case where they thought they would be pushed back, they have moved their guns; in this case they have not. They explain it very cleverly in their wireless communique. Went today to Le Touquet to a Scheme at our Hotchkiss School.

**Thursday 25 October 1917** Spent the day in the office but had a good gallop this afternoon after hares with the Corps Commander. The news from the Italian front is not good – the Boche claims 10,000 prisoners*. We knew that he had sent down three or four Divisions to bolster up the Austrians, but did not think that such a reinforcement would have such a big success. The Austrian troops must be bad, but then so must the Italians. It is a pity – but one comfort is that the Austrians must have been pretty low to force the Boche to send down Divisions so as to ensure a success.

**Monday 29 October 1917** Have been very busy with a Scheme and so have not had time to write the Diary. The Italian news is the limit* and is enough to create a great deal of despondency. Went out today and had a good look at the country in the direction of Cambrai and Bourlon – it was very interesting. The front was very quiet and the Boche hardly fired a shot.

It is difficult to see what the result of this Italian setback will be; with Russia and Italy *hors de combat*, the burden will be thrown on the West and it looks as if France, America and ourselves would be left to fight it out. I should not wonder if Germany, after the success in Italy, would try a big attack on this front. He can withdraw Divisions from the Russian front with impunity and inside the circle has practically a free hand. We are sending two Divisions† and the French four so as to help, but these are not great numbers and we can ill afford to weaken this front as we want to keep pushing for all we are worth. The papers talk about a new gas used in Italy, but it is probably the mustard gas‡ they have used over here – I think we get the benefit of every new villainy here first. We make another attack at Ypres§ tomorrow.

**Tuesday 30 October 1917** We attacked east of Ypres and got the objectives. The Canadians are close up to Passchendale and, from the Boche communique, some of their patrols must have got into the village itself. I think we shall get the ridge all right. The Italians are still retreating, but they seem to have got some sort of order into their skirmish, so I hope they will be able to check the Boche/Austrian Divisions now.

**Thursday 1 November 1917** Went out to Fins with the Corps Commander; we then walked out to the front line to have a good look at the country in the direction of Cambrai. Visibility was only fair but we saw a good bit of the country. It was very quiet, the Boche was strafing a battery but that was all.

**Friday 2 November 1917** Had a very busy day – at work on operation Schemes. General Scott of the United States Army and four Staff Officers came to lunch – we showed them some of our Signals, the horses of the 2nd Life Guards and K Battery. They had been on a mission to Russia and said that the whole place was chaotic*. The German propaganda has been very clever – the Russian soldier is very simple and also very slow in thought – the Germans said to him: 'You were fighting for your Csar – and you fought well – that was well and good. But now you have no Csar – and so why are you fighting?' This the Russian easily understands – anything beyond what is very simple he does not understand. They were very determined for the war through and tackling it very seriously, which is a comfort.

**Thursday 8 November 1917** Have not had time to write my Diary lately. Yesterday went out to the front line in the vicinity of La Vacquerie and had a good look at the country – the Boche wire is very strong and so is ours. It is very quiet indeed. A shell came over now and again but that was all. Day before yesterday we took Passchendale* – so we have got another step on the ridge. I think the Boche is going to give up the ridge and retire to the Roulers line. Eye-witnesses say that his men did not wait for the attack but bolted as soon as it started, but he still has many stout-hearted fellows who hang on with their machine guns and give a lot of trouble.

This morning I attended a conference at Army HQ and saw a lot of old friends. The Italians are still in a state of collapse and are retiring†. The Boche can surely claim a great success there – I am told he had taken close on half a million prisoners. The Italians must be pretty rotten and I am told that socialism is rife in their ranks. It has poured for the last two days – I hope the latter half of the month will be fine.

**Friday 9 November 1917** Went round and visited the 3rd and 4th Corps. The news from Italy continues to be bad and the worst part of it is that we are being forced to send troops to bolster them up. I hear that Plumer is going there so it must be something pretty big. The Germans have certainly done well.

**Saturday 10 November 1917** Had a busy day in the office, but got a lot done. We hear today from the *Daily Mail* that a Central Council* is going to run the war in the west and that Cadorna, Foche and Henry Wilson are going to be the members representing Italy, France and us. It is undoubtedly a political move and it looks as if Lloyd George would wish to have a say in the conduct of the war through Henry Wilson. How will it work, I wonder? I hate to think of the intrigue which will go on, anyhow D.H. is a strong man and will stand no nonsense and I don't think that Sir Wallie will either†. The only way to conduct a war is through one commander, there must be a military Autocrat. We have seen the advantages Germany has had and our own disadvantages when dealing with our Allies and now we go and establish a Council!‡ Our preparations go on apace.

**Wednesday 14 November 1917** Had a conference on coming operations in the morning which all Divisional Commanders attended. Things are going well and the secret has been well kept*. This foggy northerly weather is what we pray for, if it will only last us out – we ought to have a bit of luck.

**Thursday 15 November 1917** Moved our HQ from Beauquesne to Villers-Carbonnel and have gone into huts. They are at present very cold, but we shall be very comfortable once we get settled. Went and saw the 3rd and 4th Corps on my way down. The weather is still misty and it augurs well for us if it only keeps on.

**Friday 16 November 1917** Spent a very cold night last night – the first in a hut – most of the cold came through the floor which rather represents a sieve. It is very badly joined together. Our preparations for the attack are nearing completion. It is always a bad time for the Staff Officer – all work is capable of improvement – yet so great is the military machine and so complicated its cogs and wires that it is seldom the Staff can say 'Now I have finished – let the thing rip.' Once the attack starts the people who arrange things burn their boats – up to that time must be a period of anxiety. The weather is holding out well at present and I can only hope that we are going to have luck in that respect for once.

The actual plan and place of attack has been kept as secret as it is possible to keep such things. Will it succeed and will the Cavalry have a chance of real work? No man can tell. I think it has a greater chance of success than anything we have undertaken as yet. The time of the year is not good – also one could wish that we had not been forced to send Divisions to

154

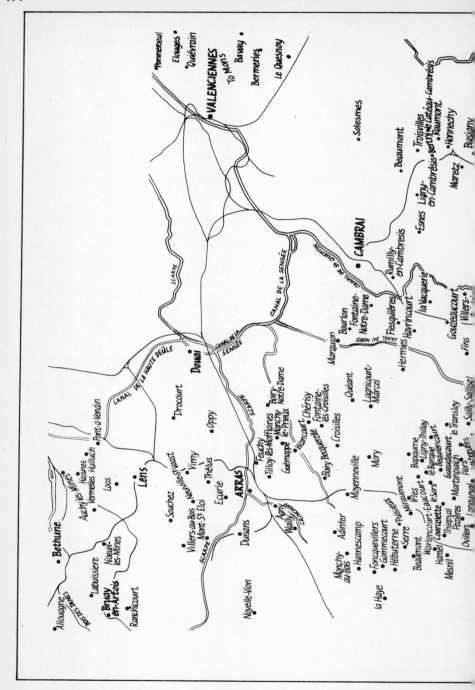

155

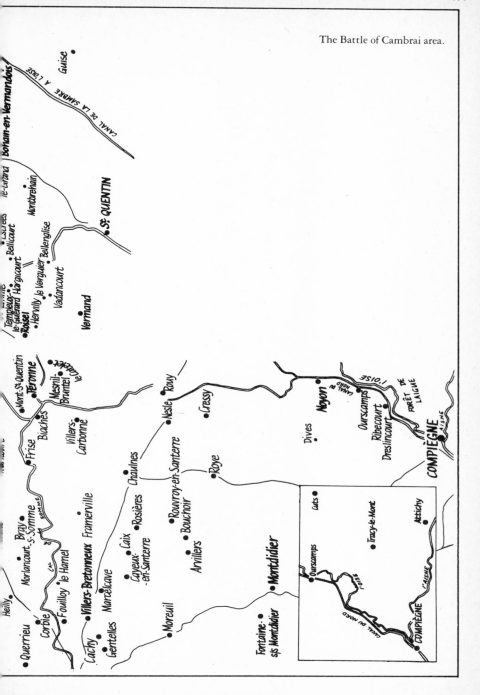

The Battle of Cambrai area.

Italy, they would have been available to support us in their attack*. It may however be for the best, as surprise is one of the greatest factors in war and the Boche may think that we are not able to undertake any offensive operations. It will be a great gallop if all goes well and I hope that it will.

**Saturday 17 November 1917** Got out for a ride this morning and saw our Pioneer Battalion practising a road-making Scheme over some old Boche wire and trenches. I hope that they will do it as well and as quickly on the day. I then rode on to Brie and saw the bridge we propose carrying on the tanks* – it is very solid and should do well if the tanks carrying it don't break down. There are many stories afloat that these coming operations are being talked of openly in London and especially among the women folk. Often one finds that things which are common gossip, are unknown by the people who ought to be the first to hear them officially. Another misty day, full of work – yet I think we may have quite a decent success with a little luck.

**Monday 19 November 1917** Spent the last two days in the office finishing up the preparations. Now everything I can do has been done and the Staff Officer stands or falls by his preparation. Tomorrow morning early we go up to our advanced HQ and the Battle of Cambrai commences. The secret has been well kept on the whole and I have great hopes of a considerable success. The weather has been fine and the country is dry, so at least we shall be going on the top of the ground – so much depends on the tanks as there has been no preliminary bombardment. If they start well, the Infantry will go like a house on fire. We shall drink success to the adventure tonight.

**Tuesday 20 November 1917** Left at 5.00 am to move to our advanced HQ at Fins. The weather which has been so kind, broke this morning and the result was a drizzle and very low clouds. The 1st, 2nd and 5th Cav.Divs moved up to their positions of forward concentration during the night. They had a 10-mile march in the darkness but came on well and were not very late, except the 5th who were blocked. The attack was a surprise on a large scale and all the preparations were kept as quiet as possible. Unfortunately the Germans raided yesterday and got four prisoners from the 36th Div. Some prisoners say that these men had given the show away and that the attack itself was not a surprise, but the scale on which it was made was a great surprise.

It went very successfully – but there were two points which affected us: the first was that the Boche had two Divisions in Reserve* behind the line where we hoped he had none; secondly, the want of confidence in some of the Infantry† in the powers of the tank. The result of both these was loss of time and therefore less time to get to our objectives. At one time it looked as if we were going to get through, but the failure of the 25th Div. to get over the Canal [de St Quentin] at Masnières and on to Rumilly-en-Cambresis before dark, did not give us the opportunity we wished for. One squadron of the Canadians‡ did get across the Canal and charged a battery which it scuppered, taking 17 prisoners, but the Boche concentrated machine guns on it and it lost heavily on its way back. It was a gallant action.

The failure of the 4th Corps to hold the village of Flesquières after taking it, delayed the action on this part of the field for several hours. The village [was] taken but badly mopped up – as our troops passed beyond, the Boche came out of his dug-outs and held on until far into the night. The result of the day was a penetration through the Hindenberg line and nearly 5,000 prisoners. The weather was bad and aeroplane observation practically nil. It had been a good day's work: a little more and I think that the Cavalry would have got through.

**Wednesday 21 November 1917** Still at Fins and another day's heavy fighting. The weather is vile and our horses get no water, so they suffer a good deal. There is no water except in the Canal and that is very near the Boche and also unhealthy. The 1st Cav.Div. have had a very heavy day's fighting today and right well they have done it too – the Bays and 4th Dragoon Guards made charges and got in with the sword and took prisoners, which is very good for the morale of the Cavalry.

The French have taken this show of ours up and are ready to pour troops through any gap we make – I wish they had started making a gap alongside us and so widened the front of attack – but alas it was not to be so. I hope that we shall get Bourlon Wood tomorrow as that place has the observation of all the country round here.

**Friday 23 November 1917** A lovely day and a successful one, we have made a good advance and taken the high ground at Bourlon Wood. I don't fancy that the Boche will like this and will probably counter attack hard to get it back. There has been a lot of train movement into and out of Cambrai – the Boche may be clearing out, or else bringing up large reinforcements with a view to counter attacking. He has quite a difficult problem to face. Is he going to bring up his heavy guns and fight us here or else go further back? One thing has been shown him – that the Hindenberg line is not a real defence. I walked round it and the line is a marvel of engineering skill – beautifully sited. The dug-outs are wonderful – regular palaces – and they are left as they stood and the Boche fled out of them.

Many stories are now afloat – the first one is that a German Gunner Major served a gun himself and knocked out eight tanks – he still lies beside his gun*. The funniest of all was the Divisional Camp Commandant [who] having collected all the Officers, servants and corps, had drawn them up and was making a speech that they must all die for the Fatherland – our men came round the corner and up went his hands at once. I think the Battle of Cambrai is finished. We have done well; we should have done much better with a bit of luck.

**Sunday 25 November 1917** Yesterday was a rather disappointing one – for us it was a day of order and counter order. At the end of the day we were ordered to push as much Cavalry as possible through Bourlon Wood and village – they wanted this done at once, the nearest Division being 10 to 12 miles away!* However, we fixed up for the Division to move this morning. Bourlon Wood and Hill is now the kernel of all the fighting. We shall have to retake it and also get beyond it so as to hold it – the Boche will not let it go without a struggle. The 1st Cav.Div. have been fighting on their feet all day, the 15th Hussars† doing well in a counter attack last night. Owing to the enemy resistance, it was not possible to push the Cavalry through and I don't know what made the Army think of it at Bourlon village. We have left the 2nd Cav.Div. at Flesquières for the night, as the situation does not look very good. It has turned very cold and they prophesy snow – I hope it will not come, as our horses will suffer very great hardships. The Infantry and tanks have done very well.

**Monday 26 November 1917** As far as the Cavalry are concerned and the chance of a breakthrough, the Battle of Cambrai is over. It behoves us now to make certain that we can hold Bourbon Hill and Wood and to take the ground on each side so as to make it less of a salient.

The main question in my mind is: could we have done better in view of after-event knowledge? [Firstly] The programme to be carried out was [retarded?] and therefore there was not enough daylight. Secondly the 29th Wessex Div. did not reach its objective, which was the last Boche line – this objective has not yet been reached. Thirdly the 1st Cav.Div. were issued fresh orders in the middle of the battle; these fresh orders were counter ordered and counter ordered again. The result was that time was wasted and time was the main factor. Critics are many – I met one this morning who is renowned as the slowest Regimental commander in the Cavalry Corps*. He said we shall never have another chance like it – we did not move fast enough!!!!

The main point was the necessity of opening the Masnières gap so as to allow the Cavalry to pass east of Cambrai: this was crucial – it failed. The 29th Div. had come a long way – had been marching all night – I don't think it could possibly [be] expected to have the final kick necessary, if it met serious opposition†. In an operation such as this, the final attack is often the most important and the necessity of saving it fatigue is paramount – it should be bussed or railed up and never marched up. As regards the Cavalry – the task assigned and method of doing it should not be changed by such a formation as a Corps, situated 12 miles behind the line. Cavalry get instructions, commanders are well informed, it is best to let them judge the situation. I don't think, as the case stands, that we could have broken through, but I think we could have made more headway on the west side of the Canal de St Quentin [Scheldt]. Rode up to Mont Havrincourt this morning and then on to Flesquières, the ground south of Fontaine-Notre-Dame and Bourlon very visible. Very cold and fine morning, but it looks like rain or snow now.

**Tuesday 27 November 1917** This morning we made another attack with a view to making our position on Bourlon Hill safe. It has not been a very propitious day – the Guards Div. attacked Fontaine and got its objectives north of it, but with heavy losses. The Boche counter attacked and drove them back to their old positions – I am afraid that they have suffered very heavily. The position in Bourlon village has been slightly improved.

Moved back from Fins to Villers-Carbonnel and that is the end as far as we are concerned – a failure. Heard tonight that we go into the line at once – that will be a better way of spending the winter than sitting in the back areas, so I am thankful for that.

**Friday 30 November 1917** This morning was woken up by a tremendous bombardment and, at 8.30 am, was told to have a Div. ready to move at short notice to support the 3rd Corps in the direction of Epehy. A few minutes after, another telephone message to say that things were looking rather black towards Villers-Guislain and that the Boche had penetrated our line as far as Gouzeaucourt. The Army wished to place the Divs under the 3rd Corps but the Corps Commander pointed out that the only way to try and restore the situation was by a counter attack from the direction of Epehy on Villers-Guislain. It was then agreed that the Corps Commander should take command and see what could be done.

We first got into a motor and went to Villers-Faucon where the 55th Div. had their HQ. Here we found that the attack had been pushed forward and had penetrated up to Gouzeaucourt. We also heard that the attack had been **expected** for two days!* To think, knowing the weakness of the line, we had not been warned – the result was that all the horses were out on exercise and the 4th Cav.Div. had a Brigade away relieving the Infantry in the line. The leading Division did not therefore get up to Epehy till about 2.00 pm and the 4th Cav.Div. till 4.00 pm. The Boche had all these precious hours to establish himself. Had we been able to get the Divisions up by 12 noon, I think an attack against Villers-Guislain would have been successful – as it was, an attempt to move forward in the dark met with a failure. The 2nd Cav.Div., being at Fins, got into action west of Gouzeaucourt and materially assisted the attack of the Guards on that place.

Early next morning, it was arranged that 14 tanks† were to attack Gauche Wood and Villers-Guislain whilst the Guards took the [Canal de St?] Quentin ridge. The 9th Hodson's Horse‡ followed the tanks on foot and took the wood – taking an Officer, five sergeants and one gunner prisoner. The others failed to get on and the advance on Villers-Guislain did not progress as it should have done. I do not think a certain Brigade pressed on as much as it should have. The Mehow Bde§, which was ordered to take advantage of the attack on Villers-Guislain, got on both mounted and dismounted in the most gallant and determined manner, but of course their left was unsupported. It was a good attempt and must have had an effect on the Boche right. Later, at 3.00 pm, another attack on the Beet Factory and Villers-Guislain was made by the 4th and 5th Cav.Divs. The Canadians made a gallant attack but, their right being not supported, they had to retire. They had 500 prisoners at one time but had to leave them owing to the Boche getting round their right. It was dark by the time this finished – we held Gauche Wood in touch with the Guards on our left. Night again fell and from that time onwards until the night [of the] 5/6th we held the line until relieved by the Infantry.

There is no doubt that the Boche effected a surprise – he ought not to have done this, his point of attack was obvious. We evacuated Bourlon Wood – this is a humbling but a good decision. We have gained some ground and killed a good many Boches, but we should have done better. Even if the Boche did surprise us, we ought not to have given the ground as we did. I hear now we are on the defensive – the main theatre is Italy!!! The Russians are making peace and so the Boche is free to bring troops over here this winter – he will give us a bad time, I expect. This is the result of Government interference with the strategy of the campaign. The main theatre of war will be this front always and people who go for the sideshows are bucking the main question. Came back to Villers-Carbonnel at 10.00 am on the 6th after quite an exciting but very cold time – there has been a hard frost for five days.

**Monday 10 December 1917** We have taken over our old line and the 24th Div. come under us, so I am pretty busy. There is a lot of talk about the Cavalry just now; people seem to think that we should have got through on 20 November. I certainly think that the 1st Cav.Div. should have got on faster. I am not sure that the lack of reinforcements has not made the Cavalry put too great a value on itself. I personally would rather lose a Division than have people say that we did not make every effort – of course it is the people who don't count that talk, but pitch will always stick. The Army Commander* is evidently disappointed, he has not been near us. Personally I am satisfied that the 5th Cav.Div. could not have done more that it did. I think the 1st Cav.Div. was much hampered by order and counter orders of the 4th Corps.

What I feel more than anything else is that the higher command do not seem to visualise a situation beyond a certain point – short of the point to carry out a really successful offensive. I hear much of probable peace rumours – are we strong enough? We have held the initiative for two years – it looks as if we were going to lose it now? If the Russians and Rumanians make peace†, we shall be hard put to it till America develops her strength. Walked round one of our switch lines today. The Boche aeroplanes were very active – I don't think they mean a big attack here. It was fine today and is freezing hard tonight.

**Tuesday 11 December 1917** A very cold day – sat in the office the whole morning. Neil Malcolm came to lunch and we come under the 5th Army I am sorry to say. They are troublesome people to deal with – too much paper flying about. We still have got the wind up as regards a German attack; it is quite possible – but we shall kill a good many if they do and that is the main thing.

**Friday 14 December 1917** Have had no time to write. Depression reigns everywhere – I do not know what has come over people. *The Times* demands an enquiry as to who to blame for the German inrush on the 30th. Somebody must be hanged – they have got someone in view I suppose, that is the English method. From all I can hear, the men were surprised after a very intense bombardment* – if you cannot trust the front lines to hold out, no defence is any good at all.

What I hate about the atmosphere is that the general trend of conjecture is 'What is the Boche going to do?' instead of 'What are we going to do to the Boche?' If the former is our line of argument, we had better make peace at once. Of course the Boche is stronger now and he had many more guns. Things don't look as rosy as they did but we fought him before and we can do so again – and we don't know how hungry he is. Poor Bertie Fisher is in the cart. He evidently said too much at a restaurant about operations and was reported. I cannot imagine him doing such a thing and am very sorry as he has lost his job and may be court-martialled. He was such a very good soldier too – but no one can tell what other people will do.

**Saturday 15 December 1917** Walked round our trenches east of Hargicourt with Duggan who commands the 73rd Inf.Btn and the Corps Commander – they are in a bad state. The Boche, if he wants to thicken his line, does so behind trenches which are good and wire which is thick. We thinned our line behind trenches and wire which were bad – the result was the reverse at Villers-Guislain. At present we are on the defensive everywhere; it is therefore necessary for us to have strong defences and this is a thing that we do not realise.

**Monday 17 December 1917** Had a busy two days. Last night it commenced to snow and we had a bad time of it. These huts are made for fine weather and not for driving snow – mine was all right as I filled the chinks with newspaper, but others were snowed out. This morning there was 8 inches of snow on the ground. It has drifted a good deal and a good many roads were quite impassable. I hope it will not go on, as if it does, our horses will have a bad time.

**Saturday 22 December 1917** Have had no time to write my Diary as have been pretty busy. There is no news here – the Boche appears to be quiet, but one does not know what devilment he is up to. The general idea seems to be that he is nearly done and does not want to go on with the war and let America come in. He has however six months before that and the Russian peace allows him to bring over men and especially guns. He has the means to put in a very big offensive – far bigger than Verdun – and it seems that his play is to put in a big throw and try to get a Division on this side. If he is successful, he is very well placed; if unsuccessful he loses his game. It is thought by many that he will put forward terms of peace before next spring and that the terms for him will be good. But whether the politicians consider them good enough, remains to be unseen. The snow is still on the ground and of course the ground is frozen hard. This makes work more difficult and our defensive line is none too strong as it is.

**Tuesday 25 December 1917** Christmas – Yesterday I went to see Sir Julian Byng at his request. He read me out a letter which he was writing at the request of the Chief as regards the action of the Cavalry. It was a fair letter which I think put the case fairly, but what struck me was that he was very sore that the thing was not a greater success than it was: ie that the Cavalry did not get through and so open up the whole theatre of war in that place. The War Cabinet, at the dictation of *The Times*, are taking the whole conduct of the operation up. I quite agree and think it is right that they should do so and on it hangs the future of the Cavalry.

I have nothing on my conscience – I don't think that, as things turned out, the original Scheme was feasible after 3.00 pm on the 20th* – I am firmly convinced that, considering the troops at our disposal, we should have stopped and made ourselves secure on the 21st†. As regards the Cavalry – people at home ask 'They had a great chance at Cambrai – is it any use keeping them? They will never have such a chance again.' That is the crux of the whole matter – on this they may do anything – make the Cavalry into latrine caretakers. I shall be glad to have a rest – that is that. This is my fourth Christmas at war – I want to beat the Boche but I also want Christmas at home with my wife and chicks.

**Thursday 27 December 1917** The ground is still covered in snow and it is still cold – there is not very much news here, we are at the usual routine of holding a line. The men are well and much prefer this cold weather to the wet and there is not much sickness. The Italians seem to be fighting hard again and there are the usual peace rumours. I think that the Boche will certainly do something in Palestine or Mesopotamia this winter, he cannot leave the Turks in the lurch* and is sure to send troops there. Had a letter from Cyril [Hankey] who was pretty sick at the talk at home and I don't wonder at it. The tongues seem to be wagging pretty freely and a good deal of mud is being thrown about.

**Monday 31 December 1917** Moved our HQ from Villers-Carbonnel to Le Catelet yesterday and so now we are permanently installed – I hope with no more changes for the present. Yesterday I took Goughie, the Army Commander, round a part of the line and we had a very interesting discussion on the power of defensive. He was quite please with what I showed him, for which I am glad. This is the last day of 1917, I wonder what 1918 will bring forth. Peace I hope – a good peace and not a Boche one.

**Sunday 27 January 1918** Went home on the 5th till the 22nd and returned to find the thaw in full blast and all the trenches fallen in. Also found orders that the 5th Cav.Div. is to go to Egypt and the 4th Cav.Div. is to be broken up*. This will leave us with a Corps of three Divisions: all British. The charge has been forced on D.H. by the War Cabinet who in turn are ruled by the Northcliffe press. They are trying to blame the Cavalry for the non-success of the Cambrai show because 10 days afterwards the Infantry were driven in at Villers-Guislain and we lost 160 guns! It is very disheartening to a soldier and must have a bad effect on the Cavalry. We are now busy with changes and the 4th and 5th Div. horses move back, so as to be ready to start for the East as soon as the arrangements have been made. The weather has been very mild and the office work in this Army is appalling. Enjoyed my trip home immensely.

**Sunday 3 February 1918** Have not had time to write – but it has been the daily routine of life and so there has not been very much in the way of news. The Boche has been very quiet and for days has done nothing. It has been very frosty with a thick fog. Today we had a conference and heard the French appreciation of the point of the Boche attack. They say that his main push will be between Arras and St Quentin and their arguments are based on the absence of preparation elsewhere. Again they say that the Boche has put the victor of Riga (Von Eutier) in command opposite us. His methods are secrecy and surprise and that no preparations will be shown. This is all very interesting, but very negative. We are hurrying on preparations as fast as we can and I think he will pay very dearly for an attack here.

Yesterday I had three hours of a French General who could not speak English – I have no doubt it must have done good to my French. Good news comes from Italy and the papers are making much of the internal situation in Germany*. I suppose that they must be in a bad way, but they are too well disciplined to break out to any great extent as yet. The French seem to be full of heart and that is good – will try to write the Diary daily in future but it is difficult just now as news is scarce.

**Friday 8 February 1918** Have had no time to write as have been more than busy – we are working hard at our defences and they are growing formidable. If only the Boche gives us time, he will have a very hard nut to crack. There is no doubt that the Boche has a large concentration of Divisions on this front; secondly Von Eutier is on this front. We want an identification badly opposite our right – I hope to get one tomorrow night when the Canadian Bde is making a raid. If we do, it will clear matters up considerably. The weather has favoured the Boche – it has been thick and flying has been impossible, [he] has therefore had a chance of concentrating Divisions where he likes with little chance of being found out. I hear the 19th Corps* relieve us here about the 20th and I shall go to a back area, it is beastly to think of it but the 5th Army are right. If there is going to be a big fight, better have an Infantry Corps here and the Cavalry as a mobile Reserve.

**Sunday 10 February 1918** The Boche is undoubtedly collecting an enormous number of Divisions behind his line, but as present there is little sign as to where he means to attack. Our line is at present quiet, although there are distinct signs of his having thickened up his line in front of us. Of course he may think that we shall strike early in the year so as to forestall his offensive – as he did at Verdun* with success. From our point of view that does not seem to be likely. They are collecting a lot of guns – I suppose that GHQ consider this is a likely point of attack. Or is this talk of attack here only a camouflage and do they mean to counter from this area, supposing the Boche has a dig at the French in Champagne? Of course we are well placed for such a counter move.

Deserters still come in – most of them are Alsatians. They talk a lot, but their information does not appear to be of great value. If there are many at other parts of the line, a good and valuable deduction may be possible. The weather has been fine I am glad to say – but low clouds and ground mist has prevented aeroplane observation.

**Tuesday 19 February 1918** Have had no time to write my Diary. On the 12th the Canadian Bde made an excellent raid and took an Officer and 13 men prisoners. They are very good at the work and real born fighters. On the 16th we had a conference here and some very straight talking about the Cavalry – the Corps Commander spoke his mind very freely and it will, I hope, do some good. There is too much talk and criticism of superiors and the morale is bound to suffer. The great excitement is the retirement of Sir William Robertson. He is going to take command of the Eastern Command*. I think he is one of the big men that we have got – he is a poor man and yet has the courage of his opinions. I wonder if the nation will allow it. This Versailles Conference† has been the cause of it. It is said that they want to make Foch Generalissimo of all the Western Armies – we know the French too well for that – but the politicians don't seem to. Whatever happens these dissensions will only raise the morale of the Boche and do us no good. Went to Daours today and saw our Schools.‡

# 12. The Spring Offensive

**26 February to 25 March 1918** Went home on 26 February to have an operation – all went well. Heard on 22 [March]* that the CC was going to be sent home, so got Barrow† to let me go out on the 26th to see what was the matter. I found that Goughie was the matter and had evidently reported badly on the CC – this was the result. Luckily the CC was in a strong position and the result is that Goughie has gone home and that Henry Rawlinson succeeds him‡. Everyone is thankful. Poor little Goughie has not stood the strain – it is a great pity with all his ability but quite unforgiveable.

There are many stories of our retirement. From what one hears on all sides, in many places it seemed to be unnecessarily fast. It is very difficult to find out the truth, one continually hears of magnificant fighting on the part of Divisons. It seems to me that where Divisions had good Officers, all was well. On all sides I hear that the Cavalry did magnificently§ and that if we only had the two Divisions which have just been disbanded, it would have made the greatest difference. The Cavalry barometer stands very high again, it was very low a month ago.

**Tuesday 26 March 1918** Had quite a good crossing and Lewenden met me at Boulogne. Found out that the Corps HQ were at Querrieu north-east of Amiens. They were bombing Amiens as we came through and doing a good deal of damage.

**Wednesday 27 March 1918** Took over my job from Kennedy who had been working it for me. We have only the 1st Div. – the other two are busy fighting in the south and doing splendidly. We have come back to one of the old lines through Albert and south of that place the Boche is further west than he had ever been before.

**Saturday 30 March 1918** Had no time to write. The 1st Cav.Div. is holding a line south of the Somme in conjunction with a collection of scalliwags – some of the 16th Div. – which have not done well. These Irish are awful. Mullens is quite cheerful, although short of sleep; he has been at it since the beginning without a rest and has done very well. Rawlinson has taken over the 5th Army and is bringing in his own Staff – I am sorry for Percy and Brooks Hambro but they have not had a chance.

The 2nd and 3rd Cav.Divs are moving up just south-east of Amiens. The French are organising a big counter stroke and I hope that it will be successful. We have now had some breathing space for three days and that will help no end. This German stroke has been a masterpiece in a way of organisation. Its object was to get a decisive success: it has not done so up to the present. It has had a great measure of success. The question is: will it satisfy the German people and Austria? If we can only put in an effective counter, it will have a great effect now.

The Boche are pushing the French south-west of Amiens and our 2nd and 3rd Cav.Divs have been drawn into the fight there. I was told that the French Divisions put in there were not expected to fight. We have got all their good ones for the counter strike. They are taking great risks – a successful counter stroke will justify them.

**Sunday 31 March 1918** The 1st Cav. Div. had a very heavy day's fighting yesterday and beat off a very determined attack by a Boche Div. on their position. They have had a good many casualties, I am afraid. Our 2nd Div. and the Canadian Bde were also engaged. The Canadians cleared Moreuil Wood*, but suffered heavily in doing so. The Corps Commander met Sir D.H. at the Army HQ and the Chief was most complimentary on the work of the Cavalry. Clemenceau the French Premier was also there and the Chief turned round to him and said 'The Cavalry are my best troops.' It is something to hear that we are good after the way people have tried to do away with us. I am told that everyone wanted Cavalry as they were really dependable in a tight corner. Our Army now is very different to the one which carried out the retreat in 1914.

Today is a quiet day up to the present. The Boche is beginning to feel that he has been stopped – of course he is tired. From what I hear, if the Boche had possessed and used a large mass of Cavalry, things would have been very black indeed. He advanced on such a big front that Cavalry in masses could be used. His lack of Cavalry saved us a disaster; just as in 1914 the lack of push in his Cavalry against the British left enabled us to get away. At present all our Divisions are away, so we have no command.

**Monday 1 April 1918** Went down to see the 2nd Cav. Div. whose HQ is at Gentelles. Their task this morning was to restore the situation south-east of that and retake a hill which gave the Boche observation over the whole country. They attacked the hill most gallantly and took the wood which crowns it. They could only muster 1,000 men from the Division. I am afraid their casualties have been rather heavy. Tommy Pitman estimates them at over 300 which at the present are hard to replace.

We went on to the Army to report progress and they were having a great conference*. Sir D.H., Clemenceau, Foch and all the Knuts were there. I hope they will come to some decision as we want to get a move on and reorganise the Cavalry – at present it will be no use until we do. We then went back to Gentelles. We were holding our ground but they thought that the Boche was going to counter attack and had turned all our guns on to them. Then we went to the 1st Cav. Div. at Fouilloy. The 14th Div. relieve the 2nd Cav. Div. tonight. I only hope they will hold on to the ground we have gained today. It has been a beautiful day and fairly warm. Saw our aeroplanes circling round and attacking the Boches this afternoon. The dirty brutes put three shells over this chateau this evening.

As regards this battle, the following questions appear to require answers:

a. We came back in places much quicker than we should have; in many cases, the Infantry walked back when the Boche appeared. Field guns did not cover the Infantry. The Horse guns on the other hand stuck it out and often continued firing after the Infantry has retired. The answer is lack of training in open warfare. Officers did not lead their men. Where the Officers were good, the men fought like tiger cats. You cannot make Officers in three months.

b. Much booty was left. The railways were not destroyed†. In the 5th Army no one knew what was happening‡. This was due to the lack of confidence in the higher command.

**Tuesday 2 April 1918** A quiet day along the whole front. It is difficult to find out what the Boche is up to. He may be meditating another surprise attack on a large scale, and is getting up his guns and fresh troops. There are no indications at present. Tomorrow the 2nd Cav. Div. comes under our orders and the next night we hope to get back the 1st and 3rd Cav. Divs so as to refit and make them up to their proper strength. With the reinforcements available, we may just be able to do this; but after that there will be no more trained Cavalrymen available. It was a great mistake to break up those two Divisions and send the Indian Regiments to Egypt. They would have been invaluable.

**Wednesday 3 April** Went down to see the 1st Cav. Div. in the morning and saw Mullens. He

The 1918 Spring Offensive area.

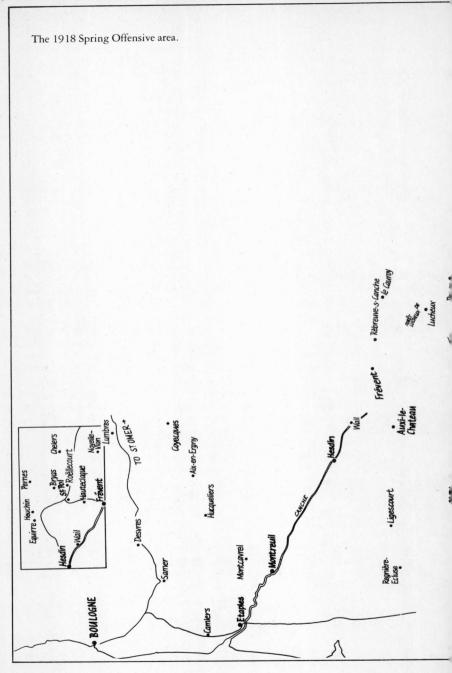

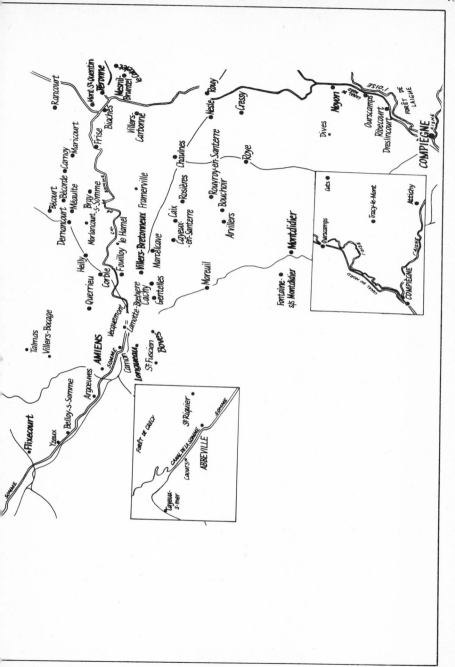

was full of grumbles, but hope that I proved a safety valve. Then went on and saw Tommy Pitman – very interesting on all his experiences. He has done very well indeed and has showed himself to be a great commander. Things have been very quiet today and the Boche has not yet disclosed his intentions. I think that he is preparing for another big attack. If it is in this direction, the lack of railways rather accounts for the delay as he will have to get guns, trench mortars and ammunition up. The Chief sent us a very complimentary wire today.

**Thursday 4 April 1918** The 14th Div. relieved the 1st Cav.Div. in the line last night, the relief not being completed until 4.00 am. At 5.00 am the Boche attacked from Marcelcave to the Somme and punched a hole in the 14th Div. line; the 3rd Cav.Div. had to go up to stop the hole. The 14th Div. were tired before they went in, but having once got into the line, they should have stayed there. The Villers-Bretonneux plateau is very commanding and, if the Boche pushes us off it, he can see for miles – that is what he is probably going for at present. I hope that a counter attack will restore the situation. It has been pouring with rain all day and looks like going on. The Boche again shelled this village today and cut our telephone wires.

**Friday 5 April 1918** The 3rd Cav.Div. are now holding the line from the Somme to the main Vermand road. The Boche has tried two attacks and never got near our trenches. The Infantry are very tired and, until we get some fresh Divs in here, the Boche will continue to make ground. As long as anyone shoots, he won't move an inch. The CC got a very nice letter from the Chief and I think that all is well now and he will continue to command the Corps. A message came from the [3rd] Army to say that we might be required to protect their right flank. It seems that the French have fallen back a bit south of Boves. They are however going to counter attack this evening, so they will get some of the ground back again but not all.

**Saturday 6 April 1918** Moved our HQ from Querrieu to the Hospice St Victor on the eastern end of Amiens. A Boche attack is expected south of Villers-Bretonneux. The 3rd Div. came out of the line last night and went into Lamotte-Brebiere and Camon east of Amiens. The 2nd Cav.Div. moved to an area between Flixecourt and Abbeville. The 1st Cav.Div. remains on the northern and western outskirts of Amiens.

**Monday 8 April 1918** Last night we were well bombed, but beyond having a few horses hit, we had no casualties. Made a liaison with the 3rd Army on our left and the 1st French Army on our right. The 3rd Army think that the Boche is massing for an attack from the River Scarpe southwards – the French think that the Boche will try and attack them driving them west and north on Amiens. If he does attack, it will probably be on a large scale and will include both the Armies and our 4th Army as well.

**Tuesday 9 April 1918** The Boche have been shelling Amiens a good deal, but it is mostly confined to the western exits. Of course they know that it is a bottleneck and that all roads lead through it. At present there have been only a few casualties. They put one shell into the Cathedral this morning. I am afraid that, if they cannot get on, they will shell it out of spite and then swear that it was used for purposes of observation. Amiens will be a very unhealthy place soon as, when the moon comes, they are bound to bomb it regularly. We made a little bit of ground this morning near Bouzencourt[?] south of the Somme, but otherwise nothing has happened.

**Wednesday 10 April 1918** The Boche has put in a strong attack between La Bassee Canal and Armentieres* and got through our line near Estaires which was held by the Portuguese† and the 40th Div.‡ This morning he attacked north of Armentieres and pushed our line back on to the Messines Ridge. There is no doubt that tired-out Divisions do not stand well now. It is owing to the lack of training of the Officers. The men are all right but want to be led, now they have no trench to stay in. Once they get out into the open, they are lost.

Owing to this fighting the Cavalry Corps were ordered north at an hour's notice with bivouacs between Auxi-le-Château and Doullens. The 3rd Div. remained in Amiens and east of it. HQ of the Corps moved to Auxi-le-Château. Whilst the move was in progress, the Corps Commander and I motored up to the 1st Army at Ranchicourt. The Chief was there, having a conference. The situation appeared none too good, but they seemed to think that this attack was for the purpose of drawing our Reserves northward and that the main blow would fall elsewhere — probably I think south of Arras and embracing the British and French front east of Amiens. The Chief told the CC that he was going to keep the Cavalry Corps as his Reserve and at midnight we got these orders. The 1st Cav.Div. was moved to the Canche Valley west of Frevent, the 3rd being brought up to between Doullens and Auxi-le-Château. We are now fairly concentrated and ready to move in any direction. Yesterday was very misty and this evening the fog came down again. All our people are full of heart and ready to take the Boche on anywhere.

**Friday 12 April 1918** Received orders over the phone from GHQ that the Cavalry Corps would move north on Aire-sur-la-Lys. So went off to the 1st Army at Ranchicourt under whose orders we are to come. Situation not very satisfactory: our troops are tired and the Boche is pushing on. The role of the Cavalry Corps is a Reserve and to protect the join between the Armies. This part of the country is a very sad sight. We were given Equirre as our HQ. It lies in a peaceful valley as yet untouched by war. The nightingales were singing in the wood. Our Divisions moved up: 2nd to Bomy, 1st [to] Heuchin, 3rd [to] Pernes. They came along well.

**Saturday 13 April 1918** Got orders this morning that we are to protect the left of the 1st Army and fill any gaps that may occur between the Army and the 2nd Army. The 2nd Cav.Div. moved to the area Sercus-Lynde-Blaringhem. First went to 11th Corps and saw General Haking and also the Army Commander who happened to arrive at the time. They have got the 5th Div. in now on the left of the Army and the situation has improved. Went on to the 15th Corps and saw De Lisle and also met Tommy Pitman there and arranged the details for him to cover the junction of the Armies. Then went to see Stevens commanding the 5th Div. He seemed happy and then on to the 31st Div.* who were not so happy. But the Australians† had come up behind them, so that ought to help. Got back to Aire, where we had temporary HQ at the Mairie. Our own HQ of the night [were] established at St André Farm just outside Aire. A long day with great trouble with our communications.

**Sunday 14 April 1918** A very cold day and our horses are going to suffer. The situation on the whole seems to be easier, although the Boche has been attacking in a north-east direction towards Strazeele and Bailleul. A great many French reinforcements* have arrived here behind the 2nd Army and one hears of others.

It is hard to understand the situation. Have we given up for the moment the plan of a large French counterstroke — or rather has the Boche forced us to give it up by his attacks and our inability to hold them? It looks as if, for the present, we stand purely on the defensive — or we may be doing so with a view to a counterstroke on a large scale later. This will not be so easy, the only thing is to catch the Boche on the rebound and the present moment does not appear favourable for such action. The atmosphere necessary will have to be created later on. Our 2nd Div. is still out covering the junction of the 1st and 2nd Armies.

**Monday 15 April 1918** The attacks in the direction of Morbecque and St Venant seem to have slackened off. The Boche is still pushing in the direction of Bailleul and Hazebrouck. He seems to have finished his attack here — he has used in all about 23 Divisions. It will be interesting to see what he intended to do here, did he mean to try to break through or was the attack intended to use up our Reserves and draw them away from the south? He again attacked a weak spot in the line, which was the Portuguese Corps. I think we may expect another big attack probably between Arras and Montdidier — or he may attack south from La Bassée so as to get the Bruay mines (which form the main coal supply of France).

Today a Brigade (7th under Portal) of the 3rd Cav.Div. were ordered up to Busnes in support of the line east of St Venant. There are no indications of an attack there as far as we know — I suppose that the Army must be nervous of that corner. A very cold day with a north wind and no sun — our horses are going to suffer pretty severely if this weather goes on. We have given up Neuve Eglise which changed hands several times before that. We are also withdrawing from the Ypres salient. It is a horrible thing to have to do when one thinks of the fighting that has taken place and the cost of hanging on to it all this time — but from a military point of view the withdrawal is absolutely right. We save a whole Corps and give the Boche the terrible devastated area. As this is the decisive year, we cannot afford to be sentimental.

**Tuesday 16 April 1918** A bad day today. The Boche took Bailleul last night and forced us back from Wytschaete this morning. This puts our line back from Ypres to the Kemmel defences and back by Dranouter. The French are going to counter attack this evening between Bailleul and Neuve Eglise, I suppose to get back the high ground between those places which overlooks all the country in the direction of Steenwerck and to the south. I hope that they will be successful as I don't like our line as far back as it is now. I am very much afraid that our troops up there are tired out. They do not fight as they used to. To think that the politicians reduced our army by about 120 Battalions only last winter* – we are now paying dearly for the folly of taking chances in war. Thank Heaven we still have three Cavalry Divisions made of the old stuff and properly officered. We can stop a break through anywhere.

Got the Army to move the 7th Cav.Bde back again to its area. They are quite handy there and can look after their horses properly. Just heard that the question of remounts is acute. There are lots of horses in England, but last winter the authorities starved them and they are not fit to come out here and work. It all hinges on the decision that Cavalry were no longer worth keeping.

**Wednesday 17 April 1918** Some better news this morning. We re-took Wytschate last night and the French have been counter attacking and have made some ground west of Bailleul. This morning went off and saw the 1st Cav.Div. A wire has just come in to say that the church tower in Albert is down. There was a local story that the war would end when the figure of the Virgin on top of the tower fell. There has been a lot of shooting today; I hear that we have been using a good deal of gas. German prisoners are boasting that they ravaged all the French women left in Merville*. They are most awful beasts and bullies, but their time will come as sure as fate. The French are moving more troops north. They are afraid of their coal mines at Bruay-en-Artois falling into Boche hands. I think the Armentieres battle is now drawing to a close. I do not know when the next phase will begin, but we have an opportunity to reorganise some of our tired Divisions so we ought to be ready for him.

**Thursday 18 April 1918** Went up in the morning and saw Pitman at 2nd Cav.Div. HQ. The 3rd Bde had been ordered forward to near Fletre to bolster up the line there. The Division is full of heart, but it wants shoeing so as to be ready to march. There has been not time to shoe horses and so we are behindhand in that respect, but this will be put right in a day or two. Went on to the 2nd Army's advanced HQ at Cassel. I was lucky enough to catch Sir Herbert Plumer and Tim Harrington who kindly told me all they knew. The French with five Divisions are taking over the 9th Corps' front.

At 2.30 pm the Chief came to see us. He was looking well, but the strain on him must have been terrific. Sir Douglas was very nice to us all and told us that we were his last Reserve and I am sure he will find us a very efficient one. He thought it practically certain that the Boche was going to put in a big attack between Arras and Montdidier. He however said that everything was prepared to meet it.

**Friday 19 April 1918** Another very cold day with snow showers. There has been hardly any shooting at all. Went to the 1st Army with the Corps Commander this afternoon. The 1st Corps had a good day yesterday and killed a lot of Boches. I am afraid the 1st Div. had rather heavy casualties, but they fought magnificently. It is rather curious; in that part of the world between La Bassée Canal and La Motte forest, there are the 1st, 3rd, 4th and 5th Divs. They all belong to the old original army and have hardly lost a trench, yet they have been wiped out times out of number. Tradition is a wonderful thing. The soldiers understand it – the politican does not and thinks he can make armies in a month or two. Went on and saw Mullens (1st Cav.Div.) at Heuchin. Hope to pull out the 2nd Cav.Div. soon. They are watching the junction of the 1st and 2nd Armies, much to the annoyance of the Australians who are on the right of the 2nd Army. But all the troops are not like the Australians!

**Saturday 20 April 1918** A very quiet day – the Boche has done nothing; on the other hand we are getting stronger every minute. I fancy that he is going to stop here and have a smack elsewhere. Am having to make some changes in my Staff. It is always unpleasant having to tell people that they have failed*, but it has to be done sometimes, although this is the first time in the war that I have had to do it.

I hear all sorts of rumours as regards changes in the higher command. People say that it is only a matter of time before our present Chief is ousted by the politicians that be. The Air Board is an example: Trenchard has the confidence of every flying man in France and it is evident that David Henderson agrees with them. The whole thing appears to be the usual political jobbery†. In politics one has to look after one's friends and thus one establishes a following. This principle applied to war means disaster! The best is really not good enough in war.

**Monday 22 April 1918** Went to a conference at the 1st Army HQ and got a lot of interesting information. They seem to think that the Boche will put in another attack against the Ypres-Kemmel-Hazebrouck line before anything against Amiens, as an attack in the former direction threatens the coast. He thus hopes to force our Reserves northwards and away from Amiens, which is the French and British point of junction and therefore still the decisive point. There appears to be no doubt that his main effort will once more come against the junction. The American troops* seem to be coming in fairly well just now and of course the Boche is wasting time. I am surprised at that, but he may have difficulties that we don't know of.

**Tuesday 23 April 1918** Spent the day down at Abbeville in our reinforcement camp and had lunch there with Sam Webster. He had a good show going when one considers all the difficulties he has had to contend with. The Officers' quarters are next to the WAAC* camp. This shows the integrity of Cavalry Officers. I hope the WAAC will not ruin their reputation! There is a good deal of night bombing going on and I think that the Germans must dread it as we are all over them. Richthofen the German crack airman has been killed. One cannot but help feeling that one would rather he had been wounded and captured. In his way he was a fine man, but his bombast was sickening.

**Wednesday 24 April 1918** Heard that the Boche had attacked and taken Villers-Bretonneaux east of Amiens. Hope our counter attacks will be successful in retaking it as it gives the Boche too much observation. He is evidently livening up on the 4th Army front. Rather disquieting news as regards our reinforcements for Infantry. The politicians state that all gaps will be made up – we know differently here and hope for the best. At the present minute we are about 10,000 short in bulk*. It is wicked to think of when there are a million men in Ireland of military age. Prisoners reports go to show that the Boche has suffered heavy casualties in the Merville salient, so that is good.

**Thursday 25 April 1918** The Boche attacked Villers-Bretonneaux with tanks yesterday and took the village. We have however retaken it. This is their first use of tanks; they are bigger than ours and are heavily gunned. Our light tanks* report great success against Infantry but could not stand up to the heavy Boche tanks. Vague rumours about the Boche having taken Kemmel Hill but these are unfounded. It is held by the Northern French Army under General Plumer and, as usual, it is difficult to find out what they hold and what they don't hold. The Boche is very puzzling just now, he is putting in attacks on a front of five or six Divisions. That will never pay as we have found out by bitter experience. He has the Divisions and his great chance is to attack on a broad front – say of 50 miles – and be ready to use his Cavalry. I think he has missed a great chance in his first effort which commenced on 21 March.

**Friday 26 April 1918** The news in the north is not so good. Evidently the Boche has attacked from Ypres to Meteren. He has forced the French Divisions holding the line back to behind Kemmel Hill and that place is in the hands of the Boche. Without in any way wishing to say anything against the French, they do not fight as well when they are wedged into our armies, as they do when they are amongst their own people. The result is that we have had to withdraw our line back to the Ypres ramparts and Canal north of that place.

**Saturday 27 April 1918** A very cold day with a heavy mist. Rode over to see the 2nd Cav.Div. at Blaringhem. There has been very heavy fighting between Locre and Ypres. The Boche still holds Kemmel and the French Divisions holding it had pretty heavy casualties.

**Monday 29 April 1918** A furious battle has been raging between Ypres and Dranouter. The Boche has been trying all he knows to get the Scherpenberg but up to present he has not succeeded in doing so. The French appear to be fighting very well now and Locre has changed hands several times during the last few days. Our troops on the right of the French have repulsed four attacks today and so I hope are killing lots of Boches. Today the 2nd Div. moved back from the Blaringhem area to an area about Coyecques. It is a better area I think, more water for the horses and they will not be so crowded. I think that on the whole the Germans must be very disappointed at their efforts of the last few days. Unsuccessful attacks mean very heavy casualties as we know to our cost.

**Thursday 2 May 1918** The first day we have had and comparatively warm. Had to go into GHQ at Montreuil – it seemed to me as if there was rather an atmosphere of depression. The general trend of things was: we do not know what the Boche intends to do. As we know there are difficulties as regards manpower, thanks to our politicians, and it seems that America is not coming in up to programme. However we are quite cheerful and hope for the best. Thank heavens the much despised Cavalry are still equal to 20 times their number of Boches! Now that the line has come back and there are a lot of French troops in our area, we are very much pinched in the way of billets.

**Friday 3 May 1918** Went out in the car and saw the 1st and 3rd Divs and had to stay in in the afternoon. Got orders for the Divs to move: 3rd Div. to 4th Army area – believe that their ultimate destination is between Albert and Amiens; 2nd Div. to go back to an area north of Montreuil; and Cavalry Corps HQ to move to Auxi-le-Château. Got the orders out late.

**Saturday 4 May 1918** Rather an interesting piece of news today. A captured airman gave away that the Boche intends to put in a big attack south of Arras. The result is that the 3rd Cav.Div. is ordered quite close up to the line and will be very uncomfortable for the time being. I only hope that the weather will not be wet as both the horses and men will be out in the open.

**Sunday 5 May 1918** Cavalry Corps' advanced HQ moved from Ferme St André near Aire to Auxi-le-Château and joined us with rear HQ. We are now in GHQ Reserve. Went down to Abbeville in the morning and inspected our reinforcement camp there. I think the show running as well as can be expected, but it is such a fluid concern that it is difficult to keep things going. We lunched at the Officers' Club and sat at a table with three full Colonels – these are rare birds as everyone is either a Lt. Colonel or else a Brigadier General. They belong to the Ordnance I think.

**Monday 6 May 1918** Went to GHQ this morning and discussed the question of Signal establishments with Fowler, the Director of Signals. The 4th Army expect a big attack between Amiens and Arras and prisoners say that it will take place on the 7th or 8th May. As far as I can make out there are signs of it – such as new hospitals and aerodromes – and also ammunition has been collected in dumps.

I have just heard a story that four [German] tanks were located by an aeroplane just south of Albert. They took the place on with a 9.2 Howitzer, fired 300 rounds into them and wiped them out. The Australians made a bit of ground just west of Morlancourt early this morning on a 2,000-yard front; this will improve their position.

**Tuesday 7 May 1918** Spent a very dull day full of work – mostly sitting at a table. Things are very quiet but an attack is expected either tomorrow or the next day. Last night was very wet and so our 3rd Cav.Div. had a hard time of it last night, having practically no shelter at all. We are getting them tents and trench shelters tonight.

**Wednesday 8 May 1918** Went down to see the 3rd Cav.Div. The men are none too comfortable and the horses are on a bog – but I hope with this dry weather things will improve. Went to the 3rd Corps and had a talk with Butler. They expect an attack on that front at any time; 3rd Div. HQ are at Contay.

The general topic of conversation is Freddy Maurice's letter to the *Morning Post*. I hear tonight that he is to be court-martialled. He is a brave man and a gentleman and he has had the pluck to put on paper what the whole Army knew — that the statements made in Parliament were false. Bonar Law, when asked whether the extension of the line was agreed to by the military powers out here, could easily have refused to answer such a question but he answered it falsely. H.W., knowing the answer was fake, should have resigned. Of course people are already saying that Freddy Maurice has been got at by the *Morning Post*. Knowing him as I do, I am sure that no paper has got at him. Knowing what he knows of the situation, I should say that he is convinced that H.W.* as CIGS cannot win the war and that Wallie is the only man for that place. It is a great thing in this war to find poor men who are dependent on their pay to take such a strong line as Wallie and Freddy have taken.

**Thursday 9 May 1918** Got out for a ride after tea with the Corps Commander and the dogs. We drew several woods for pig but had no luck. Slug Marsham joined today and is taking place of Babe Nicholson. I am sorry to lose the Babe, but he is idle and has thus lost the confidence of the Divisions and as such is no good as a Staff Officer. He has a great chance of going back and making good with his Regiment and I have arranged for his name to be kept on the Staff list. He has any amount of ability, but at present he is too indolent to use it except under the spur. There is a lot of peace talk and the story goes that the Boche has once more offered peace terms, to us this time. I think he is very disappointed at the result of his offensive.

**Saturday 11 May 1918** A very quiet day, so went joy riding round the 1st Cav.Div. Then went on and lunched with the Regiment and then on to see 2nd Cav.Bde. They were all full of heart and quite ready for anything — only wishing the Boche might attack and give them something to do. Things are very quiet on the front — too much so.

We are sending down Divisions to the Chemin des Dames, which is a quiet sector for a rest; they will be under the French. They will just have to rest and keep quiet just as the French do. We used to criticise the French for having quiet sectors where there was practically an armistice. As soon as we got into them we used to start shelling and gassing and raiding — in fact create hell's delight. I am not sure this was right in a long war as the result was that our men never got a rest. We had to hold the line thickly and our men never got any training. Of course we kept the Germans busy on our front and killed a lot of them, that goes in the balance on the other side.

**Monday 13 May 1918** This morning went up to the high ground north of Boucy to watch a scheme being carried out by the 1st and 2nd Cav.Bdes of the 1st Cav.Div. It was an instructive morning. The weather rather spoilt it as it turned out wet with a cold wind. The Boche appears to be preparing another attack against Bethune in the north and between Arras and Amiens in the south. They will probably be simultaneous.

**Thursday 16 May 1918** A real hot day. The Boche bombed Abbeville last night. I suppose we shall get it here some time or another. Our salvation is that we are not a big railway centre. Everything very quiet: rumours of a Boche peace offensive — that means another attack — as the excuse for the casualties is that we would not accept the peace offers of the Central Powers. Austria is supposed to be gingered up by the Boche to attack Italy — but nothing has as yet matured and I don't think the Austrians want to attack at all. Just heard the Canadians are dispensing with Seely's services and Patterson gets the Canadian Cav.Bde — more graft! These Canadians are awful politicians and intriguers.

**Friday 17 May 1918** Went round all the Brigades of the 2nd Cav.Div. and found them contented and well. The 3rd Cav.Div. moved their HQ to Yzeux on the Somme with two Brigades round Yzeux and Belloy-sur-Somme. The Canadians remain in the Conchy[?] Valley for another week, when they will be relieved if necessary.

**Saturday 18 May 1918** Went down to see the 3rd Cav.Div. Saw Archie Seymour in the morning, he has his HQ in the northern chateau at Belloy-sur-Somme. His Brigade is camped all around the place, which is good for the men but bad for the horses, as they have to go down 1½ miles for water. They are all very cheery and full of heart. The Boche seems to be boiling up for an attack north of the Somme – hope he will – if we cannot stop him we had better go at once and make peace. The Americans are coming in very fast they say. They ought to be good fighters. All we want is fellows who will stop and fight.

**Sunday 19 May 1918** The Australians made a good small attack this morning and advanced their line south of Albert. Otherwise all quiet.

**Tuesday 21 May 1918** Spent the morning at Cayeux-sur-Mer at our Equitation School. It is a real good show and is doing a lot of good. Rode one of their horses round the course and enjoyed it. Another Gazette out and I suppose the usual recriminations will follow. I wish that they would do away with 'Mentioned in Despatches'. It leads to a lot of heart burning and is really prostituted: one sees the same names over and over again – myself included. I shall get really hated if this goes on.

**Wednesday 22 May 1918** A very hot muggy day, but became cooler in the evening. Much bombing activity by the Germans. They bombed Etaples and could not help missing the camps as they are as thick as flies on the ground. The Life Guards had a good many casualties and they hit a couple of hospitals. They have also had several goes at Abbeville and done a good deal of damage. The 1st Cav.Div. moved from the Conchy[?] area and is now in [a] valley west of Auxi-le-Château. We are all wondering what the Boche means doing. The latest place of attack is now west of Merville.

**Friday 24 May 1918** Had a conference of Divisional Commanders this morning and successfully settled a good few points. The Boche has not yet made a move. Many of the prisoners assert that an attack on a large scale will be made shortly. If their attack is not successful: ie a breakthrough, they will have some difficulty in explaining it away at home.

**Saturday 25 May 1918** A quiet day, so had lunch with Moberley at the 6th Corps' HQ at Noyelle-Vion. Saw Harvey Kearsley there and had an interesting talk on the fighting on 21 March. They do not seem to think that an attack is imminent; on the other hand the armies seem to think so. Got my car back from the workshop for which I am thankful.

**Sunday 26 May 1918** Went round the 1st and 2nd Cav.Bdes this morning. They are quite happy in their new areas. A fine day and the ground drying up splendidly. Great arguments going on as to whether the Boche is going to attack or not. I am convinced that he is going to attack and on a very large scale. I also think that, once his position in the east is assured or he thinks it is, he will try and get peace and will offer part of Alsace-Lorraine as a sop.

**Monday 27 May 1918** Went into GHQ this morning with the CC. They seemed to be rather blue, especially as regards the manpower question. It seems that we are manufacturing so much war materiel, supplying so much coal and building so many ships that we are employing 3,000,000 men who might be soldiers and fighting. This is interesting as the ordinary soldier does not understand the necessity of such employment of fighting materiels. The Americans are coming in well, but they are untrained and not equipped. Am told that Lloyd-George said to America 'All we want is men'; but we want soldiers properly equipped to put into battle. Civilians do not understand the needs and necessities of a modern army, and that is where the Boche scores all along the line. If the Army is not permanent, then why go to war? Diplomacy should be sufficient.

We sent the 9th Corps to rest in a quiet sector west of Rheims. This morning the Boche attacked there on a 40-kilometer front and has of course pushed us back a bit – also the French*. Is this going to be his main attack? I don't think so. Prisoners taken have told of a feint at Rheims, but the main attack still to come against us in the Albert-Arras area and north of the latter place. He also made an attack north of Ypres. If either attack is really successful he may develop it. The poor old 9th Corps are having a bad time of it; the 21st Div. has had three battles this year already. I only hope they killed a lot of Boches.

My admiration for the Boche as a soldier always goes up. He is a living example of what peace training for war means and how far this will go in actual war. He is bound to be beat in the end, but that does not alter one's opinion of his management of war.

**Tuesday 28 May 1918** The news from the Soissons sector does not appear too good. As far as one can see the Boche has got across the Aisne and has driven south to the Vesle River. This means an advance of 8-10 miles in two days. Rumour has it that his best troops are in the battle there: viz. the Guards and the Brandenburg Corps. He may mean to develop this success and turn westwards on Paris – his Reserves round St Quentin are well placed for such a move. They say he has had heavy losses but they must be heavy to compensate for our loss of men and materiel.

**Wednesday 29 May 1918** Went over and saw the 2nd Cav.Div. After lunch went to GHQ, but there was not very much news. The Boche has driven the French back a pretty long way and they must [have] come back fast or else they must have held the line very lightly. I was told that they are now beginning to fight. It rather reminds one of the early stages of the war, I only hope the result will be the same: viz. a successful advance later on. It does rather make one think furiously. The Boche makes a 10-mile advance whenever he wants to. He must also have captured a good many guns as they cannot have got them away over the Aisne. I don't think there were enough bridges. It is to be seen as to whether, and to what extent, he exploits this attack and how many Divisions he uses. That will show the extent to which he means to go. I think he will go on until stopped: ie sufficient Reserves are brought up by the French. Then he will put in his main attack opposite Amiens at the junction of the French and British Armies and try to force us apart.

**Thursday 30 May 1918** The news to hand shows a further German advance. They occupy Soissons to Fere-en-Tardenois and, I am told, are all round Rheims. In the latter place there is a store of 15,000,000 bottles of champagne – which I hope the Boche will not get. I am very fond of the wine and do not like the idea of the Boche making a corner* in it! Went to see the 3rd Cav.Div. at Yzeux and met a lot of French troops moving south through Vigneuilles. The Boche is approaching the Château-Thierry railway, so I hope that Foch has his Reserves so placed that he can stop him. The French are very secretive.

**Friday 31 May 1918** Spent the morning watching a Scheme of the 9th Cav.Bde under D'Arcy Legard – a good Scheme bringing out many points of interest. The news from the battle in the south is not too good. The Boche has reached the Marne. His advance has been so rapid that the resistance cannot have been very strenuous. Of course one does not know what Reserves have been available. It seems to me that Foch, provided he has the necessary men, has a great chance of rolling up this German advance. Whether he uses his Reserves now must depend on the number of Divisions the Germans have now put into the attack. Can we afford to weaken our other front or must we still remain purely on the defensive and go on giving ground?

Again the Boche are on the Marne. The French character requires a catch phrase to send it into a victorious battle. 'The Marne' should conjure up the victories of 1914. A second Battle of the Marne will save France just as the first did. I am told today that the French are rather worried at the pace of the German advance – well they may be!

**Saturday 1 June 1918** Another glorious day. Went down to Abbeville to see our reinforcements. Saw the WAAC Camp which has been hit by a bomb. All the girls were in the trenches and, although one small bomb dropped within three yards of one trench, no one was hurt. A big bomb dropped into the centre of the camp and demolished half of it and the poor little Wacks' clothes were scattered all over the place and the trees were hung with them. It is rather a curious story: during the fighting, one of our rear echelons were sent back to Abbeville and arrived there late one evening. The Wacks were awfully good to them and gave them dinner. Later our men dug trenches for them and so saved their lives. Now the little Wacks go out every night and sleep in the woods.

This is a terrible war and women are wonderful the way they bear the strain. It is nothing new, we have only to think of our women during the Indian Mutiny and you get the same heroic fortitude. This bombing is very trying and most men one meets would rather be shelled than bombed. We went on to Le Touquet and saw the Hotchkiss School and were stopped on the way by a control who tried to find out if we were joy riding. The French are happier so I suppose they have got some Reserves up. It is still doubtful whether the Boche means to put all his eggs in the Marne basket, but revenge for the French and British victory on the Marne in 1914 may tempt him sorely. We shall know within the next few days.

**Sunday 2 June 1918** The Germans have made some progress south and west of Soissons, but the advance is not so rapid now. Probably the French Reserves are beginning to arrive and the defence is stiffening up.

**Monday 3 June 1918** No news from the French at the Marne battle, the Boche progress is slowing down now. I think he has finished and that his next attack will be against us – there are some signs of preparation Ypres way.

**Tuesday 4 June 1918** Am having awful trouble about our School at Dieppe and have to send Marsham down to French GHQ to see Woodroffe. Awful moment – the half year's honours list is out and the usual trouble commences. The CC has given me a CMG. Don't deserve it at all – but Mother* will be pleased.

**Wednesday 5 June 1918** Went down and spent the morning with the Canadian Cav.Bde and saw them at mounted work. They have improved a lot but they have still a lot to learn. They are by no means trained Cavalry yet – although the most gallant fighters in the world. They have got good ground for training on – far better than any I have seen in this country.

**Thursday 6 June 1918** Another boiling hot day. Went to see the 2nd Cav.Div. and had lunch with Bill Smyth commanding 3rd Cav.Bde. Marsham has got back from French GHQ. He says they killed a lot of Germans in the last few days and that the attack there has stopped. They seem to expect an attack southwards from the line east of Montdidier, but that has not yet developed. I am told that the Americans are coming over in large numbers, but they still want a good deal of training*. They will, I think, turn the scale in the long run. I expect the Boche will put in some more big attacks. I hope it will be against our people as then he will get a bad jolt and that will do more good than anything else.

**Friday 7 June 1981** Spent the morning watching a tactical exercise of the [1st] Cav.Bde under Sewell. He was rather nervous and the exercise contained too many controversial questions to be really instructive. The Boche attack appears to have stopped for the moment in the Marne direction, but there is a lot of evidence of great movement in the Montdidier-Roye areas. This can develop in two directions: either southwards continuing the threat on Paris or westwards in the direction of Amiens and south of that place.

**Sunday 9 June 1918** The Boche has put in another biggish attack on a front of about 30 kilometers between Noyon and Montdidier. This attack has been fully expected and is in no way a surprise. The news is that he has made some progress in places, but the exact extent cannot yet be known. I only hope that this attack will cause the Boche heavy casualties. We are not as yet involved and at present there is no reason that we should be. There is a change in the weather and I think we shall have some rain. It is badly wanted for the crops and will also stop the Boche moving across country.

**Wednesday 12 June 1918** Left here at 7.30 am and motored to Dieppe to see the Schemes – on the whole satisfactory. The instructors are good and keen and the show should run well. Stayed the night.

**Thursday 13 June 1981** Motored to Rouen and had an interview with Massenden reference the Cavalry Base Depot. Rode round and saw some of the men riding. There are many very bad horsemen, who require a good deal of training before they are fit to be called Cavalry soldiers.

**Saturday 15 June 1918** Went into GHQ and had an interview with John Fowler on the question of the increase in the Signals. I think that he is sticking his toes in the ground; on the other hand we are inclined to ask too much. Yesterday we heard that an attack on the Arras front was expected this morning, but it has not matured up to the present. Prisoners all say that there is a talk of an attack and the arrangements are pretty well forward.

**Sunday 16 June 1918** Inspected the Signals this morning and the show was very good except the horses are not yet up to the mark. It has been very cold today. The air people say a good deal of movement takes place at night in the neighbourhood of Armentieres, but the Boche at present is quiet on our front. Things in Austria look rocky, but they have done so before and nothing has happened.

**Monday 17 June 1918** The Austrians have begun their offensive against the Italians*. The news is meagre, but reading the Austrian wireless, the success has not been very great. I think the Boche has forced the Austrians to attack much against their will. We shall not know the real truth for some days. Saw the 1st Cav.Div. fire off the Finals for the ARA competition this morning – 8th Hussars, 9th Lancers, 11th Hussars left in. My Regiment won which is very gratifying. The latest news from the Italian front points to the fact that the Austrians are held. This will annoy the Boche as he must have counted with luck to force us to detach Divisions to help that front.

**Wednesday 19 June 1918** The news from Italy is fairly good and on the whole the Macaroni appear to be holding the Austrians. Yesterday I spent the morning with the 1st Cav.Div. who were carrying out a tactical exercise. Went over to the 2nd Cav.Div. this morning – they all appeared well and happy. The Boche attacked the French at Rheims with three Divisions today but got it in the neck. I cannot make out the object of this attack. Everything points to the next big attack coming in the Merville salient; but the scope of this is again limited unless it assumes a south-westerly direction. The danger point is still Amiens and Abbeville and I have no doubt that this will be the scene of his final effort.

**Thursday 20 June 1918** Went into GHQ in the morning and had a long talk with Wallace on the question of establishments. They seemed pleased with the Italian show. They expect an attack in the Merville salient at any time and say that everything points to this quarter of the front.

Am changing my Staff. The usual trouble has occurred; people come and ask why they are not chosen. It makes one sick – but I suppose if I had done it myself I should be a Major General by now. I prefer to remain as I am!!! Quite wrong according to Pelmanism* which I am studying. We have a curious epidemic – called PUO (Pyrexia† Unknown Origin). You go down with a temperature of 103°F for two or three days and then you are all right. It is very catching and whole regiments go down with it. It is a curious malady, the result of war.

**Friday 21 June 1918** Spent the morning at a Scheme with the 5th Cav.Bde under Neil Haig. It was not a very good Scheme. The Boche is putting off his attack long enough. Prisoners say he is suffering from the same epidemic as we are. In the meantime the months are slipping away and all this time we should be getting stronger and stronger. Things in Austria seem to be boiling up for trouble, the Boche will have to announce a new victory soon.

**Monday 24 June 1918** The Italians have evidently a success against the Austrians and are driving them over the Piave, which is in flood. They ought to make a good bag with any luck. It should have a bad effect on the internal situation in Austria and I am certain that the Boche will not be pleased. It might even be possible for the Italians to take the offensive and drive the Austrians back a good way before the winter, but that must depend on the effectives at their disposal. Everyone is either away or sick. This PUO is the very devil as it attacks people very suddenly.

**Tuesday 25 June 1918** Am left here quite alone. All my Staff are sick with the flu – result is that I am short of exercise. All prisoners testify to the fact that the Boche is suffering from the epidemic of PUO.

**Wednesday 26 June 1918** I think the Boche is boiling up for a big attack: he has waited so long and all this time given us the opportunity to pull ourselves together and to get reinforcements in the shape of Americans. The Italians have not taken as many prisoners as one would have thought; it looks as if the Austrians begin to retire when they saw the impossibility of holding their position on the west bank of the Piave. They may come again but I hardly think they will. The Boche is bound to try to make them do so.

**Thursday 27 June 1918** The PUO is still bad and my servant is now down with it. The CC saw the CGS today; they expect a big attack on our front. Marsham returned today and Bimbo Reynolds [his GSO(2)] is also off the sick list, so I am better off now and shall be able to get out a bit more. Mullens is still bad if his temper is any sign.

**Friday 28 June 1918** Attended a demonstration in crossing a river by the 1st Field Squadron and 9th Cav.Bde this morning. I don't think that they produced anything new. One comfort is that they did not drown anyone.

**Saturday 29 June 1918** Went in the morning and saw the 2nd Cav.Div. shooting for the ARA competition, which was won by the 5th Lancers. Our batteries are ordered forward on the 1st to be ready in case of an attack. They evidently seem to expect an attack by the Boche soon after that date. We took 450 prisoners north of Merville yesterday and it appears to have been a good show.

**Monday 1 July 1918** Went down to the Corps School. As it was the opening day, the CC gave an address which was excellent and just what was wanted. The Divisions have played the game and sent down an excellent set of students, both Officers and NCOs. It promises well for the first course. We went to the Signals School and saw them at work. They were going on well, but I am disappointed at the rate of reading the Morse.

We continue to have small shows and in every case we bring back prisoners and make ground. I hear the French are being withdrawn from the Kemmel front and I suppose we shall have to find troops to replace them. I am told that Foch thinks that any attack there is for the purpose of forcing us to use Reserves. He must therefore propose to give ground if necessary and to fall back on the inundation: ie the line Watten-Bethune. He thus gives up all that is left of Belgium and also Dunkirk. This decision must be based on the assumption that the Boche will lose heavily as compared to the ground gained. On the other hand we give up a large slice of the coast. If this gives us a superiority in the future, it is right in principle for we are fighting on the defensive/offensive – but Foch and the French must be in a strong position politically to do this without a howl from the people. It is a bold course but the right one, if the ultimate objective: viz. an offensive as soon as we are strong enough, is borne in mind.

**Thursday 4 July 1918** The Australians and American troops attached to them attacked the German positions between the Somme and Villers-Bretonneaux. They took the village of Le Hamel, a wood of the same name and the Bois de Vaire[?]. I am told that in places the Boche fought it out, much to the joy of the Australians. Sixty tanks took part in the attack and the Australians were seen riding on the top of them. This is a good thing as the Australians would not believe in tanks and the tanks as far as can be seen did well this morning*. I went to a demonstration of tanks this morning and the new ones are fast, handy, get over broad obstacles. This promises well for the future and I am certain that they will be of the utmost use to us.

**Friday 5 July 1918** Attended a conference this morning and all the Knuts present. The Austrian effort is looked on as bad and it seems as if the Boche has some difficulty in keeping up his numbers. It would appear as if the Boche is making preparations for an attack all along our front and, when these are complete, he can mount an attack anywhere at short notice. I think he will try for a decision and attack on a very big front using every man he has. The French expect an attack east of Rheims, but this is only looked on as a feint to draw away Reserves from the vital point, which undoubtedly lies about Amiens. Australians show yesterday really good – they have taken over 1,500 prisoners and repelled three counter attacks. There was heavy fighting for Le Hamel village. Six companies of Americans took part and did well.

**Thursday 11 July 1918** Went down to Varengeville-sur-Mer to the Corps School on the 9th and returned this evening. I think they are doing good work down there and they all seem to be quite happy and contented.

**Friday 12 July 1918** Attended a demonstration of tanks which was got up for the 1st and 2nd Cav.Divs. It was a good show and everyone seemed interested.

**Saturday 13 July 1918** Went down to the reinforcement camp at Abbeville and had a conference with Clinch – things are going all right down there. This afternoon attended the 19th Hussars' sports. They had them just in time, as we have just got orders to move the 1st and 2nd Cav.Divs forward in support of the 3rd and 1st Armies respectively. I suppose there is a scare somewhere. I only hope that they will not put them into trenches as they will be wasted once more.

**Sunday 14 July 1918** Went to see the 1st Army this morning and saw Hastings Anderson. The French expect an attack between Rheims and Verdun and say that the Boche has got 100 Divisions down there – evidently Foch is collecting all his Reserves at that place. It seems to me that a Boche attack there has no real objective; on the other hand it may only be an attack to draw Reserves. It is supposed to begin tomorrow morning. On our front things are very quiet, but the Boche has made such preparations that he can mount an attack at short notice.

**Tuesday 16 July 1918** The Boche attacked the French yesterday morning on a 50-mile front which has Rheims for its centre*. The most pleasing factor is that he has put several of his best Divisions into this attack. The result has not been good – he has made some ground south of the Marne but nothing to buck about. East of Rheims he has for the present failed†. Reports tonight say that 21 fresh Divisions have been identified. I personally do not think that this attack will be pushed and the next one will come against us on the Hazebrouck front within the next day or two. If it fails, I do not see the Boche undertaking any more big offensives and the initiative should pass to us. If this happens I think the Boche will retire voluntarily to the Hindenburg line – thus shortening his line, and keeping on a pure defensive. In such a case, if we wish to attack, we shall have to build all our communications forward and that will take time, labour and trouble.

**Wednesday 17 July 1918** Reading between the lines, it would appear that the French are fighting pretty hard in places, especially south-west of Rheims. No deductions can yet be made as to whether the Boche is going to push to the end in the present battlefield. The pendulum seems to be swinging northwards and people seem to think that the next attack will come on the front from Merville to the sea. This will not end the war, in fact it seems to me that the Boche cannot get a decision – so what will he do? I think go back on the defensive again this winter. Went to see the 2nd Cav.Div. in their new area – they are pretty comfortable. When will the war end? – it is a question that should be asked every three months!!!

**Thursday 18 July 1918** Foch has countered on the front Château-Thierry to Soissons with 30 Divisions and is making good progress. We are delighted as a successful advance will mean trouble for the Boche and may force him back from the Marne. I wish we were there, but if we cannot be, I only hope the French Cavalry* will be pushed up and will get a chance. This counterstroke of Foch's has great possibilities – its effect on the Boche morale should be considerable. The result of it will be that Rupprecht of Bavaria will be told to attack at once on the Messine-Ypres front so as to counter balance it.

**Monday 22 July 1918** Have been pretty busy running about, so have not had time to write. The French have been very successful, helped by the Americans and our 22nd Corps*. They have given the Crown Prince's Armies a good knock and it looks as if the German advance has been definitely stopped. It will be interesting to see if they begin to milk Rupprecht of Bavaria of his Reserve Divisions or if they have a last go for the coast. With the Americans coming in fresh and their proving themselves such good fighters, I cannot see how Germany has an earthly chance. How she can make peace and keep the domination of the Military Parties is beyond my horizon; but I suppose the diplomatists will find a way – the pure soldier cannot see it.

**Tuesday 23 July 1918** Went into GHQ this afternoon with the CC and Don Wheeler and had six rounds with John Fowler on subject of our Signal communication*. Did not get very much forrader as Fowler had his toes firmly in the ground, so the CC delivered our ultimatum and we left it at that.

**Thursday 25 July 1918** The 2nd Army, who made certain Rupprecht was going to attack, are now hedging a bit I think. The German move is awaited with much interest as it will probably give a sign of weakness or desperation. I hear from London that the U-boat* is having a very bad time and that the Boche find it difficult to get men for them as they look on them as death traps. I hope this is true.

**Friday 26 July 1918** Went down to the School at Dieppe. Things are going well there, as far as I can find out. The students seem happy; they are getting on well with their work although some of the NCOs are weak. Shall see a Scheme in the morning and then go back to Auxi-le-Château. There is another French advance reported today – it seems as if the Boche will be forced back to the Vesle.

**Thursday 1 August 1918** Had no time to write my Diary, but have simply been doing routine work, training and so on. The 2nd Div. have moved back to their old area round Montcavrel.

**Saturday 3 August 1918** The Cavalry are about to go to war again, this time under the 4th Army. It is once more a Scheme with a limited objective or GAPS Scheme*. I never like them, it will either be a walkover or the very devil. If the Boche does not reinforce this front, all will be well. Secrecy is going to be the guiding factor. I fancy we are being pushed into it as another determined attack is being made by our friends at home on the Cavalry. The proposal is to abolish the Corps, turn one Division into machine guns, one Division into Corps Cavalry and keep one Division mounted. This savours of Henry Wilson as he hates the Cavalry. People really go mad sometimes. If we make peace with the Boche on the Hindenburg line, then we don't want any Cavalry; but if we are going to beat him, we shall want every bus, car, horse, mule and donkey we can raise.

**Monday 5 August 1918** Very busy with all the preparations and it seems as if provided a surprise is effected, we shall have a real good gallop. Secrecy is the main thing nowadays and, if the Boche does not smell a rat, all will be well. We are not having the best of luck in our weather – it was very wet yesterday and has been raining again today. I hope it will clear tomorrow and then keep fine. Low cloud is a good thing as it keeps the aeroplanes away, but we don't want any more rain.

# 13. The Final Victory

**Thursday 8 August 1918** At 4.20 am this morning the battle started: the 3rd Corps attacking north of the Somme, the Australian and Canadian Corps between it and the Luce River, the French 1st Army south of that river. Last night we passed our three Divs through Amiens and the bottleneck at Longueau. A tank* stuck and delayed them for over an hour, but otherwise there was no contretemps. 18 miles of Cavalry passed one point between 10.00 pm and 6.00 am. The attack was quite successful; the enemy was surprised and overrun with considerable ease and the final objectives gained before nightfall. Corps HQ started at Longueau. The first move forward was to Cachy, then to the top of a hill just east of Lance Wood and finally on to Cayeux-en-Santerre where we spent the night. The whole of the movement was done on horseback.

The 1st and 3rd Divs led, the 1st on the left with one Brigade north of the Villers-Bretonneux to Chaulnes railway, the 3rd with its right on the main Amiens-Roye road. The 1st Cav.Bde, north of the railway, got right on to Framerville and did great execution. During the afternoon the CC put in the 2nd Cav.Div. between the 1st and 3rd, keeping the 5th Cav.Bde of that Division in Corps Reserve – a big decision to make and a right one. The result of the day's operations was that all our objectives were gained and that the absolute necessity of good and well trained Cavalry was proved.

I fetched up in Cayeux village which was filthy, the Boche having made no attempt at sanitation – the flies were awful. I saw a good many Boche dead. The prisoners came in in fifties and hundreds with two of our men guarding them, they had no real heart; some of our men told me that they put up their hands at once. It has been a great day. We might have done better of course, but in war decisions are made with eyes blindfolded. Weather perfect and going very good.

**Friday 9 August 1918** Did not get much sleep. The forward movement was to continue; the 1st and 2nd Cav.Divs closely supporting the Infantry and to push through should the situation occur – 3rd Cav.Div. brought into Reserve. The movement was to begin at 8.00 am but, in reality, did not begin till 1.00 pm owing to the difficulty of getting fresh troops forward. The advance was continued and, by the evening, the general line Rosieres/Rouvroy/Bouchoir was reached, the French taking Arvillers on our right. The Boche had considerably reinforced his line and heavy fighting took place. Towards evening the resistance weakened but it got dark.

Today's attack started too late – there was no time left in the evening for a hunt; it was a pity as I think there might have been a chance. Water for horses was a great difficulty and so the 1st and 2nd Divs were withdrawn three miles during the night and the 3rd Div. ordered forward early the next morning. It was a disappointing day, but the Boche has stiffened up considerably. A good few casualties.

**Saturday 10 August 1918** Advance to the line Roye-Chaulnes ordered for the Infantry, the 3rd Cav.Div. ready to move forward with patrols close up to the Infantry. The CC went forward early to a hill just south of Caix and HQ were established there at noon. Most optimistic reports from the Infantry so the CC ordered [the] 3rd Cav. Div to move on Roye — the 2nd on Nesle. I did not agree with this order, as it was based on information which was not confirmed; but as a commander of a force, I think he was justified in issuing it. The Divisions went forward but met with such opposition that the movement was not possible. The Boche was holding the edge of the destroyed area strongly. Orders received to push on to the Somme the next day, so I had to go to the Army to explain the matters — got back at 3.00 am.

**Sunday 11 August 1918** Conference at Villers-Bretonneux and it was decided to pause on our present line and push forward with the Infantry to the eastern edge of the destroyed area as soon as arrangements could be made. At the conference, Clemenceau and Henry Wilson turned up. The CC tackled the latter on the question of doing away with the Cavalry Corps, and H.W. said that he intended doing so. They will regret it. The 1st and 3rd Divs ordered to move back: 1st Div. to Somme Valley between Vecquemont and Amiens, 3rd Div. to south of Boves, Corps HQ to St Fuscien. The Boche bombed a lot during the night and it was rather unpleasant.

**Monday 12 August 1918** Rode back to St Fuscien and went to see No.6 Squadron. The Cavalry had a chance of doing a job and carried it out splendidly. In the papers a great deal of credit is given to the tanks, especially the Whippets*, they being the latest toy. We shall have to get a tame correspondent and have the S. African business once more: nothing but advertisement. The 1st Cav.Div. under Mullens did splendidly and so did the 3rd, the 2nd did not have the same opportunities. If they split up the Divisions, they will ruin the spirit which now exists; each Division will go its own way. The Corps Commander has built this spirit up during the last two years and the credit is his and his alone.

**Tuesday 13 August 1918** Had a quiet day. The C-in-C came to see us at 2.30 pm and was very kind and nice. He said many nice things about the Cavalry and was very pleased with the work they had done. He then rode round the 3rd Cav.Div. They gave him a great reception, I am glad to say.

**Wednesday 14 August 1918** Was sent to GHQ to arrange for the moves of the Cavalry in connection with the 5th Army. Had a real wild goose chase and found the Operations Branch in their train at [Wisy?]. Saw Lawrence the CGS who was very complimentary, as a set-off to Wigram, who said the Cavalry as a Corps was certainly to be done away with. The one consolation is that we have had a gallop before being put into the limbo of forgetfulness.

**Thursday 15 August 1918** The CC attended a conference at GHQ — the 1st and 2nd Divs move up to the 3rd Army and we go to Auxi-le-Château tomorrow morning. Weather still fine and hot. 3rd Cav.Div. move to their old area Hengest-St Omer tonight.

**Friday 16 August 1918** Moved to our old HQ at Auxi-le-Château. Went and saw the 4th Army on our way up. Had tea with Vaughan at 3rd Army HQ and had a talk reference the possible use of Cavalry on their front. Came to the conclusion that there was so much wire that movement was too restricted. Hope that they won't try to use us. It is not a good Army to be in as they don't work together — the 4th Army are quite different.

**Monday 19 August 1918** The 1st Cav.Div. is working with the 3rd Army in a show. I don't think there is a dog's chance of using Cavalry myself so I hope they will not fling them away uselessly. This Army is not too pleasant to work with — they consider horses to be machines. Thus the Batteries of the 2nd Cav. Div. had to march 40 miles unnecessarily, where a little forethought would have saved a good deal of horseflesh. I am going there to issue an ultimatum. They have little sympathy with Cavalry and know less about their possibilities.

The 4th Army ask us to send up a Staff Officer on such occasions and there is no trouble. The 3rd should take a leaf out of their book, it would save our horses. Our casualties in horses during the 3rd Somme Battle* were 2,800 odd, they have replaced 1,700 so we are still 1,100 short and not likely to get them!!! Hope the 3rd Army will have a success and kill a lot of Boches.

**Tuesday 20 August 1918** Rode over to 3rd Army and had a talk to Vaughan with reference to tomorrow's operation and spent the remainder of the day preparing for it. They do not think that it will be a Cavalry day, but one can never tell how these shows will develop. At all events the 1st Cav.Div. may have a gallop, the 2nd and 3rd are too far back to intervene tomorrow.

**Wednesday 21 August 1918** The 3rd Army attacked on a front between the Ancre River and Moyenneville, with a view to exploiting the success south-east in the direction of Bapaume. The 1st Cav.Div. was placed behind the 4th and 6th Corps with the object of exploiting a success, the remainder of the Cavalry Corps being in Reserve and ready to move at short notice. We have reached the line of the Albert-Arras railway, but the Boche has put up a good defence.

Austrian prisoners have been captured and Austrian Divisions reported behind the Boche line. This is curious. The whole attitude of the Boche is defensive. It may be therefore that he is sending down Divisions to the Italian front and making the Austrians send Divisions to this front, and is going to attack the Italians so as to end the year with a success. It won't do him any good as he is beat already. He must have a pretty good hold over the Austrians to force them to do this. On the whole it is a disappointing day – it is not yet known what prisoners we have captured. The French have had a great success and hold the Oise southern bank south of Noyon. Yesterday they took 8,000 prisoners and should have got a good few more today. Things look really well just now.

**Friday 23 August 1918** Yesterday we still advanced north of Bapaume and the 2nd Div. moved forward to Lucheux area in order to assist in today's attack which was carried out by the left of the 6th Corps. Today's operations have been very successful – we are nearing Bapaume from the north-west and we have advanced on a line astride the Somme at Bray. The French continue to make ground in the Noyon area. I think the Boche means going back to the Hindenberg line at his own time, but we are driving him there at the moment faster that he wants and the prisoners are mounting up very considerably. They are not fighting as they did. I think his morale is low and, if we can keep on pushing him, we may achieve a very decided success. I went to see the 2nd Cav.Div. in the afternoon at St Grenas and the 3rd at Yzeux this morning.

**Saturday 24 August 1918** A good day's work with about 6,000 prisoners and we are just on the western outskirts of Bapaume. Had a right royal row with the 3rd Army as regards the use of Cavalry with the result that GHQ issued an order that the Corps was the unit. From my point of view, orders are issued anyhow and the horses are not considered in the slightest.

**Monday 26 August 1918** The Canadian Corps, which has moved up to the Arras area, attacked this morning and had a considerable success, taking Monchy-le-Preux, Guemappe and Wancourt. The Corps with the 1st and 3rd Divs were ordered up at an hour's notice: Corps HQ to Hautcloque, 1st Div. to Le Cauroy area, and 3rd Div. to the valley of the Canche between Frevent and Wail.

Went up with the CC to the 1st Army. They have great hopes of breaking the Drocourt-Queant line*, and the Cavalry reaching the Canal du Nord at, and north of, Marquion, thus penetrating the Hindenburg line.

**Friday 30 August 1918** Had no time to write my Diary as I have been very busy with the arrangements for the battle. The Boche means to hold the Queant line to the last. As his strength increased, I saw the possibility of our reaching the Canal decrease[?]. It is hard to say that one thinks the Cavalry has no chance and therefore should not be employed. I was very relieved when the Army Commander came this morning and said that he had come to the conclusion that it was not the time or place for the employment of a large force of Cavalry. One can trust General Horne in these matters. So bang goes four days' hard work. I am certain the decision is a right one, as our time is coming and it is criminal to fritter us away on a useless plan.

**Sunday 1 September 1918** The Canadians attack the Drocourt-Queant line tomorrow. We have only one Regiment forward and that is the 10th Hussars*. Saw Rupert Ryan tonight and he is quite optimistic – he thinks the Boche expects an attack north-east towards Douai. We have got Peronne† once more, the Australians taking Mont-St-Quentin by a night attack and holding it against many counter attacks by the Boche. They took 2,500 prisoners in the operation.

**Monday 2 September 1918** Attack started this morning at 5.00 am. The Canadians took the trench system up to time, but progress has slowed a bit now. Cavalry Corps placed at one hour's notice to move. It appears that the Boche is putting up a big fight for it – I thought that he would. It is now 4.00 pm and I don't think that we have progressed sufficiently to make it possible to use Cavalry. A rainy and blowy day, which makes flying difficult.

**Wednesday 4 September 1918** Our attacks have succeeded in driving the enemy to the line of the Canal du Nord. It has been a heavy fighting battle but the Boche has been fairly beaten. We must now reorganise our Divisions who have been fighting since 21 August. I don't think our Allies have helped us as much as they might, but perhaps Foch means to put in a big attack the moment we get the Boche back to the Hindenberg line. The weather is fine luckily and that helps no end.

**Saturday 7 September 1918** There has been a decided lull east of Arras but east of Peronne we have been pushing forward and tonight we hear that our Australians are forward on a line north and south through Roisel. It really looks as if the Boche is making as fast as he can for the Hindenberg line. The French are getting on, on the Aillette and also on the Chemin des Dames plateau. I hope they are going to put in a big attack later, which may have a decisive effect; although it is late in the year. We had a Scheme today with Infantry in buses. It brought out many points – one of the main ones being the slowness of the Infantry in open fighting. It shows that they are still wedded to the trenches and their minds do not go beyond that. The Chief is preparing a Scheme for the Cavalry which is to take place about the 14th. I can only hope that he will not gallop the legs off our horses. We want to nurse them a bit if we have to do any fast work in the near future.

**Monday 9 September 1918** This afternoon went to Crecy to see the training people and had a long conference on a Scheme which the Chief wishes us to carry out. He expects us to cover about 50 miles in a day and, if he makes us do it, our horses won't be of much use if we have to move quickly and suddenly. [The] CC is going to see him about it tomorrow and I hope the distance will be very much reduced. It has poured all day and our horses will be over their hocks in mud. I hope it will stop tonight.

**Tuesday 10 September 1918** The Boche is nearly back on the Hindenberg line and he is bound to hold it east of it unless forced back. Another big attack against a well organised defence line such as the Hindenburg line, is a big thing to take on and one hopes that Foch has sufficient Reserves to carry it through on a large scale. It seems to me that a successful attack on the Rheims front would draw all the Boche Reserves and might develop into a decisive battle. If we could, at the same time, take Cambrai and push our Cavalry into the open plains beyond, the whole Boche defence would roll back with decisive results. A very high wind, so went and poached partridges by driving them into the telegraph wires down wind. All young birds – they were excellent eating at dinner tonight.

**Thursday 12 September 1918** Today we get news that the 1st American Army is attacking east of St Mihiel. I wonder what its objective is and what force they are putting in to the attack. It seems very far from the late battle. On the other hand there cannot be much opposition there for the moment and they may straighten out the St Mihiel salient*. It is an interesting time.

**Saturday 14 September 1918** This is the fifth Birthday that I have spent at war. It is a big slice out of one's life, especially at my age, and can never be bridged over. Went to see the Regiment this morning. They do not seem happy – I wish I could do something. Our trouble began in 1903 and since then we have been at sixes and sevens; we want to get out to India and be a happy family once more. Foch is attacking east and west of Rheims; the attacks at St Mihiel have yielded 2,000 prisoners which is good. Weather is not good as yet.

**Monday 16 September 1918** Lovely weather the last two days, so we ought to have it fine tomorrow. I hate these Schemes. They are much more difficult to arrange than actual fighting, they take up a great deal of time. I only hope that things will go all right and that the horses will not have too much of a gruelling. Dined with the 1st Army last night and met Lord Jellicoe – he is out here on a joy ride and is spoiling to see a fight. I hope he does. The tone out here is optimistic to a degree, everyone thinks the Boche is beat. If we can now put in a big attack on a broad front, I think there is a good chance of driving him out of France and that would be a good ending for a year which began so disastrously. I don't know what Reserves Foch has got now, but they should be considerable.

**Wednesday 18 September 1918** Moved our HQ to Auxi-le-Château today. The Scheme yesterday went fairly well and the Chief enjoyed his day with the Cavalry. It was luckily a fine warm day and that has a great deal to do with the tempers of the great. In the afternoon went down to our School at Dieppe.

**Friday 20 September 1918** Returned to Auxi-le-Château having given a lecture and attended two Schemes. I think that the School is doing good work as the answers given to problems were on the right lines. Yesterday the 4th and 5th Armies attacked and took 10,000 prisoners. They are now up against the old Hindenburg line. It is a sign of the times – twice last year we attempted to gain this ground and were unsuccessful. The Boche morale is certainly getting very bad and I think another attack would mean a real big defeat.

**Sunday 22 September 1918** Had to go into GHQ so I had lunch with Wallace at the Club there. The Bull is going on well in Egypt* and it looks as if he may make a big coup; they say he is nearing Bashan so he is nearly home†! The Servians are also getting on well‡ – if we can do the same here, it will be a great ending to the year.

**Tuesday 24 September 1918** Last night we got orders for the 1st and 3rd Cav.Divs to move to the Turtille Valley just north of Peronne, so I went down to the 4th Army today and saw Sir Henry Rawlinson and Archie Montgomery. They were very optimistic and had great hopes of giving the Boche a real doing. We shall not be very comfortable, but I hope that it will only be for a short time.

**Wednesday 25 September 1918** Attended a conference at the Australian Corps HQ and saw many old friends. The Boche seems to be very nervous all along the line. I think he little dreams what is in store for him in the near future. It rained hard last night but has cleared up again. We must pray hard for fine weather now.

**Friday 27 September 1918** 1st and 3rd Armies attacked today* and are making good progress towards Cambrai. We moved our HQ to a small wood about three miles north-east of Peronne. The news continues to be excellent and we hear that the Bulgars are asking for an armistice, which sounds as if they were pretty well rattled. The weather continues to be good. I think things are looking extremely promising – it is good to be under the 4th Army again as they look after us very well and help all they can.

**Sunday 29 September 1918** The morning was fine but very misty and the 4th Army attacked at 5.30 am*. All went well at first but late news shows that many pockets of Germans were left, too many. The result is that some Americans and Australians are out in the blue with Germans holding out in between†. Things were going so well that the Chief moved up the 1st and 3rd Cav.Divs to the Valley of the Cologne and Omignon rivers with a view to

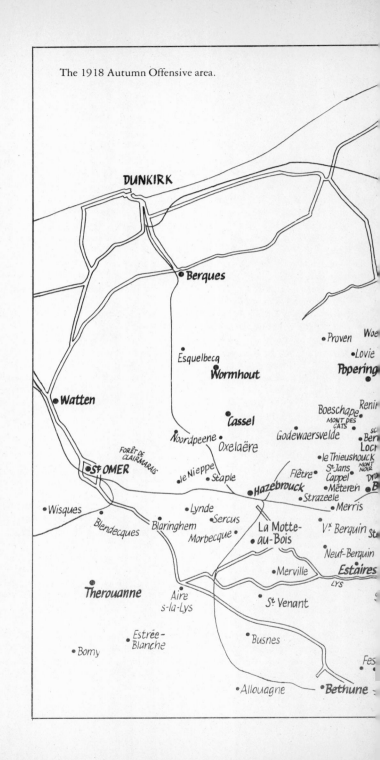

The 1918 Autumn Offensive area.

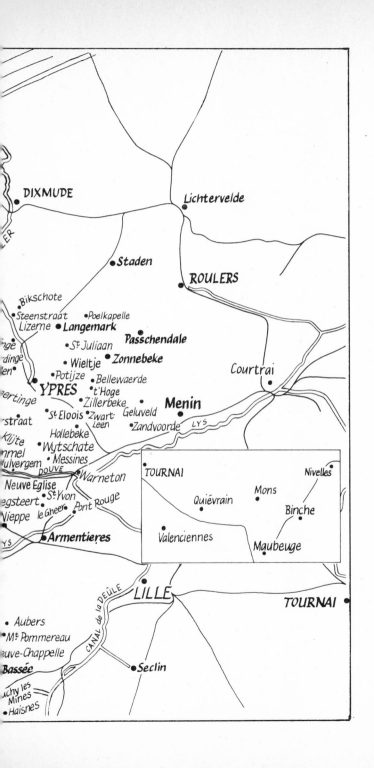

DIXMUDE

Lichtervelde

Staden

ROULERS

Bikschote
Steenstraat          Poelkapelle
Lizerne   Langemark
nge                         Passchendale
dinge      St Juliaan
en         Wieltje   Zonnebeke                   Courtrai
           Potijze  Bellewaerde
rtinge  YPRES      t'Hoge                         Menin
           Zillerbeke               Menin
strait   St Eloois  Zwart  Geluveld
                     Leen   Zandvoorde      LYS
Klijte   Hollebeke
mel     Wytschate
ulvergem  Messines
          DOUVE                    TOURNAI                    Nivelles
Neuve Eglise    Warneton
egsteert  St Yvon                      Quiévrain      Mons
Vieppe  le Gheer  Pont Rouge                                  Binche
YS                                    Valenciennes            Maubeuge
        Armentieres

                               CANAL de la DEÛLE
Aubers                    LILLE                    TOURNAI
Mt Pommereau
euve-Chappelle
Bassée                        Seclin
uchy les
Mines
Haisnes

their being able to operate in the direction of Le Cateau-Cambresis tomorrow. The Corps Commander and I went and had lunch with the Chief and he explained the plans to us. The Belgian news is really good‡, their Cavalry are approaching Roulers and the 2nd Army on their right are also advancing on Menin and the line of the Lys. It looks as if they might get the coast and drive the Boche back there. They ought to make a good bag if they do.

**Tuesday 1 October 1918** Got orders late last night that we were to turn out of our HQ to make room for the 13th Corps. We are to take two Divisional HQs in a wood just north of Templeux-la-Fosse. It was luckily a fine day so the lorries could come close up and it made the move easy. There must have been a good deal of hot air flying about at Army HQ, as between 4.00 pm and 11.00 pm we got three sets of orders.

**Wednesday 2 October 1918** Moved two Divisions to the line of the Canal [de St Quentin] between Bellenglise and Bellicourt at 7.00 am this morning and made our HQ at Bellenglise. It was very interesting to go into a place I had often looked at through glasses from our lines. There was nothing doing however and the Divisions were ordered back at 10.00 am. The Boche has, without a doubt, stiffened up this front for the moment and his machine gunners are fighting desperately. If we go on, I think the time will come when he will break and then our chance will come. We must however have patience as a premature use of the Cavalry would mean heavy losses and no compensating gain. Hope that the weather will hold.

**Thursday 3 October 1918** The 9th Corps and Australians attacked this morning and we were at one hour's notice to move. We got the order to do so at 12 noon. However the reports proved too optimistic and so we did not advance much beyond the Canal – although the 6th Cav.Bde were pushed forward towards the south of Montbrehain in the afternoon. We moved our HQ to the tumulus west of Bellenglise at 2.00 pm. Spent an interesting, but not very profitable, afternoon; luckily it was not cold. We took over 4,000 prisoners and I saw many young boys who seemed quite glad to be out of it.

**Saturday 5 October 1918** Attended a conference at the Army this morning on future movements. Yesterday we were told that Turkey has sued for peace*, but nothing official yet. It came from the King of the Belgians and is probably correct. The Boche appears to be retiring in front of the 3rd Army; it is difficult to say how far he is going back, yet every day we are taking thousands of prisoners. Hope that in the next attack we shall have a go.

**Sunday 6 October 1918** Great excitement as the papers say Germany has approached President Wilson with a view to an Armistice and the discussion of peace*. Hear that all the big boys at Versailles talking 15 to the dozen. The only answer is another attack as Germany is beat. The reason for this offer is probably that Turkey and Austria have said that they are going out and have thus forced Germany's hand†. One cannot trust the Central Powers. Our attack tomorrow has been postponed for 24 hours – I hope not on account of these peace proposals as that means an advantage to the Boche.

**Tuesday 8 October 1918** At 5.00 am we arrived at the tumulus west of Bellenglise. We could hear the guns and see the flashes of the 3rd Army on our left who started at 4.30 am. Punctually at 5.10, the guns opened [up] and the sky was lit up with the flashes. The Boche put up a good fight in places, but early on in the day we reached the line of Brancourt-le Grand/Premont/Serain villages. Here the 1st Cav.Div. tried to push through, but the Boche was holding a line east of the places strongly and many attempts made to get on failed. The 19th Hussars had a good many casualties. We made our HQ in Estrees for the night; Boche being quite active with his bombs.

**Wednesday 9 October 1918** Had a bad night, wires being down everywhere, orders being late and so on. The ball started at 5.20 am and the Boche was found to have retired during the night. We followed up and came up with him just north of Maretz – full of French inhabitants who were overjoyed at our entry. During the day our advance continued – the villages of Honnechy, Reumont and Troisvilles being taken – and at night we had the Canadian Cav.Bde in front of Le Cateau-Cambresis and on the River Selle. Spent the night in Serain. The Boche has looted all he can before he went. Roads are a trouble as he has blown a good many mine craters at crossroads. It is great to get into fresh country – few shell holes and no trenches and wire. We fought the Battle of Le Cateau here in 1914.

**Thursday 10 October 1918** Tried to force the crossing of the Selle north of Le Cateau early in the morning. The 9th Bde had a good many casualties as the Boche had a lot of guns on the north bank. It soon became apparent that it was no longer a Cavalry operation and we decided to withdraw the Divisions. All day we had no communications with 4th Army, except by wireless. Established our HQ at Bertry for the night. In the afternoon a Staff Officer brought news that Le Cateau was ours. Did not belive it, so sent Bimbo [Reynolds] in an armoured car to see. He went through the place but found several roads blown up. The Boche were close on the other side.

We have got into the industrial areas of France. It is interesting talking to the people: many of them have had no communication with kith or kin for four years. There is not a horse, cow or sheep or chicken in the countryside, the Boche has taken everything with him. Some of the people were starving when we came in. It is difficult to know what the Boche intentions are, he is retiring everywhere, but fighting his rearguards very cleverly.

**Saturday 12 October 1918** The Corps Commander attended a conference at Arras. We are moving the Divisions back to west of the Canal de St Quentin. I just hate moving back, but it is a question of roads and food. Until we get the railways on, there is not much chance of getting a move on. Heard today that the Boche accepts President Wilson's peace terms and asks for an Armistice*. It seems as if the Boche is really at his beam-ends, in fact he will give anything for peace. I only hope that the terms of the Armistice and the guarantees will be adequate and of such a nature that he cannot get round them. He is a slippery customer and I don't trust him a yard. He is now busy retiring out of the Douai and Laon salient and is thickening up in front of us here. The weather is not good, it is drizzling and the roads are like glass, the buses sliding all over the place.

**Sunday 13 October 1918** Great trouble with the moves of the Divisions as the roads are very congested. The band of the 38th Div. came and played here at lunchtime. It was a great treat.

**Monday 14 October 1918** Moved back from Bertry to our old HQ near Aizecourt-le-Bas north-east of Peronne. Went to the 4th and 5th Corps HQs on my way. Then went and had a look at Cambrai; they have destroyed the centre of the city and part of it were still smouldering. The outskirts still stand although, of course, houses are without glass and shell torn.

**Wednesday 16 October 1918** The news from the north is good. French, Belgians and Plumer's Army are all advancing, reports say that French Cavalry is advancing up [to] Lichlervelde and that Boche trains came under our fire towards Courtrai. It would seem as if there were a chance of really pushing the Boche up there and also hustling him considerably. If he is not ready to go back up there, reinforces his line and fights, then our attacks down here may have a chance of making a real good advance. The weather is again wet – oh! for six weeks' really fine weather with dry roads and dry country – it would mean everything.

**Thursday 17 October 1918** Have been married 20 years today. Spent the day in the motor going round the 4th Army Corps who are attacking today. The Boche is in great depth at Le Cateau-Cambresis and to the south of that place and the attack appeared to me to be a bit sticky. It was meeting with a good deal of resistance and there were two new Divisions in the line. Went on into Bohain-en-Vermandois to try to find the 5th Cav.Bde. The President of the French Republic* was there walking on foot through the town. The Boche has evacuated Lille I think, so he is straightening out his line. Report this evening that British sailors have landed and are in Ostend; if so I win 100 francs from Joe [Seligman?].

**Sunday 20 October 1918** 3rd Army attacked and crossed the River Selle this morning. It has been a poisonous day: heavy rain and mist. Went to GHQ and saw the CGS* and talked of the future prospects of the Cavalry. At present there does not appear to be a possible use of the Cavalry mass as the Boche has his rearguards in very great depth. But, should he take a big jump back, then we ought to be pushed forward to harass his rearguards and push them in. It is not going to be an easy job, as there are no flanks in this sort of warfare. The Boche sees to that and keeps his line very straight unless it is covered by a pretty good obstacle.

**Monday 21 October 1918** We expect the German answer any minute to Wilson's last Note*. We have advanced a good bit towards Valenciennes today and it looks as if the next Boche rearguard position is the line of the Scheldt. On the other hand we have crossed it in the north at a couple of places. It is difficult to know what the Boche is doing, but it looks as if his one idea is to get his armies back into Germany and so save them from a debacle.

**Wednesday 23 October 1918** 4th and 3rd Armies attacked today and are making good progress. We are in the suburbs of Valenciennes. It is a curious situation as every attack we make succeeds and, as a rule, several thousand prisoners are taken — yet the French and Americans are not getting on in the south*. I think the Boche is holding them with every man he has got and is slowly swinging his right back through Belgium. Alas there does not as yet appear to be a chance for us and we are sitting doing nothing. The Field Marshal's despatch came out this morning on the fighting in March and April. He gives the Cavalry the good word that they fully deserve, but I am very sorry to say does not mention the Corps Commander by name, which is a shame as he had made the Cavalry what it is.

**Thursday 24 October 1918** We attacked again this morning south of Valenciennes, drove the Boche back three miles and took a certain number of prisoners. I hope that Foch is boiling up a big attack on a large scale. We have shortened the line up a good deal and he ought to have a good few Divisions out of the line. A big attack now might have a great effect. The Boche now has no fresh Divisions in Reserve for the first time during the war.

**Friday 25 October 1918** President Wilson sent another Note to the Boche and we will now see whether they are really in a bad way or still bluffing*. It is a pretty outspoken communication. Rode over to Tertry in the morning and had lunch with 1st Cav.Div. We made ground north of Valenciennes yesterday and the Canadians are waiting to take the place, one Brigade north and one south and both betting they will be first in the place.

**Saturday 26 October 1918** Went to 3rd Army and saw Vaughan — he had no news except that we had outrun our railways and it would take time to build them up again; so for the moment the advance on that Army front would stop. Went on and saw the 1st Cav.Bde at Esnes, and also the Regiment. They are pretty comfortable. Then back to GHQ to find out their intentions as regards the Cavalry. Learnt nothing except not much chance of using us for the present, but we shall probably be moved north to an area between Arras and Bethune.

Met Clive at lunch who had just come back from Foch's HQ. They are evidently having a conference on the terms of a possible Armistice. I think our gallant Allies are not putting all in for the moment. In Paris they say the war is is over; I wish I could think so. A fine day, but the roads are bad and the delay-action mines of the Boche are working still. The level crossing at Roisel went up the day before yesterday, about 40 days after the Boche left. It is a good scientific engineering.

**Monday 28 October 1918** Just heard that the Corps Commander has been made a Commander of the Légion d'Honneur. I think he should have been made a Grand Croix. The German reply to the last Wilson Note is in today's wireless and is very humble. I think that they want peace at any price and will accept practically any Armistice terms. I sincerely hope that this is the end of the war, I believe that Germany is really beaten and it will take her a long time to recover. In the near future the Russian question will be the most difficult one. The Italians are attacking hard* and making progress and Austria is asking for peace†. It is a curious mix-up. No one could have believed in June this year that such a debacle could take place. Hope it works out all right and that we shall get home and have peace — from our enemies and from our friends the labour parties.

**Thursday 31 October 1918** The weather broke early this morning and it is raining. Yesterday and today attended Schemes carried out by the 1st Div. Yesterday's Scheme lacked ginger but today, with Mullens himself commanding, was quite a different show. Good news today — at 12.00 noon the Armistice with Turkey came into effect and 33,000 Austrians have been taken prisoners. The Central Powers have crumbled very rapidly and Austria should capitulate within the next two days or so. What Germany will do? It is interesting to see; I think she will accept any terms to get peace. I hope so, as she is beaten and no one wants to prolong this war. This peace talk does not seem to affect our troops as they are fighting better than ever. The 2nd Army, French and Belgians attacked today, but no news as yet received as to the progress made.

**Friday 1 November** 1918 We hear today that Austria has signed an Armistice with the Allies. This leaves Germany alone. On the other hand there are rumours of dissentions at the Versailles Conference*. I hope this is not true and is the result of a prolonged sitting. We must now show a united front and get an Armistice which leaves us in a position that it is impossible for Germany to resume hostilities. I am certain that the great stumbling block will be the freedom of the seas. Our Empire is dependent on and must be judged by its coastline; on this point we must be firm. At any peace conference this will become the one debatable point and our future must rest on it.

This morning saw the Canadian Cav.Bde carry out a Scheme. They did it in their usual style – plenty of dash, but not much science – it will succeed but with heavy losses. We have had many accidents lately through horses striking unexploded shells. Cyril [Hankey]'s two horses were killed and the groom lost a leg. It is a bad lookout for the future cultivators of the land.

**Saturday 2 November** 1918 A very wet morning – spent it watching a Scheme and the wet did not help it at all.

**Sunday 3 November** 1918 We attack again tomorrow on a large scale, but there does not appear to be much chance for the poor old Cavalry. I should like to have one more gallop before the end. This Armistice question is bad for troops, I am certain of that. I wish we could settle the thing one way or another.

**Monday 4 November** 1918 The 1st French Army, our 4th, 3rd and 1st Armies attacked at 6.00 am this morning; the attack has gone well and we have reached all our objectives. Tomorrow we continue and it may lead to very great things. Heard today the terms of the Armistice with Austria – give Italy Trieste and give the Allies the use of railways in Austria and the power to move troops through into southern Germany. The opinion here is that Germany will accept the Allied terms for an Armistice and I have heard that the terms are good and stiff. I hope so.

**Tuesday 5 November** 1918 Yesterday was a real good day – 15,000 prisoners and 200 guns – but this morning we are advancing with hardly any opposition. I went to see the 4th Army this morning and their Corps were advancing freely. What a thousand pities that we are not there, as touch had certainly been lost for the moment. I hope that they will put us further forward, now that we can take advantage of such a situation. It is a question of feeding. Yesterday the main line of the Army went up in three places with delay-action mines and the result was chaos – neither food or reinforcements could be taken up. I think however all is right now. It is sickening sitting back here and listening to rain on my tin roof, when we might be doing something.

**Wednesday 6 November** 1918 One of the worst days of the year – it rained for the last 36 hours and rained hard. We have orders to move north into the 5th Army area and go into an area south of Lille, with our HQ at Seclin. The 1st and 3rd Divs marched north today. They are having a bad time and will spend a very wet night. Hope it will clear.

**Thursday 7 November** 1918 Moved our HQ to Seclin today and so came under the 5th Army. Started at 8.00 am and met the Commander-in-Chief at 5th Army HQ in Lille. The Boche is still fighting on the Scheldt and we propose to put him out of it. The Chief told us that plenipotentiaries of the Boche were on their way to get the Armistice terms*.

I came through Douai which had not been much knocked about, but the Boche has cut every road he can by blowing craters in it. Lille was practically untouched and the 5th Army were in a palatial residence. Our home in Seclin is not so comfortable and the Boche have left it in a filthy state. The inhabitants are very interesting to talk to: the Boche sent them back 15 miles when we advanced, looted all the houses and then sent the inhabitants back again. They took everything such as sheets, tablecloths – leaving the poor people with nothing.

**Friday 8 November 1918** A cold day. Went to a conference in the morning. The news from Germany appears to show things in a very bad way. It seems as if the fleet has mutined and all the ports are in the hands of the revolutionaries*. This does not look as if the Boche can hold out much longer. The Boche plenipotentiaries are at Foch's HQ – they are given till Monday 11.00 am to say Yes or No. The terms went back to HQ at Spa† at 8.00 pm by special despatch carrier. It is an interesting time, but I wish it were settled one way or another as this period of waiting is very trying.

**Sunday 10 November 1918** Today we moved forward the 1st and 3rd Cav.Divs east of the Scheldt south of Tournai; HQ advanced to Genech[?]. Tomorrow we move on Nivelles.

**Monday 11 November 1918** Called at 7.00 am to the telephone and told that we're to stand fast and later heard that Armistice had been signed at 5.00 am. Had a bad morning as Divisions had started but all was well – we stopped them*. At 11.00 am, the Armistice came into force and fighting ended. Thank God†.

# FOOTNOTES

**Chapter 1: From Mons to the Marne (12-8-14 to 9-10)**
13-8 *Tommy Atkins: ie the soldiers.
15-8 *2nd Div.: then commanded by Major-General C.C. Munro and including the 4th, 5th and 6th Bdes. 19-8 *His wife: Violet Mary Bertha, née D'Arcy.
  †Unidentified. 22-8 *'Goffy' was the nickname of Hubert Gough, then commanding the 3rd Cav.Bde.
  †The 2nd Dragoon Guards, The Royal Scots Greys.
23-8 *The canal running between Condé and Mons.
  †5th Div.: then commanded by Major-General Sir G. Fergusson and including the 13th, 14th and 15th Bdes.
24-8 *This was a very famous charge and one of the few to occur on this front.
25-8 *1st Bde: then commanded by Brigadier-General F.I. Maxse and including the following Battalions: 1st Coldstream Guards; 1st Scots Guards; 1st Black Watch (Royal Highlanders); 2nd Royal Munster Fusiliers.
26-8 *4th Div.: then commanded by Major-General T.D'O. Snow and including the 10th, 11th and 12th Bdes.
27-8 *10th Bde: then commanded by Brigadier-General J.A.L. Haldane and including the following Battalions: 1st Royal Warwickshire Reg.; 2nd Seaforth Highlanders; 1st Royal Irish Fusiliers; 2nd Royal Dublin Fusiliers.
  †From the composite regiment of Household Cavalry, 4th Cav.Bde.
31-8 *ie the 1st, 2nd and 4th Cav.Bdes.
1-9-14 *1st Cav.Bde: then commanded by Brigadier-General G.J. Briggs and including the following: 2nd Dragoon Guards; 5th Dragoon Guards and 11th Hussars.
  †The 11th (Prince Albert's Own) Hussars – AFH's own Regiment.
  ‡The 2nd Dragoons (The Queen's Bays).
  §This is one of the very rare places where AFH's emotions show through his essential factual reporting. The full text is almost incoherent at this point.
3-9 *The Cavalry lost practically all their equipment during the Retreat from Mons. AFH told his daughter (TMV Briscoe) that General Allenby had had to borrow his razor as it was the only one left among the Cav.Div. Staff!
5-9 *Henry Wilson.
  †This was the furthest point south of the Retreat from Mons.
6-9 *1st Corps: then commanded by Lieutenant-General D. Haig and including the 1st and 2nd Divs.
  †German name for lancers.
  ‡Unidentified.
7-9 *Hutchinson, the BG.GS of the 1st Cav.Bde.
  †2nd Cav.Bde: then commanded by Brigadier-General H.de B. De Lisle and including the following: 4th Dragoon Guards; 9th Lancers; 18th Hussars.
8-9 *Johnson of the King's Royal Rifle Corps.
  †The 4th Dragoon Guards charged, supported by the 1st Battalion the Black Watch. An artist's

impression of this action is on the jacket of this book.

10-9 *Marceline was a famous clown who was notorious for arriving with profuse offers of help just as all the work was finished. He was a particular favourite of AFH.

12-9 *5th Bde: then commanded by Brigadier-General R.C.B. Haking and including the following Battalions: 2nd Worcester Reg.; 2nd Oxford and Bucks Light Infantry; 2nd Highland Light Infantry; 2nd Connaught Rangers.

13-9 *Allenby, then commanding the Cav.Div.

15-9 *Slang for the shellburst from a 5.9 or heavier high explosive shell fired from a German Howitzer. See also 24-9‡.

†Zouaves were a type of French Light Infantry; the soldiers were French but wore an Arab-style uniform. Turcos were Algerian native Light Infantry, serving in the French army.

‡1st the Black Watch (Royal Highlanders), attached to the 1st Bde.

16-9 *4th Cav.Bde: then commanded by Brigadier-General Hon.C.E. Bingham and including the following: Household Cavalry (composite reg.); 6th Dragoon Guards; 3rd Hussars.

†Royal Field Artillery.

‡The Sugar Factory, also known as the Sucrerie, was near Troyon.

17-9 *Possibly General Mitaud, commanding the French 38th Div. See 19-9. 18-9 *The Queen's Own (Royal West Kent Regiment), attached to the 13th Bde.

19-9 *General Mitaud.

†Mutes were professional attendants at funerals and so looked permanently miserable.

20-9 *Douglas Haig.

†Probably Lomax who was commanding the 1st Div.

24-9 *VIPs.

†Prince Arthur, Duke of Connaught.

‡As 15-9*. Interestingly *Soldiers' Songs and Slang* says that this is an earlier usage than 'Black Maria'.

§A bar or insignia attached to a medal ribbon to indicate the bearer had been involved in a specific battle or campaign.

‖This was probably the first they had heard of General Maunoury's strike against General von Kluck's 1st Army on 5-7 Sept.

¶ Rum and water possibly?

25-9 *AFH describes this as 'Got up at 7.00 am and shaved and dressed quite leisurely, then loafed around in the sun.'

†Assistant Quartermaster General.

‡'Buck' is defined as vigourous cheerfulness or exaggeration. 'To buck' is to gossip and perhaps to brag and/or complain about one's doings.

§The Army Remount Service.

‖This was the famous message which referred to the British Expeditionary Force as the 'contemptible little army'.

26-9 *2nd Bde: then commanded by Brigadier-General E.S. Bulfin and including the following Battalions: 2nd Royal Sussex Reg.: 1st Northamptonshire Reg.; 1st North Lanscashire Reg.; 2nd King's Royal Rifle Corps.

27-9 *1st Div.: then commanded by Major-General S.H. Lomax and including the 1st, 2nd and 3rd Bdes.

29-9 *Brigadier-General Royal Horse Artillery to the Cav.Div; B.F. Drake.

7-10-14 *Possibly Jack Ainsworth; see 13-10.

8-10 *His wife, Violet.

9-10 *Allenby. He had just been appointed to command the newly-formed Cavalry Corps.

## Chapter 2: The First Battle of Ypres (10-10-14 to 18-11)

11-10 *2nd Corps: then commanded by Lieutenant-General Sir H.L. Smith-Dorrien and including the 3rd and 5th Divs.

13-10 *6th Div.: then commanded by Major-General J.L. Keir and including the 16th, 17th and 18th Bdes.

14-10 *Light Infantryman in the German army.

†She was a Roman Catholic; he was an Anglican.

20-10 *4th (Guards) Bde: then commanded by Brigadier-General Scott-Kerr and including the following Battalions: 2nd Grenadier Guards; 2nd and 3rd Coldstream Guards; 1st Irish Guards.

21-10 *11th Bde: then commanded by Brigadier-General A.G. Hunter-Weston and including the following Battalions: 1st Somerset Light Infantry; 1st East Lancashire Reg.; 1st Hampshire Reg.; 1st Rifle Bde.

†2nd Battalion, Essex Regiment, attached to the 12th Bde.

‡2nd Cav.Div.: then commanded by Major-General H.de la P. Gough and including the 3rd, 4th and 5th Cav.Bdes.

22-10 *De Lisle. All such references will be to the same person, until indicated otherwise.

†Possibly a report of the Battle of Tannenberg; however this was hardly a big success for the Russians.

23-10 *The Lahore and Meerut Divs.

†The 57th (Wilde's) Rifles were attached to the Ferozepore Bde; AFH wrote 61st, but this must be a mistake.

‡Usually considered to be typical 1920s slang, this actually dates from about 1903.

25-10 *De Lisle presumably, although AFH usually means the Commander-in-Chief (at this time, Sir John French).

†7th Div.: then commanded by Major-General T. Capper and including the 20th, 21st & 22nd Bdes.

‡A patriotic German song, written by Schneckenberger.

26-10 *3rd Cav.Div.: then commanded by Major-General Hon. J. Byng and including the 6th and 7th Cav.Bdes.

†2nd Battalion, the Connaught Rangers, from the 5th Bde.

28-10 *Probably Frederick Coleman who drove them to Messines that day. He has an almost identical remark in his book *From Mons to Ypres with French* (p.225); see 30-10†.

2-11-14 *The Royal Theatre, Drury Lane who used to specialise in spectacular effects such as trains and ships on stage as well as earthquakes.

†'The President' was Coleman's nickname. He says it was 'bestowed to mark my nationality'. An American journalist and photographer, he was one of 25 volunteer drivers from the Royal Automobile Club who brought their own cars to France in August 1914 to act as liaison for the GHQ Staff. Coleman was attached to Allenby's Cavalry Division and then to De Lisle's 1st Cav.Div. until De Lisle left for Gallipoli in May 1915. His first book covers from August to December 1914, while his second book *With Cavalry in 1915* covers January to May 1915. Many of the photos in this book from 1914 and 1915 were taken by him.

‡Oxfordshire Hussars were a Yeomanry Regiment, then attached to the 2nd Cav.Bde.

§14th London (London Scottish) Regiment, then attached to the 1st Bde.

8-11 *Breastplate and backplate.

†7th Cav. Bde: then commanded by Brigadier-General C.T.McM. Kavanagh and including the following: 1st & 2nd Life Guards; Royal Horse Guards (The Blues).

‡The Russians held most of Poland by this point, despite the defeat at Tannenberg.

§The Austrian armies had been driven back by the Russians in Galicia and their invasion force had been thrown out of Serbia. Italy was then allied to Germany and Austria, but negotiating with the Allies.

10-11 *De Lisle; judging by Coleman's descriptions, he was reckless in the extreme.

11-11 *1st Queen's Own (Royal West Kent Regiment), attached to the 13th Bde.

†Either the 1st or the 4th Bde.

‡Unidentified.

14-11 *9th Bde: then commanded by Brigadier-General F.C. Shaw and including the following Battalions: 1st Northumbrian Fusiliers; 1st Lincolnshire Reg.; 1st Royal Scots Fusiliers; 4th Royal Fusiliers (City of London).

†15th Bde: then commanded by Brigadier-General Count A.E.W. Gleichen and including the following Battalions: 1st Norfolk Reg.; 1st Cheshire Reg.; 1st Bedfordshire Reg.; 1st Dorset Reg.

‡Château .

194

§3rd Div.: then commanded by Major-General H.I.W. Hamilton and including the 7th, 8th & 9th Bdes.

‖AFH's own horse.

¶French Cavalry.

15-11 *Probably a reference to Hindenburg's Polish offensive, which had been launched on 11-11.

## Chapter 3: Stalemate (19-11-14 to 21-2-15)

20-11 *End of Volume I of the full Diaries.

27-11 *A type of tyre.

†Probably the action at Lodz when the Russian 5th Army managed to cut off a substantial portion of the German 9th Army.

5-12 *The Kiel Canal lay about 300 miles north as the crow flies! It was vital, strategically, to the German Navy because it allowed even the super-dreadnaughts to pass from the Baltic to the North Sea and vice-versa in complete safety.

7-12 *Lodz fell to the Germans on 6-12, while the Russians retreated some 30 miles to the Rivers Rawka and Bzura.

10-12 *Serbians. The country then known as Serbia now lies mostly within the Socialist Republics of Serbia and Macedonia (minus the province of Vojvodina) in Yugoslavia.

12-12 *Typhoid fever.

17-12 *Admiral Hipper had already launched one raid on Great Yarmouth (3-11) before his battle-cruiser squadron, supported by the High Seas Fleet (with 14 dreadnaughts and 8 older battleships), raided both Scarborough and Hartlepool on 16-12. Over 500 civilians were killed in the bombardment. They also laid a large minefield north of Scarborough.

21-12 *2nd Battalion Durham Light Infantry, attached to the 18th Bde.

†In charge of Musketry instruction; AFH had been involved in this area also.

22-12 *Kitchener's Army of volunteers were training and being equipped in England. The Territorial forces were being sent out during this period to make up for the (approximately) 45% casualties of the original BEF.

28-12 *Turkey had declared war on the Allies on 1-11, whereupon Egypt became a British protectorate. Turkey had been collecting troops and supplies in southern Palestine before the declaration of war, so an attack on the Suez Canal and Egypt was anticipated.

29-12 *It has not been possible to identify which action this might refer to.

†From the 1st Field Squadron, Royal Engineers, attached to the 1st Cav.Div.

31-12 *Wilson's Note.

2-1-15 *Sir John French?

†De Lisle.

4-1 *Bylaugh Hall belonged to W.K. D'Arcy (AFH's father-in-law); it was his shooting home in Norfolk.

12-1 *27th Div.: then commanded by Major-General T.D'O. Snow and including the 80th, 81st & 82nd Bdes.

15-1 *Unidentified.

18-1 *He was the Divisional Assistant Quartermaster General.

24-1 *3rd Cav.Bde: then commanded by Brigadier-General J. Vaughan and including the following: 4th Hussars; 5th Lancers; 16th Lancers.

†Japan had declared war on Germany on 21-8-14.

30-1 *On 14-1, General von Lochow had stormed the French positions near Soissons on the north bank of the Aisne, taking 5,000 men and 35 guns.

5-2-15 *28th Div.: then commanded by Major-General E.S. Bulfin and including the 83rd, 84th & 85th Bdes.

7-2 *King Albert.

8-2 *Cicerone: a guide who shows the curiosities of the place to strangers.

12-2 *This may relate to the attacks on the Carpathian Mountains or to initial reports of Ludendorff's attack with the German 10th Army towards the Masurian Lakes.

17-2 *'Cavan's House' was named after Lord Cavan (4th (Guards) Bde) who had used it as his Field HQ during the 1st Battle of Ypres; it lay at an important intersection of the trench system.

20-2 *Companion of St Michael & St George.

21-2 *Probably refers to the German 10th Army's campaign; they drove the Russians back to the River Niemen.

## Chapter 4: The Second Battle of Ypres (22-2-15 to 25-5)

22-2 *The Maxim was a type of machine-gun; see 13-12-15*.

26-2 *Nickname of General Allenby.

27-2 *He was Assistant Provost Marshal for the 1st Cav.Div. so spy-catching came within his duties.

28-2 *Saps are deep and narrow trenches used for communication or for undermining the enemy's defences.

1-3-15 *Probably relates to the offensive in the Carpathians.

3-3 *Probably refers to the 1st Battle of Champagne which had started with Joffre's shell barrage (the first ever) on 16-2.

5-3 *End of Volume II of the full Diaries.

7-3 *At Neuve Chapelle.

†23rd Bde: then commanded by Brigadier-General R.J. Pinney and including the following Battalions:2nd Devonshire; 2nd West Yorks; 2nd Scottish Rifles; 2nd Middlesex.

‡25th Bde: then commanded by Brigadier-General A.W.G. Lowry Cole and including the following Battalions: 2nd Lincolnshire; 1st Royal Irisuh Rifles; 13th London (TF); 2nd Royal Berkshire; 2nd Rifle Bde.

§Garhwal Bde: then commanded by Brigadier-General G.G. Blackader and including the following Battalions: 2nd Leicestershire; 1st & 2nd/39th Garhwalis; 3rd London (TF); 2nd/3rd Gurkhas.

12-3 *2nd Battalion, Rifle Bde, then attached to 25th Bde.

13-3 *Magor-General F.J. Davies, commanding the 8th Div.

†To be superceded and sent home, more or less in disgrace, but not cashiered. Comes from the relevant camp in South Africa during the Boer War.

18-3 *Probably refers to the reduction of the outer forts of the Dardanelles, which had been completed by 9-3.

21-3 *Refers to the initial bombardment and attack on the Narrows on 18-3; this was abandoned after one French and three British ships had been disabled or sunk by mines.22-3 *It fell to the Russians on this day, after a prolonged siege.

24-3 *AFH had arranged for the burial after he was killed on 17-10-14.

†Originally thieves' slang for a place of public amusement, hence a music hall or concert entertainment.

‡There is a programme pasted into this volume for a concert on 22/23 March which included a Mr Barrington Foote, who was probably the person concerned.

30-3 *The negotiations for the Treaty of London (signed 26-4-15) were going on at this point.

†Its name meant 'dove' and it was used for reconnaisance and training. Powered by a 100hp Mercedes DI engine, it had two crew armed with rifles or revolvers and a top speed of about 71mph.

31-3 *3rd Corps: then commanded by Lieutenant-General W.P. Pulteney and including the 4th & 6th Divs.

3-4-15 *The Queen Elizabeth was a superdreadnaught equipped with 15in. guns.They could hit a target accurately over 9 miles away.

11-4 *The French attacks on the St Mihiel salient began on ? but failed to make any progress.

14-4 *5th Corps: then commanded by Lieutenant-General Sir H. Plumer and including the 27th, 28th & Canadian Divs.

19-4 *Gough was notoriously quarrelsome, see 31-7-16 (if this is indeed Gough).

20-4 *To distinguish one side from the other.

22-4 *Start of the 2nd Battle of Ypres.

23-4 *Chlorine: this was the first time that such a weapon was used on the Western Front.

†Canadian Div.: then commanded by Major-General E.A.H. Alderson and including the 1st, 2nd & 3rd Canadian Bdes.

‡The 87th (Territorial) Div. and the 45th (Algerian) Div.

§50th (1st/Northumbrian) Div.: then commanded by Major-General M.G. Lindsay and including the 149th, 150th & 151st Bdes.

26-4 *Lahore Div.: then commanded by Major-General H.D'U. Keary and including the Ferozepore, Jullundur & Sirlind Bdes.

†Northumbrian Bde: AFH probably meant the 50th (1st/Northumbrian) Division.

27-4 *Colonel, Royal Horse Artillery.

30-4 *Possibly Philip Howell.

4-5-15 *Mackensen's attack with the German 11th Army in the Gorlice/Tarnow sector of the Carpathians.

6-5 *Smith-Dorrien; he was placed in an untenable position by the antagonism of Sir John French and so resigned.

7-5 *They had made the initial beach-head on 25-4, but had failed to exploit their opportunities while also being pinned down at certain points by the Turkish counterattacks.

9-5 *Almost certainly De Lisle.

10-5 *According to his account (*With Cavalry in 1915*, p.203), it was thoroughly flea-ridden but safer than outside.

†Assistant Provost Marshal, presumably 'Mouse' Tomlinson.

13-5 *6th Cav.Bde: then commanded by Brigadier-General D. Campbell and including the following: 3rd Dragoon Guards; 1st Dragoons (The Royals); North Somerset Yeomanry.

†8th Cav.Bde: then commanded by Brigadier-General Bulkeley-Johnston and including the following: Royal Horse Guards (The Blues); 10th Hussars; Essex Yeomanry.

16-5 *80th Bde: then commanded by Brigadier-General W.E.B. Smith and including the following Battalions: 2nd King's Shropshire Light Infantry; 4th King's Royal Rifles; 4th Rifle Bde.

18-5 *81st Bde: then commanded by Brigadier-General H.L. Croker and including the following Battalions: 1st & 9th(TF) Royal Scots; 2nd Camerons; 2nd Gloucestershires; 1st & 9th (TF) Argyll & Sutherland Highlanders.

19-5 *Territorial.

20-5 *Shells from a German small-calibre, high-velocity (usually 7.7) gun.

22-5 *De Lisle.

†At Esquelbecque.

24-5 *84th Bde: then commanded by Brigadier-General L.J. Bols and including the following Battalions: 2nd Northumbrian Fusiliers; 2nd Cheshire; 12th (London) Rangers (TF); 1st Monmouthshire(TF); 1st Suffolk; 1st Welch.

25-5 *29th Div.: then commanded by Major-General A.G. Hunter-Weston and including the 86th, 87th & 88th Bdes.

## Chapter 5: The Dismounted Division (27-5-15 to 21-8)

27-5 *Of the 1st Cav.Div.; compare AFH's remarks on 23-3 with his future attitude towards Bingham.

29-5 *Italy had declared war on Austria on 24-5.

†From now on, Bingham.

‡End of Volume III of the full Diaries.

31-5 *Cavalry Club, in Piccadilly.

†Przemysl actually fell to the German 11th Army on 3-6; either AFH wrote this after that date or it was the prospect of the fall causing the depression.

‡A Coalition Cabinet had been formed on 26-5 in which Liberals and Conservatives shared power under Asquith as Prime Minister.

§Probably Field Marshal Sir John French, Commander-in-Chief of the BEF.

‖Probably Sir William Robertson, French's Chief of the General Staff.

8-6 A French offensive (the Battle of Souchez) had been launched between Lens and Arras on 9-5. The British attack around Festubert on the same day had been a disaster.

10-6 *Kitchener.

†It is not possible to pinpoint which event might have caused this rumour.

14-6 *Sir John French.

15-6 *51st (Highland) Div.(TF): then commanded by Major-General R. Bannatine-Allason and including the 152nd, 153rd & 154th Bdes.

16-6 *The owner of the chateau at Esquelbecque.

18-6 *Probably relates to the German advance on Lemberg. The Russians had retired from the whole of Galicia since the offensive started on 1-5.

21-6 *They had lost 102,500 men in the attacks in the Lens/Arras area.

24-6 *Richard III by William Shakespeare (I.i.24).

†Now L'vov in the Ukraine; it fell on 22-6.

‡A brevet is a document entitling a commissioned officer temporarily to hold a higher military rank, but without the additional pay and allowances.

28-6 *Stanmore Hall in Middlesex was the country home of W.K. D'Arcy (AFH's father-in-law).

†The equerry on duty.

3-7-15 *The nickname of Richard Howard-Vyse; he was supposed to look like one.

9-7 *This was a particularly effective remark as French had been complaining bitterly to the War Cabinet about the lack of ammunition for the guns; during the initial Festubert attack, the bombardment only lasted 46 minutes and was over 90% shrapnel instead of high-explosive.

16-7 *The Germans had tried to envelop the Warsaw salient, but Grand-Duke Nicholas had managed to extract the Russian armies in time.

17-7 *Naval slang for rough weather.

†Chief of the General Staff.

18-7 *Ceuta lies on the southern side of the Straits of Gibralter with a total area of about 5 sq.miles.

†Aden lies at the southern end of the Red Sea and was an important staging port on the way to India via the Suez Canal. It now forms part of the People's Democratic Republic of Yemen.

20-7 *This was the French subsidiary attack on Vimy under Foch in conjunction with the British offensive known as the Battle of Loos. The main French attack was to be in Champagne.

26-7 *King Albert of the Belgians had ordered the sluices on the Yser opened during the last week of October 1914. Sea water then flooded the area between the Yzer and the railway embankment linking Dixmude and Nieupoort to a depth of 3-4 feet.

1-8-15 *This was the first time the Germans had used this new weapon.

2-8-15 *Sir William Robertson. His usual nickname was 'Wullie', but AFH quite clearly writes 'Wallie' whenever he uses it. It may have been a private joke between him and AFH, or it may have been a specifically Cavalry nickname.

5-8 *He was killed in a motor accident.

7-8 *AFH's only son: Archibald Frederick (Freddie) Douglas (1901-1981). 'Gen' was the family's nickname for him – it was a diminutive of 'General'. He joined the Coldstream Guards in 1924, rising to Major in 1940. He went to France with the BEF in September 1939 as GSO(3) to the 3rd Div. On obtaining his majority he went to Egypt with the 3rd Bn.Coldstream Guards. He joined General Wilson's Staff after Halfyah and later commanded a school of infiltrators in Palestine, returning to London in 1944 where he did a number of jobs in the Defence Ministry. He retired in 1946.

†Warsaw fell on 4-8 and the Russians were still retreating.

9-8 *18th Bde: then temporarily commanded by Lieutenant-Colonel F.W. Tewsey and including the following Battalions: 2nd Durham Light Infantry; 2nd Sherwood Foresters; 1st East Yorks; 1st West Yorks; 1/16th London (Queen's Westminster Rifles).

11-8 *From lack of attention and exercise.

†The second landings at Sulva and Anzac started on 6-8; see 19-8-15.

16-8 *Bingham.

17-8 *The Duke of Sutherland Hospital.

18-8 *Now Kaunas, on the River Niemen in Lithuania.

19-8 *The new attack in Gallipoli had been launched on 6-8. Sir Bryan Mahon (commanding the 10th Div.), General Hammersley (commanding the 11th Div.) and General Stopford (commanding the ? Corps) seem to have been quite as bad as AFH makes out.

200

## Chapter 6: The Battle of Loos (23-8-15 to 23-10)

24-8 *Naval fight near Riga.

25-8 *The second day of the Retreat from Mons.

26-8 *Fanshawe from now on, until further notice.

27-8 *First mention of the preparations for the Battle of Loos.

5-9-15 *The Royal Flying Corps.

10-9 *Sialkot is now in Pakistan. It lies about 25 miles south-west of Jammu in Kashmir.

11-9 *Probably Fanshawe.

12-9 *Sworn to secrecy.

16-9 *Unidentified.

†Louis-Napoleon, Prince Imperial, was the only son of Napoleon III born in 1856. He fled to England with his father in 1870, entered the Woolwich Military Academy in 1874 and was duly commissioned in the Royal Artillery. He saw active service in South Africa where he was killed on 1 June 1879 in an ambush at Itelezi during the Zulu Wars.

20-9 *Sir William Robertson.

25-9 *The Battle of Loos.

†4th Corps: then commanded by Lieutenant-General Sir H.S. Rawlinson and including the 1st, 15th (Scottish) & 47th (London) Divs.

26-9 *11th Corps: then commanded by Lieutenant-General and including the Guards, 19th (Western), 21st, 46th (North Midlands), Lahore & Meerut Divs.

†Probably the 2nd Worcestershire Reg. attached to the 5th Bde in the 2nd Div.

‡21st Div.: then commanded by Major-General Forestier-Walker and including the 62nd, 63rd & 64th Bdes.

§24th Div.: then commanded by Major-General Sir J.G. Ramsay and including the 71st, 72nd & 73rd Bdes.

28-9 *12th (Eastern) Div.: then commanded by Major-General F.D.V. Wing and including the 35th, 36th & 37th Bdes.

†47th (London TF) Div.: then commanded by Major-General C.St.L. Baxter and including the 140th, 141st & 142nd Bdes.

5-10-15 *British troops from Gallipoli and French troops were being sent to help the Serbians who were about to be attacked by Austro-German and Bulgarian Armies; the former crossed the Serbian frontier on 6-10. The allied expedition was commanded by the French General Serrail.

†Csar of Bulgaria was King Ferdinand.

10-10 *Bulgaria was about to attack Serbia, having signed a treaty with the Central Powers. serbia wanted to attack Bulgaria while the latter was still mobilising; but the Allies refused to countenance such tactics.

13-10 *It has not been possible to explain this remark.

19-10 *Gambling tables are usually covered in green baise.

21-10 *End of Volume IV of the full Diaries.

# Chapter 7: Waiting for a Chance (1-11-15 to 13-3-16)

1-11 *Constantine I (1868-1923) was King of the Hellenes (ie Greece) from 1913-17 and from 1920-2. His wife, Sophia, was the sister of Kaiser Wilhelm II. He abdicated in 1917, but as recalled to the throne by plebiscite in 1920. He abdicated for a second time after the disasterous Greek attack on the Turks in 1922.

3-11 *Prince Arthur, Duke of Connaught.

5-11 *Eleutherios Venezelos (1864-1936) was Premier of Greece from October 1910 to August 1915 when he resigned as a result of the opposition of the pro-German King Constantine. He helped to establish the so-called 'provisional government of national defence' at Salonika in 1916 and returned to the Premiership on 27-6-17 after Constantine's abdication.

8-11 *Then commanded by General Sir H.C.O. Plumer.

10-11 *Then commanded by General Sir D. Haig.

†Acclimatise the new troops and get them used to shelling and trench life without putting them in the front line.

11-11 *Bingham from now on until further notice. He had taken over command on 22-10-15

12-11 *W.S. Churchill had resigned as 1st Lord of the Admiralty as a result of the failure of the Dardannelles Expedition. Troops were to be evacuated on 18-12 from Sulva and Anzac Cove and from Helles on 8-1-16.

†See Biographical Note on AFH. AFH did not like Churchill much, see 30-5-17.

15-11 *Princess Margaret of Connaught (1882-1920) had married Gustaf Crown Prince of Sweden in 1905. Although strongly pro-German, Sweden observed strict neutrality during World War I.

22-11 *These experiments had begun in about February 1915. The first French group were under the control of M. Guirand de Scevola, an artist then serving with the French Artillery, who may be the person mentioned by AFH. The first British group was started in April 1916.

23-11 *Out of condition: ie puffing and wheezing like leaky bellows.

5-12-15 *Name of a Muslim sect based among the tribes of the western desert of Egypt and Libya. They had responded to the Turkish proclamation of a Jehad (Holy War), particularly because their Sheikh saw political possibilities in supporting Turkey. It took 18 months to subdue them after General Maxwell's campaign began in 11-15.

†During the Mahdi's rebellion in 1884-5.

‡Sir Douglas Haig. AFH was obviously unaware of the complaints Haig had been making about French's conduct during the Battle of Loos, to the War Cabinet and Lord Kitchener.

12-12 *Bulgaria had invaded southern Serbia and captured the Vardar Valley, thereby cutting off the serbs from the Allied Forces and their camp at Salonika. The Serbs had decided to retreat through the Albanian mountains but the first snow had fallen on 17-11 and they were encumbered with many civilians and 25,000 Austrian prisoners. They were also stricken by a typhus epidemic, so that only about 100,000 men reached the Albanian coast, whence they were transferred to Corfu.

13-12 *The Lewis machine gun weighed 28½lbs and was fed from 47-round drums. The Maxim machine gun and carriage weighed about 9½cwt (1045lbs) and fired 500 rounds per minute. Each carried 3500 rounds plus 8000 in reserve.

†A Non-Commissioned Officer.

18-12 *Probably the 6pdr rather than the machine gun.

20-12 *Chief of the Imperial General Staff; Sir William Robertson had just been appointed to that post.

†German for 'Civilisation'; applied ironically as a comment on their authoritarianism or derisively on their methods of waging war, etc.

‡German for 'World Politics'; ie the Kaiser's drive to make Germany a world power with influence everywhere.

§Deus Vult: ie God willing.

8-1-16 *The Military Service Bill was introduced by Asquith on 6-1-16 and it passed its first reading on that date. However it did not become law until 25-5-16 after a very stormy passage.

18-1 *Now Vilnius in Lithuania.

†The German Cavalry had made a huge raid eastwards in conjunction with the Autumn 1915 push in Poland. They had got close to the Minsk railway (about 90 miles south-east of Vilna) but had not been able to consolidate this thrust and so had withdrawn.

23-1 *This is a rather peculiar entry in view of AFH's description of Sir Hubert being knighted (see 2-12-14). I have not been able to establish why AFH calls him 'Goughy' from now on instead of 'Goffy' (as in 1914-15). It may be that Hubert had inherited the nickname spelling of his elder brother John who had been GSO(1) to Allenby and the Cavalry Division, then BG.GS to Haig and the 1st Corps. He had been killed by sniper fire in 2-15 while visiting his old regiment in the front line. AFH was extremely fond of John, but never really forgave Hubert for his conduct during the Curragh Mutiny in 3-14. (Gough was commanding the 3rd Cav.Bde at the Curragh. John Seeley (of the Canadian Bde!) was Secretary of State for War at the time and had given those officers who had 'direct family connection with the disturbed area in Ulster' a special dispensation to 'disappear' in the event of a conflict without losing their commissions. Gough then announced with 57 of his subordinates that they would prefer to accept dismissal rather than undertake ' active military operations against Ulster'.) AFH considered that this had shown disloyalty to his oath to King and Country.

27-1 *Raymond Poincaré (1860-1934) was the President of France (1913-20) while Aristide Briand (1862-1932) was then head of the Coalition Government.

†Edward, Viscount Grey of Fallodon (1862-1933) was the then Secretary of State for Foreign Affairs.

4-2-16 *F.E. Smith (1872-1930), then Attorney General.

†The Provost Marshal was responsible for all police duties for the armies in the field.

5-2 *Ground communications were mainly by telephone, by coded messages sent by cable using the Morse code, and by messengers whether on foot, horse, bicycle or motorcycle, or by car. 'Wireless' communications were available but the machines were cumbersome, unreliable and in short supply.

11-2 *35th (Bantam) Div. was recruited from physically-fit men who were under the army's minimum height (they all measured between 5ft and 5ft 3in.). The Division was reconstituted at the end of 1916 with men of normal height due to the lack of suitable replacements for their casualties.

24-2 *This was the start of Falkenheyn's 'attrition' offensive which involved attacking by methodical stages, each having a limited objective.

†Now Erzurum, in eastern Turkey. The Russians captured it on 15-2.

7-3-16 *Possibly a reference to the Algerian Division which had broken under a massed German attack on the slopes around the Fort de Douaumont on 25-2.

8-3 *'Cis' Bingham.

†*Character of the Happy Warrior* by William Wordsworth.

13-3 *End of Volume V of the full Diaries.

# Chapter 8: The Infantry on the Somme (8-4-16 to 2-9)

12-4 *A flame thrower: this was the first time that the Germans had used such a weapon, although the French had experiemented with something similar in 1914.

15-4 *The Mesopotamian Expedition was originally formed to protect the oil-fields around Basra. Due to the optimism of various experts, the 6th Div. (Major-General C. Townsend) and the 12th Div. (Major-General S. Gorringe) under General Sir John Nixon were pushed up the Euphrates and Tigris towards Bagdad. Early successes led to them occupying Kut-el-Amara and Nasiriya, thereby securing the Shatt-el-Hai link between the two rivers. On 20-11-15 they set out for Bagdad but were defeated at Ctesiphon on 22-11 and retreated to Kut by 3-12. The Turks invested Kut on 5-12 and the relief forces sent in January, March and April 1916 were unable to reach Kut. The surviving defenders eventually surrendered on 29-4-16.

19-4 *Now Trabzon, a Turkish port on the Black Sea.

20-4 *To establish which German Division they were facing.

22-4 *Stuart-Wortley.

23-4 *138th Bde: then including the following Battalions: 1/4th &1/5th Lincolnshire; 1/4th & 1/5th Leicestershires.

26-4 *Army slang for high-ranking officers, derived from the gold-lace decoration on the peaks of their caps.

29-4 *7th Corps: then commanded by Lieutenant-General Sir T.D'O. Snow and including the 4th, 37th & 55th Divs.

†At this point, the Germans changed their tactics from 'nibbling' attcks to wider ones. However the battle is considered to continue to at least 24-6 when Falkenhayn stopped the flow of ammunition to the Verdun front in preparation for the attack on the Somme. Crown Prince Rupprecht was not ordered to stand solely on the defensive until 11-7.

30-4 *See AFH's remarks on 11-5-18.

6-5-16 *Stuart-Wortley, from now on until further notice.

†In Latvia in the USSR, it lies near the mouth of the River Daugava where it empties into the Gulf of Riga in the Baltic Sea.

7-5 *56th Div.: then commanded by Major-General C.P.A. Hull and including the 167th, 168th & 169th Bdes.

†137th Bde: then commanded by Brigadier-General H.B. Williams and including the following Battalions: 1/5th & 1/6th South Staffordshire; 1/5th & 1/6th North Staffordshires.

8-5 *37th Div.: then commanded by Major-General Lord Edward Gleichen and including the 110th, 111th & 112th Bdes. He had renounced his German title as part of the British royal family's disengagement from its German connections.

†Brigadier-General H.B. Williams, see †7-5-16.9-5 *139th Bde: then commanded by Brigadier-General G.T. Shipley and including the following Battalions: 1/5th, 1/6th, 1/7th & 1/8th Sherwood Foresters.

12-5 *Devise the plan of action.

15-5 *Army slang for punishment or a verbal dressing-down, extended to artillery barrages, etc. Adapted from a phrase from a German song: *Gott stafe England*. (God punish England); see also 21-5-16.

21-5 *See 15-5-16.

29-5 *Nickname for the Sherwood Foresters, a territorial regiment.

31-5 *Brigadier-General, Royal Artillery.

†General Von Hötzendorf of Austria had launched an offensive against Italy in the Trentino around Asiago on 15-5. The Italians appealed to the Russians to prevent the Austrians reinforcing this attack, which led to General Brusilov starting his 'little tap' at the Austrians on 4-6-16. Meanwhile Cadorna retreated to the Piave River and prepared a counter offensive.

1-6-16 *1/1st Monmouthshire Pioneers.

†Dug like an ordinary sap, but leaving the supported topsoil and grass in place. They were mostly used to enable raiders to make a surprise entry into a nearby trench or post.

2-6 *First report of the Battle of Jutland, which had taken place on 31-5.

7-6 *The final score was in fact 11 German (*Pommern* (battleship); 4 light cruisers; 5 destroyers) and 14 British (*Queen Mary, Indefatigable, Invincible* (battlecruisers); 3 armoured cruisers; 8 destroyers).

†Kitchener was on his way to Russia to inspect the Eastern situation when his ship was torpedoed on 5-6.

‡Almost certainly Stuart-Wortley.

8-6 *Army slang for artillery shelling.

9-6 *First report of Brusilov's offensive in the Carpathians on 4-6. The 7th, 8th, 9th and 11th Russian armies were in the process of destroying the 4th and 7th Austrian armies, taking over 350,000 prisoners and recapturing the Bukovina and Eastern Galicia.

22-6 *ie all wire.

27-6 *Hamilton-Gordon.

28-6 *The start of the Battle of the Somme.

29-6 *AFH was right!

30-6 *Almost certainly Burnett Hitchcock, the 'Head of the Q side' in the 9th Corps.

†Probably Philip Howell who, according to AFH, resented having been passed over for the command of the 11th Hussars. AFH thought that he had no cause for complaint and had been very lucky to do as well as he had. (Complete Diary transcript 27-9-14)

1-7-16 *The Battle of the Somme.

†13th Corps: then commanded by Lieutenant-General W.N. Congreve and including the 18th & 30th Divs. They attacked between Maricourt and Fricourt, taking Montauban.

‡15th Corps: then commanded by Lieutenant-General H.S. Horne and including the 7th & 21st Divs. They attacked Fricourt village and wood.

§8th Corps: then commanded by Lieutenant-General Hon. J.H.G. Byng and including the 4th, 29th & 31st Divs. They were attacking on the left flank.

‖10th Corps: then commanded by Lieutenant-General Sir T.N.L. Morland and including the 32nd & 36th Divs. They attacked Thiepval.

¶Interestingly AFH does not mention the 3rd Corps (Pulteney) who were attacking near La Boiselle and Ovilliers. Perhaps he had no contacts in that Corps; or the wireless communique may not have mentioned them.

**Stuart-Wortley.

2-7 *The French 20th Corps were taking the German second line and high ground overlooking Peronne. Their official prisoner count for this day was just over 4000.

†This never really happened due to the inaction of General Evert.

3-7 *Was this the 1st or 2nd Anzac Corps?

7-7 *Probably a mistake for the 36th Div., see 14-7-16.

9-7 *The 46th Div. had been very badly shelled the night before the attack and had had to wait in flodded trenches. The heavy smoke screen had added to the problems of navigating across No Man's Land so that only small parties had reached the German front line. The result was that when the 56th (London) Div. had bombed their way up to meet the 46th, they were not there and the 56th had to retreat.

14-7 *36th (Ulster) Div.: then commanded by Major-General O.S.W. Nugent and including the 107th, 108th & 109th Bdes.

†I have not been able to confirm this figure, but as AFH undoubtedly talked to Staff Officers of the Division, it is likely it was as accurate as was possible at that date.

17-7 *Hamilton-Gordon.

19-7 *Delville Wood lies immediately to the north-east of Longueval.

†Ovilliers fell on 15-7.

20-7 *High Wood lies about halfway between Martinpuich and Longueval. It was taken on 14-7, but evacuated late on 15-7. The 7th Div. used two squadrons of Cavalry on the flank during the evening of 14-7 while taking the wood.

22-7 *The 1st Australian Div.: then commanded by Major-General and including the Bdes.

23-7 *This may refer to Brusilov's continuing campaign in Eastern Galicia or to the attacks on Brody (in the Ukraine) and Lemberg which had just started.

25-7 *14th Corps: then commanded by Lieutenant-General Lord Cavan.

30-7 *Now L'vov in the Ukraine.

31-7 *Then commanding the 10th Corps.

†Presumably G. is Gough, although it would make more sense if AFH meant Hamilton-Gordon. Why AFH should be able to keep Gough in order is not clear.

1-8-16 *48th Div.: then commanded by Major-General R. Fanshawe and including the 143rd, 144th & 145th Bdes. This is not the Fanshawe under whom AFH served in 1915 with the Cavalry Corps.

5-8 *France, Great Britain and Russia.

7-8 *Colonel von Kressenstein, the German commander in the Sinai peninsula, with some 16,000 men had been defeated at Romani some 20 miles east of the Suez Canal. After this battle, power passed to the Allies in Sinai.

9-8 First report of Cadorna's success at Gorizia, to the north of Trieste.

14-8 *4th Canadian Div.: then commanded by Major-General and including the Bdes.

†19th (Western) Div.: then commanded by Major-General G.T.M. Bridges and including the 56th, 57th & 58th Bdes.

21-8 *23rd Div.: then commanded by Major-General J.M. Babington.

23-8 *Rumania declared war on 27-8; troops moved on the night or 27/28-8.

25-8 *See 20-10-14.

†See 2-11-14.

1-9-16 *It is not clear from this whether this had prevented them from reaching their gas masks easily or whether they had walked back after being gassed with their packs on.

†Deputy Assistant Quartermaster General.

## Chapter 9: The Cavalry Corps Revived (8-9-16 to 31-12)

8-9 *The Heavy Section, Machine Gun Corps had been training near Thetford in Norfolk with their 140 armoured caterpillar tractors, code-named 'tanks', since January. They had just arrived amid great secrecy to assist in the attack on the German last line between Morval and Le Sars. 60 arrived, but only 32 were actually deployed during the battle.

16-9 *A system of trenches.

†Rubbish; it derives from 'an exclamation or derision, remonstrance or surprise' (*Shorter O.E.D.*)

18-9 *They had been involved in the capture of Flers and the clearing of captured ground; however 14 had either broken down or been ditched in craters.

19-9 *This ran from Sailly-Sailliset, past Le Transloy and in front of Bapaume.

22-9 *New Zealand Div.: then commanded by Major-General Sir A.H. Russell and including the 1st, 2nd & 3rd New Zealand Bdes.

†Many bodies were not retrieved from No Man's Land until 2-17, when the Germans retreated to the Hindenberg Line.

8-10-16 *It is not possible to identify the plane from this description.

18-10 *Rumania had declared war on 27-8-16. She had attacked Transylvania, despite her lack of equipment and ammunition, but the slowness of the attack allowed the Austro-German forces under General Falkenhayn to gather troops for a counter-offensive. He managed to turn the Rumanian southern flank by breaking through the Carpathian Mountains and forcing them to retreat from Sibin (Hermannstadt). Meanwhile Mackensen had attacked the southern frontier from Bulgaria and had crossed the Danube at Turtucaia. Falkenhayn then forced the central Rumanian column to retreat from Brasor (Kronstadt), although they still held the mountain passes by 9-10.

29-10 *Canadian Bde: then commanded by Brigadier-General J.E.B. Seeley.

31-10 *At this date, General Falkenhayn was being baulked in his attempts to force a passage across the Carpathian Mountains.

4-11-16 *Presumably from horses going lame.

†This probably refers to one of the follow-up attacks in the Isonzo region, following the Italian successes in 8-16. Sadly they failed to gain much ground and had high casualties.

9-11 *The Austro-German forces were about to achieve the breakthough into Wallachia.

13-11 *This attack, which captured Beaumont-Hamel and Beaumont-sur-Ancre but failed to take Serre, was the last of the Battle of the Somme.

†Probably refers to the recapture of Monastir, the capital of Macedonia, by the reconstituted Serbian army in co-operation with the French forces at Salonika.

15-11 *Lloyd George.

†Probably Admiral Lord Fisher.

‡Winston Churchill.

§Probably Ian Hamilton. He was an Infantry Officer, who had crossed Haig towards the end of the Boer War when he pointed out, in an official memorandum, that the old Cavalry tactics were dead and that the true function of the horse was to convey a rifleman to a point of attack or move him rapidly through a zone of fire. He was quite right but neither Sir John French nor Haig relished being taught their business by the Infantry and training methods were not changed.

19-11 *Falkenhayn had driven the Rumanian armies back to the River Alt.

†End of Volume VI of the full Diaries.

2-12-16 *Mackensen had forced the crossing of the Danube at Sistora and so had turned the Rumanian flank on the Alt. Despite a counter-attack by General Presan, the Austro-German forces were converging on Bucharest, which was to fall on 6-12-16.

6-12 *GHQ had appointed Major Solly-Flood to organise a proper Training Scheme for all the armies and services and to co-ordinate training generally.

†This is a reference to a story that Asquith, while on a tour of inspection of Irish prisons in 5-16 had shaken hands with IRA murderers and promised them leniency. He resigned on the evening of 5-12.

10-12 *Admiral Dartige du Fournet, Commander-in-Chief of the Allied naval forces in the Mediterranean, had been instructed to seize the light craft of the Greek navy and to demand an equal quantity of materiel to that abandoned to the Bulgars as a result of Constantine's earlier policies. Constantine had at first acquiesced and then refused. A French-British landing party had been instructed to seize the key points of Athens on 2-12-16, on the understanding that they would not be opposed. However Greek troops ambushed the landing party and many were killed. The navies were forced to shell the Greek royal palace before the landing party could be withdrawn.

12-12 *Lieutenant-General C.T.McM. Kavanagh.
15-12 *Unidentified.
17-12 *Probably General Mangin's action when the French lines advanced almost two miles; 11,000 prisoners and 115 guns were taken.
'31-12 *By this date, two-thirds of Rumania was occupied by Austro-German and Bulgarian troops. Despite Russian support, only the northern third was still supporting the Allies.

208

## Chapter 10: In the Line at Arras (18-1-17 to 11-7)

18-1 *AFH wrote Edward, but this must be an error.

2-2-17 *A famous Parisian restaurant.

4-2 *Probably a reference to the German proclaimation on 1-2-17 which announced that all approaches to the British Isles, the western coast of France and the Mediterranean were under blockade and that any vessel found within these waters would be sunk on sight.

15-2 *Nickname of his then only daughter, Esther Mary Philomena (1906-1972).

†There was a major epidemic of flu in England in 1917; AFH was quite right to be worried as many people died from it.

18-2 *7th Div.: then commanded by Major-General G. Barrow and including the 20th, 22nd & 91st Bdes.

†I have not been able to trace who or what this was.

19-2 *General Maude, with the reorganised Mesopotamian Expeditionary Force, had begun an attack on 12-2-16 by digging new trenches around Kut. He had cleared the west bank of the Tigris by 22-2-17, so this is presumably a reference to initial reports of his final attack.

25-2 *First mention of the Retreat to the Hindenberg (or Siegfried) Line. This ran from just east of Arras, via St Quentin and La Fere, to just east of Soissons (see 19-3-17).

9-3-17 *The standard ration per horse per day in the British Cavalry was 10lb oats, plus 10lb of hay or forage. The oats were an essential part of the horse's diet and, on half rations, they would not have been able to gallop so fast or march so far as British horses.

15-3 *This proposal had been made at a conference in Calais on 26-2-17, although it is not clear who originated it. Haig eventually agreed to work under Nivelle's direction, but with the right of appeal to the British Government. There was a further conference in London on 12-3-17, after an appeal from Haig, to sort out problems and to agree the form of Nivelle's instructions.

18-3 *First mention of the Russian Revolution; the Tsar had abdicated on 15-3.

19-3 *This destruction was part of Operation Alberich and involved burning houses, contaminating wells and laying numerous explosive booby-traps. See also AFH's comments on 27-3 and 29-3.

2-4-17 *For the Battle of Arras. The Cavalry Corps were intended to sweep through, once the 3rd Army had broken the first line of the German defence, and drive towards the Switch line of trenches which had been dug from Drocourt to Quéant in order to protect the rear of their old defences north of Arras. If they could take the Switch line, the Hindenberg Line would automatically be taken in flank and rear. However the lack of surprise (see below) made this move impossible.

†Allenby had wanted only a two-day bombardment, but GHQ had promoted the Artillery adviser who supported him and supplied a new adviser who shared their views. The result was that any possibility of surprise was lost and the Germans had nearly three weeks to prepare for the attack.

9-4 *Despite a 3-week preliminary 'wire-cutting' bombardment!

†Cavalry was used around Monchy-le-Preux but to no end and great mounds of dead horses remained for days afterwards. There were a few squadrons in action along the Scarpe as well. This was the last time that mounted troops were used in a cratered battlefield. 19-4 *Nivelle's offensive on the Aisne, to east and west of Rheims, had started on 16-4. While the German reserves were still on hand, and without the element of surprise, a rapid breakthrough was impossible; also the French troops were sick of being thrown against uncut wire and active machine guns.

22-4 *The Oxfordshire Hussars, a Yeomanry regiment.

†This was 'in order to assist our Allies' (Haig).

29-4 *The Provisional Government was wrestling with an impossible overload of work, while the Russian armies were melting away as the peasants deserted to claim land in their home region. The Soviet [Council] of Workers and Soldiers was also working to destroy the existing system of discipline in the armies and actively encouraged the rank and file to defy their officers.

2-5-17 *End of Volume VII of the complete Diaries.

11-5 *William Knox D'Arcy was his father-in-law; see the Biographical Note.

13-5 *Howard-Vyse.

22-5 *There had been a series of mutinies in the French armies during May as a result of Nivelle's offensive. On 15-5, Pétain was appointed to replace Nivelle and he was engaged in re-inspiring and reorganising the demoralised forces. However Pétain was not to undertake another large offensive until the following year.

†I have not managed to pinpoint any event which might have inspired this comment.

‡By the end of 4-17, one in every four ships which left Britain never returned; nearly a million tons of

Allied shipping was sunk. The convoy system was introduced finally in early May and proved unmistakably successful, while the introduction of special submarine chasers and new mines helped to decrease the number of U-boats in action (148 at the start of the 1917 campaign). However the 'bag' of 21 submarines in a week is an implausible figure.

26-5 *Raid; I have not been able to trace the origin of this slang word.

28-5 *At this date, Churchill was Minister for Munitions.

30-5 *They had presumably relieved the 11th Corps under General Mandhui.

4-6-85 *In fact the bombardment had started on 21-5 for wire-cutting and was developed into a 7-day intensive bombardment.

9-6 *The 2nd Dragoon Guards, the Royal Scots Greys.

15-6 *The 29th Lancers, the Deccan Horse.

24-6 *For the 3rd Battle of Ypres.

5-7-17 *34th Div.: then commanded by Major-General C.L. Nicholson and including the 101st, 102nd & 103rd Bdes.

†55th Div.: then commanded by Major-General H.S. Jeudwine and including the 164th, 165th & 166th Bdes.

‡This was the final Russian effort of the war. As a result of Kerensky's oratory, General Brussilov had managed to gather about 200,000 men in Galicia to attack an Austrian army. However, without the necessary discipline, the attack was hopeless. Many of the most able officers sacrificed themselves trying to lead their men; while the Germans forewarned of the attack by deserters and well aware of the impending Bolshevik uprising in St Petersberg (Petrograd/Leningrad), were able to prepare an overwhelming counter attack. The Russian army disintegrated in the face of this.

11-7 *Just south of St Omer.

## Chapter 11: Passchendale to Cambrai (15-7-17 to 19-2-18)

24-7 *General Allenby had been appointed Commander-in-Chief in Egypt in early July. He was currently engaged in extensive preparations for his Autumn offensive in Palestine; most of his Cavalry troops were from Yeomanry regiments.

26-7 *The 2nd Lancers (Gardner's Horse) were an Indian regiment.

†Pertab Singh (1845-1922) as the British called him, was Sir Pratap Singh, Maharaja of Idar. He was famous as a most fearless warrior and a renowned sportsman. He acted as regent of Johdpur during the minority of his nephew and commanded the Jodhpur Lancers in France and Palestine throughout World War I.

31-7 *Otherwise known as Passchendale.

3-8-17 *The prolonged bombardment had totally destroyed the drainage system of dykes around Ypres, with the result that the countryside had reverted to its original swamp.

†While the remains of the Russian army were retreating through Galicia in terrible disorder, the Germans under von Eutier were preparing to take Riga on 3-9-17, rightly judging that its loss would compromise the already shaky government of Kerensky irretrievably.

13-8 *Polygon Wood lies east and slightly north of Beselare, between it and Wieltje.

20-8 *The 9th Corps had been in the centre of this most successful attack on 7-6-17.

†8th Div.: then commanded by Major-General H. Hudson and including the 23rd, 25th and 70th Bdes.

‡The second major attack of Passchendale (or the 3rd Battle of Ypres) had taken place on 16-8.

22-8 *A reference to the strongpoints, nicknamed 'pill-boxes', which were both inconspicuous and strong enough to resist a direct hit from a field gun. Well sited to take advantage of the flooding, they were almost impossible for Infantry to capture, except by crawling close enough to throw a grenade through the machine gun slits.

†General Cadorna had just launched the '11th Battle of the Isonzo', during which General Capello's 2nd army had taken much of the Bainsizza plateau north of Gorizia.

8-9-17 *The Hanseatic League was a commercial association of towns in northern Germany, formed in the mid-14th century to protect and regulate trade. It was most powerful in the 15th century.

14-9 *Following his success at Messines, General Plumer and the 2nd Army were called upon to take over the Menin Road sector of the Battle of Passchendale from Gough and the 5th Army, and therefore to make the main advance towards the ridge east of Ypres.

†Sir Douglas Haig.

18-9 *The 5th (Royal Irish) Lancers.

†The 1st Australian Division probably.

25-9 *These may have been connected to the Schemes being advocated by General Sir Julian Byng (3rd Army) and Colonel Fuller of the Tank Corps. The tactics evolved were eventually used in the Battle of Cambrai in 11-17.

26-9 *Possibly from the naval term 'boxing the compass' and so figuratively 'going round in circles'.

30-9 *General Kiggell.

2-10-17 *The British forces under General Maude had taken Bagdad on 11-3-17; Enver Pasha had been collecting troops for an attempt to recapture it, but they had been diverted to Palestine to meet the danger of Allenby's new offensive.

8-10 *The horses would be exhausted by plodding through the mud and therefore would not be able to perform a long gallop.

9-10 *In fact this was not the case; only the targets on the low ground on the left of the 8-mile attack were achieved.

12-10 *They were preparing for another attack on 12-10 which made practically no headway at all.

25-10 *First report of the Battle of Caporetto on 24-10, which was followed by the collapse of the Italian frontline.

29-10 *The remains of the entire Italian army was retreating to the line of the River Piave, thereby abandoning the province of Friuli to the Austro-German forces.

†The British sent the 5th, 7th, 23rd, 41st and 48th Divs, all of which arrived in Italy between 6-11 and 27-11.

‡Mustard gas was seldom fatal, but caused blindness plus great blisters and very painful burns which took a long time to heal. It also seeped into the soil and remained potent for several days after release, so that anyone who touched the ground in a previously gassed area could get burnt. It had first been used earlier in the Passchendale campaign.

§There had been other attacks on 22-10 and 26-10, involving the Canadian Corps as well, but with minimal progress.

2-11-17 *Lenin and Trotsky had overthrown the Kerensky government on 24-10 in the October Revolution; meanwhile the Russian economy was totally devestated.

8-11 *This was the final push of the 3rd Battle of Ypres and marks the official end of the battle.

†Cadorna had withdrawn all the troops he could behind the Tagliamento by 1-11 and was reorganising the remains of the 2nd and 3rd Armies. He had decided to withdraw to the Piave by 2-11 and this move was complete by 10-11.

10-11 *Actually entitled the Supreme War Council.

†He eventually resigned as CIGS and was replaced by General Sir Henry Wilson; see 19-2-18.

‡These were very much Haig's sentiments when he announced: 'I can deal with a man but not with a Committee'.

14-11 *First mention of the preparations for the Battle of Cambrai. I would guess that AFH was first informed of the plans on 24-10; it is clear by 29-10 that he was making active plans for the Cavalry Corps.

16-11 *The lack of Reserves seems to be the major point which all commentators stress. To all intents and purposes, the Cavalry Corps was the only Reserve that Byng had available.

17-11 *Probably the brushwood bundles which were carried on the nose of each tank and released into the Hindenburg Line trenches.

20-11 *A British telephone message – 'Tuesday Flanders' – was intercepted by General von der Marwitz. Sounding like a codeword, he was alarmed and deployed an extra Division to strengthen his defenses.

†General Harper of the 51st (Highland) Division refused to use the new tank tactics as he did not believe they would work. The result was that the Infantry could not keep up with the tanks and so their attack, in the centre of the battle, was held up at Flesquières. What is incomprehensible is that this salient was not pinched out, because troops on both sides had advanced well beyond it. Probably the answer was that the extraordinarily rapid advance had played havoc with communications.

‡From the Fort Garry Horse.

23-11 *Lieutenant Muller of the 108th Regiment apparently scored hits on five tanks singlehanded; however three batteries had been involved initially. The action is principally famous because Haig's dispatch gave a unique mention to a German officer: 'The great bravery of this officer aroused the admiration of all ranks.'

25-11 *A horse in good condition can cover about 12 miles per hour at the trot; however it would be tired after such heavy exercise and in no fit state for a charge over badly churned-up ground.

†The 15th (King's) Hussars.

26-11 *Sadly unidentified.

†They had been held up by machine guns in the houses on the steep slope beyond the canal. This was probably General de Lisle's opinion, who was the commander of the 29th Div. As an old friend of AFH, he may well have said something to him in private which he could not admit publicly.

30-11 *General Jeudwine, commanding the 55th Div., had asked the 3rd Corps to bombard the area around Banteux (just south of La Vacquerie) on the morning of 30-11 as a counter preparation, but this was refused.

†From the 2nd Tank Bde.

‡An Indian Cavalry regiment.

§Mehow Bde: then including the following Regiments: 6th Inniskilling Dragoons, 2nd Lancers (Gardner's Horse), & 38th (King George's Own) Central Indian Horse.

10-12-17 *Sir Julian Byng.

†The Russians were to sign an Armistice with the Central Powers on 17-12-17. The Peace of Brest-Litovsk was signed on 3-3-18. Rumania also made peace in 3-18, although King Ferdinand kept his throne.

14-12 *This included smoke, gas and a machine gun attack from low-flying aeroplanes.

25-12 *The Cavalry were intended to seize Cambrai and the passage over the River Sensee, thereby cutting off the German forces south of the river and west of the Canal du Nord. They were then to exploit this success towards Valenciennes.

†The attack had been continued in an effort to take Bourlon Wood and Hill which menaced the new British positions.

27-12 *Allenby had climaxed a brilliant campaign in Palestine by taking Jerusalem on 6-12, just before the rainy season started. Meanwhile the Arab irregulars under Colonel T.E. Lawrence were harrassing the Hejaz railway to Damascus.

27-1-18 *Previously the 1st and 2nd Indian Cavalry Divisions.

3-2-18 *Over half a million workmen had gone on strike in German, mostly in Berlin. There was a desperate food shortage in both Germany and Austria which was only relieved by the ceding of the Ukraine in 3-18.

8-2 *19th Corps: then commanded by Lieutenant-General H.E. Wells and including the 24th & 66th Divs.

10-2 *At Verdun in 1916.

19-2 *He did not in fact do so.

†The Supreme War Council.

‡End of Volume VIII of the full Diaries.

## Chapter 12: The Spring Offensive (26-2-18 to 5-8)

26-3 *This was the day after the German Spring Offensive started. Interestingly, AFH's youngest daughter (Teresa Mary Violet) was born on 22-12-18.

†His surgeon.

‡This is a slightly eccentric description of Gough's dismissal, which occurred on 29-3 and was principally due to the retreat of the 5th Army in the face of the German offensive. Presumably Gough's dismissal allowed Kavanagh to shake off the former's criticisms. The whole thing may be in cryptic form, so that AFH could remember what actually happened.

§The Cavalry Corps, then attached to the 3rd Army, had provided a cordon across the gaps during the retreat. They had provided invaluable service by holding up the German advance guard and maintaining contact between the Infantry Divisions.

31-3 *This wood was a most important point as it not only formed the junction between the French and British armies, but also commanded the crossings of the Rivers Avre and Luce at their confluence, which in turn commanded the manin Amiens to Paris railway.

1-4-18 *At a previous conference on 26-3 at Doullens, Foch had been evelated over Pétain to 'co-ordinate the operations of the Allies on the Western Front'. He was eventually appointed Commander-in-Chief on 24-4.

†Apparently the French had had responsibility for destroying the railway bridges and had failed to do this properly – most crucially at Peronne over the Somme.

‡The efficient but complicated telephone system, based on more or less static fromt lines, was totally unable to cope with the rapid retreat. The result was that even less information than usual reached the 5th Army HQ.

10-4 *First report of the Flanders Offensive, codenamed 'Georgette'.

†The 2nd Portuguese Div. had been stretched to cover a whole Corps sector (6 miles) and were about to be relieved by two British Divisions when the attack started. They were at a low ebb in morale and regretably broke under the intense bombardment and mustard gas attacks.

‡40th Div.: then commanded by Major-General J. Ponsonby and including the 119th, 120th & 121st Bdes.

13-4 *General Sir Henry Horne.

†31st Div.: then commanded by Major-General R.J. Bridgford and including the 4th (Guards), 92nd & 93rd Bdes.

‡The 1st Australian Div.

14-4 *In fact it was five French Divisions.

16-4 *Lloyd-George had refused to allow the 300,000 general service men in England, or troops from other theatres, to be sent to France to make up the losses of 1917 (about 760,000 men). As a result, Divisions had had to be reduced from 12 to nine Battalions each, which seriously interfered with the organisation of the Divisions and the tactical handling of Brigades.

17-4 *The Germans, starved of food and essentials, had pillaged Merville on the night of 11-4. Such events happened several times during these offensives and each time caused a serious delay in the German advance.

20-4 *This may be 'Babe' Nicholson; see 9-5-18.

†A reference to the machinations surrounding the formation of the Royal Air Force.

22-4 *About 12 American Divisions had arrived by this date.

23-4 *Women's Army Auxilary Corps.

24-4 *It was during this period that the conscription age was raised to 50 and men under the age of 19 wer sent to France. Irish conscription was eventually introduced during this month.

25-4 *This was the first battle in which tank faced tank. The British light tank was the 'Whippet'.

27-5-18 *First report of the German attack on the Chemin des Dames.

30-5 *Obtain a monopoly of; from the commercial usage whereby a combination buys up the whole, or all available supplies, of a commodity in order to fix their own price for it.

4-6-18 *His wife, Violet.

6-6 *The US 2nd Div. were to counter attack with the French at Château-Thierry on 10-6; although their methods were described as clumsy and amateur, their attacks were extremely vigorous.

17-6 *They attacked from Asiago and against Montello and Monte Grappa on the Piave, thereby dissipating their effort over far too wide a front. All attacks were repelled and the armies returned to their former lines.

20-6 *Pelmanism was a system of training to improve the memory.

214

†A technical name for a fever.

4-7-18 *This was a most important, if small, action because it demonstrated that systematic rehearsed co-operation between tanks and Infantry could minimise casualties. The use of a barrage just ahead of the tank advance made German retaliation very difficult. It also foreshadowed the tactics used in the Autumn advances.

16-7 *This was Ludendorff's *Friedensturm*; his final diversion attack designed to pull British Reserves south to support the French.

†The German troops had to cross more than two miles of evacuated lines, booby-trapped with gas and land mines and under continuous bombardment, to reach the main French resistance. The attack failed totally.

18-7 *The French Cavalry Corps was then in the second line of Mangin's 10th Army, which also included the American 1st and 2nd Divs.

22-7 *This then included the 15th, 34th, 51st & 62nd Divs.

23-7 *I have not been able to establish what this argument was about; perhaps about allocation of wireless equipment in view of AFH's previous comments.

25-7 *Their main bases at Ostende and Zeebrugge had been partially blocked by the British actions under Sir Roger Keyes on 22/3-4-18 and 10-5-18. In May alone, 14 out of 125 boats in service were sunk.

3-8-18 *First mention of Haig's planned attack which was only revealed to the Divisional Commanders on 31-7. It is clear that the Cavalry Corps had not been informed of their role before this day or just possibly 2-8.

## Chapter 13: The Final Victory (8-8-18 to 11-11)

8-8 *456 tanks were used in this offensive. There appears to have been a liaison problem between the tanks and Cavalry – probably due to lack of experience in co-operation. The Whippets could not keep up with the Cavalry cross-country when not under fire; while the Cavalry could not keep up with the tanks while under fire.

12-8 *These were the light tanks which had failed against the heavier German tanks in April; see 25-4*.

19-8 *In March/April 1918.

26-8 *This was the Switch line that protected the northern end of the Hindenberg Line.

1-9-18 * 10th (Prince of Wales' Own Royal) Hussars.

†Three Battalions under General Monash had taken Mont St Quentin, while other units stormed Peronne in the face of fierce resistance.

12-9 *This was the first action faught by an American Army, under general Pershing, as opposed to Divisions fighting with Allied Armies. The salient lay between Verdun and Nancy.

22-9 *Allenby's new offensive had opened on 19-9; by 21-9, the Palestine force had destroyed two Turkish armies.

†From Psalm XXII, v. 12: 'Many oxen come about me: fat bulls of Bashan close me in on every side.'

‡Serbian and French troops had attacked Bulgaria successfully on 15-9; while the British attack at Doiran had been repulsed. King Ferdinand abdicated on ?-9 and left the country, while a surrender at discretion was arranged on 30-9.

27-9 *Over the Canal du Nord.

29-9 *To take the southern sector of the Hindenberg Line.

†The American troops in their enthusiasm, failed to clear the maze of galleries where the Canal de St Quentin goes underground for some 6,000 yards. The Germans were therefore able to lay down a cordon of fire between them and the Australian Corps supporting them.

‡They had attacked on 28-9 and took Passchendale and the forest to the north of Langermarck that day. However they then got bogged down in the mud and the attack fizzled out on 2-10.

1-10-18 *13th Corps: then commanded by Lietenant-General Sir T.L.N. Morland and including the 19th & 46th Divs.

5-10 *The Capitulation came on 30-10. Damascus had been taken by Lawrence and the Arabs on 1-10 and Aleppo on 22-10.

6-10 *Prince Max of Baden, the new German Chancellor, had sent a Note to President Wilson of the USA on 3-10 accepting the 14 Points, which had been laid down by Wilson on 8-1-18 as a basis for peace negotiations, and requesting an immediate armistice.

†In fact Ludendorff had decided on 29-9 that Germany was in an untenable position and would have to make the best terms she could.

12-10 *Probably refers to the German Chancellor's second Note, which explicitly renounced any rights of negotiation on the principles of the 14 Points.

17-10 *Aristide Poincaré.

20-10 *The Chief of the General Staff, then General Lawrence.

21-10 *Following the sinking of the *Leinster* (a passenger ship sunk in the Irish Channel), Wilson had refused to consider any armistice while the German forces continued such practices. He also demanded guarantees of continuing military superiority for the Allies and a limitation on the powers of the Kaiser.

23-10 *The Offensive in the Meuse-Argonne region had been hampered by lack of transport and the natural barrier of the Forest of Argonne.

25-10 *He had said on 23-10 that, if he had to deal with 'military masters and monarchial autocrats', he must demand surrender, not permit negotiations.

28-10 *The Battle of Vittorio Veneto had started on 24-10 with an attack on the crossings of the Piave. These had been forced by a Anglo-Italian force on 27-10 and the Cavalry and armoured cars were thrusting for Vittorio Veneto which they reached on 30-10.

†The Emperor Karl had written to the Kaiser on 27-10 announcing his intention of demanding a separate armistice immediately.

1-11-18 *Foch and Haig were arguing over what should be demanded of the Germany Army, while the British Admiralty was pushing for the internment, if not the surrender, of all U-boats and most of the German superdreadnoughts.

7-11 *The German Armistice Commission had crossed the lines on that day and Foch had communicated the terms to them.

216

8-11 *The sailors had mutinied when Admiral von Scheer had announced his plan for a final raid on Dover and the mouth of the Thames. By 4-11, the port of Kiel was in their hands.

†The Kaiser was now at Spa and had ordered Hindenberg to prepare for civil war against those who were seeking peace. Hindenberg told him that it was impossible because the armies would ignore such an order. The Kaiser eventually abdicated on 9-11 and fled to Holland the next morning.

11-11 *AFH suffered from neuralgia in his right hand for the rest of his life. He once said to TMVB that he thought it had been caused by the strain of hand-writing the orders to stop the Divisions on that morning, since he had never had it before that date.

†End of Book IX of the full Diaries.

# INDEX

Seligman, Joe 2/7/17; 17/10/18
Sewell, Major 24/2/15; 7/6/18
Seymour, Archie 18/5/18
Shannon, Pat 9/4/17
Shea, Colonel J.S.M. 25, 27/9/14, 3, 7/10/14, 27/11/14
Sloane 4/3/15
Smith-Dorrien, General Sir Horace 11/12/14; 12/1/15, 6/5/15, 20/11/15
Smith, F.E. 30/1/16
Smyth, Bill 6/6/16
Smythe 30/11/14, 5/12/14
Snow, General Sir T. D'O. 12/1/15; 30/4/16, 16, 24/5/16, 10/6/16
Solly-Flood, Major 22, 26/7/15; 19/7/17
Sordet, General 21/8/14
Spiers, Louis 15, 21/8/15
Squires 19/12/14
Stevens 13/4/18
Stopford 19/8/15
Stuart, Jack 27, 29/9/16
Stuart-Wortley, General E. 4/4/16, 5/7/16
Teck, Prince Alexander, Duke of 8/2/15, 27/11/15
Thorpe, Gervase 9, 21, 26/4/16, 15, 16/5/16
'Tino' (Constantine I, King of the Hellenes) 1, 5/11/15; 10/12/16
Tomkinson, Capt. 'Mouse' 30/9/14; 27/2/15
Townsend 14/4/16
Trenchard, General H.M. (RFC) 6/9/15; 8/20/16; 20/4/18
Vanderbyl 24/6/17
Vandeleur 30/1/15
Vaughan, John 22/10/14; 13/10/15; 9/1/16, 25/7/16; 16/8/18, 26/10/18
Venezelos 5/11/15
Vesey 2/11/15; 30/1/16
Vincent, Berkely 28/4/16, 8/5/16, 8/6/16
Von Richthofen, Baron 23/4/18
Von Eutier, General O. 3/8/2/18
Walker, Colonel 22/6/17
Wallace 20/6/18, 22/9/18
Walters 22/7/16
Ward, John 3/1/16
Watson 12/11/14
Webster, Sam 23/4/18
Weir 28/1/15
Weston 1/7/16
Wheeler, Don 23/7/18
Whigham, Bob 8/11/15, 20/12/15; 24/2/16
White, The Hon. Luke 2/4/15
White, Thompson 20/7/15
Wigram, Clive 3/12/14; 8/2/15; 28/6/15; 11/7/17; 14/8/18, 26/10/18
Wilberforce 27/2/15
Williams, Bruce 17/7/15, 5, 24/8/15
Wilson, General Sir Henry 10/11/17; 3, 11/8/18
Wilson, Woodrow 4/2/17; 6, 12, 21, 25, 28/10/18
Woodroffe 5/6/18
Wormald, 'Scrubbs' 4/10/15
Wrangles, General Baron 29/6/17, 3, 6/8/17
Yates, Camperdown 19/4/15